JÓN LEIFS AND THE MUSICAL INVENTION OF ICELAND

MUSIC, NATURE, PLACE
Sabine Feisst and Denise Von Glahn

JÓN LEIFS AND THE MUSICAL INVENTION OF ICELAND

ÁRNI HEIMIR INGÓLFSSON

INDIANA UNIVERSITY PRESS

This book is a publication of

Indiana University Press
Office of Scholarly Publishing
Herman B Wells Library 350
1320 East 10th Street
Bloomington, Indiana 47405 USA

iupress.indiana.edu

© 2019 by Árni Heimir Ingólfsson

All rights reserved
No part of this book may be reproduced or utilized in any form or by any means, electronic or mechanical, including photocopying and recording, or by any information storage and retrieval system, without permission in writing from the publisher. The paper used in this publication meets the minimum requirements of the American National Standard for Information Sciences—Permanence of Paper for Printed Library Materials, ANSI Z39.48-1992.

Manufactured in the United States of America

Library of Congress Cataloging-in-Publication Data

Names: Árni Heimir Ingólfsson, author.
Title: Jón Leifs and the musical invention of Iceland / Árni Heimir Ingólfsson.
Description: Bloomington : Indiana University Press, 2019. | Series: Music, nature, place
Identifiers: LCCN 2018049685 (print) | LCCN 2018051364 (ebook) | ISBN 9780253044075 (e-book) | ISBN 9780253044044 (cl : alk. paper) | ISBN 9780253044051 (pb : alk. paper)
Subjects: LCSH: Jón Leifs. | Composers—Iceland—Biography. | Jón Leifs—Criticism and interpretation. | Music—Iceland—History and criticsim.
Classification: LCC ML410.J73 (ebook) | LCC ML410.J73 A75 2019 (print) | DDC 780.92 [B] —dc23
LC record available at https://lccn.loc.gov/2018049685

1 2 3 4 5   24 23 22 21 20 19

CONTENTS

Acknowledgments vii

Note on Spelling and Naming xi

Introduction 1
1. The Land without Music (1899–1916) 9
2. Years of Study (1916–21) 29
3. Composer and Conductor (1921–29) 56
4. Leifs and the Elements of an Icelandic Style 103
5. Icelandic Nation-Building and the 1930 Alþingi Festival (1929–33) 134
6. "This Music Belongs to Us" (1933–37) 159
7. Dinosaurs in Berlin (1937–44) 195
8. Guilt and Retribution (1944–55) 242
9. The Final Years (1955–68) 287
    Postlude: Revival and Influence 335

Appendix: List of Jón Leifs's Completed Works 343

Selected Bibliography 365

Index 375

ACKNOWLEDGMENTS

THIS BOOK IS A REWORKING of my earlier biography of Leifs (pronounced "Layfs"), which was published in Icelandic in 2009 as *Jón Leifs—Líf í tónum*. In the current version, I have eliminated much that seemed of limited interest to non-Icelandic readers while augmenting the discussion of Icelandic literature, landscape, and cultural identity. I remain indebted to everyone whom I thanked in the earlier iteration of the book, not least Hjálmar H. Ragnarsson, whose 1980 MFA thesis from Cornell University was the only serious study of Leifs's music when I began my research as an undergraduate at Oberlin College in 1996. Ragnarsson has provided unfailing support and encouragement and generously shared his materials and insights with me. The same is true of Carl-Gunnar Åhlén, the author of a Leifs biography that appeared in Icelandic translation in 1999 and then in the original Swedish in 2002.

Other scholars have been no less generous. Ásgeir Guðmundsson, Halldór Guðmundsson, and Þór Whitehead shared materials from German archives. Bjarki Sveinbjörnsson, Ingunn Þóra Magnúsdóttir, Michael Hillenstedt, and Sif Sigmarsdóttir gave me permission to cite their unpublished theses. Two descendants of Josef Rindskopf, Albert Rode of Florida (United States) and Frederick Ridley of Liverpool (England), graciously shared their memories of the Riethof family in Teplitz. To the library staff at the National and University Library in Reykjavík, home to the voluminous Leifs archives, I owe an enormous debt. Also, my thanks to the staff at the National Archives (Reykjavík), Rigsarkivet (Copenhagen), Bundesarchiv, Stiftung Archiv der Akademie der Künste, Archiv Berliner Philharmoniker, and Staatsbibliothek zu Berlin (Berlin), Archiv Gewandhaus zu Leipzig and Hochschule für Musik und Theater "Felix Mendelssohn Bartholdy," Hochschulbibliothek/Archiv (Leipzig), the New York Public Library, Jean Gray Hargrove Music Library at the University of California (Berkeley), and Eda Kuhn Loeb Music Library at Harvard University.

I am deeply indebted to Sabine Feisst and Denise Von Glahn, who originally requested this book for the present series; to an anonymous reviewer for thoughtful and constructive comments; and to the staff at Indiana University Press, especially Janice Frisch and Nancy Lila Lightfoot for their admirable patience and helpful remarks, as well as to Elise Vaz for her expert copyediting. My gratitude also goes to other colleagues and friends who have discussed with me various topics and ideas relating to Leifs: Alan Steinweis, Atli Heimir Sveinsson, Claudia Macdonald, Egill Guðmundsson, Finnur Karlsson, Helga Bahr, Helga Kress, Joel Sachs, Kimberly Cannady, Klaus Erlendur Kroner, Nico Muhly, Osmo Vänskä, Oswald Georg Bauer, Paul Zukofsky, Petra Garberding, Pétur H. Ármannsson, Pétur Óli Gíslason, Reinhold Brinkmann, Rüdiger Kläring, Selma Guðmundsdóttir, Sigríður Steinunn Lúðvígsdóttir, Þorkell Sigurbjörnsson, and Örn Magnússon. Andrew Wawn kindly assisted with my own translations of Icelandic poetry, and Össur Geirsson typeset music examples. Extracts from Leifs's works appear by kind permission of the Iceland Music Information Center; translations by Bernard Scudder appear by kind permission of Sigrún Eiríksdóttir.

Support for the English version of this book came from Hagþenkir (the Association of Icelandic Non-Fiction Writers) and STEF, the Performing Rights Society of Iceland. The music department at Harvard University graciously appointed me a Visiting Fellow in the 2014–15 academic year, which allowed me to complete the first draft of the English version. Last but not least, I am grateful to my family, who have endured life with Leifs for more than two decades and have been unfailingly supportive from start to finish.

NOTE ON SPELLING AND NAMING

THIS BOOK USES ICELANDIC SPELLINGS of all Icelandic names and texts. The special characters used to write Icelandic are preserved here, not transliterated to an approximate English spelling. The special characters used are the consonants þ (uppercase Þ) and ð (lowercase only), pronounced as the first sound in English "thin" and "this" respectively and often spelled with *th* or *d* in English transliteration. Also, æ [ai̯] and ö [œ] are considered letters in their own right, as are the diphthongs represented by acute accent marks over the letters á [au̯], é [jɛ], í [i], ó [ou̯], and ú [u].

In general, Icelanders employ a patronymic system in which the suffix *-son* or *-dóttir* is added to the genitive form of a parent's (most commonly the father's) first name. Although Icelanders refer to each other by first name, this book refers to them by patronymic and treats these in the same manner as family names. However, members of Leifs's immediate family (his parents, siblings, wives, and children) are referred to by their first names throughout.

JÓN LEIFS AND THE MUSICAL INVENTION OF
ICELAND

INTRODUCTION

ICELAND IS A LAND OF extremes: of ice and fire, of glaciers and volcanoes, of majestic mountains and vast expanses of tundra and sand. In winter, the land is shrouded in darkness; in the summer months it is bathed in never-ending sunlight. In recent years, as Iceland has become increasingly known for fostering a vibrant culture of composition and performance, its music—whether classical or rock, ambient or experimental—has often been described in terms that associate it with the unique nature of its land of origin. The usefulness of such descriptions is often a matter of debate, but one native whose music certainly invites being heard in terms of nature and landscape is Jón Leifs (1899–1968), the first Icelander to devote himself fully to composition. He was a fervent nationalist in his art, fashioning an idiosyncratic and uncompromising Icelandic sound from traditions of vernacular music. Many of his compositions depict local landscapes or set the nation's ancient literary epics, yet their style is strangely novel, and the raw quality of his orchestral music is often enhanced by a greatly expanded percussion section. In terms of the details of his style, Leifs has not had many imitators, yet in a larger sense, he marked the beginning of an internationally viable Icelandic music.

Leifs was a maverick in other ways as well. Along with other artists of his generation, he championed the assimilation of the

Western tradition of "art music" in a country that had for centuries been virtually without any musical instruments or systematic music education yet wished to adopt such music as part of its effort to become a legitimate and modern European nation state.[1] Through his enthusiastic promotion of cultural exchange between Iceland and Germany, Leifs contributed significantly to this development. He procured talented German performers and teachers who made important contributions to musical culture in Iceland, and he organized and conducted a concert tour to Reykjavík with the Hamburg Philharmonic in 1926—the first concerts to be given there by a full symphony orchestra. He also fought tenaciously to secure composers' rights in his homeland, founding both the Icelandic Composers' Society and the Performing Rights Society as well as the Federation of Icelandic Artists.

There are thornier aspects to Leifs's career and his reception as a composer. He studied in Germany from 1916 to 1921 and lived there until 1944 with his wife, who was a Jewish-born pianist, and their two daughters. Although not a Nazi sympathizer, Leifs sought accommodation with the regime to a certain degree. His works were largely welcomed in the early years of the Third Reich due to a burgeoning interest in Nordic music as well as literature and mythology, but these doors closed after 1937, both because of his wife's racial origin and the Nazis' disdain for his peculiar musical language. Leifs does not, in this as well as certain other periods in his life, emerge as a wholly sympathetic figure. Of his intelligence there is no doubt, but he could be narcissistic and self-serving, too caught up in his own ideology of a "re-birth of Nordic music" to see its considerable flaws.[2]

Leifs's work was directly influenced by Icelandic nineteenth-century nationalism and the campaign for increased political independence. After nearly four hundred years of colonial rule over Iceland by Denmark, many Icelanders were eager to renegotiate their economic and political relationships with the Danish crown on more equal terms. A distinct Icelandic cultural nationalism began to manifest itself, largely justified by the important heritage of literature written down in the twelfth and thirteenth centuries. At the same time, nationalist writers and poets extolled the wonders of the Icelandic landscape, particularly the majestic and sublime qualities of its natural phenomena. In drawing inspiration from literature and nature, Leifs was fully in line with the broader trend of cultural nationalism that had been cultivated in Iceland since the 1830s and that aimed for the nation's full independence. His advocacy was premised on the belief that Iceland could be fully sovereign in the eyes of the outside world only if its culture, including music, was substantial enough to sustain the claim for nationhood.

The development of Leifs's ideology was also shaped in part by the challenge of finding his own voice as a foreign musician within the rich artistic heritage of Germany, where he was faced with marginalization and cultural and geographical distance. Leifs's response was the creation of a strongly individual, nationally tinged music, through which he aimed to legitimize Iceland as an independent, culturally empowered nation. In many ways, this was a typical "national music" project such as many European composers had undertaken in the nineteenth century, intended to bring forth positive ideas of a nation and emphasizing internal characteristics such as landscape, language, and historical experiences.[3] For all his opportunism during his years in Nazi Germany, Leifs's ideology always had more in common with the Icelandic cultural nationalism of the nineteenth century than with the German national socialism of the 1930s.

While acknowledgment of Iceland's significant literary past was central to its nationalist movement, other art forms did not enjoy any sort of elevated status in this codification of national heritage. Instead, they were viewed as primitive and in need of modernization and internationalization. This was particularly true in the case of music: folk songs and hymns cultivated in the nineteenth century were perceived by Icelanders in the early twentieth century as frozen relics from the past.[4] As Kimberly Cannady has noted, Icelandic nationalism in the nineteenth century took a different route in this regard from continental European Romantic nationalism.

Whereas key thinkers such as Johann Gottfried Herder viewed vernacular singing, or "folk songs," to use his own term, as central to any nation, such singing in Iceland was more likely to be seen as an embarrassing remnant of isolation and stagnation.[5] Leifs was a key advocate for Icelandic vernacular music, particularly in the 1920s, when he wrote articles on the subject to alert his compatriots to their own national culture and undertook local gathering expeditions, making invaluable field recordings and transcriptions. In terms of his Icelandic audience, Leifs's challenge was to promote both the local and international, encouraging a more positive appraisal of the native heritage while at the same time attempting to modernize Icelandic musical life through the Austro-German symphonic tradition.

Leifs's uncompromising scores can be heard as a fusion of competing musical discourses: the folklorist, the nationalist, and the modernist/primitivist.[6] His reception at home was hampered by two elements of his style that Icelanders regarded with skepticism: the vernacular (viewed as embarrassing) and the modernist, for which they showed little sympathy. Although Leifs sought inspiration in native folk music, landscape, and medieval epics, it should be kept in mind that he wrote his music largely for an international audience, in the hope that his nationally colored Nordic style would eventually encourage a more widespread school of composition.

It is fitting that Leifs was born in 1899, on the brink of a new century. While his music initiated a novel soundscape, it also contains echoes of nineteenth-century aesthetics. For example, he frequently sought inspiration through texts or images—most often from nature—in order to bring his music fully to life. Some of his most famous instrumental works portray landscape or render extramusical narratives in a manner reminiscent of the nineteenth-century tone poem (*Hekla, Geysir*) or programmatic symphony (the *Saga Symphony*). Others have a strong biographical element, including four hauntingly beautiful works he composed after the tragic death of his daughter in 1947. Occasionally the elements of biography and landscape coincide, for example in *Landfall*, inspired by his journey to Iceland after the war ended in 1945 and seeing the landscape gradually emerge in the distance. The notion that the creations and the biography of an artist are inextricably linked is a cornerstone of nineteenth-century criticism, but, as Alexander Rehding has pointed out, the strategy of mapping a composer's life onto his works, or vice versa, "smacks of unbridled Romanticism and is viewed with considerable suspicion in contemporary scholarship."[7] However, Leifs remained beholden to Romantic views of artistic inspiration and creativity. Many of his works do indeed appear to have sprung unequivocally from his concurrent biographical situation, yet the relationship between life, art, and place is complex and should not be reduced to facile interpretation.

Leifs's individuality did little to endear him to the musical public in Iceland, where he was largely neglected and ridiculed during his own lifetime. His abrasive and quarrelsome personality did not help, nor did his predilection for composing massive orchestral and choral scores for which the performing forces and facilities simply did not exist. At the time of his death in 1968, many of his most demanding compositions remained unperformed. Leifs has more recently been lauded as a creative personality "among the most radical and original of the 20th century," and because of his nationalist stance he has been seen as a figure comparable to Bartók or Sibelius.[8] The individual visionary quality of his oeuvre has invited parallels with eccentric outsider figures such as Charles Ives and Havergal Brian; others hear in his music echoes of Carl Ruggles, Alan Hovhaness, and Roy Harris.[9] In the past two decades, Leifs's own works have finally become more prominent on the international concert scene, and much of his output has now been released on CD—the Swedish record label BIS has a complete set in progress.

The purpose of this book is threefold. Firstly, it offers a broad summary of Leifs's life and work. As there is no other book-length study of Leifs in the English language, I have attempted to give as much relevant information as possible, including translations of important sources and a cultural context for his reception in Iceland and abroad. Secondly, the book examines the role of landscape, literature, and vernacular music as key elements of his nationalistic style. As Nicola Dibben has noted, the elision of the Icelandic nation with landscape and nature is frequently evoked in discussions of contemporary music in various genres.[10] The historical roots of this connection can be traced back to Leifs himself, who encouraged it by consistently evoking in his writings a Nordic exoticism based primarily on landscape and literature. His music still frequently recalls such imagery among critics and audiences alike. John Pickard has likened the counterpoint of the *Saga Symphony*'s opening to "two geological plates, grinding against one another"; for others, Leifs's music is "hewn out of granite," and images of volcanoes and geysers are ubiquitous in writings on his works.[11] In this book I seek to explore the historical background of such imagery as well as its role in the reception of Leifs's music, but I also attempt to discuss his works in terms of specific musical elements: quotation or imitation of characteristic genres of Icelandic folk song and the vertical progressions of third- and tritone-related harmonies that exert an uncanny effect on the listener.

The third main purpose of this book is to place this music within a broader context of nation building and the emergence of an Icelandic musical identity in the first decades of the twentieth century. An awareness of the historical moment out of which Leifs's music was born is crucial in placing his aesthetics in a larger perspective. Iceland's steps toward independence from Denmark were accompanied by an earnest effort to legitimize the nation's sovereignty through culture, an enterprise in which Leifs enthusiastically participated and one that had a profound impact on the development of the local arts scene. A more nuanced understanding of the historical context also allows us to distinguish between Leifs's homegrown brand of Icelandic nationalism—fully in line with local developments—and the far more extreme form of racism in Nazi Germany, where his music did briefly gain a modicum of attention and respect. A substantial part of this book is devoted to Leifs's career in the Third Reich. His modest ascent and precipitous decline there raise important questions about music's relationship with political extremism and offer a valuable case study of the ideology and reception of Nordic music during that period. Leifs does not fit the traditional black-and-white categories of perpetrator and victim, and I have attempted to present as much of the relevant material as possible, for the reader to draw his or her own conclusions. All in all, then, this book presents a multipronged approach—the weaving together of landscape, literature, nation building, cultural identity, and politics into a biographical narrative.

For his admirers, Leifs can be a difficult object of affection. He is a character full of paradoxes, his output is inconsistent, and his nationalist ideology seems to border on zealotry. His letters and contemporary accounts depict both an ardent visionary and a cantankerous narcissist. For all his faults, Leifs was a unique composer, driven by the ambition to create an Icelandic sound that might intrigue and inspire the world by bringing to life the country's literature, landscape, and vernacular songs. His friend, the writer and diplomat Kristján Albertsson, who was unusually cognizant of the composer's strengths and weaknesses, wrote that Leifs's purpose had been to give Iceland "a voice among the musics of the world, to let the cool, strong gale of the Icelandic weather rush into the world's music—and to remind ourselves who we are, what we are, can be or become if we choose to be ourselves, true to our origins and character—and not simply epigones in the world of art."[12] In his best works, Leifs achieved his goal. They are born of a deep personal conviction and epitomize the unique soundscape of his country: roaring ocean, erupting mountains, cracking icebergs, trembling earth.

NOTES

Unless otherwise stated, all archival material cited is part of the Jón Leifs collection at the National and University Library, Reykjavík, Iceland.

1. Kimberly Cannady and Kristín Loftsdóttir, "'A Nation without Music?': Symphonic Music and Nation-Building," in *Sounds Icelandic*, eds. Þorbjörg Daphne Hall, Nicola Dibben, Árni Heimir Ingólfsson, and Tony Mitchell (Sheffield: Equinox, 2019), 28.

2. A brief note on terminology is in order. In this book, I generally use the term *Nordic* to refer in a neutral way to the countries consisting of

Scandinavia (Sweden, Norway, Denmark) as well as Finland and Iceland. In the context of Nazi cultural aesthetics, however, *Nordic* (or its German equivalent, *nordisch*) is a loaded term that implies cultural superiority and often includes Germany in addition to the countries mentioned above. In what follows, the meaning should in each case be clear from the context.

3. Philip Bohlman, quoted in Matthew Riley and Anthony D. Smith, *Nation and Classical Music from Handel to Copland* (Woodbridge: Boydell, 2016), 9.

4. Kristín Jónína Taylor, "Northern Lights: Indigenous Icelandic Aspects of Jón Nordal's Piano Concerto" (DMA diss., University of Cincinnati, 2006), cited in Cannady and Loftsdóttir, "'A Nation without Music?,'" 24.

5. Cannady and Loftsdóttir, "'A Nation without Music?,'" 24.

6. The same is true of Edvard Grieg, as Daniel M. Grimley has ably explored; see his *Grieg: Music, Landscape, and Norwegian Identity* (Woodbridge: Boydell, 2006), ix.

7. Alexander Rehding, "Liszt's Musical Monuments," *19th Century Music* 26, no. 1 (Summer 2002): 53.

8. John Pickard, "Jón Leifs (1899–1968)," *Tempo*, New Series, no. 208 (April 1999): 9.

9. Guy Rickards, "Music of Fire and Ice: a Survey of Icelandic Music on Record," *Tempo*, New Series, no. 181 (June 1992): 53; see also Andrew Clements, "BBCSO/Oramo Review—Elemental Sibelius to Buoyant Beethoven," *Guardian*, August 23, 2015, http://www.theguardian.com/music/2015/aug/23/bbcsooramo-review-elemental-sibelius-to-buoyant-beethoven; Rob Barnett, review of *Hekla and Other Orchestral Works*, BIS-CD 1030, http://www.musicweb-international.com/classrev/2001/Aug01/Leifs_Hekla.htm; Rob Barnett, review of *Dettifoss and Other Orchestral Works*, BIS-CD 930, http://www.musicweb-international.com/classrev/2001/Aug01/Leifs_organ.htm.

10. Nicola Dibben, *Björk* (Sheffield: Equinox, 2009), quoted in Tony Mitchell, "Music and Landscape in Iceland," in *The Oxford Handbook of Popular Music in the Nordic Countries*, eds. Fabian Holt and Antti-Ville Kärjä (Oxford: Oxford University Press, 2017), 146.

11. Pickard, "Jón Leifs," 10; Rob Barnett, review of *Baldr*, BIS-CD 1230/1231, http://www.musicweb-international.com/classrev/2002/Aug02/Liefs_Baldr.htm.

12. Kristján Albertsson, "Sextugur í dag: Jón Leifs tónskáld," *Morgunblaðið*, May 1, 1959.

ONE

THE LAND WITHOUT MUSIC (1899–1916)

WHEN JÓN ÞORLEIFSSON (WHO LATER took the surname Leifs) was born at Sólheimar farm in northwestern Iceland in 1899, Iceland was virtually a "land without music."[1] This island of roughly forty thousand square miles had for centuries been among the most economically deprived regions of Europe. Its economy was largely dependent on farming, a risky endeavor in a country with infertile soil and a volatile climate; the majority of its population of roughly seventy thousand still lived in houses made of turf. Brutal weather conditions, a volcanic eruption, and an increase in population led to a massive emigration of Icelanders between 1860 and 1914, when an estimated quarter of the total population chose to start a new life in Canada, the United States, and Brazil.

The musical scene in nineteenth-century Iceland was equally humble. It consisted largely of folk songs, unaccompanied hymn singing in church, and performance on a single type of indigenous instrument, a bowed zither known as a *langspil* (similar to the Norwegian *langeleik*). But while musical activity in Iceland was at a low point in the nineteenth century, sources suggest that it had been more vibrant at earlier stages in its history. During the Roman Catholic era (1000–1550), nine monasteries and nunneries existed in Iceland, and, like their counterparts elsewhere in Europe, these were centers of culture and learning. Gregorian chant and simple polyphony were sung at mass and office, including a liturgy for Þorlákur, Iceland's patron saint, which survives in a manuscript from around 1400.[2] After the Lutheran Reformation (completed with the beheading of the last Catholic bishop in 1550), church authorities published hymnals in which the new liturgy, largely derived from Danish and German sources, was adapted to local use. Domestic singing seems also to have been widespread, judging from the considerable number of manuscript songbooks surviving from the seventeenth and eighteenth centuries. Some of these demonstrate a surprisingly active transmission of both sacred and secular polyphony from distant shores. One Icelandic songbook from the 1660s contains local contrafacta—new lyrics to preexisting music—to a medieval pilgrim song from the Catalan manuscript *Llibre vermell*, a well-known French *chanson spirituelle* first published in 1548, a lighthearted *canzonetta* by the sixteenth-century Florentine composer Francesco Corteccia, and secular songs by the Swiss and Austrian composers Ludwig Senfl and Paul Hofhaimer.[3] Such imported polyphony was in all likelihood mostly cultivated at the country's two Latin schools—at Skálholt in southern Iceland and at Hólar in the north. Each school housed roughly twenty students, and music was part of the curriculum, although the precise nature and quality of the instruction seem to have varied over time.[4]

By the early 1800s, this eclectic type of music making had all but evaporated. Violent volcanic eruptions in 1784–85, along with a destructive earthquake in southern Iceland, signaled the end of the Latin schools in their age-old form. When a new school was established in Reykjavík a few years later, music was no longer part of the curriculum. The consequences of such neglect were quickly felt, for in the ensuing decades only a handful of figures among the cultural elite acquired any proficiency in music. When the pioneer of the Icelandic enlightenment, Magnús Stephensen, died in 1830, an organ formerly in his possession was shipped back to Copenhagen, as no one on the island knew how to play it.[5]

A decade later, Pétur Guðjohnsen, the first Icelander to have formally studied church music in Denmark, returned to Reykjavík and was promptly rewarded with an appointment as cathedral organist. Gradually, a fledgling music scene began to take shape. Most of the activity centered on church music and choral singing; a new hymnal appeared in print in 1861, and a men's chorus was founded the following year. A leading advocate of progress was Olufa Finsen, the wife of the Danish governor, who resided in Reykjavík between 1865 and 1882. She taught piano and singing, formed a small choir that rehearsed twice weekly at her home, and in 1880 conducted her own cantata for voices and organ at the funeral of Icelandic nationalist hero Jón Sigurðsson.[6]

Songs with simple piano accompaniment were a staple of the burgeoning household music making, and a handful of local composers—all amateurs with limited musical training—achieved considerable popularity in this field in the last decades of the nineteenth century. Jónas Helgason was a blacksmith who later developed a career in music and was an influential teacher; Árni Thorsteinson was a photographer; Bjarni Þorsteinsson was a priest. A more experienced musician was Sveinbjörn Sveinbjörnsson (1847–1927), who studied music with Carl Reinecke in Leipzig and lived in Edinburgh for most of his career. His works are well crafted, with echoes of Mendelssohn, Grieg, and Niels Gade, but Sveinbjörnsson remained largely unaffected by nationalist spirit. His output includes the first Icelandic works of chamber music (two piano trios and a violin sonata) as well as the choral hymn "Ó, Guð vors lands" ("O, God of Our Country").

This piece, which later became the national anthem, was composed for an event that greatly stimulated the development of the local music scene. In 1874, to mark the one-thousand-year anniversary of the Norwegian settlement, Iceland celebrated with a national festival. King Christian IX of Denmark was among the guests and presented Icelanders with their first constitution, granting the parliamentary Alþingi legislative power with the crown in matters of exclusively Icelandic concern. This was a milestone in Iceland's claim for independence from Denmark, the main topic of political discussion in the last decades of the nineteenth century. When Norwegians had settled in Iceland in the 870s, they had founded a free country, but decades of civil unrest in the early thirteenth century had led the country to the brink of collapse, and Iceland lost its independence to Norway in 1262. Royal succession eventually brought Norway under Danish rule, and by the nineteenth century, Iceland was little more than a Danish colony, with no local representation within the Danish government.[7]

In the years following the 1874 festival, Icelanders were buoyed by a new optimism, which led to a revitalization of society and the urge to create a better and more advanced life for the Icelandic people. This was also true of music, which, like other art forms, plays a crucial role in the formation of a national identity. The development of Iceland's musical infrastructure in the late nineteenth and early twentieth centuries was directly related to the burgeoning nationalist movement. The Reykjavík Brass Society (*Lúðurþeytarafélag Reykjavíkur*) performed for the first time in 1876, the first public concert by a mixed choir was given in 1883, and a program for improving church music by installing small harmoniums in rural churches was adopted throughout the country between 1874 and the 1890s.[8] But progress was slow; catching up with centuries of continental developments would not be achieved overnight. During the first two decades of the twentieth century, music in Reykjavík consisted mostly of the cathedral choir leading hymn singing during worship, occasional song recitals or choral concerts, and a few local ensembles that performed salon music in the town's cafés. Satisfactory instruments were scarce; as late as 1914, a critic lamented that a visiting pianist had no choice but to perform his recital—which included Beethoven's *Appassionata* sonata—on an upright piano.[9]

FROM COUNTRYSIDE TO VILLAGE

While Jón Þorleifsson (later Leifs) was not born in the capital, his parents moved from the countryside to Reykjavík in 1900, when he was just over one year old. Iceland was still a rural society of farmers and fishermen; out of a total of seventy-eight thousand inhabitants, only five thousand lived in the capital.¹⁰ Leifs's parents had been raised in the countryside, and both came from relatively well-to-do families. His father, Þorleifur Jónsson (1855–1929), had been born at the farm Sólheimar ("Sun-worlds") in the northern county of Húnavatnssýsla, the son of a prosperous farmer who had served as a member of parliament. After graduating from the Reykjavík Latin school in 1881, Þorleifur departed for Copenhagen, where he commenced studies in law at the university. His time there was cut short by a dangerous infection, for which he was hospitalized for nearly a year, often in serious condition, before returning to Iceland, where he spent another year convalescing at his parents' farm. In 1886, having regained full strength, he began his career in earnest. He purchased a weekly Reykjavík journal called *Þjóðólfur*, which he managed and edited for six years, and he also became an elected member of the Icelandic parliament, following in his father's footsteps. In his aspirations as both journal editor and parliamentarian, he was a staunch supporter of the burgeoning revivalist movement that sought national emancipation and dreamed of a better, more enlightened, and more prosperous society. For a while, he enjoyed the strong backing of his constituents, who admired, in the words of a friend, his "rare conscientiousness" in working "for the benefit of the nation and its people."¹¹

Þorleifur was a confirmed bachelor until September 1893, when, at age thirty-eight, he married the twenty-year-old Ragnheiður Bjarnadóttir. She had been born and raised at Reykhólar, an ancient farm site in northwestern Iceland, whose name ("Smoke Hills") refers to the nearby hot springs used for washing clothes and occasionally for cooking. Her parents, Bjarni Þórðarson and Þórey Pálsdóttir, had no fewer than thirteen children and hired a schoolteacher from Reykjavík each winter to ensure the best education available for all of them. At age eighteen, Ragnheiður continued her studies in Copenhagen, and the following year she received her first job, teaching Danish and needlework at an all-girls school in northern Iceland. Her career was truncated by what seems to have been a hastily arranged wedding to Þorleifur Jónsson; their

Figure 1.1. Ragnheiður Bjarnadóttir and Þorleifur Jónsson in Reykjavík, ca. 1900. © Leifs Archives, National and University Library of Iceland.

first child, a son named Bjarni, was born after only seven months of marriage. During their first year of matrimony, the couple lived with Ragnheiður's parents at Reykhólar. Later, they farmed for a while on land owned by Þorleifur's family farther east, in Húnavatnssýsla, before relocating yet again to another nearby farm. Their letters suggest that they had their doubts about whether they were cut out for the farming life, not least because Þorleifur's frequent absence during parliament sessions in Reykjavík put a strain on the running of the household.[12]

After thirteen successful years, Þorleifur's career as a parliamentarian came to an abrupt end when he took a contested standpoint on a heated political topic. While Iceland's bid for independence from Denmark had gained considerable momentum in the second half of the nineteenth century, the post of minister of Iceland was still occupied by a Danish government official. Many Icelanders wanted to press for the establishment of a local minister's post in Reykjavík, but others believed that the Danes might be more easily swayed if the native minister were to be based in Copenhagen. This more cautious plan was known as *Valtýska*, after its leading advocate, Valtýr Guðmundsson, professor at Copenhagen University and Þorleifur's former classmate. In the end, the home rule framework prevailed, and Iceland received its first home minister in 1904. Þorleifur's support for the alternative Valtýska movement caused a falling out with his constituents, who in 1899 appealed to him to either support home rule or resign from parliament. The forty-five-year-old Þorleifur chose not to run for reelection the following year, accepting instead a position as clerk at the Reykjavík post office. For a former parliamentarian, this was certainly a step down the social ladder, but the prospect of being able to make his home in the capital with his family may have outweighed the short-term negative social and financial impact. Thus, in the summer of 1900, he moved from Húnavatnssýsla to Reykjavík with his wife and their four children: Bjarni, age six; Þórey, age five; Salóme, age three; and Jón, at a little over one year old.

On arriving in the capital, they settled at Bókhlöðustígur 2, a modest three-story house in the heart of the small town. Despite the difference in their personalities, Þorleifur and Ragnheiður seem to have enjoyed a happy marriage. Þorleifur was an introvert who, in his own words, kept his "feelings, joys and frustrations" to himself; Leifs would later remark that he found his paternal relatives "too timid and lacking in self-confidence."[13] Ragnheiður, on the other hand, was self-assured, decisive, and outspoken. Both were admired for their generosity to the poor and needy, and their house soon became a kind of social center. Shortly after they moved

Figure 1.2. Leifs and three of his siblings, ca. 1912. From left to right: Þórey, Páll, Salóme, and Jón. © Leifs Archives, National and University Library, Reykjavík.

to Reykjavík, the couple took Ragnheiður's niece under their wing, and when a few years later Þorleifur's brother passed away, his three children also moved into the Bókhlöðustígur home. There was also a new addition to the family proper: a son named Páll was born in May 1902. Þorleifur's salary as postal clerk hardly sufficed to feed such a large extended family. This emboldened the energetic Ragnheiður to start her own store, Silkibúðin (the Silk Shop), in 1906, specializing in ladies' clothing and knitting supplies. For decades it was located in nearby Bankastræti, but in 1951 it moved to the basement of her home at Bókhlöðustígur. She managed it herself until her old age, with help from Leifs's sister Þórey, and the profits would to a considerable extent sustain her son during his years in Germany.

Two tragedies befell the family during Leifs's childhood. Ragnheiður suffered a miscarriage in 1910, and three years later the eldest son, Bjarni, died in Bíldudalur, a small village in the Western fjords, of acute appendicitis—three days before his nineteenth birthday. The family's losses fueled their interest in spiritualism, the belief that spirits of the dead had the ability and inclination to communicate with the living. This was a significant trend in Icelandic society in the early years of the twentieth century, and like its counterpart in English-speaking countries, it was typically a middle-class phenomenon. The family's initial interest in spiritualism had been awakened in 1906, when Þorleifur's brother, terminally ill with cancer, attempted various supernatural cures. After Bjarni's death, his parents hosted séances at their home in attempts to contact him. While these were not attended by the children except for the oldest, Þórey, the younger children experimented on their own with séances, automatic writing, and talking boards; a notebook in Leifs's handwriting, dated March 1915, is titled "Experiments to Prove Man's Immortality." At one session, he noted, he played "Nearer, My God, To Thee"—the choice presumably inspired by reports of the sinking of the *Titanic* three years earlier—on the piano while a friend tried to connect with the afterlife. Although the experiments were unsuccessful, Leifs observed that they had led him to contemplate the more important things in life, "selflessness, charity, and such things," and he resolved that he would "lose [himself] in compassion for others."[14]

DISCOVERING MUSIC

Leifs, or Nonni as he was called by the family in those days—a common Icelandic nickname for Jón—was a small, slender, rather fragile lad who enjoyed books and music and was an avid stamp collector. It was most likely in 1909, when he was ten years old, that an upright piano was brought into the family home. It was primarily intended for Þórey, the older of the two girls, who received lessons and practiced diligently. Playing the piano was primarily a female occupation in Iceland at this time. The semiprofessional pianists and piano teachers in Reykjavík were all women, and it was only in 1912 that two young male pianists gave their first public concerts in town. But Leifs was fascinated by the instrument, and before long he was taking lessons from Martha María Stephensen, a septuagenarian who was a friend of his mother's. No sources besides Leifs's own biographical notes describe Stephensen as a piano teacher, so lessons with her may have been perfunctory. In any case, he found a more reliable instructor before long. Herdís Matthíasdóttir, in her midtwenties, was the daughter of the renowned Icelandic pastor and poet Matthías Jochumsson—the author of the words to Iceland's national anthem. She had studied at the Royal Conservatory in Copenhagen on a scholarship offered to her by King Frederick VIII himself and then returned to Reykjavík, where she taught piano and voice.[15] Her brief career came to a tragic end when she died in the flu pandemic of 1918, which claimed the lives of nearly three hundred inhabitants in the small town of Reykjavík alone.

The young Leifs also briefly studied the violin. In an interview later in life, he recalled that his parents allowed him to take up the instrument after he had "cried an entire day for not being allowed to get a violin."[16] He took lessons from the Danish violinist Oscar Johansen, who arrived in Reykjavík in 1910 and performed at one of the town's leading hotels, Hótel Ísland. Johansen was a seasoned performer whose concerts included more ambitious fare than was common in Reykjavík at the time, but he did not remain there for long. After two years he left for New York City, and Leifs gave up the violin.[17]

In January 1915, fifteen-year-old Leifs began a diary that chronicles his intellectual and emotional development as a teenager. He seems to have been aware of the instability of his adolescent temperament and noted that he wished to preserve in his notebook not mundane incidents but rather the "extreme sadness, extreme joy or some other intense emotions" that consumed his mind.[18] The diary portrays a sensitive, introverted young man who preferred reading dramatic novels to doing homework—Goethe's *Faust* and *Die Leiden des jungen Werthers* were among his favorites. He had commenced studies at the Reykjavík Grammar School (*Menntaskólinn í Reykjavík*), also known in Iceland as the Latin school or the learned school, conveniently located across the street from his home on Bókhlöðustígur. At the time, this was the only grammar school

Figure 1.3. Jón Þorleifsson on his confirmation day, May 1912.
© Leifs Archives, National and University Library, Reykjavík.

in the country. Its history dates back to the founding of the first Icelandic Latin school in Skálholt in 1056; that school was moved to Reykjavík in the eighteenth century, but the present building, which still houses the school, was inaugurated in 1846.

Leifs's diary entries and school notebooks offer glimpses of his interests and his personality, both of which are remarkably indicative of his future leanings. His love for nature, for example, was instilled at an early age. In 1914, in a school essay titled "Mountains," he proclaimed that "our mountains are the most beautiful and sublime that nature can offer. I remember that when I was a child, I could sit outside and stare at the mountains for hours at a time." He recalled that in times of "terrible sadness, terrible despair," he would run into the mountains, and the effect was like "washing away all the sorrow and sadness."[19] Here he is presumably recalling the summers of 1910–13, when he was sent to live and work at Reynifell, a farm in southern Iceland, near the palagonite mountain Þríhyrningur (Three Peaks Mountain) with its yellow-brown hue. (The tradition of sending urban youngsters into the country for summer work was common in Iceland throughout the twentieth century.) Leifs's letters suggest that he enjoyed his stay there, at least for the first few summers; he delighted in horseback riding and splashing in the nearby river.[20] Still, the reminiscence quoted above suggests, as do many of Leifs's diary entries, a temperamental youngster seeking an outlet for his intense emotions.

The adolescent Leifs also expressed his admiration for medieval Icelandic culture, seeing it as a reflection of an enlightened connection with the landscape itself as well as a model for the more depraved modern society. In February 1915, he penned an essay called "The Virtues of the Ancients in Iceland," the most important of which, he argued, were bravery, athleticism, and noble-mindedness, and he surmised that medieval Icelanders had been "in better harmony with the land, than we are today." The essay continued: "I believe that men such as they could not have existed anywhere but in a country where mountains and glaciers stare out into the wilderness, terrifying and powerful; where the rivers and waterfalls sing, the mountains rattle, fire rages and the sun casts a golden flush on the clear blue sky, for all of this seems to be reflected in the souls of the ancient Icelanders. Should not their descendants also reflect this?"[21]

Strongly influenced by the revivalist language of the early twentieth century, the young Leifs sounds remarkably like his adult self in his reverence for the Icelandic landscape and the country's medieval heroes. His notions of Icelandic exceptionalism, always somewhat naïve and unreflective, were rooted in those of the teenager, expressing his thoughts in what was then still an economically disadvantaged Danish colony.

Music had already become a passion for Leifs by age fourteen. For a school journal, Leifs shared his ideas in an article titled "Poetry and Music": "Music is the art form with which I have become most familiar. And now that I have familiarized myself with it *a little*, I am intrigued by it beyond words. It is without a doubt the most beautiful and magnificent of all the arts (of those that I know) and it can reach *the highest degree of perfection*."[22]

For the young Leifs, music seems to have been primarily an emotional outlet. In summer 1915 he confided in his diary that "there is some yearning in my heart that is trying to break out," and he found the piano to be the ideal vehicle to express feelings.[23] He was also eager to expand his musical horizons. Reykjavík was a town without a music shop, but Leifs, undeterred, penned letters to music publishers abroad, ordering Mozart sonatas and concertos from Wilhelm Hansen in Copenhagen and four-hand arrangements of Beethoven's symphonies from Breitkopf und Härtel in Leipzig.

He gradually gained proficiency as a pianist under Matthíasdóttir's guidance, and at Christmas 1914 his performance was one of the main events at a variety program at his school; he played three *Lyric Pieces* by Grieg and movements from Beethoven's *Pathétique* and op. 26 sonatas. A diary entry from a few weeks later stresses the fifteen-year-old's continued infatuation with music and also indicates his progress in terms of repertoire: "I had a piano lesson tonight. Now I am playing: scales in contrary motion, Carl Czerny Etudes III and Beethoven sonatas. I have already played his sonatas no. 1, no. 8 (*Pathétique*), no. 9, and am starting no. 14 (*Moonlight*). Tonight I played the last part of *Pathétique* and the opening of no. 14 (*Moonlight*). I am now so inclined towards music, that I find no other art form to be as beautiful."[24]

Later that year he began learning Beethoven's *Appassionata* sonata, although he admitted that he was only able to "glean an inkling of it, compared to what one can reach with practice, dexterity, and knowledge—of course preferably guided by one's own temperament. One day I will really master them, all of these sonatas, and then I will *give them my all*—or so I hope."[25] Besides the young Leifs's passion for Beethoven, he particularly admired Grieg, whose *Lyric Pieces* were a staple of the pianistic diet during his student days. Later in life, he blamed "childish innocence" for his infatuation with Grieg while also confessing that he had failed to grasp the full extent of Beethoven's genius.[26]

Leifs's goal was to practice for six hours a day, but usually he managed only three or four. He confided to his diary one reason for this: "Sometimes, when I have begun to practice, I start to rattle away (some gibberish of my own) and forget all about practicing."[27] A more detailed account appears in another diary entry, dated September 30, 1915: "Tonight, when I was outside and saw the northern lights, I suddenly got the idea to try to depict them in music; how glorious this would be. And I saw in my mind's eye how it could be done. When I got home and had eaten dinner, I again thought of the northern lights. I sat down at the piano and tried, again and again, but it didn't sound the way I felt it should, and so I stopped."[28]

This passage is remarkable in light of Leifs's future compositional work. Even at such an early age, with no compositional training, he was motivated to depict nature through music. Witnessing the northern lights inspired an attempt at creating a novel soundscape, although in this case, sadly, one left unrealized due to his own lack of skill (which he duly acknowledges). In his mature works, Leifs would return again and again to representing natural phenomena through music: volcanic eruptions in *Baldr* and *Hekla* and hot springs, waterfalls, and icebergs in *Geysir, Dettifoss,* and *Hafís*. He never again explored his youthful subject of the northern lights, but the ideas of nature, the north, and the juxtaposition of light and shade would define his works throughout his career.

The teenage Leifs may have been inclined to improvise, but he rarely put his flights of fancy to paper. Only one composition has survived from his student years in Iceland: a brief, tender piano piece written in 1913 and titled *Reverie/Meditation* (*Vökudraumur/ Hugleiðing*). Its twenty-four measures seem to betray a rather uncertain grasp of music theory; harmonically it hovers between a second-inversion F-sharp major tonic and its subdominant, without a single dominant chord. Given Leifs's later predilection for loud and forceful music, a notable feature of this work is its prevailingly soft dynamic, *pianissimo* and *una corda*. Its simplicity and tenderness are typical for the Icelandic songs published in the first years of the twentieth century, written for an amateur audience by part-time composers such as Bjarni Þorsteinsson and Jón Laxdal.

Leifs's desire to devote himself fully to music only grew stronger. In July 1915, his teacher invited him for evening coffee at her home along with Haraldur Sigurðsson, who was at the time Iceland's most advanced pianist. Sigurðsson was completing his studies in Dresden and later became a professor at the Copenhagen Conservatory. He was in Reykjavík for a brief visit, performing a recital of four Beethoven sonatas (on a "new Hornung & Møller grand piano," it was noted in local newspapers), which may have been the first proper piano recital Leifs attended.[29] Matthíasdóttir presented Leifs as a "future colleague," which suggests that she had faith in his talent, but he himself was riddled with worries and self-doubt: "I know well that this is a path strewn with rocks, but this seems to only make it even more desirable."[30]

As the autumn semester began, Leifs became increasingly despondent at the thought of having to devote his time to school, which he regarded as a "*deadly* chore."[31] He wished his studies were "nothing but music" but also found himself socially isolated. In his diary, he noted that his schoolmates had accused him of arrogance and of disparaging his friends' playing: "'Oh, the genius. He can't listen to anyone play but himself. My, he thinks he's superior,' they think. I know it. Last year at school I heard people say that I supposed myself 'so musically gifted' that I couldn't 'bear to hear a single note that was out of tune.'"[32]

One senses here, perhaps, something of the sense of superiority and of antipathy toward others that would become a mark of

Leifs's character. The mental strain of his dissatisfaction at school even began to manifest itself physically, for he suffered from nosebleeds and headaches that prevented him from taking his Christmas exams. "Perhaps I am losing my mind," he wrote in February 1916. "Either I want to cry loudly in front of everyone, or be sullen and mean, and quarrel furiously. I do more of the latter, I think."[33] These bouts of extreme irritation were followed by intense reflections on self-improvement, influenced by the spiritualist inclination of the entire household: "We are here to become spiritually mature—I am the spirit, not the body—we live to ennoble our spirit (so that we can then ennoble the spirits of others), *this and nothing else is what we live for*."[34]

A few weeks later, Leifs experienced an epiphany that would change the course of his life. A key event in Reykjavík's humdrum music scene was a recital given at the cathedral on March 5, 1916, by Páll Ísólfsson, a young organist enrolled at the Leipzig Conservatory of Music. Ísólfsson, six years Leifs's senior, had begun music studies at an early age with his father, who was an organist and choirmaster at Stokkseyri, a seaside village roughly forty miles south of Reykjavík. He continued his studies in the capital with Sigfús Einarsson, the cathedral organist and one of the town's most proficient musicians, before moving abroad. Ísólfsson had been studying in Leipzig for three years, and his debut recital in his hometown was eagerly anticipated; it consisted of works by J. S. Bach as well as Liszt's *Prelude and Fugue on B–A–C–H*, and the church was filled to capacity.[35] In the audience on that Sunday evening happened to be two teenagers who would later become leading artists in their own right: Jón Þorleifsson and Halldór Laxness, the Icelandic novelist who later won the Nobel Prize for Literature.[36]

Although Ísólfsson was only a few years older than Leifs, he had received from an early age the finest instruction Iceland could offer, and the difference in their backgrounds must have been obvious to the younger student. Still, Leifs was enraptured by his playing and now envisioned that with proper training and diligence, he might achieve something comparable. Returning home after the concert, he announced to his parents his intention to quit school and devote himself fully to music. His parents refused to grant their consent, and, as Leifs confided to his diary, he retired to bed in a despondent mood: "I cried. I think my grief has never been more acute." He refused to attend school the following day but instead spent the morning playing Chopin, with tears running down his cheeks (again, according to his somewhat overwrought diary account). Later that day, after conferring with his piano teacher, his parents proposed a compromise. They had both studied in Copenhagen, and they must have been aware of Reykjavík's shortcomings when compared to what major cultural hubs could offer. Their son would be allowed to attend a conservatory abroad on the condition that he complete his spring exams at the Reykjavík *menntaskóli*. His diary entry that evening was jubilant and concise: "Victory."

After passing his exams in June, Leifs spent the summer practicing at home. His admiration for Beethoven was boundless, and at midsummer he confided to his diary the sublime effect the Ninth Symphony had had on him a few weeks earlier: "I cannot put into words the fervor that took hold of me. It was as if my soul had entered Paradise and a heavenly fire burned in my chest—and then when this comes: *Alle Menschen werden Brüder wo dein sanfter Flügel weilt*—then I wanted to fall down on my knees, lift my hands and praise God—and this does not happen frequently. What power this music has! Perhaps this symphony can really make brothers of all men?"[37]

Although Leifs himself was overjoyed, his intention to study in Germany caused his parents grave concern. With a war raging on the continent, Icelandic newspapers frequently carried reports of food shortages and other hardships facing the German population. However, the family was reassured when he at last summoned the courage to introduce himself to Ísólfsson, who agreed to take him under his wing and accompany him to Leipzig in the autumn. For Leifs, Ísólfsson's advice and support would prove invaluable. They enjoyed a close friendship during their time in Leipzig—for a while they were virtually inseparable—but they were fundamentally different personalities, and their relationship later in life would be fraught with disputes and rivalry.

Shortly before the young musician departed for Germany in autumn 1916, he was advised that his patronymic, Þorleifsson, might cause trouble with foreign immigration officers. Abroad, the Icelandic letter Þ was sometimes spelled *Th* but could also be incorrectly rendered as *P*, and papers with conflicting spellings were bound to raise suspicion in wartime. Thus he applied for, and received, special dispensation from the Icelandic government to adopt a proper surname, Leifs—derived from the second syllable of his patronymic, Þor*leifs*son.[38] It was both a practical gesture and a symbolic one: an act of rebirth, a refashioning of the self before departing on the journey that would shape his destiny. From then on, his sole ambition was to become something still virtually unheard of in Iceland—a professional musician.

NOTES

1. The famously derisive comment "Das Land ohne Musik" was directed at England by the German critic Oscar Adolf Hermann Schmitz in 1904; see Richard Taruskin, *Music in the Nineteenth Century* (Oxford: Oxford University Press, 2010), 803.

2. A study and edition of the St. Þorlákur liturgy is Róbert Abraham Ottósson, *Sancti Thorlaci Episcopi Officia Rhythmica et Proprium Missae* (Copenhagen: Ejnar Munksgaard, 1959).

3. This manuscript, Rask 98, is in the Arnamagnaean collection at Copenhagen University. See my article "Fimm 'Ütlendsker Tonar' í Rask 98," *Gripla* 23 (2012): 7–52, and "Íslenskt tvísöngslag og Maríusöngur frá Montserrat," *Gripla* 15 (2004): 195–208.

4. On music instruction at the Latin schools, see Guðlaugur R. Guðmundsson, *Skólalíf: Starf og siðir í latínuskólunum á Íslandi* (Reykjavík: Iðnú, 2000), 174–84.

5. Ólafur Davíðsson, *Íslenzkar skemtanir* (Copenhagen, 1888–92), 271–72.

6. Þóra Friðriksson, "Frú Olufa Finsen," *Óðinn* 4 (1909): 90–92.

7. For a nuanced discussion of Iceland's status within the Danish realm, see Gavin Lucas and Angelos Parigoris, "Icelandic Archeology and the Ambiguities of Colonialism," in *Scandinavian Colonialism and the Rise of Modernity*, eds. Magdalena Naum and Jonas M. Nordin (New York: Springer, 2013), 92.

8. Hallgrímur Helgason, *Tónmenntasaga Íslands* (Reykjavík: Skákprent, 1992), 61–63; "Samsöngur í Reykjavíkurdómkirkju," *Suðri*, January 3, 1884.
9. Árni Thorsteinson, "Piano-hljómleikar," *Morgunblaðið*, October 25, 1914.
10. Guðmundur Jónsson and Magnús S. Magnússon, eds., *Hagskinna, Sögulegar hagtölur um Ísland* (Reykjavík: Hagstofa Íslands, 1997), 93.
11. Páll Steingrímsson, "Þorleifur Jónsson póstmeistari," *Vísir*, April 10, 1929.
12. See, for example, Þorleifur Jónsson to Ragnheiður Bjarnadóttir, August 1, 1895 (National and University Library, Reykjavík, Lbs 4072 4to).
13. Þorleifur Jónsson to Leifs, April 23, 1922; Leifs to Jón Jónsson, September 19, 1931.
14. Leifs, diary entries, April 16 and 29, 1915.
15. Þórunn Erlu Valdimarsdóttir, *Upp á Sigurhæðir—Saga Matthíasar Jochumssonar* (Reykjavík: JPV, 2006), 555.
16. Leifs, interview by Þorkell Sigurbjörnsson in "Tónskáld mánaðarins," Iceland National Radio, DB-567-1.
17. Ingólfur Kristjánsson, *Harpa minninganna* (Reykjavík: Ísafoldarprentsmiðja, 1955), 385–86; Ingólfur Kristjánsson, *Strokið um strengi* (Reykjavík: Setberg, 1966), 44. After arriving in New York, Johansen took the stage name William Oscar, performed with the Philharmonic Society of New York from 1916 to 1919, and made several recordings, including some of the first commercial recordings of Icelandic instrumental music (for Columbia Records in 1919); see "Oskar Johansen," *Morgunblaðið*, December 11, 1919.
18. Leifs, diary entry, January 10, 1915.
19. Leifs, "Íslenzka," notebook, 1.
20. Leifs, letters to parents, August 4, 1910 and August 7, 1911; letter to Salóme Þorleifsdóttir, August 20, 1910. National and University Library, Reykjavík, Lbs 4072 4to.
21. Leifs, "Dyggðir fornmanna á Íslandi," in "Íslenzka," notebook, February 4, 1915.
22. *Dagrenningarblaðið Bragi* (student publication, Menntaskólinn í Reykjavík), October 31, 1914, copy in the Leifs collection, box 16.
23. Leifs, diary entry, June 8, 1915.
24. Leifs, diary entry, January 12, 1915.
25. Leifs, diary entry, September 11, 1915.
26. Leifs, *Islands künstlerische Anregung. Bekenntnisse eines nordischen Musikers* (Reykjavík: Islandia Edition, 1951 [recte 1950]), 18.
27. Leifs, diary entry, July 15, 1915.
28. Leifs, diary entry, September 30, 1915.
29. Ego, "Haralds-hljómleikar," *Ísafold*, June 12, 1915. Only a handful of proper piano recitals had been given in Reykjavík earlier. The American

pianist Arthur Shattuck, a former pupil of Theodor Leschetizky's, gave a well-received recital (on a piano that he brought with him on a ship) in July 1910—presumably too early to have captured Leifs's attention. Another American pianist, Edward Weiss, performed in Reykjavík in October 1914, and Haraldur Sigurðsson performed in 1912 and 1914. For more on Sigurðsson's early career, see Þórður Kristleifsson, "Haraldur Sigurðsson píanóleikari," *Vísir*, November 19, 1944.

30. Leifs, diary entry, July 16, 1915.
31. Leifs, diary entry, September 11, 1915.
32. Leifs, diary entry, September 11, 1915.
33. Leifs, diary entry, February 24, 1916.
34. Leifs, diary entry, January 3, 1916.
35. Árni Thorsteinson, "Orgel-leikur," *Morgunblaðið*, March 8, 1916.
36. Laxness recalled the event in an article celebrating Ísólfsson's fiftieth birthday: "Páll Ísólfsson fimmtugur," *Tímarit Máls og menningar* 2 (1943): 148.
37. Leifs, diary entry, June 22, 1916.
38. Leifs, diary entry, September 23, 1916; Cabinet of Iceland to Þorleifur Jónsson, August 28, 1916 (National and University Library, Reykjavík, Lbs 700 fol.). The use of surnames instead of patronymics became something of a fad in Iceland in the 1910s and '20s; this both influenced and enabled Leifs's decision. In January 1915, a new law took effect that allowed Icelanders to adopt new surnames for a small fee. In 1925, this law was revoked, and the invention of new surnames has been illegal ever since. See Páll Sigurðsson, *Lagaþættir III: Greinar af ýmsum réttarsviðum* (Reykjavík: Háskólaútgáfan, 1994), 404–05.

TWO

YEARS OF STUDY (1916–21)

ON THE BRISK AUTUMN EVENING of September 27, 1916, the steamship *Botnía* departed from Reykjavík harbor, bound for Copenhagen. Among its passengers were three young musicians whose final destination was Leipzig: Páll Ísólfsson, Jón Leifs, and Sigurður Þórðarson, a violin student four years Leifs's senior who had also decided to join Ísólfsson on his return to Leipzig and to apply for the conservatory. This was Leifs's first journey abroad, and it was not without its complications; the trio were delayed for four days in Copenhagen while awaiting a permit to cross the border. Because of the war, they were required to present a signed declaration from the Icelandic consul to establish that they were not suspected of espionage.[1]

Their destination had for centuries been one of Germany's great cultural and commercial capitals. Leipzig University had been founded in 1409, and the city's musical legacy included the onetime residents J. S. Bach, Schumann, and Mendelssohn—the last of which had founded the city's conservatory in 1843. The Royal Conservatory of Music of Leipzig, as it was called from 1876, was housed in large, imposing quarters in Grassistraße, south of the city center. Leifs and Ísólfsson rented rooms in a house nearby (Fürstenstraße 11) and obtained both an upright and a grand piano so that they could practice simultaneously.[2]

Leifs's entrance exam took place on October 19. He played a Beethoven sonata but was dissatisfied with the outcome; in a letter to his parents he lamented that his training in Reykjavík had not prepared him adequately for such an ordeal, even though his piano teacher was "among the best there."[3] Nevertheless, he was admitted as a piano major. It was his good fortune that enrollment at the conservatory was low due to the war, and Ísólfsson had put in a good word for his friend. He was placed in the studio of one the school's most highly regarded professors, Robert Teichmüller, from whom Ísólfsson had also taken secondary piano lessons. Leifs developed a closer relationship with Teichmüller than with any of his other teachers, and Teichmüller later became the godfather of his first child. Leifs had nothing but praise for Teichmüller's pedagogical approach, noting that he "had no method, or to be more precise, had a new method for each and every student."[4]

The conservatory's curriculum was divided into three levels, according to competence: *Unter-, Mittel-* and *Oberstufe*. Leifs was placed in the *Mittelstufe* but soon began to question whether the jury had overestimated his abilities. Having completed his first lesson, he conveyed Teichmüller's verdict to his parents: "He said that I was musical but completely lacking in technique, so now I shall only practice technique. Had I begun my studies with him when I was twelve, I would be a good pianist by now."[5] Although Leifs practiced diligently, he was at times frustrated by the strict regimen of etudes and scales; he was allowed to proceed to J. S. Bach's two-part inventions only in early December. At least the effort seemed to be paying off, for at Christmas, Ísólfsson wrote to Leifs's parents that Teichmüller was "very pleased with him."[6] Ísólfsson was himself making splendid progress, and in 1917 he became assistant to his teacher, the renowned organist Karl Straube, at the Thomaskirche.

Leifs's studies abroad proved far costlier than his family had predicted, putting considerable strain on his parents' household. Tuition cost 360 marks a year, and Leifs had estimated his living expenses at roughly 200 marks a month. But he had little financial self-control and was usually in need of at least 50 additional

Figure 2.1. Leifs (*right*) and Páll Ísólfsson (*left*) in Leipzig, ca. 1918. From the collection of Þuríður Pálsdóttir.

marks each month, mostly for purchasing clothes or scores. Luckily, Ragnheiður's business at *Silkibúðin* was thriving, and Leifs's parents were able to comply with his frequent requests for more money. Their main concern was that he had enough to eat, since food was in short supply due to the war, but Leifs urged them not to worry. Each day, he and Ísólfsson ate a decent lunch at a cafeteria nearby, but evenings were spent at home with frugal fare: sardines, bread, marmalade, cocoa, and four sugar cubes each.[7] Occasionally they would receive butter and sausages from friends in Denmark, and by Christmas 1916 the slight-framed Leifs (his full adult size was five feet eight inches) announced that he had gained a bit of weight and was now 118 pounds. As the war dragged on, though, food rations were reduced, and by December 1917 the city's restaurants had little to offer beyond mashed turnips.[8] Twice that same year, Leifs journeyed by train all the way to Copenhagen for the sole purpose of eating his fill; from there he cheerfully informed his parents that he was consuming "1–2 glasses of cream each day and delicious cakes too."[9]

On arriving from humble Reykjavík, Leifs was thoroughly overwhelmed by the splendor of old Europe, which he found "unfamiliar in every way." Even the towering trees that lined the streets of Leipzig were a new experience, far beyond anything he had seen in his barren homeland:

> Everything was alien to me, both daily life and the loftiest art.... For the first time in my life I saw streetcars, trains, and countless other things.... My first walk through the alleys lined with tall trees was typical: autumn leaves were falling and blowing in the wind. I had never seen anything like it and had never even imagined such a thing. It was equally symbolic when I heard the sound of a symphony orchestra for the first time: Franz Liszt's *Faust Symphony*. I felt as if I could throw myself on the floor and scream loudly in amazement.[10]

This particular concert took place on October 26, little more than a week after Leifs's arrival. The renowned Gewandhaus orchestra held its concerts in the New Gewandhaus hall, opened in 1884 and destroyed in World War II. Its principal conductor, and at the helm of the *Faust Symphony* concert, was the legendary Arthur Nikisch, whose control of the orchestra, as well as his seemingly improvisatory, "gypsy-like" musicianship, mesmerized Leifs.[11]

For the young Icelander, his initial encounter with the cultural milieu of central Europe was an adventure, but it also had its disadvantages. Even decades later, the more negative aspects of his experience remained lodged in Leifs's memory: "It seemed to me as if central Europeans were of a different race and I thus became quiet and shy, and it took me many years to understand their daily behavior and conduct."[12]

> Some were not even familiar with the name Iceland, and believed that I was perhaps from Estonia or Ireland or perhaps some island in the Baltic Sea. Some had heard of Icelandic herring that was supposedly better than herring from other countries. Others, more knowledgeable, had heard of Geysir and perhaps also Hekla, but they asked in astonishment: "Iceland! Is it possible? Do humans actually live there?—But you're not Icelandic, are you?"—Yes, I replied that I was. "But your parents must be Danes or Europeans?" they asked. When I replied in the negative, my interlocutor would sometimes give me a strange look and say: "Well, but at least you are a mix of—an Icelander and a European?" When I also gave a negative reply, the next question came with an awkward glance: "But where in Iceland do the Eskimos live?"[13]

Leifs, who had been raised in the spirit of nineteenth-century nationalism, and who was convinced that Iceland was (in his words) "the greatest country in all the world," found his schoolmates' ignorance difficult to comprehend. Still, this cultural and physical marginalization of his native land only strengthened his resolve. His vision, later in life, of Iceland assuming a leading role in the world's culture can be traced not only to his upbringing in a country claiming independence but also to his frustration when confronting a Europe to which his native land hardly seemed to belong.

As a staunch nationalist, Leifs had developed a hatred of Danes and all that reminded him of the old colonial power. In 1917, when Germans banned all foreign correspondence in Icelandic, Leifs chose to write to his family in German rather than Danish, stating that he despised "everything that is Danish. . . . I hate the Danes even more because here everyone thinks that we *belong* to Denmark (!!!), that we speak Danish (!!!) and that the Old Norse language, which is still spoken in Iceland, is nothing more than a *dialect* (!!!)."[14] A major victory, and one that Leifs fervently desired, was the Act of Union of 1918, which established Iceland as a fully sovereign state in personal union with the Danish king. (When this agreement expired twenty-five years later, Denmark was under Nazi occupation, and Icelanders voted in a plebiscite to abandon the union unilaterally in favor of a republic.) A few years later, Leifs expressed in a letter his complete identification with his homeland and the national pride that would—for better or worse—define his lifelong artistic pursuit: "I stand or fall as an Icelander, I can only be understood as an Icelander, for I have always, as long as I remember, loved Iceland more than anything else in this world, almost more than my art or my family."[15]

ROMANCE AND ILLNESS

During his student years, Leifs fell in love. Annie Riethof was a fellow Teichmüller student two years Leifs's senior, born on June 11, 1897 (see fig. 2.2). Her father, Edwin Riethof, was an affluent businessman from Teplitz (now Teplice) in Bohemia, whose own father, Josef Rindskopf, had established a glass factory there in the 1860s. After Rindskopf's death, four of his sons, some of who had adopted different last names (Riethof and Rode), founded a new company, Josef Rindskopf's Söhne A.G., which became one of the leading manufacturers of colorful art nouveau glass objects around the turn of the twentieth century. Edwin married the twenty-three-year-old Gabriele (or Gabi) Perlman in 1894; like him, she was of Jewish descent, from a wealthy merchant's family in Prague. Theirs was an artistic household. Gabi was a talented pianist in her youth, and Edwin enjoyed singing and painting. Annie's older sister, Marie, had studied voice at the Leipzig Conservatory, although by the time Leifs came into their lives she had enrolled at the Academy of Visual Arts. Since they were both in Teichmüller's class, Leifs and Annie must have become acquainted soon after his arrival in Leipzig, but they began their relationship formally on March 23, 1918. To mark their first anniversary a year later, Leifs completed his first original composition, *Torrek* for piano, with a dedication to Annie (he would later arrange it for orchestra as part of *Trilogia*

Figure 2.2. Annie Riethof, ca. 1918. © Leifs Archives, National and University Library, Reykjavík.

piccola op. 1; see chap. 3). The title, *Torrek*, already suggests the influence of Old Icelandic literature. The word means "deep sorrow" but is also used to mean "eulogy"; the most famous eulogy found in the ancient sagas—a text that Leifs would later set as op. 33a—is known as *Sonatorrek*—that is, the *torrek* of the poet's loss of two sons.

We know little of Leifs's specific musical experiences during his student years, since his letters to his parents, our main source of information regarding his daily activities, are silent on such matters. However, since Leifs traveled back to Iceland in summer 1918 (his first trip home after arriving in Germany), his correspondence with Ísólfsson reveals that it was the latter's responsibility to purchase subscription tickets for the two at the Gewandhaus and Alberthalle, a large concert hall at the Leipzig Crystal Palace; it is possible that they subscribed to other seasons as well.[16] While Nikisch was no admirer of the avant-garde, his programs provided a steady staple of Austro-German music from Mozart to Bruckner, along with more recent compositions by Mahler and Strauss. The 1918–19 season would have given Leifs the opportunity to hear works such as Beethoven's symphonies no. 3, 5, 7, and 9, Brahms's symphonies no. 2 and 4, Bruckner's Sixth, and excerpts from Wagner's *Parsifal* and *Tristan und Isolde*. In light of Leifs's later development as a composer, it is tempting to speculate whether he also heard Nikisch conduct Strauss's *Eine Alpensinfonie* in November 1916, shortly after his arrival in Leipzig, or Mahler's Sixth Symphony near the end of his residence there, in December 1921.[17]

In spring 1919 Leifs traveled to Copenhagen to attend the Nordic Music Days—a festival of Scandinavian music that had been held regularly for more than three decades. The Copenhagen festival consisted of eight concerts, and Leifs was able to hear works that were not standard fare in Leipzig's concert halls. It also prompted his first newspaper article, a festival report for the Icelandic *Morgunblaðið*. He considered Ture Rangström (Symphony no. 1) and Carl Nielsen (Symphony no. 4) to be the most interesting composers presented at the festival, whereas he found Sibelius mediocre at best. His Second Symphony, Leifs declared, contained "hardly any original ideas, and I must consider his work harmless prattle, sometimes pure nonsense."[18] Leifs would later form a more sympathetic opinion of Sibelius, whose works he praised in 1957 as being "inspired by landscape and the forces of nature, and humility before them."[19]

The Copenhagen festival in 1919 prompted Leifs to consider Iceland's position in the music world. Though still ruled by the Danish king, Iceland was now a sovereign nation—yet no Icelandic music had been performed during the festival. Leifs concluded his report by urging his countrymen to raise the level of music culture in Iceland so that the country would not again have to endure such disgrace abroad. The first step, he suggested, would be to found a music school in Reykjavík (which, according to his plans, would eventually become the "Icelandic Conservatory") and, in conjunction, a performing ensemble that would introduce the masterpieces of the Western canon to local audiences. He also encouraged the forming of a youth choir on the model of Leipzig's Thomanerchor or Berlin's cathedral choir, along with a new position for a choral director, who should first be sent to Germany to observe "how the best conductors drill each and every schoolboy, day after day."[20] Here Leifs emerges in a role that would become increasingly familiar, as a passionate (though sometimes obstinate) instigator of musical progress in his native land. For the time being, however, his ideas seem to have had little impact at home.

Leifs's main obstacle during his years of study was not his lack of previous training but the feeble state of his health, which prevented him from attending school for long stretches at a time. In spring 1917 he was in severe pain for days, and a doctor suggested it might be heart-related or possibly "chest rheumatism caused by too much practicing."[21] His health again turned precarious in 1919. In May he suffered a headache for ten days and nights with no relief, and in September a stay in the Harz mountains, during which he had hoped to recuperate in the country air, came to a regrettable end. He had been there for two weeks when he once again fell seriously ill, and on October 1 he was transported by ambulance to Leipzig, where he spent the next few months in various hospitals and sanatoriums. The diagnosis was pulmonary inflammation, and doctors recommended total rest, thus ruling out the possibility of resuming his studies in the fall.

Having graduated from the conservatory in summer 1919, Annie remained in Leipzig for private lessons. She was already giving solo recitals: a program in Teplitz in April 1920 included Mendelssohn's

Variations sérieuses, Schubert's A minor sonata D. 537, Schumann's *Kinderszenen*, and smaller works by Handel, Reger, and Rachmaninoff. Annie and her mother were a godsend to Leifs in his illness, but Annie's father opposed her relationship with the young musician. He feared that the couple would move to Iceland (which he saw, rightly, as a dire career choice for a promising pianist), and even if they remained in Germany, the chronically ill Leifs might never be able to provide for his daughter. Leifs, on the other hand, refused even to meet with Riethof, since he found it "impossible to put my trust in someone who values people according to their bourgeois status."[22] He had hoped to wed Annie on May 1, 1920—his twenty-first birthday—but now his parents also expressed their reservations, advising him to launch his career before starting a family. In the end, Leifs's poor health put a halt to their plans. He continued to suffer from pains in the lungs and stomach, and from February 1920 until that summer he received treatment from a Leipzig gastroenterologist who prescribed complete rest.[23]

When he was well enough to return to the conservatory, Leifs studied piano as well as score reading, orchestration, and theory and also took composition lessons from Paul Graener, who had been appointed as successor to the recently deceased Max Reger. Leifs's composition notebooks suggest a strict regimen of counterpoint exercises, fugues, and canons, but they also reveal a distinctive musical personality taking shape. Although intended as academic exercises, the two-part inventions he wrote in January 1918 occasionally demonstrate his flair for the dramatic gesture: one culminates in a "Grave" section in which the two parts explode into octaves, marked *fortissimo* and *pomposo*.[24] Another sketchbook, marked "Übungen bei Graener," contains a string quartet movement on a cantus firmus, the Lutheran chorale *Ein' feste Burg ist unser Gott*—a tune that Leifs would employ decades later in *Viking's Answer* (see chap. 9).

Leifs also studied orchestration with the Hungarian conductor Aladár Szendrei, making steady progress in the subject. In June 1918, he arranged the *Adagio sostenuto* from Beethoven's

Hammerklavier sonata for string orchestra, and in 1920 there followed more sonata movements by Beethoven: the slow movements of the *Pathétique* and op. 26 sonatas arranged for strings and the opening movement of op. 31 no. 3 for winds. His sketchbooks also contain drafts of original works: a dramatic movement for piano titled "In memoriam"—in memory of a gifted young Icelandic pianist, Jón Norðmann, who had succumbed to tuberculosis in Berlin—and another mournful sketch for violin and piano in G minor marked "Andante lamentoso." Leifs also completed, in October 1920, the first draft (in short score) of a larger work, originally titled *Symphonische Trilogie*, although he later settled on the more modest title of *Trilogia piccola*. It would take him four years to further revise and orchestrate the work, and by then his composing style had taken quite a different direction (see chap. 3). Leifs had for a while been attempting to contact the renowned pianist-composer Ferruccio Busoni, hoping that the latter might agree to give him composition lessons, and at their single meeting, in Berlin in autumn 1920, Leifs showed Busoni the first two movements of this work. Busoni remarked that this was interesting and original music but advised him to study Mozart intensively—advice that, according to an account published by Leifs's friend and colleague, the musicologist Hallgrímur Helgason, somewhat perturbed the young composer.[25]

By spring 1920, Leifs had missed nearly a year of school because of his illness. It is difficult to gauge whether he used his infirmity as an excuse to devote himself to composition—as Carl-Gunnar Åhlén suggests in his biography—or whether his extended hospital stays led him to reconsider his options for a career in music.[26] After his first year at the conservatory he had fretted to his parents about his "nervousness, both when performing and in other things," and a psychosomatic explanation for his disease does not seem farfetched.[27] He had arrived in Leipzig with the hope of becoming a professional pianist, but after three years it seemed clear that he would attain neither the technical skill nor the fluency of a virtuoso. In autumn 1919, having just begun to practice again after months away from the instrument, he confessed to his parents that he had felt more incompetent than he could ever have imagined.[28]

Leifs attended the six-week Munich Opera Festival in late summer 1920, and again his report in an Icelandic newspaper gives an indication of his musical tastes. He was particularly impressed with Karl Muck's conducting of Wagner's *Siegfried*, less so with Leo Blech and Bruno Walter, both of whom he found to be diligent but dull. He attended Strauss's *Die Frau ohne Schatten* (which had premiered earlier that year) and was delighted by the music and the orchestration, although he found the execution less than perfect. In his mind, the highlights of the festival were Franz Schreker's *Die Gezeichneten* and Hans Pfitzner's *Palestrina*, the act I climax of which he described as "burning with conviction."[29]

After yet another health incident in autumn 1920, Leifs finally recommenced his formal studies in spring 1921, after a hiatus of a year and a half. Although still a piano major, he now also took formal conducting lessons with Otto Lohse, director of the Leipzig Stadttheater and a former student of the legendary conductor Hans Richter. Leifs had begun to view conducting as the path most likely to lead to a stable and artistically fulfilling career, and by summer 1921 he had already had his first actual conducting experience, at rehearsals of the Leipzig Philharmonic and the Grotrian-Steinweg orchestra. The latter, intended as a low-price alternative to the Gewandhaus orchestra, operated under the leadership of the maverick conductor Hermann Scherchen. Leifs's piano teacher Teichmüller had been instrumental in luring Scherchen to Leipzig and presumably introduced him to Leifs, who promptly began taking conducting lessons from him. Scherchen's anti-Romantic views of the classical repertoire would have a profound influence on Leifs (see chap. 3).[30] But the experience of conducting an orchestra came at a steep cost, and Leifs's father had to foot the bill—250 marks for the Philharmonic and 125 for Grotrian-Steinweg. Leifs kept his parents updated on his progress: "And now I know I can conduct an orchestra," he proudly declared following his debut in May.[31]

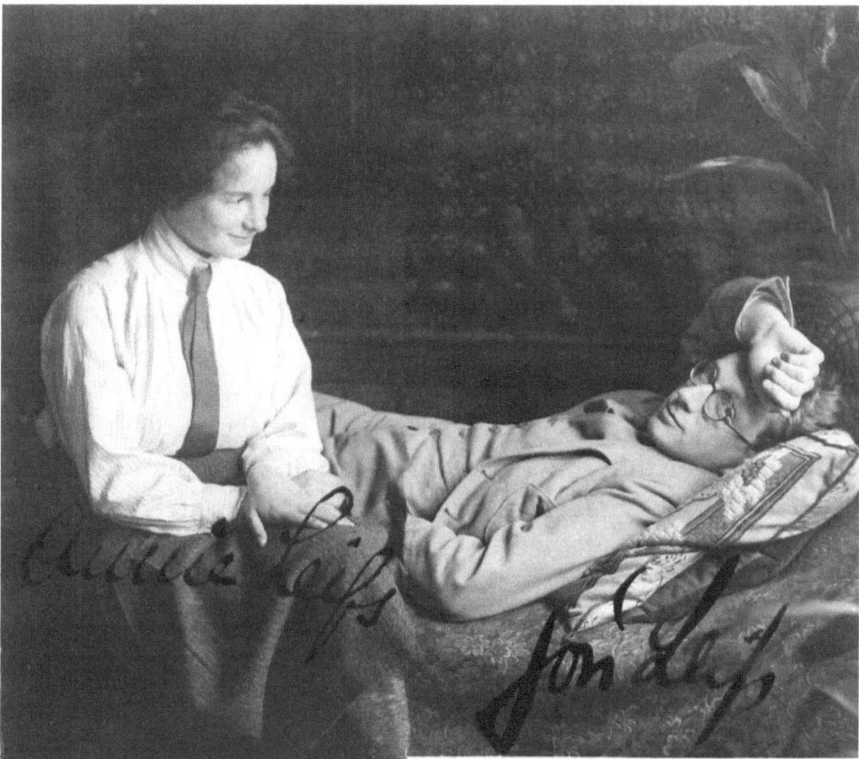

Figure 2.3. Jón and Annie Leifs in Leipzig, spring 1921. © Photographic Collection, National Museum of Iceland.

Leifs graduated from the Leipzig Conservatory on June 17, 1921. It was the fulfillment of a long-held wish, but he must have harbored mixed feelings all the same. In the four years since commencing his studies, he had been repeatedly sidelined by illness, and a career as a pianist seemed unlikely. Leifs's student records at the conservatory show that his formal education consisted of two and a half years in *Mittelstufe* (October 1916 to Easter 1919) and only a few months in *Oberstufe* (from Easter 1921), although he evidently took private lessons from 1919 through 1921 as his health allowed. His graduation recital was not even a full program and, somewhat remarkably, contained not a single solo piece: he performed J. S. Bach's Concerto in F minor BWV 1056 with a student orchestra and took the piano part in a sonata for violin and piano by Paul Graener, his composition teacher. Still, the concert appears to have been a success. A review in a Leipzig journal, *Der Drache*, praised Leifs's "admirable understanding of style," and Teichmüller wrote him a glowing recommendation, stating that he had thoroughly enjoyed teaching "such a talented musician with a personal flair."[32]

HONEYMOON IN ICELAND

A week after his graduation recital, Leifs and Annie Riethof were married. Although his parents had given their consent, Edwin Riethof still objected on the grounds of their uncertain economic future. The newlyweds sailed to Iceland for their honeymoon, arriving on July 22, and Leifs immediately set in motion a plan to invigorate the local music scene in Reykjavík. He hoped to establish a small string ensemble that might later be expanded into a full orchestra, but finding capable players who were willing to take part was a challenge. The previous year, Leifs's former schoolmate Sigurður Þórðarson had reported to him on the forces available in town: five to six good violinists, three clarinetists, one cellist, two double bassists, two flautists, and a few horn players. Although these were limited resources at best, he encouraged Leifs to go ahead with his plan, declaring it "a scandal" that no such ensemble existed in a town of sixteen thousand inhabitants. Leifs, his friend suggested, should "wake the citizens of Reykjavík from their sleep" and make them appreciate "the ennobling effect that music has on each man's soul."[33]

The task proved more challenging than Leifs had imagined, not least because Reykjavík's two leading violinists refused to cooperate. The Dane Paul Bernburg, who had settled in Iceland in 1905 and was a popular performer in the town's cafés, dismissed Leifs's strategy as unrealistic, while Þórarinn Guðmundsson, a local violinist and graduate of the Copenhagen Conservatory, had plans for an orchestra of his own. Earlier that summer, he had rehearsed a small ensemble to perform at the Icelandic visit of King Christian X. Seeing potential for further development, Guðmundsson founded The Reykjavík Orchestra (*Hljómsveit Reykjavíkur*), which had roughly twenty members and was the city's only such regularly performing ensemble until the Iceland Symphony Orchestra was established in 1950. Although Leifs had to make do without the two top players in town, he did convince a group of ten amateurs to form an ensemble that rehearsed four times a week, with the goal of performing a short program at his concert with Annie on September 23. After a rough start, Leifs was heartened by their progress, but he saw no choice but to cancel the entire enterprise when the band's only violist withdrew. Disillusioned, Leifs explained the project's failure from his perspective in a newspaper article, stressing his sacrifice of time and talent and taking a rather superior attitude toward the local players: "Without love for my nation and faith in her abilities, my patience would never have carried me this far."[34]

Another of Leifs's ambitions was to found a music school in Iceland. A short article of his on the subject had already appeared in *Morgunblaðið* the previous year, but now he laid out his ideas in more detail. He suggested that a music school in Reykjavík could function with a mere three teachers at the outset: a pianist, a violinist, and a cellist. They could form a piano trio and give public concerts, and the group would eventually be expanded to a larger ensemble as more locals acquired the necessary skills. He hoped that a small coterie of well-to-do benefactors might assist in financing the school, alongside other contributions from ordinary music lovers. While many of Leifs's ideas were commendable, the article's disdainful tone won him nothing but enemies. For example, he declared that the local church music could "make no man pious" and that most Icelandic compositions were "the skimmed milk of a syrupy Danish music" that he wished had never seen the light of day.[35] With his pugnacious attitude, Leifs infuriated virtually all of Reykjavík's leading musicians, especially Sigfús Einarsson, the cathedral organist, who retorted with an article of his own.[36]

Leifs had another tactic for cultivating interest in music among his countrymen. Few books on music had ever been published in Icelandic, and in any case these were long out of print. To address this lack, in summer 1921, Leifs wrote a twenty-eight-page pamphlet on the fundamentals of music, in the hope that this would encourage the locals' appreciation of the art. The resulting volume, *Techniques of Music* (*Tónlistarhættir*), was an overly ambitious crash course in music theory, including fugue, double counterpoint, canon, and cantus firmus technique, and it proved too demanding for an amateur readership. The ever ambitious Leifs had the volume printed in Leipzig by the venerable Breitkopf und Härtel press, but sales in Iceland were abysmal, and the proposed second volume never materialized.[37]

All things considered, Leifs's 1921 trip to Iceland must be viewed as a failure. He had arrived in Reykjavík with all odds in his favor: he was a homegrown talent with a prestigious conservatory degree, accompanied by his charming and talented wife, yet his prickly personality and ostentatious ideas earned him the animosity of local musicians and adversely affected his future possibilities as an artist there. The only truly successful enterprise of the couple's honeymoon to Iceland was their concertizing. They gave a two-piano recital at one of the town's main concert venues, Báran—a wooden house near the lake Tjörnin in central Reykjavík, on the site of what is now Reykjavík's city hall. On the program were Bach's F minor Concerto, with Leifs taking the solo part in what had been his graduation piece, Mozart's Piano Concerto in A major, K. 488 (with Annie as soloist), and Bach's double harpsichord concerto BWV 1060, in Reger's arrangement for two pianos. Annie also gave solo recitals in both Báran and the newly constructed Nýja bíó (The new cinema), to great acclaim, with critics lauding her "supple and gentle playing" and "unusually cultivated taste."[38]

DISCOVERING ICELANDIC FOLK MUSIC

Even though the journey to Reykjavík was largely a failure, in one respect it proved decisive for Leifs's future, for it was then that he stumbled on Icelandic folk music as the foundation of his art as a composer. It began with the discovery of a volume on his parents' bookshelf that had gone more or less unnoticed during his childhood: *Íslenzk þjóðlög* (Icelandic folk songs), a massive tome of music collected and transcribed by the Icelandic pastor and amateur composer Bjarni Þorsteinsson and published in 1906–09.[39] While it may seem odd that Leifs had ignored this collection during his adolescent years, this is most likely explained by the negative perception, common among Icelandic nationalists, of native music as "primitive" and "stagnated" in comparison with the Austro-German tradition that had been Leifs's staple diet as a piano student. Although he had composed, or at least begun, a handful of pieces during his student years in Leipzig, it was only when he discovered Þorsteinsson's book that he resolved to try his hand seriously at composition and to employ vernacular tunes as the basis of an Icelandic style. In a newspaper interview in 1959, he reminisced about his internal conflict and uncertainty at this point in his career: "But to compose music... no, I didn't dare. It demanded that I re-live the entire human experience. It demanded everything. But still, I wanted to try. And then I began searching, in an attempt to answer the question whether we in Iceland had some material like other countries, which might be reworked into a new music—some spark that might ignite that big flame."[40]

The book that provided Leifs with his spark, Þorsteinsson's *Íslenzk þjóðlög*, is a curious hybrid, and less than half of it consists of folk songs. It is divided into three main sections: transcriptions of music from manuscripts dating from roughly the fourteenth century until around 1800 (pp. 76–408); music from Lutheran hymnals printed in Iceland (pp. 409–520); and over five hundred Icelandic folk songs, transcribed around the turn of the twentieth century by Þorsteinsson himself and a few dozen collaborators in various locations throughout the country (pp. 521–919). Although Þorsteinsson was a beloved amateur composer, he had no systematic training in music. His original compositions are graced with a lyrical gift, though sometimes hampered by a limited harmonic range and predominantly homophonic texture. Þorsteinsson only rarely arranged Icelandic folk songs and never wrote any large-scale works of his own, but he did predict a future in which composers would draw on the vernacular tradition in creating their own styles. In the preface to his collection, he observed that composers in other countries had immersed themselves in "the spirit of folk song, and so can let their new work descend from the fatherland and the nation. In this regard, Icelandic composers of the future have a large task ahead of them."[41]

In recognizing the value of the native material, Þorsteinsson went against the general viewpoint in Iceland. He found little support for his enterprise among local intellectuals, as is demonstrated by the fact that the Icelandic Literary Society (*Hið íslenzka bókmenntafélag*), at that time virtually the only publisher of scholarly books in Icelandic, rejected his proposal for publication. It was only through a generous grant from the Danish Carlsberg Foundation—established by the founder of the eponymous brewery—that his volume saw the light of day.[42] A rare endorsement came from the Danish musicologist Angul Hammerich, who declared Iceland to be a "musical treasure-chest," echoing claims generally reserved for the country's literary heritage.[43] Another enthusiastic proponent of the native folk song practice was the renowned Icelandic poet Einar Benediktsson, who would soon encourage Leifs on his path to a national music (see chap. 3).

Leifs made a careful study of Þorsteinsson's entire tome, as his heavily annotated copy (now part of his collection at the National/University Library in Reykjavík) shows. He was most intrigued by two primary types of nineteenth-century folk music found at the very end of the volume: *tvísöngur* and *rímur*. In order to better understand Leifs's musical style, it is necessary to explain the characteristics of each in some detail.

Rímur (rhymes, sing. *ríma*) are a form of epic poetry that appears to have developed in the fourteenth century. A ríma will be in one of various rímur meters (*rímnahættir*) and consists of two to four lines per stanza. Rhyme and alliteration are prevalent features of the genre, as example 2.1 demonstrates—in a favorite quatrain meter called *ferskeytt*.

Example 2.1. Rímur melody (from Leifs, 25 *Icelandic Folk Songs* no. 3).

Andskotann ég **á**ðan *sá*	I saw Satan just now
uppi á fjalla *brúnum,*	up on the mountain side,
hafði **h**att og parruk *á,*	he had a hat on and a wig,
hann var að gá að *kúnum.*	and was tending the cows.

Here, the first two lines alliterate through vowels (vowels can alliterate with each other: *andskotann/áðan/uppi*), while the latter two emphasize h (*hafði/hatt/hann*). End rhymes (here sá/á; brúnum/kúnum) are characteristic of most quatrains; internal rhymes can also occur in rímur poetry and were considered the mark of a particularly talented versifier. As seen above, another characteristic of many rímur melodies in performance was a kind of mixed meter (often 4–3–4–2) that results from the close alignment of poetic and melodic rhythm.

Rímur are a kind of Icelandic *chanson de geste*; the oldest surviving such poem is found in *Flateyjarbók,* a manuscript believed to have been copied in the 1390s. Rímur were a mainstay of Icelandic poetry for centuries and were often composed in cycles on an already existing story. *Núma rímur,* for example, relate the story of the Roman king Numa Pompilius while *Ólafs ríma Haraldssonar* tells the legend of St. Olaf of Norway. Hundreds of rímur cycles have survived—roughly 250 from the eighteenth century and 500 from the nineteenth.[44] As late as the nineteenth century, rímur were a mainstay of evening gatherings (known as *kvöldvaka*) on rural farms, where people would gather round to enjoy some kind of recitation. In some cases, rímur singers went from farm to farm, receiving food and accommodation in exchange for their performances.[45] In the later nineteenth century, the popularity of rímur

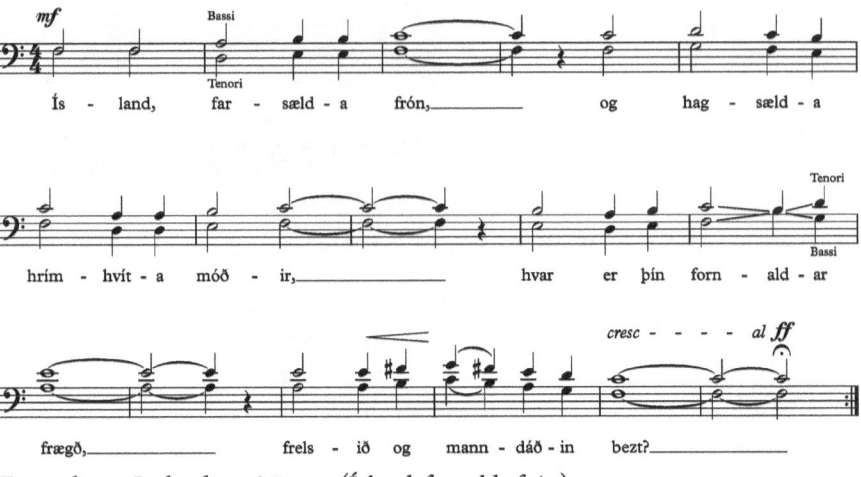

Example 2.2. Icelandic tvísöngur (Ísland, farsælda frón).

diminished sharply, in part due to criticism from a younger generation of Romantic poets who saw it as unworthy of a nation aspiring to independence and requiring a more expressly "cultured" poetry.

The other main genre of Icelandic folk music was *tvísöngur* (twin song or two-part song; see example 2.2). Here, a main tune is doubled at the fifth, with the accompanying voice beginning a fifth below the tune, then converging with the melody at the close of the penultimate phrase and moving to the upper fifth for the conclusion.

In the preface to his folk song volume, Þorsteinsson was eager to demonstrate the ancient origins of both rímur and tvísöngur genres. Of the latter, he postulated that two-part singing in parallel fifths had, just like the Icelandic language itself, been "brought here by the early settlers; both were first distorted, then disappeared in all of Scandinavia, but both survived, with remarkably few changes, on our remote native land right up to the present day."[46] Although tvísöngur is certainly an important Icelandic tradition, the evidence suggests that Þorsteinsson was mistaken in his view of its origin. Practiced in Iceland from at least the thirteenth century, tvísöngur seems to have been an imported tradition of church singing from continental Europe, a kind of note-against-note counterpoint commonly referred to as *cantus planus binatim* or "doubled plainsong."[47] It seems that this tradition was largely—though not exclusively—confined to the two Latin schools, in Skálholt and Hólar. Only in the late eighteenth century, when the schools were temporarily shut down due to a series of devastating natural disasters, was the written tradition of tvísöngur transformed into the orally transmitted ("folk") one documented in Þorsteinsson's transcriptions.[48]

After his epiphany in the summer of 1921, Leifs immersed himself in the Icelandic folk material. Within a few months he had completed new compositions based on folk songs (*Four Pieces for Piano* op. 2, see chap. 3) as well as an article in which he attempted to elucidate "The Character of Icelandic Music" through an analysis of melodies from Þorsteinsson's collection. It appeared in 1922 in *Skírnir*, a prestigious journal primarily devoted to literature; it is still the oldest continuously published journal in the Nordic countries.[49] Here Leifs laid down what he considered the main elements of Icelandic folk music: irregular rhythm, parallel fifths, modal melodies (most frequently Dorian and Lydian) with "missing" notes, narrow ambitus, and recurring motivic patterns. One of Leifs's remarks on the characteristics of Icelandic vernacular song holds the key to his aesthetic approach during the 1920s. He declared that the scarcity of leading-tone and dominant functions in Icelandic folk songs could be seen as a kind of "free tonality or atonality." This fit nicely with his own aesthetic preferences and formed the justification for his developing style. Leifs predicted that the new music of the twentieth century, which he noted was "breaking off the shackles of earlier times," would justify the existence of Icelandic music. Thus, like Bartók, Leifs found elements in his native folk music that he saw pave the way to a musical modernism.[50]

Until Leifs came along, Icelandic composers had largely ignored folk song as a musical influence. For example, the songs of Cathedral organist Sigfús Einarsson are firmly anchored in the nineteenth century, written in a lyrical parlor style with traces of Schumann and Mendelssohn. Einarsson turned his attention to Icelandic folk song only in 1907, when he included four arrangements in a volume of his own songs, and five years later he published another volume that included still more folk song arrangements.⁵¹ One of these was *Ísland, farsælda frón* (see example 2.2), a well-known tvísöngur to a nationalistic poem by Jónas Hallgrímsson, one of Iceland's leading nineteenth-century poets (see chap. 4). This song had been given pride of place in Þorsteinsson's collection, where it opens the chapter on tvísöngur and has ever since been cited as the most common and authoritative example of the genre. In its original form *Ísland, farsælda frón* bears all the hallmarks of the nineteenth-century tvísöngur tradition, but none of these are evident in Einarsson's arrangement, which was reprinted in 1915 in the popular volume *Íslenzkt söngvasafn* (*Icelandic Songbook*; see example 2.3). Here Einarsson focuses on the melody itself, abandoning the parallel fifths in favor of a harmonically conventional setting. His arrangement neatly accommodates most of the melody's unusual features, but occasionally this results in awkward harmonic progressions—for example, the false relation between B-natural and B-flat in the penultimate measure.

Sveinbjörn Sveinbjörnsson, who composed the Icelandic national anthem and was the grand old man of the Reykjavík music scene, took even longer to warm to native folk songs. His volume of *20 Icelandic Folk Songs* arranged for voice and piano was published in 1924 and was well received; some of the items have never left the repertoire of young Icelandic singers.⁵² His approach was a decidedly old-fashioned one, as he took great care to make the modal material conform with a tonal harmonic framework. An advertisement for the volume in local newspapers stated that Sveinbjörnsson had "given these old and peculiar Icelandic folk songs a new costume that fits them extremely well, so that many find that they stand equal to the best in this category amongst any other nation."⁵³ In short, the purpose of these arrangements was to clothe the strange and unusual Icelandic melodies in continental garb so that they might be considered equal to—or even be confused with—vernacular tunes of other nations.

Although these conventional arrangements by Sveinbjörnsson and Einarsson were well received at home, others felt that

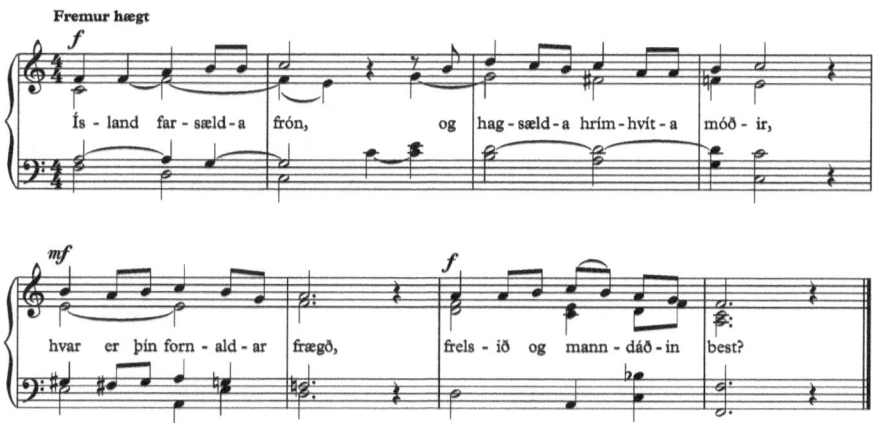

Example 2.3. Sigfús Einarsson, arrangement of *Ísland, farsælda frón*.

the moment had arrived for the birth of a truly national style of music. Þorsteinsson's remark on the "large task" awaiting nationally minded Icelandic composers of the future was quoted above, and in a 1915 lecture on "Iceland and the Scandinavian Influence," the lexicographer Sigfús Blöndal lamented the Danish influence on local music, claiming that Icelandic folk songs were still "awaiting the arrival of someone like Grieg, who can use them as the basis for compositions that could be profitable to the musical life of the entire world."[54] The impact of Danish music on the earlier generation of composers had been considerable, but Leifs took a different path.

Leifs often remarked that he did not regard folk music as "true art, but as material for art"—that is, as inspiration. He observed in it the "genial flashes of nationality and nature, a neglected soil, which can be brought to fruition as 'music of nature.'"[55] His goal was to integrate the essential features of Icelandic vernacular music with his own compositional voice. The majority of examples of Leifs's use of actual folk melodies date from the first eight years of his active composing career, from 1922 to 1930. In the latter year, this phase of his compositional development came to an end with the Organ Concerto op. 7, with its triumphant climax of the old Icelandic chorale *Allt eins og blómstrið eina*.

As he departed Iceland in autumn 1921, Leifs had discovered an uncommon path to explore as a composer. Since illness had prevented him from fully taking advantage of the Leipzig Conservatory's curriculum, his opportunities as a professional musician in war-ravaged, economically challenged Germany were limited at best. He would never pursue fame as a pianist but instead attempted to launch a dual (and no less arduous) career as conductor and composer. From then on, Leifs was determined to become Iceland's first truly national composer, to draw from the country and its songs a kind of music never before imagined.

NOTES

1. Leifs to parents, Copenhagen, October 10, 1916.
2. "Tónlistarhátíð Norðurlanda," *Morgunblaðið*, September 19, 1967.
3. Leifs to parents, Leipzig, November 28, 1916.
4. Leifs, "Robert Teichmüller †, Erinnerungen eines Auslands-Schülers," *Zeitschrift für Musik* 106 (1939): 748–49.
5. Leifs to parents, Leipzig, October 21 and 24, 1916.
6. Páll Ísólfsson to Þorleifur Jónsson, December 8, 1916.
7. Leifs to parents, Leipzig October 18 and 21, 1916.
8. Leifs to parents, Leipzig, January 1, 1918; Gunnar M. Magnúss, *Sigurðar bók Þórðarsonar* (Reykjavík: Setberg, 1979), 32; Matthías Johannessen, *Hundaþúfan og hafið* (Reykjavík: Bókfellsútgáfan, 1961), 130.
9. Leifs to parents, September 22, 1917.
10. Leifs, *Islands künstlerische Anregung*, 19–20.
11. Leifs, "Erinnerungen an Karl Muck," *Zeitschrift für Musik* 107 (1940): 290.
12. Leifs, *Islands künstlerische Anregung*, 19.
13. Leifs, "Ísland frá erlendu sjónarmiði," *Iðunn* 20 (1937): 49–50.
14. Leifs to parents, January 30, 1917.
15. Leifs to Rolf Cunz, February 26, 1926.
16. Páll Ísólfsson to Leifs, September 30, 1918.
17. Johannes Forner, *Die Gewandhauskonzerte zu Leipzig, 1781–1981* (Leipzig: VEB Deutscher Verlag für Musik, 1981), 441–45.
18. Leifs, "Norræn tónlistarhátíð í Kaupm.höfn 13.–21. júní 1919," *Morgunblaðið*, July 20, 1920.
19. See Leifs, "Minning Jean Sibelíusar," *Alþýðublaðið*, September 24, 1957. The two got along well at a cocktail party at the latter's country residence,

Ainola, in 1956, and a year later Leifs attended Sibelius's funeral on behalf of the Icelandic Composers' Society.

20. Leifs, "Norræn tónlistarhátíð í Kaupm.höfn 13.–21. júní 1919."
21. Leifs to parents, March 21, 1917.
22. Leifs to Edwin Riethof, May 16, 1921.
23. Medical note from Dr. Pascal Deuel (Leipzig), July 4, 1920.
24. Leifs, Leipzig sketchbooks.
25. Hallgrímur Helgason, "Jón Leifs," in *Tónskáld og tónmenntir* (Reykjavík: Skákprent, 1993), 109. Helgason suggests that Leifs and Busoni met during Leifs's twentieth year (i.e., in 1919 or early 1920), but the meeting took place later in 1920, when the opus 1 movements were ready in full score; see Carl-Gunnar Åhlén, *Jón Leifs—Tónskáld í mótbyr* (Reykjavík: Mál og menning, 1999), 73. Leifs had been attempting to make contact with the composer since 1918. That year, he wrote to the musicologist Hugo Leichtentritt, who sent him Busoni's address in Zürich (card from Leichtentritt, May 4, 1918), but Leifs appears to have waited until Busoni had returned to Berlin. A letter from Leifs to Busoni, dated October 1, 1920, has survived (Staatsbibliothek zu Berlin, Musikabteilung; Mus.Nachl. F. Busoni B II, 2774+2774a), in which he asks to meet Busoni and also requests lessons from him in composition and orchestration; their meeting presumably took place in October or November that year.
26. Åhlén, *Jón Leifs—Tónskáld í mótbyr*, 70.
27. Leifs to parents, September 22, 1917. Whatever the cause of Leifs's illness, it must have seemed to his parents that he might share the fate of his father, who himself had returned to Iceland from Copenhagen without a university degree following an extended ailment (see chap. 1).
28. Þorleifur Jónsson to Leifs, December 11, 1919.
29. Leifs, "Söngleikahátíðin í München," *Lögrétta*, October 20, 1920.
30. Hermann Scherchen, *Werke und Briefe*, (Berlin: P. Lang: 1991), 19, 179.
31. Leifs to parents, June 1, 1921 (National and University Library, Reykjavík, Lbs 4070 4to).
32. Teichmüller, recommendation for Leifs, June 5, 1921.
33. Sigurður Þórðarson to Leifs, August 3, 1920.
34. Leifs, "Tónlistarlíf Rvíkur.—Tilraun," *Morgunblaðið*, September 25, 1921.
35. Leifs, "Íslenskt tónlistarlíf," *Morgunblaðið*, August 14, 1921.
36. Sigfús Einarsson, "Örfá orð," *Morgunblaðið*, September 22, 1921.
37. Þorleifur Jónsson to Leifs, May 3, 1923.
38. "Hljómleikar," *Alþýðublaðið*, September 7, 1921; "Hljómleikar," *Vísir*, October 6, 1921.
39. Þorsteinsson's volume was—and still is—the definitive collection of Icelandic folk music. Yet it was not the first attempt to collect songs from

Iceland. The Frenchman Jean-Benjamin de Laborde had obtained five Icelandic songs for his encyclopedic *Essai sur la Musique Ancienne et Moderne* (Paris, 1780); the Scottish traveler George Mackenzie included in his book, *Travels in Iceland, 1810*, six "Specimens of the ancient Sacred Music of Iceland." These transcriptions, and others that appeared in the nineteenth century, are problematic from a scholarly perspective, and although Leifs did make use of one of Laborde's melodies, it was Þorsteinsson's collection that gave him the basis for his musical language. For a full account of the circumstances behind the Laborde transcriptions, see Jón Helgason, "Eddasáng," *Gardar* 3 (1972): 15–49. An Icelandic publication that included several folk song transcriptions was *Íslenzkar skemtanir* (vol. 2), published in 1888–92. These are also of questionable accuracy, though generally more reliable than the others mentioned here.

40. Matthías Johannessen, "Lögmálin í hrúgunni. Spjallað við Jón Leifs," *Morgunblaðið*, May 5, 1959.

41. Bjarni Þorsteinsson, *Íslenzk þjóðlög* (Copenhagen: S.L. Møller, 1906–9), 2.

42. Ibid., viii–ix.

43. Angul Hammerich, "Studier over islandsk musik," *Aarbøger for nordisk Oldkyndighed og Historie* 14 (1899): 273.

44. Finnur Sigmundsson, *Rímnatal* (Reykjavík: Rímnafélagið, 1966).

45. Þorsteinsson, *Íslenzk þjóðlög*, 807.

46. Ibid., 767–68; also published in Bjarni Þorsteinsson, "Íslenzk þjóðlög," *Skírnir* 80 (1906): 292.

47. The oldest surviving source for tvísöngur is a two-part *Credo* and *Agnus Dei* found in a fragment of a manuscript written in northern Iceland in 1473 (AM 80 b 8vo, in the collection of the Árni Magnússon Institute for Icelandic Studies, Reykjavík).

48. For a detailed account of the development of tvísöngur, see my doctoral dissertation, "These Are the Things You Never Forget: The Written and Oral Transmission of Icelandic *Tvísöngur*" (PhD diss., Harvard University, 2003).

49. Leifs, "Íslenskt tónlistareðli," *Skírnir* 96 (1922), 130–43. A year later, Leifs translated this article into German, and it was published as "Isländische Volksmusik und germanische Empfindungsart," *Die Musik* 16 (1923): 43–52.

50. Leifs, "Íslenskt tónlistareðli," 141; Leifs, "Isländische Volksmusik," 46,

51. See also Pamela M. Potter, *Most German of the Arts: Musicology and Society from the Weimar Republic to the End of Hitler's Reich* (New Haven: Yale University Press, 1998), 217.

51. Sigfús Einarsson, *Hörpuhljómar* (Reykjavík: Bókaverslun Guðm. Gamalíelssonar, 1907).

52. Sveinbjörnsson also used folk songs in instrumental arrangements, such as *Vikivaki* (Góða veislu gjöra skal) and *Islandsk Rhapsodie* (Fagurt galaði fuglinn sá), both of which are undated but probably were written around 1920 and thus postdate Þorsteinsson's collection. The earliest reference to them in an Icelandic newspaper is in an article about his performance of them in Winnipeg in August 1922 (see "Kveðju-hljómleikar," *Heimskringla*, August 16, 1922). These two pieces (along with a third one, *Idyl*) were recorded by the composer three years later (see *Morgunblaðið*, September 25, 1925) and were the first instrumental works based on Icelandic folk music to be released on record (Polyphon Musik Z.S.67002).

53. *Heimir*, January 1, 1924, flyleaf.

54. Sigfús Blöndal, "Ísland og Norðurlönd—Fyrirlestur haldinn á 5. norræna stúdentafundinum á Eiðsvelli 1915," *Skírnir* 91 (1917): 149.

55. Leifs, "Íslensku þjóðlögin," *Vörður*, August 29, 1925.

THREE

COMPOSER AND CONDUCTOR
(1921–29)

WHEN LEIFS AND ANNIE RETURNED to Leipzig in October 1921, both continued their private lessons with Teichmüller. Leifs also took occasional conducting lessons from Scherchen and hoped that his skills as pianist and conductor might land him a job as a repetiteur. As for his efforts in composition, he drew on material from Þorsteinsson's folk song collection to create music that is often a strikingly innovative fusion of central-European and Icelandic influences. His first opus, the *Trilogia piccola*, was still not complete, but in January and February 1922 he wrote four short movements that would be published as *Four Pieces for Piano* op. 2. Despite their brevity, they were an important step on Leifs's path toward a national sound. The opening *Valse lento* is unique among the set in that it does not contain folk melodies. It is a simple rounded binary form, with a gentle theme in triple time, supported by harmonies that constantly cloud over, moving from major to minor. The frequent third-related progressions foreshadow what would later become a favorite Leifsian harmonic device, and they explain his alternative title, preserved only in the manuscript: *Der Querstand* ("The Cross-Relation"). The brief central section, on the other hand, consists of sharp discords and austere parallel fifths in tvísöngur style, as if the refined central-European atmosphere has suddenly yielded to the rugged climate of the north.

Example 3.1. Leifs, *Isländisches Präludium* op. 2 no. 2, mm. 19–25. © Iceland Music Information Center.

The second piece of the set, titled *Icelandic Prelude*, is a fiercely dissonant and modern arrangement of the well-known tvísöngur melody *Ísland, farsælda frón*. With it, Leifs announces firmly his departure from the conservative style cultivated by Sigfús Einarsson and other Icelandic composers in their vernacular arrangements. He presents the tune in its traditional parallel-fifth guise, over an open-fifth drone on D (see example 3.1). The radical element is the punctuation of each phrase by cluster-like sonorities, for which Leifs employs only four pitch classes throughout the piece: C-sharp and G-sharp, E-flat and B-flat. These frame the central D-A fifth by a semitone on each side, and Leifs arranges them to achieve the effect of maximum dissonance.

Leifs also employs tunes from Þorsteinsson's collection in the third and fourth pieces. An *Icelandic Ballade* (no. 3) is the most technically demanding of the set, growing from a soft, unadorned theme in the bass register to a dramatic climax. The concluding *Icelandic Scherzo* is far more accessible than the preceding movements, both technically and in terms of harmony. It is a rondo on four well-known folk songs, and the subtitle, *Scherzo im klassischen Stil*, emphasizes Leifs's conservative approach.

These piano pieces were not the success Leifs had hoped for. On their publication in 1924, two hundred copies were shipped to a Reykjavík bookseller, but six weeks later not a single one had been sold.[1] Leifs also sent a copy to the renowned pianist Walter Gieseking, who found his treatment of the vernacular tunes "very interesting" and encouraged him to keep composing but never performed them.[2] A rare vote of confidence came in 1929 from the author Halldór Laxness, who was then living in California; he told Leifs that he had played the jarring arrangement of *Ísland, farsælda frón* frequently during the Christmas holidays, much to his own delight but to the profound annoyance of his neighbors.[3] When an Icelandic pianist performed that same piece at a concert in Reykjavík in 1930, the stunned audience greeted it with silence until one of Leifs's closest friends, Kristján Albertsson, began what became only a lukewarm round of applause. He described the incident in a letter to Leifs and did not mince words: "There's no point in arguing about it; the Icelanders don't understand you yet—based on the little they have heard of your music, they don't care for you as a composer."[4]

MISERY IN GERMANY: 1922–25

With hyperinflation rampant and unemployment high, Leifs found himself in the midst of troublesome times in Germany. While this dire situation was a curse for him, he saw that it could be a blessing for Iceland in that impoverished but talented German musicians might be persuaded to relocate there and contribute to its fledgling music scene. In 1922, he arranged for Otto Böttcher, a fellow recent graduate from the Leipzig Conservatory, to sail to Reykjavík to assume a teaching post. Böttcher was a dedicated teacher and was proficient on virtually any instrument, a valuable asset in a small town like Reykjavík. His stay proved highly beneficial. He merged the two competing local wind bands into one larger group, the Reykjavík Town Band (*Lúðrasveit Reykjavíkur*), and in autumn 1922 he and Páll Ísólfsson founded a small music school where Böttcher taught strings, winds, and brass while Ísólfsson was responsible for piano and music theory. Encouraged by Böttcher's success, Leifs next convinced the pianist Kurt Haeser, a former Teichmüller student and teacher at the Dortmund Conservatory, to take a teaching position in the town of Akureyri in northern Iceland. He also arranged for three German musicians to relocate to Reykjavík in autumn 1923, where they performed as a trio at Hótel Skjaldbreið: the violinist Fritz Peppermüller, who later became a member of the Berlin Philharmonic, the cellist Paul Plenge, and pianist Ernst Schacht. In just over one year, Leifs arranged for five talented Germans to join the ranks of Icelandic musicians, thereby making a substantial contribution to musical development in Reykjavík and Akureyri in the 1920s.

In May 1922 Leifs and Annie traveled to Norderney, one of the Frisian islands near Germany's Dutch border, with the intention of permanently settling there. Norderney was a small town with a northerly climate, but in the summertime the population multiplied as tens of thousands of vacationers gathered there. It was in Norderney that Leifs wrote to the renowned Icelandic poet Einar Benediktsson, who, in the preface to his volume *Hrannir* (*Waves*, 1913), had encouraged poets and singers to revive the neglected native genres of music, particularly that of rímur, and called on musicians to employ them as material for large and ambitious works—to "elevate these national songs to the same level as other music composed in our country."[5] In his letter, Leifs requested a poem that might serve as a "true national anthem" for Iceland. Benediktsson replied by sending him *Rise Up, Banner of Young Iceland* (*Rís þú, unga Íslands merki*), a poem in seven stanzas written in 1906 with the intention that it become a "flag song"—the poet had recently suggested a distinctive flag for Iceland, much to the chagrin of Danish officials, since it was a visible symbol of the desire for self-rule.[6] This flag, a white cross on a blue field (intended as a symbol of heavenly azure and the white of the glaciers), was employed in the early years of the century, and a modified version (a red and white cross on a blue field) was later adopted as the national flag.

Rís þú, unga Íslands merki,	Rise up, banner of young Iceland!
upp með þúsund radda brag.	with a thousand voices to the skies.
Tengdu í oss að einu verki	Unite in us, for a single goal,
anda, kraft og hjartalag.	heart, soul, and spirit.
Rís þú, Íslands stóri, sterki	Rise up, Iceland's strong and stout
stofn, með nýjan frægðardag.	stem, to a new day of glory.

Leifs set these words in an energetic *alla marcia* style, with a tritone-laden melody harmonized largely with third- and tritone-related chords. His setting never gained the popularity he hoped for, no doubt largely due to its modern flair, but by this time Icelanders had received their own flag by royal decree, so the poem had lost some of its political urgency. In 1924, two years after he composed his setting, Leifs met with Benediktsson in Berlin, and the latter pledged to support his efforts on behalf of Icelandic vernacular music. Perhaps it was at this meeting that the poet emboldened Leifs to collect folk songs himself, since nothing suggests that this had been Leifs's intention previously. Shortly afterward, Benediktsson penned a flattering article on Leifs for the Icelandic right-wing journal *Vörður*, publicly rousing the composer to gather native songs throughout the island, claiming that he was "the only Icelander who is undoubtedly qualified to save what he can, before it is lost forever."[7]

Leifs's stay in Norderney was short and unpleasant. He had hoped for a conducting post with the town orchestra, but when it was offered to another candidate he and his wife moved again, this time to Halle, near Leipzig.[8] Here, Leifs dreamed of establishing his own orchestra, but his plans came to nothing, and he had no luck with other engagements. His scheduled Beethoven concert with the Leipzig Philharmonic was cancelled at short notice in December, as was his debut with the Halle City Orchestra a few weeks later.[9] When he did get a chance to conduct, the reviews were fairly positive. He led a Mozart evening with the Buckeburg City Orchestra on November 17, 1922, where one critic praised him as a "serious artist" with a distinctive interpretation; in December he conducted Reger, Brahms, and Beethoven's *Eroica* symphony in Dortmund, where critics lauded his "technical prowess" and "sound musical sensibility" but found his tempos in the symphony too fast and unyielding, particularly in the funeral march and finale.[10] Leifs's propensity for lively tempos was likely a result of his studies with the objective, neoclassically inclined Scherchen, whose interpretation of the *Eroica* was for decades the fastest committed to disc.[11] Much of Leifs's aesthetic in matters of orchestral performance seems to have been inspired by Scherchen, including brisk and steady tempos, the carefully considered application of vibrato, and attention to the polyphony of inner voices.[12]

After a concert with the Dresden Philharmonic in March 1923, critics were less kind. "One of these mediocre conductors who choose popular works only to guarantee a positive reception," said the *Sächsische Volkszeitung*; another remarked that the orchestra had been conducting Leifs rather than vice versa.[13] A week later, a concert with the Berlin Symphony Orchestra was even less encouraging. A review in one of the city's leading music journals, *Signale für die musikalische Welt*, found him "lacking in personality" and unable to free himself of the written score.[14] In managing his fledgling career, Leifs had proved himself to be too ambitious and had not allowed himself time to mature. Smaller cities like Dortmund and Buckeburg might have been quite content with talent such as his, but conducting in Dresden and Berlin was a different game altogether. Now that critics in two of Germany's cultural capitals had voiced their displeasure, it became virtually impossible for Leifs to secure any further conducting engagements.

This downturn in Leifs's career came at the worst possible time, for he had never been more in need of employment. On March 2, 1923, Annie gave birth to a girl who was christened Snót—the old Icelandic word means "girl" but is rarely used as a given name. They had assistance from Leifs's sister, Salóme, who had arrived in Halle a few months earlier to study German. Her rapport with her brother would soon become strained, as she began a romance with Dr. Erich Nagel, a talented linguist, to which Leifs adamantly objected.[15] He could be controlling both with family members and friends, but Salóme stood firm; she and Nagel were married in 1931 and ran a language school in Leipzig until World War II. Their relationship with Leifs remained cool, and Nagel refused to even be in the same room with him for years.[16] After Snót was born, Leifs and Annie hired a nanny to assist with the household: the meticulous Frieda Zapp, who remained in their service for eighteen years and eventually became an extension of the family. They also employed a domestic servant for most of their marriage, and while this may seem a frivolous expense given their financial constraints, it was a lifestyle to which both were accustomed from their own upbringings.

When it became clear that a position in Halle would not materialize, the family relocated again, to Wernigerode in the Harz mountains. It seems perplexing that two unemployed musicians should choose to move to a remote town of only twenty thousand inhabitants, but they may have done so simply to avoid the reach of Halle authorities. The local police had visited the family's single-room apartment in December 1922, questioning Leifs on his immigration status and demanding that he leave Prussia within eight days.[17] At least Wernigerode was inexpensive, and Leifs had plenty of time to compose and study scores, but his friend Kristján Albertsson predicted that he would soon tire of the solitude and move to a metropolis like Vienna.[18]

Leifs's income in the mid-1920s, such as it was, came mostly from newspapers and music journals. He had already published a preliminary study of Icelandic folk songs in *Die Musik* in 1923 (derived from his Icelandic article from the previous year) and was now able to get a steady stream of articles printed in *Rheinisch-Westfälische Zeitung* and *Signale für die musikalische Welt*. The latter periodical's advertising manager was an Icelandophile by the name of Fritz Jaritz, who penned an encomium expressing great faith in Leifs, lauding him as a genius who combined in his art "Nordic and *ur*-Germanic temperament, spiritual depth, austere masculinity and affirmation for life"—rhetoric that also anticipates the discourse on the composer and his music during the Third Reich.[19]

The only opportunities for Leifs and his wife to concertize came through renting halls and orchestras at their own cost. Leifs procured the Leipziger Volksakademie for performances in October 1923 (Bach, Handel, Mozart) and February 1924 (Beethoven's *Eroica* and Schubert's *Unfinished*) while Annie rented halls for recitals in Magdeburg and Braunschweig.[20] Her performances were generally well received, although critics had little sympathy for the "ultra-modernist" sounds of her husband's op. 2.[21] With hyperinflation soaring, the piano recitals came at a cost of 100 million marks each; Leifs had to put up 664 million marks for the orchestra concerts, though this was the equivalent of only 70 Danish kroner.[22] The couple would have never been able to take such steps had they not received financial assistance each month from their respective fathers in Reykjavík and Teplitz. Leifs's father had recently been promoted to postmaster in Reykjavík, and in 1923 he usually transferred around 300 Icelandic krónur monthly—roughly half of his salary.[23]

Ensconced in the serene Harz area, Leifs devoted himself fully to composition in spring and summer 1924. He had never before been so productive, completing four works in five months: *Trilogia piccola* op. 1, *Prelude and Fughetta* for solo violin op. 3, *Three Verses from Hávamál* op. 4, and *Kyrie* for choir and organ op. 5. Although each has a distinctive character and can be seen as a further exploration on the path toward his own musical style, all are in one way or another characterized by the novel combination of modernism and Icelandic vernacular elements that Leifs had already espoused in the piano pieces op. 2. Leifs allowed himself a break from composing only in order to attend an inspiring concert at the other end of Germany, enduring a twenty-four-hour third-class train ride from Wernigerode to Hamburg with the sole purpose of hearing Karl Muck conduct Beethoven's Ninth. He was delighted to witness a performance that echoed his own ideals and later reminisced fondly about Muck's interpretation, which he found stringent, austere, and faithful to the score.[24]

Of the works Leifs completed in spring and summer 1924, he was particularly proud of *Trilogia piccola*, which had taken him no less than five years to complete. This was also—apart from a couple of short *Icelandic Rhapsodies* by Sveinbjörn Sveinbjörnsson—the first orchestral work composed by an Icelander. Inspired by his reading of Nietzsche's *Also sprach Zarathustra*, each of the three movements of Leifs's "dramatic trilogy" originally bore a heading taken from the book—*Das Grablied / Von den grossen Sehnsucht, Die stillste Stunde,* and *Vom höheren Menschen*—although Leifs later abandoned this plan. The first two movements of *Trilogia piccola* were composed before he discovered Icelandic folk song; he drafted the first movement in 1920, and the second movement is *Torrek,* his piano piece for Annie from 1919, in orchestral guise. The music, forged out of slow buildups and shattering contrasts, demonstrates Leifs's flair for dramatic gestures. The harmony is ambiguous and densely chromatic: the first half of the opening movement carries a key signature of six flats, suggesting E-flat minor, but the music mostly unfolds on the dominant. A tremendous *ffff* climax is followed by *ppp* D-major harmony in the violins, a glimpse of hope that is immediately shattered by a dissonant brass entry, *feroce ed energico*. Toward the end, the atmosphere brightens, and the lush orchestral sound suggests the influence of Bruckner. More than anything else, this work shows how Leifs *could* have developed—into a composer in dialogue with the late-Romantic Austrian symphonic legacy. Only in the finale do parallel fifths and the shifting meter of rímur appear, although Leifs does not cite specific folk tunes.

The *Three Verses from Hávamál* for voice and piano, written in May 1924, are notable for their economy of means—each song is only a little over one minute in duration. Leifs wished to mirror the terse and concise Icelandic poetry (in this case, the gnomic texts from the Viking Age known as *Sayings of the High One*), noting that this resulted in music that might be "10 times shorter than a corresponding work by another composer."[25] Parallel fifths abound in this piece, but Leifs employs them in an atonal manner. The third song has a funebrial character and is marked, in an early version, *Grave maestoso, funebre ed eroico*; the marking, if not the music itself, betrays the influence of Beethoven's *Eroica* symphony. The songs have never been published or recorded in their original version; Leifs revised them in 1926 and again (more extensively) in 1932, virtually rewriting the piano part in its entirety.

The *Prelude and Fughetta* for solo violin op. 3 and the *Kyrie* op. 5 are inspired by older models (Bach in the former, Renaissance polyphony in the latter) but with an abundance of dissonance within a controlled part-writing framework. The *Kyrie* consists of two movements: an organ prelude and a movement for *a cappella* chorus, both of which employ a plaintive tune taken from an Icelandic music manuscript from the seventeenth century (*Melodia*, now part of the Arnamagnæan collection in Copenhagen) with an anonymous text:

Grátandi kem ég nú, Guð minn, til þín,	Weeping, o Lord, I come to thee,
glæpum hlaðinn og þungri pín.	Burdened with crimes and painful smart.
Lít við, ljúfi faðir líknargjarn,	Dear merciful father, look on me,
hér er ég, þitt auma hjartans barn.	Here I am, poor child of your heart.[26]

In the organ prelude, this melody appears in the pedals, supporting a four-part fugal elaboration of another theme (by Leifs himself) in the manuals. The choral movement, to the text of "Kyrie eleison" in Icelandic (*Drottinn, miskunna þú oss*), begins as an exposition on Leifs's own theme from the prelude. As the movement reaches its climax, a boys' choir joins with the ancient hymn tune in soprano register—thus complementing the organ prelude, where the tune occupied the low end of the texture. In a sense, Leifs would repeat the overall trajectory of the choral *Kyrie* on a much larger scale in his Organ Concerto six years later—both involve the unfolding of an old Icelandic melody as the culmination of a more traditionally central European work.

Leifs's *Kyrie* was possibly intended for Ísólfsson, who had recently returned to Reykjavík and formed a mixed chorus there, presenting choral works by Handel, Brahms, and others for the first time in Iceland. In August 1923 he had requested from Leifs "something to play or rehearse with my choir," but this was a mediocre group, and Ísólfsson admitted that getting them to sing in tune had nearly cost him his wits.[27] Leifs must have sensed that his music was too demanding for the Reykjavík chorus. He added the option of singing the *Kyrie eleison* in Greek or German in order to make the work more feasible for continental ensembles, but to little avail—the work received its first performance a full decade later. The organ prelude fared better; Ísólfsson premiered it in Reykjavík in 1925 and revived it on occasion, including in a radio broadcast in 1934.[28]

Snót had been diagnosed with congenital hip dislocation, a birth defect that required extensive treatment, and the family moved to Berlin in August 1924 so that she might receive the best available care. Although Leifs was still at odds with his father-in-law, Edwin Riethof did agree to pay the hospital bills as well as for the family's apartment in Eislebenerstrasse until Snót was fully cured. Berlin was a metropolis teeming with technology and new art, but Leifs made no headway in promoting his music or his conducting skills. "All kinds of worries and stress," Annie wrote in her diary while Leifs confided to his parents that the past few months had been "the most miserable period in my entire life and it pains me to have to write you that it is so. Everything I do seems futile. Everything that I witness in the musical world around me is so rotten, unhealthy, and devoid of artistic sensibility, that it often seems to me pointless to live longer on this earth.... I have hardly been able to convince anyone to even *look at* my compositions.... I have had moments where I have lost the courage to live."[29]

Leifs had become convinced that the Berlin music scene was controlled only by money and an insider clique.[30] He called on some of the city's top music agents, including Norbert Salter, who represented Wilhelm Furtwängler and had been Mahler's impresario; he was willing to add Leifs to his roster for a down payment of three thousand US dollars, with the guarantee of a respectable conducting position or the money would be returned without interest.[31] After several months of negotiations, Riethof decided against subsidizing his son-in-law, and so the plan came to nothing.[32] Despite local advertising, Leifs and Annie failed to procure even a single student, and for a while it seemed like the only option would be to move to Iceland and for him to take over the Reykjavík Town Band, whose organization had already extended an offer to him.[33]

Leifs felt he was at a crossroads: he could lead a simple, artistically unfulfilling life in Iceland or attempt success in Germany at any cost. In the end, he botched the negotiations with the wind band by demanding a five-year contract, according to which he would be required to dwell in Reykjavík only six months a year, excluding the winter months, which was when most of the rehearsing traditionally took place.[34]

Part of Leifs's problem was that he had still not decided on a single career path. In the early months of 1925, he purchased nearly thirty opera scores and studied them intensely, reviving his old notion of becoming a repetiteur. For a while it seemed like he might receive an offer as second *Kapellmeister* in Gleiwitz (Gliwice) in Upper Silesia, but the principal conductor, after meeting with Leifs for only a few minutes, decided that his command of the opera repertoire was insufficient. When another offer came for a second Kapellmeister position, this time in Sonderhausen, where his main duty would be to conduct operettas, he hesitated, and when he finally replied, the post had been given to someone else.[35] Leifs himself admitted to his father-in-law that the theater was not really close to his heart and that he regarded it only as a means of making a living.[36]

Leifs's preparations for a career in the theater may have directly influenced his compositional work at this time, for his main project in 1925 was incidental music to *Galdra-Loftr (Loftur the Magician)* by the Icelandic playwright Jóhann Sigurjónsson (1880–1919). This was Leifs's largest score to date, consisting of fifteen numbers distributed among the play's three acts. He had been fascinated by the play ever since he had seen the first production in Reykjavík in 1915 and vowed that he would one day write music for it. Decades later, Leifs penned the following recollections for a concert program: "*Galdra-Loftr* is the drama of my pubescent years. I saw it on stage in Reykjavík when I was 15 or 16 years old, three times in a row, and was elated, as I felt instantly that music belonged with the drama.... Of course I knew nothing about composition at the time, but as soon as I had learned the fundamentals of the craft, I wrote the music, and completed the orchestration in 1924–25."[37]

Sigurjónsson based his play on a folktale that appears to reference historical events in the early eighteenth century.[38] It tells the story of Loftur, a young student at the Latin school in Hólar in northern Iceland, who is fascinated with black magic. He has previously seduced a chambermaid, Steinunn, but when the play begins he has turned his affections toward the bishop's daughter. Steinunn reveals that she is carrying Loftur's child, and in despair he chants a magic spell for her death—with success, it seems, as she is later seen drowning herself in a nearby river. At night, Loftur enters the cathedral to summon the spirit of a deceased bishop who is in possession of a book of magic spells. The play's climax is his dramatic plea to the supernatural forces to make his "heart powerful in evil," but it all proves too much for him. He falls dead as he reaches for the book, overcome by the strength of his own spell. For all the Gothic horror of its finale, Sigurjónsson's play now reads like a stilted melodrama with Nietzschean overtones, a tragedy about a failed attempt at turning the superman into a reality. From this angle, the sorcerer's fate is the playwright's confrontation with—and rejection of—the superman ideal.[39]

While the incidental music occasionally betrays Leifs's lack of experience in the theater, he ably sets the tone for some of the play's most memorable scenes. Particularly effective is his use of two traditional Icelandic melodies, both found in Þorsteinsson's collection. Appropriately, the tune to the chorale *Allt eins og blómstrið eina* appears in the substantial funeral march that opens act III and depicts Steinunn's burial; the melody is of German origin and was part of the Icelandic Lutheran hymnals from 1589 onward. The verse is from a hymn by the seventeenth-century pastor Hallgrímur Pétursson, Iceland's most revered poet of the Protestant Baroque era:[40]

Allt eins og blómstrið eina	Just as a single flower
upp vex á sléttri grund,	flourishing in an even field,
fagurt með frjóvgun hreina	fair in its fresh fertility
fyrst um dags morgunstund,	in the first hours of morning,
á snöggu augabragði	is cut down in a trice,
af skorið verður fljótt,	in the twinkle of an eye,

lit og blöð niður lagði,	its color and leaves laid low;
líf mannlegt endar skjótt.	so, suddenly, ends the life of man.

Both music and text have traditionally been sung at most Icelandic funerals, and this remains the custom. Leifs was fond of the chorale and employed it frequently, particularly between 1925 and 1930 (see chap. 5). Toward the conclusion of act II, as Loftur offers his soul to the devil, Leifs quotes another traditional tune, *Night Has Entered the World* (*Kvöld er komið í heim*), from a 1742 manuscript hymnal.[41] Yet another prominent theme is Leifs's own: a rímur tune heard at the beginning of the play sung by a group of beggars at the cathedral and later echoed in some of the instrumental interludes. Both the funeral march and the play itself conclude with the pealing of the cathedral bells, confirming the catastrophe that has cost two youngsters their lives.

LEIFS AS FOLK SONG COLLECTOR: THE 1925 JOURNEY

Encouraged by the nationalist poet Benediktsson, Leifs's interest in Icelandic folk material led him to seek out remnants of such singing himself. In August 1925—his first visit to Iceland in four years—he and Annie traveled to his own native county of Húnavatnssýsla in northwestern Iceland, going largely by foot or on horseback between farms (see fig. 3.1). In a span of ten days, they heard ten singers perform over two hundred songs, but the expedition was only a qualified success. The traditional manner of performing the vernacular songs included microtonal inflections and extensive, rapid ornamentation, but Leifs, who had only paper and pencil to notate the tunes as they were being sung, soon realized that meticulous transcription would be impossible. Instead, he focused on the constantly changing metric structure and dynamic shadings, making diagrams from tunes such as those sung to him by the farmers Jón Ásmundsson, who had learned them from his mother, and Sigurbjörn Bjarnarson, who insisted that his memory and singing would greatly improve if he were able to "oil his throat" with

Figure 3.1. Leifs and Annie traveling by horseback on the folk song collecting trip, 1925. © Leifs Archives, National and University Library, Reykjavík.

alcohol—a request that Leifs, due to prohibition, was unable to fulfill.[42]

Although the journey was not the success Leifs had hoped, it did inspire him artistically, for on his return to Reykjavík, he compiled *25 Icelandic Folk Songs*, a volume of simple arrangements for piano. Despite the title, the volume consists of only twenty-four legitimate folk songs, since Leifs included a tune of his own without acknowledging his authorship: *Rís þú, unga Íslands merki* (no. 10), his setting of Benediktsson's flag poem discussed above. For the *25 Icelandic Folk Songs*, Leifs drew almost exclusively on the earlier publication *Íslenzk þjóðlög*. Mostly he chose tvísöngvar and rímur collected by Þorsteinsson and his associates but also the funeral hymn *Allt eins og blómstrið eina*, three songs from Icelandic seventeenth- and eighteenth-century manuscripts, and one from Jean-Benjamin de Laborde's 1780 collection *Essai sur la musique ancienne et moderne*, all of which are found in Þorsteinsson's volume.[43] Leifs characteristically presented the songs in a stark, primitive guise, with unisons or octaves punctuated with phrases in parallel fifths, or fifth drones in the left hand. Three songs were given full triadic harmonization (nos. 10, 11, and 20), and these were characterized by a novel approach to harmony, in which chords related by seconds, thirds, and augmented fourths were more prevalent than fifth relations. This harmonic technique, which later became a crucial feature of Leifs's fully developed musical language, was seen here for the first time in his works.

For ten of his arrangements, Leifs employed lyrics different from those found in Þorsteinsson's collection. This was in accordance with standard practice in the rímur tradition, where a tune could be sung to any poem that shared its particular meter. In most cases, Leifs substituted one text for another found nearby in Þorsteinsson's volume. For example, he took the tune *Lífið gerist þungt og þreytt* from the folk song volume (p. 907) but found the text on the facing page (p. 906), where it was accompanied by a different melody. In another case, Leifs took the tune given to *Hann er að skera haus af kú* (p. 905) and fitted it to the verse of the preceding song (*Daga alla drottinn minn*). One wonders if Leifs, disappointed by the meager results of his song-gathering journey, wished to disguise his reliance on Þorsteinsson's collection by employing other texts.

Perhaps Leifs intended the inclusion of his own "flag song" partly as an homage to his supporter, for the first performance of the 25 *Icelandic Folk Songs* took place at Benediktsson's residence on Laufásvegur in Reykjavík, just a few buildings down the street from Leifs's childhood home. This informal concert took place on a Saturday evening, September 12, 1925, and was a social event in its own right, attended by Reykjavík's elite—including Prime Minister Jón Magnússon, Finance Minister Jóhannes Þorláksson, and the renowned painter Jóhannes Kjarval. The town's leading composers were also present: Árni Thorsteinson, who as a music critic admitted to being baffled by some of Leifs's music, and Sigfús Einarsson, whose relationship with Leifs had been tense since their 1921 newspaper spat regarding the latter's proposal for an orchestra and music school in Reykjavík. Leifs's performance at Benediktsson's house concert cemented his reputation as a bona fide national composer, not least as it was hosted by the poet who more than a decade earlier had encouraged Icelandic musicians to engage in a national style. Before his performance, Leifs gave a brief introduction to the work, pointing out that he did not consider the arrangements "*art* in the true sense of the word, but rather an attempt to make the Icelandic folk songs known to the wider public in piano guise. At the same time, I have tried to be true to their character as much as possible."[44] The concert was well received and was even reviewed in *Morgunblaðið*, where it was described as an "important event in the history of Icelandic music."[45] Another critic predicted that Leifs's attempt would begin a "renaissance of our folk songs, which have suffered humiliation for an entire lifetime."[46] Encouraged by the positive reaction, Leifs and Annie followed up with a sold-out public appearance in Nýja bíó on October 2. Here, she played piano pieces by Chopin, Debussy, and Paul Graener while Leifs again performed the *25 Icelandic Folk Songs*, and the two of them shared movements from his piano pieces op. 2.

In autumn 1925, Leifs's arrangements sparked a debate about whether Icelandic folk music constituted proper material for serious-minded composers and whether it was compatible with the rules of music theory and counterpoint—or even good taste. This should be seen, again, as a manifestation of the tension between the vernacular tradition, regarded by many as a distressing reminder of Iceland's "unrefined" past, and the ongoing project of modernization, which in music largely meant deference to the nineteenth-century Austro-German tradition. In his review of the October 2 concert, Árni Thorsteinson maintained that the native tunes should not be performed on instruments at all but simply sung in the old style, as had been the custom for centuries; yet he also admonished Leifs for being too modern in his treatment, getting "lost in the wasteland of fashion ... which I do not comprehend and which pains my old ears."⁴⁷ Shortly afterward, in the conservative weekly journal *Vörður*, Sveinbjörn Sveinbjörnsson—the grand old man of Icelandic music—condemned the use of parallel fifths in new compositions, declaring them aesthetically unpleasant as well as forbidden due to long-standing tradition: "To compose music inspired by the so-called Icelandic tvísöngur is impossible, unless people's tastes change so that they enjoy hearing parallel fifths, which until now have been thought harsh and impossible to use. But if this should be the case, we would require new rules in harmony and counterpoint, completely contrary to those now in use; we would need a new foundation, and would have to reject everything that the greatest musical minds of the world have taught us."⁴⁸

Sveinbjörnsson reluctantly agreed that the Lydian or Dorian modes might be appropriately employed, but only because such modes could be found in "some of the best and strangest Icelandic folk songs." His disdain for parallel fifths provoked reactions from two musicians of the younger generation, both of whom dismissed it as anachronistic. One of these writers was, not surprisingly, Leifs himself, who maintained that the perception of parallel fifths as beautiful or ugly was a matter of taste but insisted that the historical importance of the Icelandic tvísöngur was—like the nation's ancient literature—too great to ignore in contemporary composition.⁴⁹ The other response to Sveinbjörnsson's article came from composer-pianist Emil Thoroddsen, who was one year Leifs's senior and had recently returned to Reykjavík after several years of music study in Leipzig and Dresden. Thoroddsen had his doubts about Leifs's style; only a few months earlier he had lashed out at Leifs's arrangement of *Ísland, farsælda frón* (op. 2) as a "Schoenberg-influenced" piece that would "never become the foundation of a national art."⁵⁰ Yet on this occasion, he joined forces with Leifs in a vigorous defense of the latter's modern, national style. Thoroddsen wrote that

> no one expects parallel fifths to be made a *conditio sine qua non* of nationally colored composition. Many of the younger foreign composers have already used them, and thus Icelanders would already be behind the times in this, no less than in other things. Yet I do find it

conceivable that fifths, along with the Lydian mode and other characteristics of Icelandic folk song, might give our music the color it needs—but only if these elements fall into the hands of a great musician, who will make the character of Icelandic music his own. Then one could, for the first time, speak of an Icelandic national music, but it would be quite useless for every composer of average talent to start gushing out fifths and Lydian scales.[51]

Only in the concluding sentence does one sense a hint of irony pointed in Leifs's direction. Leifs's compositions had left Thoroddsen unimpressed, and his review of op. 2 makes clear that he regarded Leifs as little more than a mediocre composer. Still, when faced with opposition from the dean of Icelandic composers, the younger generation closed ranks in a spirited defense of modern music.

The set of 25 *Icelandic Folk Songs* was published by the Georg Kallmeyer-Verlag in 1929, with a preface by Erik Eggen, a noted scholar of Norwegian folk music with whom Leifs had corresponded during his research. Among the volume's admirers was the Hungarian composer Imre Weisshaus, Bartók's former student, who encountered it while traveling in California in 1930 at the invitation of Henry Cowell. A San Francisco music patron and friend of Halldór Laxness had lent Weisshaus her copy of the score and found that he "was so taken with the arrangement of these songs that he would have carried them away with him to Europe if I had not insisted at the last moment that I really wished them *very* much myself. He reluctantly relinquished them to me but I let him copy those he was most interested in."[52] Incidentally, selections from the 25 *Icelandic Folk Songs* were the first music by Leifs to be performed in public in the United States. Through the instigation of Thorstina Jackson Walters, the daughter of Icelandic immigrants, the Women's University Glee Club sang five numbers from the set at a concert in New York's Town Hall in May 1930.[53]

Leifs and Annie sailed back to the Continent in mid-October 1925, on the same ship as the violin virtuoso Emil Telmányi (Carl Nielsen's son-in-law), who had just given a recital in Reykjavík.

Never one to miss an opportunity to promote his works, Leifs gave Telmányi a copy of his *Prelude and Fughetta* for violin, but the latter never played it in public.[54] Leifs and Annie took up residence in Vienna for a few months, and from there Leifs traveled to Munich for a meeting with Siegmund von Hausegger, conductor of the Philharmonic, who had been impressed by his recent article in *Zeitschrift für Musik* on Beethoven's *Eroica* (see below). Leifs hoped that Hausegger might be able to engage him as a conductor, perhaps for a program including *Trilogia piccola*, but their meeting proved a disappointment, and Leifs wrote him a scathing letter before leaving the city.[55] *Trilogia piccola* was first performed in Karlsbad by the local Kurorchester in November 1925. Leifs attended a rehearsal but found the orchestra's playing "very bad" and left town before the concert.[56] Reviews were mixed, but there was general agreement that the work was a poetic rendering of a strange, Nordic soundscape and a promising start for the young composer.[57]

Earlier in 1925, desperate for money and prestige, Leifs had considered dedicating *Trilogia piccola* to King Christian X of Denmark and Iceland or his brother, King Haakon of Norway, which Leifs's Norwegian acquaintance Eggen advised against.[58] Two years later, Leifs had not given up hope of attaching royal prestige to his orchestral score and receiving some remuneration in return. He requested permission to dedicate the work to the prince of Liechtenstein, but the prince's cabinet director declined, pointing out that His Highness had never even visited Iceland.[59] Through these rather baffling inquiries, one gets an early sense of Leifs's weakness for power, particularly when it could be harnessed for financial gain or promoting his own music—something that would affect his career far more negatively later in life.

As a conductor, Leifs's anti-Romantic stance led him to oppose traditional early twentieth-century approaches to performance of the symphonic repertoire. He lamented the "distortion" or "romanticization" of music in the classical style, and while he had been spellbound by the charismatic Nikisch's interpretations during his student years, he now advocated a more analytical approach based on a careful study of the composer's score.⁶⁰ Influenced by Scherchen's ideals, Leifs proposed a stylistically "pure" manner of performance that did away with inaccurate editions and old, unquestioned performing traditions. Leifs predicted the "downfall of Romanticism" and encouraged performers to be more scrupulous in their attention to details of tempo, phrasing, and dynamics.⁶¹ In November 1925, the venerable journal *Zeitschrift für Musik* published Leifs's first extensive exposé on the subject, an analysis of the opening movement of Beethoven's *Eroica* symphony, titled "Against the Romanticization of Classical Music." Leifs continued to expound on the subject, writing articles on "Classical Interpretation" and "Orchestral Score Material" as well as a larger survey titled *Orchesterkultur*, sixty typewritten pages that remained unpublished. He also continued his study of the *Eroica*, and in 1927, the centenary of Beethoven's death, the *Neues Beethoven-Jahrbuch* issued his analysis of the symphony's funeral march and finale.⁶²

AN ORCHESTRAL ENTERPRISE

Although Leifs's plan to establish an orchestra in Reykjavík had foundered, he clung to his dream of Icelanders being able to experience symphonic music in live performance. The twenty-member Reykjavík Orchestra (*Hljómsveit Reykjavíkur*) consisted mostly of amateurs, and because of its small size, it performed the classical and Romantic repertoire in modified arrangements, with piano or harmonium filling in the missing parts. The internal balance left much to be desired: one critic complained (understandably) of having to hear nine violins pitted against a single cello and a double bass, without any violas at all.⁶³ In its early years, the Reykjavík Orchestra did introduce to local audiences some key works of the symphonic repertoire such as overtures and symphonies by Haydn, Mozart, and Beethoven, but its concerts were also laced with more popular salon fare, such as the Norwegian Ole Bull's *The Herd-girl's Sunday*.

Leifs knew that first-class symphonic performances could, for the time being, be presented in Iceland only by a foreign group willing to travel there at minimal cost. In the spring of 1925, he was invited to conduct the so-called Academic Orchestra of the State Universities of Berlin (*Akademisches Orchester der Staatlichen Hochschulen Berlin*), which was made up of university students and academics ranging in age from nineteen to fifty-seven, lawyers, engineers, and philosophers as well as four music students.[64] This was considered one of Berlin's finest amateur orchestras, and after a well-received debut with them in Berlin, Leifs suggested a tour of Iceland the following year. The idea was not as absurd as it might seem, for he knew that the ensemble had toured Sweden and Norway with success a few years earlier. The orchestra members agreed to waive their fees as long as travel expenses were paid in full. The plan was to give concerts in Sweden (Malmö, Gothenburg), Norway (Oslo, Bergen), and Iceland, with a program consisting of symphonies and other orchestral works by Mozart, Beethoven, and Schubert. Leifs's friends in Reykjavík were skeptical of the entire enterprise, but a 10,000 krónur subsidy from the Reykjavík town council guaranteed its financial viability.[65]

In March 1926 Leifs was already in Berlin rehearsing the Academic Orchestra when things took an unexpected turn. German newspapers had reported on the upcoming tour, and Leifs now received several inquiries from professional orchestras regarding the possibility of touring Iceland. Among them was the Hamburg Philharmonic, one of Germany's finest ensembles, currently under the leadership of Karl Muck, former music director of the Boston Symphony and much admired by Leifs for his interpretation of Beethoven and Wagner. Members from the Hamburg Philharmonic typically joined colleagues from other leading German ensembles to make up the pit orchestra at the Wagner festival in Bayreuth, but this had not yet become an annual event, and there was no festival in 1926. Thus it happened that Leifs, to his astonishment, received a phone call from the Philharmonic's manager informing him that a substantial segment of the orchestra was willing to travel to Iceland under the same conditions as the Berlin amateurs: no fee, with third-class travel and accommodation.

Although the Berlin players were understandably disgruntled by this turn of events, no contract had been signed, and the Hamburg offer was too tempting to refuse. In a newspaper article printed in Reykjavík in advance of their arrival, Leifs urged the local townspeople to attend the concerts, emphasizing the artistic impact such an outstanding ensemble could have: "The musical culture of Iceland will suddenly be thrust forward an entire lifetime!"[66]

The tour was not an official undertaking by the Hamburg Philharmonic but a private arrangement entered into with the consent of its management. The full orchestra consisted of ninety-seven players, forty of whom traveled to Iceland. Shortly before their departure, Leifs arrived in Hamburg to rehearse with the orchestra each morning. He was enthralled by their immaculate sound and enthused to Annie, "I have never in my life heard *staccato* played the way they do in the first movement of [Beethoven's] Seventh."[67] In ten rehearsals, they put together an extensive program including Beethoven's symphonies nos. 2, 3, and 7, the *Coriolan* and *Egmont* overtures; Mozart's late symphonies in G minor and C major, the Piano Concerto in A major K. 488 (with Annie as soloist), and Horn Concerto in E-flat K. 495; and numerous smaller works, such as Handel's Concerto Grosso no. 6, Weber's *Preziosa* overture, an entire concert devoted to Johann Strauss Jr. in honor of his centenary the previous year, and Wagner's *Siegfried Idyll*—the only time Leifs conducted a work by the composer, most of whose output he dismissed on the grounds that Wagner had "misunderstood the Nordic character" (see chap. 6).[68]

The tour's first concerts, in Oslo on May 26 and in Bergen the following evening, included music by Leifs himself: the premiere of two movements from the incidental music to *Galdra-Loftr* as well as the *Iceland Overture* (*Minni Íslands*) op. 9. Composed especially for the journey, the twelve-minute overture is scored for small orchestra with mixed and children's choirs *ad libitum*. The music is typical for Leifs at that point in his career: simple folk and folk-inspired themes are given dissonant treatment in a primitive style, with little or no development or elaboration. Leifs claimed that his goal had been to present in the overture "the key features of Icelandic folk music, without any attempt to improve the melodies, or to employ any kind of compositional craftsmanship."[69] The atmospheric opening measures include loud timpani strokes, clashing minor seconds in the brass, and shrieking high notes in the piccolo, piercingly dissonant against a cello and double bass tremolo. Later in the work, Leifs gives prominence to the timpani, including a ferocious solo passage that can be seen as an intimation of his later percussion-heavy style. The conspicuous timpani part perhaps suggests the influence, conscious or not, of Nielsen's Fourth Symphony (*The Inextinguishable*), which Leifs had heard and admired in Copenhagen in 1919. That work's explosive final movement includes dueling sets of timpani and a particular emphasis on tritones, an interval that is also prominent in Leifs's *Iceland Overture*.

The overture's melodic material consists of six folk tunes from Þorsteinsson's collection as well as two written by Leifs himself in vernacular style. Only one of these was composed specifically for the overture; the other is *Rís þú, unga Íslands merki*, which he had also incorporated into his set of 25 *Icelandic Folk Songs* for piano. Five of the genuine folk songs are also found in the latter collection, and a sixth one had appeared in the last of Leifs's *Four Piano Pieces* op. 2:

1. *Ísland, farsælda frón* (BÞ 775; 25 *Folk Songs* no. 1)
2. *Hani, krummi, hundur, svín* (BÞ 849; op. 2 no. 4)
3. Original rímur theme
4. *Ég að öllum háska hlæ* (BÞ 847; 25 *Folk Songs* no. 14)
5. *Fjalla hrynja stallar steins* (BÞ 848; 25 *Folk Songs* no. 9)
6. *Rís þú, unga Íslands merki* (Leifs original; 25 *Folk Songs* no. 10)
7. *Kvölda tekur, sest er sól* (BÞ 865)
8. *Aldurinn þótt ei sé hár* (BÞ 825; 25 *Folk Songs* no. 12)

Themes 2–6 are in the mixed meter of rímur while the opening *Ísland, farsælda frón* is a stately tvísöngur in duple time. Tune 7 stands out for its slow tempo and its regular triple meter as well as its mournful minor mode. Leifs relishes juxtaposing his themes polyphonically. For example, tune 6 appears in celli and basses against tune 3 in bassoon (mm. 175ff), and tune 7 is played by violas and celli against tune 8 in English horn (mm. 225ff). Since the frequent meter changes do not coincide, the outcome is often polymetric as well as polymodal. Leifs even employs canon, setting theme 7 against itself at the distance of one measure (mm. 209ff).

In his program notes for the *Iceland Overture*, Leifs explained that he had sought inspiration in both the Icelandic landscape and the nation's history. His description of the work is fully in line with the local nationalist view of Iceland's past propounded in the early twentieth century—for example, by the influential historian Jón Jónsson Aðils, who traced its history from the glory of the commonwealth era through the humiliation of Danish rule, to its revitalization through celebration of Iceland's "ancient glory."[70] The overture's defiant, dissonant opening, Leifs suggested, can be heard as an echo of the golden age of the Vikings, the lachrymose central section was meant to depict the doleful period of foreign oppression, and the finale "promises rebirth."[71] In the rousing conclusion, both *Ísland, farsælda frón* and *Rís þú, unga Íslands merki* return to suggest a brighter future for Iceland, their texts glorifying the landscape (glaciers, blue sky) and the new Icelandic flag, respectively.

After a brief stop and a concert in the Faroe Islands, the Hamburg Philharmonic arrived in Reykjavík on May 31 and gave fourteen concerts in seventeen days. Most were held in Iðnó, a theater by the lake Tjörnin in central Reykjavík, but the ensemble also performed in the Reykjavík Cathedral and at Vífilsstaðir, a tuberculosis sanatorium a short drive from town. The concerts were a local sensation, and reviews were unanimously positive. The critic-composer Árni Thorsteinson described the opening concert as "the greatest event in the history of the arts in this country"; Emil Thoroddsen, who had earlier expressed his doubts about Leifs's talent, wrote that "that old wooden shack Iðnó has become the Parthenon; for a few days Reykjavík has become a metropolis; this music brings us all the kingdoms of this world and their glory."[72] Reviews of Leifs's

Figure 3.2. Leifs and the Hamburg Philharmonic in Iðnó, Reykjavík, 1926. © Leifs Archives, National and University Library, Reykjavík.

compositions were sympathetic, if not ecstatic. Thorsteinson wrote that no music written by an Icelander had yet sounded "so strange" but acknowledged that it might "gradually, upon further hearing, become clearer and more understandable."[73] The painter Kjarval, on the other hand, was elated, suggesting to Leifs that the citizens of Reykjavík should be allowed to hear his overture "at least once a week—then it would be easier to wake up."[74] As the orchestra sailed off on June 17, over one thousand people assembled at the Reykjavík pier to express their gratitude; the town's wind band performed the German national anthem, and the crowd joined in a quadruple hurrah. One journalist struck a wistful note in his account of the farewell ceremony: "It will be a while before the citizens of Reykjavík again have the opportunity to hear orchestral playing as good as this."[75]

Despite local enthusiasm for the orchestra, the Reykjavík concerts were not an unqualified success for Leifs himself. Rumors had begun to spread that his conducting had been panned by critics in

Norway. This was not quite true, although reviews had certainly been mixed. Some praised his conducting as "full of talent, temperament, and understanding of structure," while others lamented his "lack of technique and routine."[76] More embarrassingly for Leifs, one Reykjavík critic claimed that orchestra members themselves had also disparaged his conducting, saying that "it didn't matter whether he waived his stick or not."[77] This claim is substantiated by a memorandum in the Hamburg Philharmonic Archives. It was addressed to Karl Muck, the orchestra's chief conductor, by an unnamed player who castigated Leifs for having been "in no way equal to his artistic task."[78] In all fairness, it was a considerable task. The relatively inexperienced Leifs not only had to learn and rehearse a vast repertoire in a short amount of time, he also simultaneously had to plan the details of the tour, arrange travel schedules, book concert venues, compose a substantial new work and write out orchestra parts. It is quite conceivable that his performance on the podium was of a considerably lower caliber than that to which the members of the Hamburg orchestra were accustomed.

A RETURN TO SONG-COLLECTING, AND A FAILED PROPOSAL

Leifs remained in Reykjavík after the Philharmonic's departure, and now resumed his activities as folk song collector. He had learned from his trip the previous year that no attempt to transcribe songs on the spot would yield satisfactory results, given the Icelandic singers' propensity for ornamentation and microtonal inflections. He had therefore, in November 1925, met with Erich Moritz von Hornbostel, director of the Berlin Phonograph Archives (*Berliner Phonogramm-Archiv*) and a prominent representative of the discipline then known as comparative musicology, which combined systematic and ethnological studies with the goal of establishing relationships between the music of various countries and peoples.[79] Hornbostel and his colleague, the ethnomusicologist Carl Stumpf, had begun their collection of Edison wax cylinders in 1900, when they recorded a Siamese ensemble visiting Berlin. By the mid-1920s their archive had grown into an invaluable resource containing over 10,000 cylinders, including music-making from remote places such as Angola and Australia, China and Kazakhstan.[80]

Hornbostel provided Leifs with a phonograph and a supply of cylinders at no cost, with the proviso that the original cylinders would be deposited in his collection, while copies would be made available for Leifs's own use. Leifs had originally intended to travel to the north of Iceland, but when the parliament declined his request for funding he decided to stay in Reykjavík and advertised for singers in local newspapers, requesting "anyone who knows some rímur, old hymn tunes, tvísöngur or other old folk songs" to contact him.[81] He was somewhat disappointed by the results, particularly since some of the singers had resided for decades in Reykjavík and he suspected that vernacular singing in the south was not as "authentic" as in the north. Yet some of the material he recorded in 1926—a total of 28 cylinders—would eventually come to good use. An elderly lady from northwestern Iceland sang an ornamented version of the hymn tune *Allt eins og blómstrið eina* which Leifs would later quote in two of his works (the Organ Concerto and the *Three Hymns* op. 12a), and he also recorded tunes that appeared in his *Icelandic Dances* for piano three years later.[82]

Leifs's local success with the Hamburg Philharmonic opened no doors for him as a conductor in Germany. Quite the contrary, for on his return in autumn 1926, there unfolded one of the most despondent periods of his career. Leifs had decided to launch a new project, the idea for which had been born during the tour. He found most professional orchestras to be a hodgepodge of different playing methods and backgrounds, which made it difficult to unify details of technique, musical expression, and artistic vision. He now hoped to establish an academy for young performers, the *Westdeutsche Orchesterakademie*, a cooperative enterprise of many smaller cities with the goal of raising orchestral performance in Germany to a new level of perfection. Leifs would himself direct the orchestra's rehearsals and concerts while each member would receive private lessons from acknowledged soloists.[83] Leifs worked

Figure 3.3. Leifs, his daughter Snót, his mother, and his maternal grandmother during his stay in Reykjavík in 1926. © Leifs Archives, National and University Library, Reykjavík.

tirelessly to gather support for the academy, writing up to sixty letters each day in the hope of gaining interest and financing from municipalities in the Rhine-Ruhr area.[84] In September 1926, he and Annie left Berlin for Cologne, and in early October they had leased a small room in Düsseldorf. He went from city to city—Dortmund, Gelsenkirchen, Essen, Mülheim, Duisburg, Bonn—but met with rejection everywhere. He tried to explain the purpose of his undertaking to his parents, taking on the role of martyr:

> It is difficult to explain to you the project I am now working on. It is an attempt to bring orchestral playing, organization, and conducting

to a higher level than has previously been known. This attempt has already gained some support and is bound to be successful and set a new standard in orchestral performance, if I can ensure the right conditions. The preparation will be long and difficult and the results are not yet certain; but after all, it is my fate to be a trailblazer, so I must accept this cross and the burdens that go along with it.[85]

In 1926–27, Leifs came as close as ever to actually being reduced to poverty. He and Annie were without any income for months, spending only a few pfennigs on food each day, and Annie lost an alarming amount of weight. Leifs admitted to his parents that the final weeks of 1926 had been "the worst that I have ever lived."[86] Leifs and Annie dismissed the nanny temporarily, sending Snót to live with Annie's parents in Teplitz for six months, and only an 1,100 mark loan from the piano manufacturer Bechstein allowed them to put food on the table again.[87]

The *Westdeutsche Orchesterakademie* was in many ways a worthwhile idea, and Leifs was here ahead of his time, for orchestra academies have in the past several decades become an important part of training young musicians in both Europe and the United States. But Leifs was completely unknown in this part of Germany, and his timing was abysmal. Replying to his request for funding, a representative of the German Musicians' Union (*Deutscher Musiker-Verband*) stressed the outrageous cost of such an undertaking, which he estimated at no less than half a million reichsmark annually, at a time when local ensembles were fighting for grants of only 1,000 marks.[88] With Germany's economy in ruins, municipal authorities in the industrial Ruhr area could hardly be expected to invest large sums of money in revolutionizing the world's orchestra culture.

Six months had gone to waste, and in February 1927 Leifs gave up on the idea altogether. He and Annie now moved to Baden-Baden, the wealthy spa resort town that was home to one of Europe's largest casinos. Around eighty thousand guests visited the town each year, many of them millionaires, and this ensured a lively if sometimes ostentatious cultural scene. It is unclear why Leifs chose to relocate there; he told his parents that he expected to find peace and quiet for composing, but he also may have hoped to attract a wealthy patron who might be willing to finance his artistic pursuits.[89] The family resided in an apartment at Tiergartenweg 3 where Leifs was finally able to resume composing. In March he wrote to his parents that he was busy with three large works that had been in progress for some time—presumably the Organ Concerto, *Variazioni Pastorali on a Theme by Beethoven,* and the overture to *Galdra-Loftr.*[90] The overture is a stand-alone work with a separate opus number (op. 10), and while it borrows some musical ideas from the incidental music, it synthesizes them into a larger and more coherent whole. There is plenty of drama in this overture; it begins with tolling bells and a folklike rímur theme while quicksilver runs in the violins spread throughout the orchestra. Loud and forceful episodes suggest the deranged magician, but a quiet central section evokes the funeral march from act III and its accompanying chorale tune.

Even with all its wealth, Baden-Baden had little to offer Leifs, who found himself yet again in unfamiliar surroundings, with no professional contacts. Annie was able to attract one piano student who paid twenty marks an hour; she got up at seven each morning and practiced until noon in a rented studio space.[91] In March 1927 the Bochum Symphony, under the direction of Leopold Reichwein (Bruno Walter's successor at the Vienna State Opera), performed *Trilogia piccola,* but Leifs was unable to attend because he did not have 100 marks to pay for the journey.[92] Disaster was once again averted by financial assistance from both their parents as well as the encouraging news that the Icelandic government had awarded Leifs a composing stipend of 2,000 krónur (roughly 1,000 marks).[93]

In July 1927, Baden-Baden hosted the German Chamber Music Festival (*Deutsche Kammermusik*), which was something of a misnomer, since the festival, now newly relocated from Donaueschingen, had been expanded to include chamber operas as well as motion pictures with music. Leifs was in attendance and wrote an extensive two-part review for *Signale für die musikalische Welt,* declaring the strongest musical statements to have been the nationally tinged works of Martinů (String Quartet no. 2) and Bartók, who gave the first performance of his own Piano Sonata—Leifs's first documented encounter with his music. He was less impressed with Alban Berg's *Lyric Suite* and found the premiere of the *Mahagonny Songspiel* by Kurt Weill and Bertolt Brecht to be "unfunny and boring," remarking that better "jazz music" could be heard even at mediocre coffee shops.[94]

The family celebrated Christmas in Teplitz, where Leifs once again felt awkward and distressed in the company of his father-in-law. Edwin Riethof was still not convinced about Leifs's pursuit of a career as a freelance composer and accused him of neglecting to provide for his family.[95] Leifs, on the other hand, felt that Riethof failed to grasp his artistic calling and that he saw money as the measure of all things.[96] Nevertheless, Riethof's financing soon provided Annie with the big break of her career. On March 21, 1928, she performed her favorite concerto, Mozart's A major K. 488, at Salle Pleyel in Paris, at the Festival of Romantic and Classical Music, conducted by the Munich-based Friedrich Munter.[97] The audience responded enthusiastically, and reviews were positive, lauding her "confident technique and agreeable tone," but Annie's Parisian debut proved to be her last major concert appearance.[98] All her and Leifs's attempts later in 1928 to attract the attention of German concert agents proved futile, and it seems no coincidence that by the end of the year Annie had again become pregnant. From then on she would devote herself unconditionally to her family and to advancing her husband's career.[99]

In April 1928, Leifs was Iceland's self-appointed representative at an international meeting of composers and authors in Berlin. Representatives from twenty countries were in attendance, and there Leifs and Annie attended cocktail parties and mingled with leading artists such as Max Reinhardt, who expressed interest in the Icelandic playwright Jóhann Sigurjónsson (author of *Galdra-Loftr*). The most memorable event was their first journey on an airplane, a tour organized by Lufthansa following the Berlin city council's reception at Tempelhof airport.[100] While their Berlin experience a few years earlier had been abysmal, Leifs now felt that all doors were open to him and his art.¹⁰¹ This positive response may have influenced their decision, five years later, to permanently return to the greater Berlin area.

FOLK SONG GATHERING, SUMMER 1928

Leifs returned to Iceland in summer 1928 to continue his folk song collecting. Hornbostel had again provided him with a recording device as well as a fresh supply of thirty cylinders; a grant from the *Notgemeinschaft der Deutschen Wissenschaft* (Emergency Association of German Science) ensured that he could undertake a substantial journey into the countryside, unlike his attempt in Reykjavík two years previously. This would be Leifs's longest collecting trip, a total of twenty-five days in northern and northwestern Iceland. The journey, which began on September 8, also took him through the western part of the country, where a farmer in the town of Borgarnes sang a "fine rímur tune" that later became the basis of Leifs's *Icelandic Dance* op. 14b no. 2.¹⁰² In another village, a local priest's rendition of a tune called *Breiðafjörður* captured the composer's imagination; he believed that it might be the remnants of an ancient tvísöngur and later arranged it for voice and piano. On September 12 Leifs arrived at Skarð, an ancient farmstead in the northwest, where an entire family was willing to share their music: the farmer, Kristinn Indriðason, chanted tvísöngur with his brother, and their parents also contributed to the growing cylinder collection. Still, Leifs was most impressed with a "completely authentic" performance by an old farmhand, Búi Oddsson (b. 1863), who sang with microtonal shadings that would have been impossible to transcribe with complete accuracy.¹⁰³

In other areas, Leifs was less fortunate. Locals in Akurey, Flatey, and Reykhólar (his mother's birthplace) insisted they knew no folk songs at all. Leifs made a stop at the small fishing village of Siglufjörður to meet the dean of Icelandic folk song collectors, the sixty-six-year old Bjarni Þorsteinsson, who gave a frosty welcome. He insisted that Icelandic folk song was already dying and that collecting it was a waste of time and effort and refused to give Leifs the names of local singers. While Þorsteinsson may have wished to fend off an assumed competitor, his words did contain a grain of truth. When Leifs attempted to record two of Iceland's legendary tvísöngur singers, the septuagenarians Kristján Blöndal and Böðvar Þorláksson, they had trouble recalling the tunes and had to consult Þorsteinsson's printed volume.[104] Still, Leifs was pleased with the overall outcome and received an encouraging response from Hornbostel, who was convinced that the few tvísöngvar Leifs had captured were "certainly tunes from the 10th century!"[105] Hornbostel transcribed the tvísöngur recordings himself and published the findings in an article two years later.[106]

Leifs and Hornbostel were not the only ones to study these recordings with great interest. In 1932, the American composer Henry Cowell traveled to Berlin on a Guggenheim fellowship to research Hornbostel's collection and was particularly enthralled by the songs found on the Icelandic cylinders. He brought copies of some of the recordings back to the United States and wrote an essay on Icelandic folk music for *The Musical Mercury*, enthusing about the "weird fascination" of this music, "which should be more known and heard, both for its bleak loveliness, and for its historical scientific value."[107] Cowell's fascination even led him, in 1938–40, to record his own cylinders of Icelandic expatriates in San Francisco.[108] In 1941, he wrote to Leifs in Germany, hoping to obtain further recordings and transcriptions of Icelandic folk songs, but this proved impossible because of the war.[109] Much later, when commissioned to write a new work for the Iceland Symphony Orchestra, Cowell's recollection of the old recordings prompted him to write a symphony "in the spirit of national Icelandic music," aptly termed the *Icelandic Symphony* (no. 16).[110]

Leifs recorded his last cylinders for Hornbostel's collection in 1934, on the steps of his mother's house in Reykjavík. (He was captured in a photograph by the renowned Dutch photojournalist Willem van de Poll, who happened to be visiting Iceland on assignment from Associated Press, see fig. 3.4.) By then, the future of the Berlin

Figure 3.4. Jón Leifs on the steps of his childhood home in Reykjavík, 1934, recording the singing of Icelandic fisherman Oddur Sigurgeirsson (1879–1953). Photograph: Willem van de Poll. National Archives of the Netherlands, Public domain.

archive was uncertain, and the half-Jewish Hornbostel had been forced to leave Germany. In any case, Leifs himself was ready to move on as a composer, having already integrated the vernacular material into his own mature style. The *Two Icelandic Folk Songs* op. 19b, arranged for voice and piano around 1934, were, in a sense, his farewell to the genre of folk song arrangement.[111] His use of folk tunes in later large-scale works is limited to his first string quartet (*Mors et vita*, 1939), two choral pieces from 1943, and *Spring Song* for choir and orchestra (1958). From the time Leifs began serious work on *Edda I*, the massive oratorio that took up much of his composing energies in the 1930s, actual quotation, arrangement, or reworking of folk melodies was no longer of prime interest. While the spirit of Icelandic vernacular music remained a decisive influence on his overall style, it did not dictate the actual content of his works.

On his arrival in Iceland in August 1928, Leifs had been the main instigator in founding the Federation of Icelandic Artists (*Bandalag íslenskra listamanna*), whose goal was to protect artists' rights, encourage their cooperation, and promote Icelandic art at home and abroad. At that time, artists were a newly emerging group in Icelandic society, and this seemed a propitious time for them to band together, since earlier that year the Icelandic state had guaranteed financial resources to artists through the newly established Culture Fund (*Menningarsjóður*), which was funded by prohibition fines.[112] Still, many of the country's traditional-minded farmers and fishermen were suspicious of this new development. Some feared that Iceland might become overpopulated with artists, with one claiming that they were "beggars or fools, who have no real right to exist in a bourgeois society."[113] The Federation of Icelandic Artists was Leifs's brainchild. He had mentioned the idea to the artist Guðmundur Einarsson around 1925 and traveled to Denmark in 1928 to meet with the novelist Gunnar Gunnarsson, whom he convinced to preside over the society, with Leifs and Einarsson completing the three-member board.[114] A large percentage of the founding members were authors, and just a year after its founding, the society had obtained membership to the PEN Club as well as the Nordic Association of Writers, thanks to the efforts of Leifs and Gunnarsson. The Federation of Icelandic Artists remains active and serves an important role as a common mouthpiece for various individual societies, particularly regarding government policy and regulations.

PRAYERS AND LULLABIES

The year 1929 was one of loss and renewal: it saw the birth of a child and the death of a parent. Leifs's father passed away on April 2, having battled cancer since the previous year. At his mother's request,

Leifs did not travel to Iceland for the funeral; instead, he eulogized his father in *Three Hymns* for voice and piano op. 12a, to texts by the seventeenth-century poet Hallgrímur Pétursson. The first and third are original compositions while the second draws on one of Leifs's 1926 field recordings, an ornamented version of his beloved funeral chorale *Allt eins og blómstrið eina*. The third hymn (*Up, Up, My Soul*) is the liveliest of the set, "bright and free, striving towards light and victory," as Leifs reported to his family in Reykjavík.[115]

The opening hymn, composed on April 4, is particularly remarkable. Its text is a common children's prayer in Iceland to this day; Leifs had learned it from his father and had already passed it on to Snót:[116]

Vertu, Guð faðir, faðir minn	Father God, be my father
í frelsarans Jesú nafni,	in the savior Jesus's name,
hönd þín leiði mig út og inn	may thy hand lead me out and in,
svo allri synd ég hafni.	so that I shun all sin.

Leifs's setting, marked *dolcissimo* and *molto intimo*, is simple yet hauntingly atmospheric; he noted that it was "best suited to a boy soprano." Over an open-fifth drone in the piano, the voice spins expansive *legato* phrases that alternately touch on the major and minor third of the scale, creating a fragile luminosity that would become a hallmark of Leifs's more intimate style. He would employ this oscillating-third motion in two further compositions from 1929, the *Lullaby* and the fifth movement from the *Iceland Cantata*—which, not coincidentally, is written for a boys' chorus. This major/minor oscillation is also a key element of some of Leifs's later works, such as the *Requiem* and *A Hymn to the Setting Sun*, many of which, like the 1929 settings, suggest childlike innocence mingled with loss.

It was becoming obvious that the move to Baden-Baden had been a mistake. Leifs had fallen out with local musicians early on and had admitted to his parents in 1927 that the casino town had "completely failed" his and Annie's expectations.[117] His constitution also did not agree with the summer heat of southern Germany;

he had spent most of the summer of 1928 in bed with a stomach flu, subsisting on porridge and tea.[118] In June 1929 the family relocated yet again—their eighth move in as many years—this time to Travemünde by the Baltic Sea, roughly ten miles north of Lübeck. This was a popular tourist destination in summer but had only 3,500 year-round inhabitants. Leifs delighted in its "nearly Icelandic" climate—the town is about as far north as one can get in Germany—and enjoyed taking a daily swim in the sea.[119]

It was in Travemünde that Leifs and Annie's second daughter was born on August 20, 1929. For Leifs, who had recently lost his father, it was a potent reminder of the cycle of life and death. She was christened Líf—the Icelandic word for life, and, like Snót, an uncommon name at the time. Among the greetings the family received after her birth was a poem from Jóhann Jónsson, a Leipzig-based poet three years Leifs's senior, who, despite a protracted battle with tuberculosis that would soon claim his life, wrote some of the most impressive and influential modernist poetry in Icelandic. He had become good friends with the couple a few years earlier and had even penned a short but flattering poem in praise of "Frau Annie."[120] He now enclosed in a letter to the composer another poem, this one with a dedication to young Líf, expressing the hope that Leifs might set it to music. Jónsson remarked that he had tried to capture in his delicate verse "some of that classical reticence that graced the poets of old, when they had better taste."[121]

Þei, þei og ró.	Hush, husha-bye.
Þögn breiðist yfir allt.	Silence reigns over all.
Hnigin er sól í sjó.	The sun sinks to the sea.
Sof þú í blíðri ró.	Now slumber peacefully.
Við höfum vakað nóg.	We have been long awake.
Værðar þú njóta skalt.	Sleep on your eyelids fall.
Þei, þei og ró.	Hush, husha-bye.
Þögn breiðist yfir allt.	Silence reigns over all.[122]

Leifs's *Lullaby* is dated September 5, two weeks after Líf's birth. It is one of his most haunting creations and demonstrates how he could employ the most limited means to great effect. The vocal line

Example 3.2. Jón Leifs, *Lullaby* op. 14a no. 2, mm. 1–10. © Iceland Music Information Center.

for the most part spans only a perfect fifth, with additional half steps above and below (see example 3.2). The accompaniment is sparse: over a tolling F-sharp in the left hand, the right provides an evolving kaleidoscope of harmonies that can be reduced to four basic voice-leading patterns. The most notable feature of this music—as in the hymn op. 12a no. 1—is the oscillation between major and minor thirds, suggesting the flickering of light and shadows. The three occurrences of the major third are strategically placed at the end of a phrase, each given the softest dynamic (*ppp*) in a song that is otherwise marked *pianissimo* throughout.

Leifs experienced a short-lived spiritual awakening in the months following his father's death. As a teenager, he had been confirmed as a Lutheran (in accordance with Icelandic tradition), but he had never been devoutly religious. Now he began attending church and reading the Bible, although he confessed to his mother that he was "not a fundamentalist, and I find the Catholic church much more humane and beneficial than the Lutheran."[123] In August 1929 he wrote a setting of *The Lord's Prayer* (*Faðir vor*, op. 12b) for soprano or tenor and organ. While this is a far more elaborate composition than the *Three Hymns* from a few months earlier, the joint opus number suggests that it should also be considered a tribute to Leifs's (terrestrial) father. The music is as clear an example as any of Leifs's delight in word painting. "Forgive us" (*Fyrirgef oss*) is set to serene major triads while "temptation" (*freistni*) is accompanied by menacingly low pedal notes, and "trespasses" (*skuldir*) by biting dissonances made up of two fully diminished seventh chords; this same dissonance would also serve as a referential harmony in Leifs's Organ Concerto, completed a few months later. The religious awakening of the summer of 1929 did not last. *The Lord's Prayer* would be Leifs's last original composition based on a sacred text, and later that year he chose not to set any lines alluding to Christianity in Davíð Stefánsson's libretto to the *Iceland Cantata* (see chap. 5).

Leifs's first decade as a professional musician was in many ways decisive for his future career. His prospects in Reykjavík had been substantially damaged by what local musicians perceived as a combative stance during his stay there in 1921. Even the success of the Hamburg Philharmonic tour five years later did not alter the local perception of Leifs as a prickly personality endowed with more confidence than talent, and his conducting career in Germany had never truly materialized. Meanwhile, he had paved a new path for himself as a composer-collector. He had undertaken three important trips gathering folk songs and had completed a dozen works of significant promise. Although his earliest works exhibit a varied stylistic approach, by 1929 Leifs was well on his way to developing a consistent musical language based largely on the vernacular style. Before turning to the landmark year (for Leifs and for Iceland) of 1930, it is worth briefly suspending the chronological narrative in order to consider the essential elements—derived from literature, history, music, and nature—of the unique style that was about to emerge from his crucible.

NOTES

1. Þorleifur Jónsson to Leifs, May 6, 1925.
2. Walter Gieseking to Leifs, April 20, 1922.
3. Halldór Laxness to Leifs, January 1, 1929.
4. Kristján Albertsson to Leifs, October 25, 1930; see also Sigfús Einarsson's review of the concert, "Hljómleikar," *Morgunblaðið*, August 13, 1930.
5. Einar Benediktsson, *Hrannir* (Reykjavík: Sigurður Kristjánsson, 1913), ix.
6. Heimir Pálsson, "Einar Benediktsson," in *Icelandic Writers*, Dictionary of Literary Biography vol. 293, ed. Patrick J. Stevens (Detroit: Gale, 2004), 38.
7. Einar Benediktsson, "Tónment Íslendinga," *Vörður*, January 10, 1925.
8. Josef Frischen (Königl. Musikdirektor, Kgl. Kur-Orchester Norderney) to Leifs, May 1922 (undated); Annie Leifs, biographical sketch of Leifs.
9. *Hallische Nachrichten*, January 8, 1923; Åhlén, *Jón Leifs—Tónskáld í mótbyr*, 34.
10. "Kunst und Wissenschaft," *General-Anzeiger Dortmund*, December 30, 1922; "Konzert der westfälischen Konzertdirektion," *Rheinisch-Westfälische Zeitung*, December 30, 1922; *Dortmunder Zeitung*, January 3, 1923.
11. On Scherchen's interpretation of the *Eroica*, see Martin Zenck, "Zum Begriff des Klassischen in der Musik," *Archiv für Musikwissenschaft* 39 (1982): 276–79; for a historical perspective of his neo-objective approach, see Jürg Stenzl, trans. Irene Zedlacher, "In Search of a History of Musical Interpretation," *The Musical Quarterly* 79 (1995): 689–90.
12. Program note by Leifs, Leipziger Volksakademie, February 24, 1924.
13. *Sächsische Volkszeitung* (undated) and *Dresdner Nachrichten* (undated), both in Leifs's scrapbook, 1923.
14. *Signale für die musikalische Welt Berlin*, March 21, 1923.
15. Leifs to Erich Nagel, September 19, 1923.
16. Salóme Þorleifsdóttir to Leifs, July 1927 and June 7, 1931.
17. Leifs to Danish-Icelandic embassy in Berlin, July 8, 1922 (Rigsarkivet Copenhagen, Berlin, diplomatisk ræpresentation og militærmission, Gruppeordnede sager 1930–45, 81.A.10).
18. Kristján Albertsson to Leifs, September 9, 1923.
19. Fritz Jaritz, "John [sic] Leifs," *Wernigeröder Zeitung und Intelligenzenblatt*, June 23, 1923; also printed in *Der Chorleiter*, July 15, 1923, and *Die Tonkunst*, October 15, 1923.
20. Verband der konzertierenden Künstler Deutschlands to Leifs, September 5, 1923; invoice from Leipziger Volksakademie to Leifs, October 18, 1923.
21. *Magdeburger Tageszeitung*, November 16, 1923; *Volksstimme Magdeburg*, November 16, 1923.

22. Verband der konzertierenden Künstler Deutschlands to Leifs, September 5, 1923; invoice from Leipziger Volksakademie to Leifs, October 18, 1923.
23. Þorleifur Jónsson to Leifs, September 24, 1923.
24. Leifs, "Erinnerungen an Karl Muck," *Zeitschrift für Musik* 107 (1940): 290.
25. Leifs, "Til Emils Thoroddsens," *Alþýðublaðið*, October 13, 1925.
26. Bernard Scudder, translation for *Melodia*, Carmina Chamber Choir, Smekkleysa SMK 56, 2007, compact disc. The original text and tune are found in the manuscript Rask 98 (14v–15r), in the collection of The Arnamagnaean Institute (Department of Nordic Research, Copenhagen University).
27. Páll Ísólfsson to Leifs, March 1923 and August 8, 1923.
28. "Dagskrá útvarpsins," *Nýja dagblaðið*, March 11, 1934.
29. Leifs to his parents, November 23, 1924.
30. Leifs to Edwin Riethof, November 26, 1924.
31. Leifs to Edwin Riethof, November 26, 1924.
32. Leifs to Edwin Riethof, December 4 and 12, 1924.
33. Leifs to Edwin Riethof, November 26, 1924.
34. Björn Jónsson to Leifs, November 15, 1924.
35. Leifs to Edwin Riethof, May 3, 1925.
36. Leifs to Edwin Riethof, February 11 and March 19, 1925.
37. Leifs, Program note for *Galdra-Loftr*, performance on March 21, 1963, Iceland Symphony Orchestra Archives, Reykjavík.
38. Galdra-Loftur (Loftur the Sorcerer) is the subject of a well-known folktale (see Jón Árnason; on the historical background to the story and the life of Loftur Þorsteinsson, who graduated from the Latin school in Hólar in 1722, see Hannes Þorsteinsson, "Galdra-Loptur, söguleg rannsókn eptir Hannes Þorsteinsson," *Huld, Safn alþýðlegra fræða íslenzkra*, vol. 2, (Reykjavík: Snæbjörn Jónsson, 1936), 214–32.
39. Guðni Elísson, "From Realism to Neoromanticism," in *A History of Icelandic Literature*, Histories of Scandinavian Literature, vol. 5, ed. Daisy Neijmann (Lincoln: University of Nebraska Press, 2006), 349.
40. The tune was originally sung to the text *Dagur í austri öllum*, an Icelandic translation of a Danish morning hymn; see Páll Eggert Ólason, *Upptök sálma og sálmalaga í lútherskum sið á Íslandi* (Reykjavík: Árbók Háskóla Íslands, 1924), 185.
41. The melody is transmitted in Lbs 1927 4to ("Hymnodia sacra"), a manuscript written by the priest Guðmundur Högnason; its contents were published in Bjarni Þorsteinsson, *Íslenzk þjóðlög*, and this was Leifs's source for the tune. On the manuscript and its history, see my article "*Hymnodia Sacra* and Its Influence on the 1772 Icelandic Hymnal," in *Mirrors of Virtue:*

Manuscript and Print in Late Pre-Modern Iceland, ed. Margrét Eggertsdóttir and Matthew James Driscoll (Copenhagen: Museum Tusculanum, 2017), 31–56.

42. Leifs, "Isländische Volkslieder: Zwei Forschungsberichte," *Zeitschrift für Musikwissenschaft* 11 (1929): 366–67.

43. Melodia (Rask 98) is held at the Nordisk forskningsinstitut, Copenhagen University; Hymnodia sacra is at the National and University Library, Reykjavík (Lbs 1927 4to).

44. Leifs's notes from the gathering survive in his collection of letters, in the National and University Library, Reykjavík. See also "Íslensk þjóðlög, brot úr ræðu eftir Jón Leifs," *Ísafold*, September 24, 1925.

45. "Íslensk þjóðlög," *Morgunblaðið*, September 20, 1925.

46. The article, published under the pseudonym *Þjóðlaga-vinur* (friend of folk songs), appeared in *Vísir*, September 26, 1926.

47. Árni Thorsteinson, "Annie Leifs. Jón Leifs," *Morgunblaðið*, October 6, 1925.

48. Sveinbjörn Sveinbjörnsson, "Fáein orð um íslenskan tvísöng," *Vörður*, December 12, 1925.

49. Leifs, "Tvísöngurinn," *Vörður*, January 23, 1926.

50. Emil Thoroddsen, "Tónleikar Annie og Jóns Leifs," *Alþýðublaðið*, October 10, 1925.

51. Emil Thoroddsen, "Ungir listamenn og forn tónfræði," *Vörður*, January 23, 1926.

52. Halldór Laxness to Annie Leifs, April 2, 1930. The original letter, from Harriet Jessup Wilson (dated March 10, 1930), is in the Laxness collection, National and University Library, Reykjavík.

53. Thorstina Walters Jackson to Leifs, March 8, 1930; F.D.P., "University Glee Club of Women Offers Novelties," *New York Herald Tribune*, May 9, 1930. The Chicago-based Icelandic tenor Guðmundur Kristjánsson sang Leifs's songs in concert, including the *Lullaby* and op. 12a no. 1, at a recital at Steinway Hall, New York, on October 20, 1937.

54. Emil Telmányi to Leifs, September 19, 1925.

55. Siegmund von Hausegger to Leifs, November 20 and 26, 1925; Leifs, draft letter to Hausegger, December 14, 1925.

56. Leifs to his parents, December 24, 1925.

57. M. Kaufmann, "Bühne und Kunst," *Karlsbader Tageblatt*, December 1, 1925; "Dhc," "Das dritte volkstümliche Symphoniekonzert," *Deutsche Tageszeitung Karlsbad*, December 4, 1925.

58. Erik Eggen to Leifs, March 19, 1925.

59. Fürstlich Liechtenstein'sche Kabinetskanzlei to Leifs, July 23, 1927.

60. See Leifs, *Islands künstlerische Anregung*, 51–53.
61. Leifs, "Klassische Interpretation," *Rheinische Musik- und Theaterzeitung* 30, October 5, 1929; Leifs, "Das Orchesternotenmaterial," *Zeitschrift für Musik* 97 (1930): 268–70.
62. Leifs, "Gegen die Romantisierung klassischer Musik," *Zeitschrift für Musik* 92 (1925): 633–39; "Grundlagen klassischer Interpretation," *Zeitschrift für Musik* 95 (1928): 257–61, 329–32; "Interpretationsstudien (Der Eroica-Trauermarsch / Das Eroica-Finale)," *Neues Beethoven-Jahrbuch* 3 (1927): 62–90.
63. "ln," "Hljómsveit Reykjavíkur. 1. hljómleikar," *Alþýðublaðið*, November 12, 1925.
64. Dr. Mantze, Akademisches Orchester der Staatl. Hochschulen Berlin to Leifs, February 7, 1925.
65. Þorleifur Jónsson to Jón and Annie Leifs, December 22, 1925.
66. Leifs, "Þýzka hljómsveitin," article draft, April 29, 1926.
67. Leifs to Annie Leifs, May 10, 1926.
68. Leifs, "Ég mótmæli—Ég ákæri, Orðsending frá tónskáldi mánaðarins," typewritten document, March 1, 1968.
69. Leifs, *Islands künstlerische Anregung*, 30–31.
70. Sigríður Matthíasdóttir, "Réttlæting þjóðernis: samanburður á alþýðufyrirlestrum Jóns Aðils og hugmyndum Johanns Gottlieb Fichte," *Skírnir* 169 (1995): 55–56.
71. Quoted in Hjálmar Helgi Ragnarsson, "Jón Leifs, Icelandic Composer: Historical Background, Biography, Analysis of Selected Works" (MFA thesis, Cornell University, 1980), 143.
72. Árni Thorsteinson, "Hamburger Philharmonisches Orchester," *Morgunblaðið*, June 4, 1926; Emil Thoroddsen, "Fyrstu hljómleikar Hamburger philharmonischen Orkesters," *Vörður*, June 5, 1926.
73. Árni Thorsteinson, "Kirkjuhljómleikar," *Morgunblaðið*, June 8, 1926.
74. Jóhannes Kjarval, "Meistari Jón Leifs," Leifs collection, scrapbook V.
75. "Hljómsveitin þýzka," *Alþýðublaðið*, June 18, 1926. The Hamburg Philharmonic's visit left a more personal kind of impact on one of its members, the cellist Paul Moth. Concerned that the Nazis might discover the Jewish origins of his family, in spring 1939 he encouraged his twenty-five-year old daughter, Helga, to sail to Iceland, where she married, raised a family, and lived until her death in 2002 (see "Helga Moth Jónsson," *Morgunblaðið*, April 20, 2002). The Hamburg Philharmonic would also visit Iceland again in June 1952.
76. Sverre Jordan, "Koncert," *Morgenavisen*, May 28, 1926; Arne van Erpekum Sem, "Konsert og operette," *Tidens tegn*, May 27, 1926.
77. Guðbrandur Jónsson, "Tónlistadómar," *Vísir*, August 31, 1926.

78. This correspondence is quoted in Michael Hillenstedt, "Das "isländische" als ästhetische Komponente in der Musik von Jón Leifs," 177–79. Hillenstedt suggests that the author of the memo may have been Johannes Rieckmann, who was the orchestra's chairman (*Vorstand*).

79. Albrecht Schneider, "Germany and Austria," in Helen Myers, ed., *Ethnomusicology: Historical and Regional Studies* (New York: W.W. Norton & Company, 1993), 80–81.

80. For accounts of the collection and its history, see Susanne Ziegler, *Die Wachszylinder des Berliner Phonogramm-Archivs* (Berlin, Staatliche Museen zu Berlin, Preußischer Kulturbesitz, 2006), and Artur Simon, ed., *Das Berliner Phonogramm-Archiv 1900–2000* (Berlin: VWB-Verlag, 2000). All of Leifs's cylinder recordings can be heard online at http://www.ismus.is/i/collection/id-1000002, accessed July 11, 2017.

81. "Bæjarfréttir," *Vísir*, August 21, 1926.

82. Leifs reported on his 1925 and 1926 field trips in "Isländische Volkslieder: Zwei Forschungsberichte," *Zeitschrift für Musikwissenschaft* 11 (1929): 365–73. The recordings made in 1928 were the subject of two further articles, "Isländische Volkslieder I: Dritter Bericht," *Mitteilungen der Islandfreunde* 19 (1931): 2–12; "Isländische Volkslieder II: Dritter Bericht," *Mitteilungen der Islandfreunde* 19 (1931): 32–41.

83. Leifs, "Zur Entwicklung der Orchester-Interpretation," *Rheinisch-Westfälische Zeitung*, July 18, 1926; "Provisorischer Entwurf zu einem Prospekt," undated proposal for an orchestra academy, autumn 1926.

84. Leifs to his parents, October 13, 1926.

85. Leifs to his parents, November 3, 1926.

86. Leifs to his parents, December 5, 1926.

87. Leifs to his parents, March 24, 1927.

88. Deutscher Musiker-Verband to Leifs, December 7, 1926.

89. Leifs to his parents, March 6, 1927.

90. Leifs to his parents, March 6, 1927.

91. Leifs to his parents, May 14, 1927.

92. Leifs to his parents, March 24, 1927.

93. Leifs to his parents, May 28, 1927.

94. Leifs, "'Deutsche Kammermusik' in Baden-Baden," *Signale für die musikalische Welt* 85 (1927): 1107–08, 1130.

95. See, for example, Leifs to Edwin Riethof, August 8, 1930.

96. Leifs to his parents, March 30, 1920; Leifs to Páll Ísólfsson, May 30, 1928.

97. Positive reviews of Annie's performance appeared in the Paris papers *Le Gaulois* (March 25, 1928) and *Le Journal* (March 27, 1928).

98. *Le Gaulois*, March 25, 1928.

99. Cf. letters from Konzertdirektion Otto Eckermann, May 15, 1928; Konzert-Direktion Hermann Wolf und Jules Sachs, June 4, 1928, and others of a similar date.
100. Leifs, "Alþjóðafundur," *Vörður*, June 30, 1928.
101. Leifs to his parents, April 9, 1928.
102. Leifs, "Isländische Volkslieder I: Dritter Bericht," *Mitteilungen der Islandfreunde* 19 (1931–32): 3.
103. Leifs, "Isländische Volkslieder I: Dritter Bericht," 6.
104. Leifs, "Isländische Volkslieder I: Dritter Bericht," 35.
105. Erich M. von Hornbostel to Leifs, December 1, 1928.
106. Erich M. von Hornbostel, "Phonographierte isländische Zwiegesänge," in *Deutsche Islandforschung 1930*, vol. I, ed. Walther Heinrich Vogt (Breslau: Ferdinand Hirt, 1930), 300–20.
107. Henry Cowell, "The Music of Iceland," *The Musical Mercury* 3/3 (September 1936): 50.
108. These recordings are now in the Library of Congress and can be heard through their website, http://memory.loc.gov/ammem/help/view.html (search term: rimur), accessed December 16, 2014.
109. Leifs to Henry Cowell, May 26, 1941, New York Public Library, Henry Cowell Papers.
110. *Þjóðviljinn*, March 19, 1963, 12.
111. The *Two Icelandic Folk Songs* op. 19a are *Blómi fagur kvenna klár* (recorded by Leifs in 1928) and *Sofðu unga ástin mín* (recorded in 1934).
112. Ingunn Þóra Magnúsdóttir, "Ágrip af sögu Bandalags íslenskra listamanna frá upphafi og til ársloka 1942" (MA thesis, University of Iceland, 1991), 12.
113. Björn Th. Björnsson, *Íslenzk myndlist á 19. og 20. öld II* (Reykjavík: Helgafell, 1973), 8–9; "Íslendingar þurfa að bæta kjör og aðbúnað listamanna sinna," *Morgunblaðið*, September 10, 1936.
114. Leifs to Guðmundur Einarsson, March 29, 1925; quoted in Ingunn Þóra Magnúsdóttir, "Ágrip af sögu Bandalags íslenskra listamanna," 15–16; Gunnar Gunnarsson, "Jón Leifs kvaddur," *Þjóðviljinn*, August 7, 1968.
115. Leifs to Þórey Þorleifsdóttir, April 9, 1929; Leifs to Ragnheiður Bjarnadóttir, April 11, 1929.
116. Leifs to Þórey Þorleifsdóttir, April 5, 1929.
117. Leifs to his parents, November 11, 1927; see also Leifs to Carl Flesch, September 6, 1927; Leifs to Kristján Albertsson, January 4, 1928.
118. Leifs to Ragnheiður Bjarnadóttir, May 11, 1929.
119. Leifs to Ragnheiður Bjarnadóttir, July 18, 1929.

120. The poem is printed in Jóhann Jónsson, *Kvæði og ritgerðir* (Reykjavík: Heimskringla, 1952) and in my biography, *Jón Leifs. Líf í tónum* (Reykjavík: Mál og menning, 2009), 130.

121. Jóhann Jónsson to Leifs, August 23, 1929.

122. Ruth L. Magnússon, translation for *Jón Leifs: Söngvar/Complete Songs*, Finnur Bjarnason and Örn Magnússon, Smekkleysa SMK 20, 2001, compact disc.

123. Leifs to Ragnheiður Bjarnadóttir, June 3, 1929.

FOUR

LEIFS AND THE ELEMENTS OF AN ICELANDIC STYLE

IN HIS AESTHETICS AND IDEOLOGY, Leifs was strongly influenced by Icelandic nationalist thought. The forming of a national identity through the arts, a project largely begun in the nineteenth century and taking on increased political weight during the 1920s, had a decisive impact on his work. Icelandic nationalism was—and, to a degree, still is—founded on its linguistic and literary heritage as well as its history and landscape. Leifs drew inspiration from precisely these elements in forging his archaic and primitive national sound.

LEIFS AND THE MEDIEVAL TRADITION

Sentiments about the distinctiveness of its culture were at the core of Icelandic claims to nationhood. Iceland had its own language and possessed a large corpus of medieval literature of significant cultural value, the so-called Eddic poetry and family sagas, discussed below. This historical and cultural memory, embodied in the literary tradition, was central to the formation of collective identity and the claim to political independence.[1] The international recognition of its language and literary history helped to set Iceland apart from Denmark's other North Atlantic colonies, Greenland and the Faroe Islands, with their strong oral traditions and relatively new written local languages. The historical situation left for Icelanders a rich legacy, and its revival for purposes of independence was both prudent and practical. As historian Gunnar Karlsson has suggested, "Iceland felt the need for a revival because it had unusually good material in its past on which to base it."[2]

The view of Iceland as a "treasure chest" of ancient Nordic/Germanic culture, particularly with regard to literature and the language in which it has been preserved, was a common trope of Icelandic nationalism from the nineteenth century up to the present day. In a 1930 speech, Ásgeir Ásgeirsson, then parliamentary speaker and later president of the republic, argued that the ancient legacy had "saved the nation from ruin, at times when the paw of foreign domination, bad harvest, and misery had nearly cut her life's thread in two."[3] The influence of the ancient "golden age" on the present historical moment was seen as a key factor in Icelandic nation building. Iceland's former glory justified its revival as an independent state; through impending statehood, the country would finally fulfill the promise of its medieval heritage. Furthermore, the emphasis on ancient culture as national symbol encouraged Iceland, even before its independence from Denmark in 1918, to demand the repatriation of medieval Icelandic manuscripts to Reykjavík from Copenhagen, where they had been stored for centuries. After strenuous rounds of negotiations that lasted until the 1960s, this led to the return of roughly 1,800 items—an unprecedented outcome justified not by judicial right but by what was seen instead as a moral obligation, given the importance of the material for Iceland's cultural identity.[4]

By claiming the local medieval heritage as the root of his artistic philosophy, Leifs drew on and embodied the nineteenth-century nationalist sentiment in which he had been raised. He saw in the medieval tradition the promise of a "Nordic Renaissance," not only in Iceland but throughout the world, for he claimed that the "true culture of the collective North" had never developed to its full potential.[5] Instead of becoming a dominant force within the wider European cultural domain, Icelandic literature had come to a standstill around 1300, together with the demise of the free republic and the pledge of fealty to the Norwegian king in 1262.[6] In Leifs's view, political independence and artistic creativity were mutually dependent. Iceland's political autonomy could be won and sustained only through artistic creation, as it had in the Middle Ages. Speaking on the radio in 1933, he urged his countrymen to bear in mind that "it is the arts, and only they, that can justify the existence of Iceland as a distinct nation—our ancient language and literature of course being the obvious foundation."[7]

EDDAS AND SAGAS

The influence of the medieval tradition on Leifs was most apparent in his choice of texts. Much of the renowned poetry of medieval Iceland is preserved in a handful of manuscripts written in the thirteenth century, although the material is believed to be older. Poems about Óðinn and other Norse gods, and about the major characters in the heroic story of the Völsungs, are transmitted in an anthology known as *Codex Regius* (the *King's Book*), written in about 1270 and traditionally referred to in English as the *Poetic Edda*. Another substantial and slightly older text is the *Prose Edda* (or *Snorra Edda*, as it is known in Icelandic), believed to have been written ca. 1225 by the chieftain Snorri Sturluson. This work combines a treatise on poetry with an account of the myths and legends also contained in the *Poetic Edda*. Both the *Poetic Edda* and the *Prose Edda* have been described as antiquarian efforts, as they testify to an impulse to collect and preserve what was left of the culture of pagan antiquity, through the perspective of thirteenth-century Christian scholarship.[8]

Two types of unrhymed alliterative prosody are prevalent in the Eddas: *fornyrðislag* ("way of ancient words," the measure in which a majority of Eddic poems are composed) and *ljóðaháttur* ("song meter").[9] Fornyrðislag typically consists of eight half lines per stanza, and the two halves of a strophe are usually syntactically independent. Each pair of lines shares alliteration, and each line is a metrically self-contained unit consisting of two stressed syllables and a variable number of unstressed ones:

Hljóðs bið ég allar	Hear me, all ye
helgar kindir	hallowed beings
meiri og **m**inni	both high and low
mögu Heimdallar.	of Heimdall's children:
Viltu, að ég, **V**alföður,	thou wilt, Valfather,
vel fyr telja	that I well set forth
forn spjöll **f**ira,	the fates of the world
þau er **f**remst um man.	which as first I recall.[10]

(*Völuspá*; Leifs op. 20/i)

Ljóðaháttur typically consists of two symmetrical half stanzas of three lines each. The first two lines of each share alliteration, whereas the third alliterates singly.

Deyr fé,	Beasts die,
deyja frændr,	kinsmen die,
deyr **s**jalfr it **s**ama,	you will die yourself.
ek veit **e**inn,	But a well-earned
at **a**ldrei deyr:	reputation
dómr um **d**auðan hvern.	will never perish.[11]

(*Hávamál*; Leifs op. 4 no. 3)

These two principal Eddic meters form the backbone of Leifs's vocal music. He employed them not only in the three *Edda* oratorios but also in two sets of songs with piano (opp. 4 and 18b) and three smaller settings for voice and orchestra (*The Lay of Guðrún, The Lay of Helgi the Hunding-Slayer,* and *Gróa's Spell*).

Yet another ancient meter is *dróttkvætt* ("lordly verse"), also known as *skaldic* poetry (from the Icelandic word *skáld*, or poet). This was courtly verse presented by the Icelandic poets to kings and other members of the nobility, and it is considerably more complex in its expression than Eddic verse. Skaldic poetry frequently departs from conventional prose word order and uses riddle-like metaphors and periphrases to convey its meaning. Each stanza consists of eight lines of six syllables each; besides alliteration, each line contains two internal rhymes (typically, half rhymes in odd lines, full rhymes in even lines):

Hlóðu hugprúðir	Skilled were our soldiers
hrings at brynþingi	who silenced this leader;
varir vegstórir	with swarming weapons
virðar baugnirðir.	they swathed the sovereign;
Fylldusk fjölselldum	feast did the ravens
frammi valgammar	on battlefield fare.
hverr man hringþverris	Who will seek vengeance
hefna auðstefni.	for the vanquished noble?[12]

(*Sturla Þórðarson, 1214–1284*; Leifs op. 31 no. 3)

Leifs did not employ skaldic poetry as frequently as Eddic verse. It appears in only three sets of solo songs with piano: *Three Songs from Icelandic Sagas* op. 24, *Songs of the Saga Symphony* op. 25, and *Old Skaldic Verses from Iceland* op. 31.

The skaldic genre of poetry is most often found in *sagas*—around forty original works that constitute Iceland's greatest contribution to medieval narrative art. These are epic, fictionalized accounts of events that took place during the time of the Vikings, from shortly before the settlement of Iceland in 874 to somewhat after the conversion to Christianity in the year 1000. Written mainly in the thirteenth and fourteenth centuries, they concern characters and events in Iceland, and to some extent the larger Norse world, three hundred years earlier. Known in Icelandic as *Íslendinga sögur* (sagas of Icelanders), they are often referred to in English as "family sagas."

In many ways, the Eddas and sagas provide the key to Leifs's entire artistic enterprise. He shaped his vocal music according to their terse, straightforward style and diction, and in a wider sense the rhythmic gestures of his instrumental music were also influenced by the taut rhythm and crisp accents of the ancient literature. The structure of Eddic verse suggested to Leifs "an almost symphonic preparation ... a presentiment of majestic, musical motives with their bold, rhythmic rise and fall, their intensification and relaxation."[13] The same was true of the sagas; in *Njáls saga* he heard the "expression of musical rhythm in virtually every sentence."[14] He also admired their laconic style and lack of excess: "Not a single word appears here to be superfluous." The sagas' complex plots and intertwining of narratives into a single whole brought to mind "the lines of counterpoint in music, the voice-leading logical yet severe."[15]

Although the Icelandic sagas are not without prominent women characters, they mostly valorize masculinity and heroism—defined by virtues such as honor, fortitude, and athletic ability. They are populated with strong-willed characters who display little external emotion and maintain distance through the terse, often ironic dialogue—which Leifs regarded as a vital aesthetic element, expressing the "laws of heroic souls."[16] The emphasis on hero worship was a common trope of the sagas' reception long before Leifs. In the words of one scholar, it had the value of "emboldening people, not only when chieftains required supporters, but also and more often in the conflicts with the forces of nature that were daily occurrences among the common folk."[17] Yet, whereas for nineteenth-century Icelanders the saga characters were models of bravery and fortitude, natives born in the early twentieth century showed a growing skepticism of or disdain for the heroics of the saga world. The deconstruction of the ancient hero worship became a common theme in twentieth-century Icelandic literature, most memorably expressed in Halldór Laxness's 1952 novel *Gerpla* (see chap. 9). Yet no one doubted the historical importance of saga literature for the spiritual and material autonomy of the Icelandic nation. Even Laxness himself, writing in 1945, in the wake of Iceland's declaration of full independence, remarked that the saga was "our undefeatable fortress, and thanks to its influence we are today an independent nation."[18]

Leifs was virtually the first Icelandic composer to engage with the poetry and subject matter of the ancient literature. Native amateur composers of the early twentieth century showed little interest in actual saga poetry, instead favoring modern retellings. In 1916, the composer Jón Laxdal published two song cycles to paraphrases by a contemporary lyricist, written in modern poetic meters: one is for mezzo-soprano and titled *Helga the Fair* (*Helga in fagra*, after the female heroine of *The Saga of Gunnlaugur Serpent-Tongue*); the other is *Gunnar at Hlíðarendi*, after one of the heroes of *Njáls saga*.[19] These are, by and large, in the typical Icelandic song style of the period: tuneful melodies with simple accompaniment that could be rendered on either harmonium or piano. Also based on a saga theme was *Skarphéðinn in the Flames* (*Skarphéðinn í brennunni*) a short, popular setting for male choir written in the 1890s by (appropriately enough) the Reykjavík fire chief Helgi Helgason, to a Romantic poem depicting the hero that Leifs would later portray in his *Saga Symphony*.

Only one composer, Árni Thorsteinson, had set an original saga poem to music when Leifs began his career. His song with piano accompaniment *Skin-cloaked Ingjaldur* (*Ingjaldur í skinnfeldi*, to a verse from the lesser-known *Saga of Bárður Snæfellsás*) is undated but must have been composed sometime before 1920, as it was released that year on a 78 rpm record and published in score in 1922.[20] Leifs, on the other hand, was the first composer to set verses from the *Poetic Edda* to music, in his *Three Verses from Hávamál* (1924). All in all, Leifs based eight of his works on Eddic poetry, including the three *Edda* oratorios. His settings of saga poetry are somewhat fewer in number: the three skaldic song cycles mentioned above, as well as *Torrek* op. 33a and *Song of Dorrud* (*Darraðarljóð*), but he was also inspired by saga narratives on a far more expansive scale in the *Saga Symphony* of 1941–42.

BEETHOVEN AND THE HEROIC IMPULSE

Leifs's impulse to represent a heroic attitude in his music was derived not only from valiant saga characters but also from Ludwig van Beethoven, the only composer for whom he expressed unqualified affinity and admiration in his adult years. The notion of Beethoven's style as "heroic"—of leading, in a compelling, narrative sweep, through a trajectory of struggle and conflict to glorious consummation—had a long history by the early twentieth century. This is epitomized by the *Eroica* symphony (on which there is more below), not only a work that is said to have changed the course of music history but one that in the nineteenth century also established a symbolic conjunction of work and artist. Beethoven was thus transformed, in the words of Scott Burnham, from "the portrayer of heroes to hero himself."[21] As David B. Dennis has shown, Beethoven's works became ever more firmly associated with German nationalist goals and military values in the late nineteenth century, a trend that continued during World War I and into the Third Reich.[22] Nazi ideologues praised Beethoven's "Nordic depth" and "titanic greatness" and took up the task of cleansing the composer of any "biological blemishes" (due to his Flemish background) to guarantee his eligibility for Nazi hero status.[23]

Leifs was familiar with Beethoven's works from an early age (see chap. 1). In the 1920s he conducted several of his symphonies and overtures, wrote a cadenza to the Piano Concerto no. 3 for Annie, and composed the *Variazioni Pastorali* on a theme from Beethoven's op. 8. The centenary of Beethoven's death in 1927 prompted a translation of the Heiligenstadt testament into Icelandic as well as several articles in German on the composer and his works. One of these, titled "The Nordic Beethoven" and published in the *Rheinisch-Westfälische Zeitung*, is an early illustration of Leifs's ideology of Nordic art and its characteristics, influenced by the *völkisch* pseudoscience of racial anthropology (see chap. 6). Here he argued that prior to Beethoven, music had been mostly a "southern" phenomenon, a kind of a form-play or "superficial entertainment." Beethoven, on the other hand, had "opened up the entire world of human emotion in music," and Leifs maintained that many things in the composer's art were specifically "Nordic." He felt that an artistic continuation of Beethoven's work along these lines still had not been achieved (i.e., the "Nordic Renaissance" that he himself promulgated) but predicted that this would in due course disclose Beethoven's (and, presumably, his own) true greatness.[24]

Leifs's most extensive analysis of Beethoven's music is found in his two articles on the *Eroica* symphony. He found the work to be an outstanding example of Beethoven's "Nordic musical sensibility," not least the well-known hammer blows toward the end of the exposition, where he described the music as being "torn to bits with the heavy blows of the Nordic hero."[25] Leifs later recalled, "I could have jumped from my seat when I heard this passage for the first time."[26] He even compared the varying rhythmic stress of two versus three beats in the first movement of *Eroica* to that of the Icelandic rímur melodies. The funeral march from *Eroica* was also profoundly influential. For Leifs, the pregnant rests inserted into the final statement of the main theme were a symbol of "affliction conquered with pride," and he found the effect reminiscent of pauses in Old Icelandic poetry.[27]

As a conductor, Leifs seems to have been most successful as an interpreter of Beethoven's works. During the Hamburg Philharmonic tour in 1926, the critic-composer Emil Thoroddsen wrote that, in Leifs's hands, Beethoven had become "a Nordic titan, stronger and more magnificent than others make him out to be, and yet at the same time colder and more rigid. This Beethoven has nothing to do with Vienna. He is blood of our blood, a wild, fully bearded Teuton from the depths of a German forest."[28] Leifs's ideal interpretation of Beethoven had much in common with that of his own music. His conducting scores of Beethoven's symphonies contain frequent pencil markings of added *marcato* articulation, *sff* accents, and extreme dynamic contrasts—a "Leifsification" of Beethoven, or, more precisely, the German master's influence coming full circle in exaggerated form.[29]

Leifs's writings reveal that he was well aware of—and even emphasized—the extent to which he had modeled his own artistic persona as well as his music on that of Beethoven: rough, irascible, adversarial, a misunderstood genius whose demanding works were understood fully only after his death. In the preface to his translation of the Heiligenstadt testament, Leifs noted that "long after Beethoven's death it still occurred that members of renowned orchestras mocked his works during rehearsal"—a strangely portentous comment given the reception, later in his own career, of works like the Organ Concerto, the *Saga Symphony*, and *Edda I*.[30] Another telling remark comes from a radio broadcast on Beethoven's music, in which Leifs praised the composer's single-minded commitment to his artistic goal: "A mark of true artists is that they are like vessels made to carry out the command of higher powers, no matter what and against all odds, even though their life and work only brings suffering for their closest relatives, children and wife, even though no one comprehends them or their work."[31] Such notions of the suffering genius are also found in Leifs's letters to family members in which he laments his own plight.

Leifs drew inspiration from Beethoven in other, more subtle ways in his compositions, for example in his fondness for extremes in dynamics and register. This is perhaps most obvious in his choral writing: the stratospheric soprano part in *Hafís*, for example, seems like an attempt to outdo Beethoven's notorious demands in his Ninth Symphony. For Leifs, the aesthetic category of the sublime was best accessed through performers having to overcome extreme technical difficulties in his music.

The most bizarre testament to Leifs's identification with Beethoven is a dream that he chronicled in 1958. Perhaps as a lingering effect of growing up in a spiritualist household, Leifs believed in prophetic dreams. In this particular case, his faith in the dream's meaning led him to publish the recollection in a local periodical devoted to spiritual matters, along with an older dream of his, which he believed had already come true. The gist of Leifs's 1958 dream was that Beethoven was still alive and in Iceland on some kind of official visit, staying at what is known as the "minister's residence" (*Ráðherrabústaðurinn*), a late nineteenth-century building in central Reykjavík that was once the residence of Iceland's minister to Denmark but has for decades been used for official government receptions. Naturally, Leifs paid Beethoven a visit, finding him to be "friendly, calm, and content," but their conversation was brief, as Leifs felt it inconsiderate to disturb the master for too long. His account then continues:

> As I am making my way back through a crowd of inquisitive observers, all of whom wish to pay their respects to him, it is as if I am told by an invisible voice: "He intends to settle in Iceland and will make his home here for the next twenty years." This elates me, but I am also somewhat distressed, fearing that people would be allowed to disturb him. I feel a strong urge to make this known and to ensure that he be left alone. I also surmise: *"For this, Iceland will become a world-renowned country; this has already secured her independence. This must be made known throughout the world as soon as possible."*[32]

This extraordinary narrative is perhaps best explained by the Freudian theory that dreams reveal hidden truths, providing a gateway into the unconscious mind. In this case, the wish fulfillment centers around Beethoven (a displaced Leifs figure), who has been offered an official residence—a sign of the government support that Leifs himself so ardently desired (see chap. 9). Furthermore, Beethoven's sojourn earns Iceland fame and respect throughout the world, thus fulfilling Leifs's ultimate artistic goal. More than thirty years earlier, Leifs wrote that Icelandic culture "must be both national and international in the artistic sense, to such a degree that we may earn the respect of the entire world. This and nothing else can deliver Iceland's independence and secure it for all time."[33] That Leifs would publish his dream, along with another one whose prophecy he believed to have come true, suggests that he hoped for its fulfillment, presumably through his own international renown as well as the Icelandic state's official recognition of his artistic rank. Through his Beethoven fantasy, Leifs could finally—albeit only for a fleeting moment—achieve his life's goal of Iceland playing, through music, a leading role in the world's culture.

LEIFS AND HIS POETS

Aside from his frequent use of anonymous medieval and folk poetry, Leifs set to music texts by seventeen Icelandic poets. These span a wide range both in terms of style and chronology, from the tenth-century warrior Egill Skallagrímsson and the Baroque hymns of Hallgrímur Pétursson to a single setting of the twentieth-century novelist Halldór Laxness. Two poets were particularly close to his heart, and he set their texts more frequently than those of any others: Jónas Hallgrímsson and Einar Benediktsson. Although different in style, both expressed in their poetry a deeply felt nationalist spirit and sentiment for nature—elements that spoke directly to Leifs, influenced his views and inspired him in his settings.

Jónas Hallgrímsson (1807–45) was an early exponent of Romanticism in Iceland, but his career came to a sudden and premature end: he fell down a staircase at his home in Copenhagen and died of blood poisoning, aged 37. He has been described as the most admired poet of modern Iceland, and his status is underscored by the designation of his birthday as the official "Icelandic Language Day."[34] Leifs employed Hallgrímsson's poetry in twelve of his works, enthused about his innate understanding of "the laws of music," and saw in his output a unique manifestation of the Icelandic national character.[35] Other contemporaries were in full agreement. Laxness, in his 1929 volume of essays *The Book of the People* (*Alþýðubókin*), extolled him as "our most Icelandic poet" and his entire work as "an uninterrupted song about Icelandic destiny."[36]

In his promotion of artistic nationalism, Hallgrímsson focused on what has since been termed the "Icelandic trinity" of history, literature, and nature. Many of his poems have an archaizing quality, harking back to the metrics and syntax of the Eddas while promoting the agenda of nineteenth-century nationalism. Inspired by Iceland's history and surging nationalist sentiment, Hallgrímsson saw a "pure" Icelandic style as the ideal vehicle for reviving the medieval "golden age."[37] He was on the editorial team of the journal *Fjölnir*, an influential mouthpiece for nationalism in Iceland, published annually from 1835 to 1847.[38] Its editors drew their readers' attention to the poor state of affairs in Icelandic society and were eager for their countrymen to cast away apathy and superstition. They proposed three objectives intended to encourage progress and kindle patriotism among the populace: the reestablishment of the Alþingi at Þingvellir (see chap. 5) as a national assembly, a more thorough knowledge of the old sagas and the language that they preserved, and a careful examination of Icelandic nature.[39] They extolled the landscape for its clear streams, green valleys, and clear sky and regarded the sagas as means to inspire the patriotism and achieving spirit that their countrymen, in their opinion, lacked: "Whoever reads the Icelandic sagas carefully, in him must be lit the most burning love of his country, or he does not understand them as he should."[40] Each of these objectives was in harmony with Leifs's own ideals; he was, at heart, a national Romantic fashioned after the *Fjölnir* model.

Fjölnir's inaugural volume contained Hallgrímsson's own paean to Iceland and exhortation to his countrymen, *Ísland, farsælda frón (Iceland, Fortunate Isle)*, which became a symbol for nineteenth-century patriotism and was commonly sung in tvísöngur (see example 2.2). Thus, it was the perfect vehicle for Leifs, who employed the melody more frequently in his works than any other vernacular tune. *Ísland, farsælda frón* consists of fourteen elegiac distichs and has been described as a manifesto for Iceland's cultural and economic revival "based on a greater measure of political independence and restoration of the Alþingi at Þingvellir."[41] It begins as a lament, for the country has lost its power and prestige of old:

> Ísland! farsælda frón og hagsælda hrímhvíta móðir!
> Hvar er þín fornaldar frægð, frelsið og manndáðin best?

> Iceland, fortunate isle! Our beautiful, bountiful mother!
> Where are your fortune and fame, freedom and happiness now?

Although old Alþingi is gone, there is still hope for a nation willing to shake off its shackles of sloth, lethargy, and prejudice. The basis for Iceland's rejuvenation, in Hallgrímsson's poem as in Leifs's music, is its nature, which still retains its beauty:

> Landið er fagurt og frítt, og fannhvítir jöklanna tindar,
> himinninn heiður og blár, hafið er skínandi bjart.

Comely still is our country crested with snow-whited glaciers,
azure and empty the sky, ocean resplendently bright.[42]

Hallgrímsson was a natural scientist as well as a poet and wrote extensively on Icelandic nature. Scholars have pointed to the influence of the scientific outlook on his poetic works, among the recurring themes of which are nature and man's interaction with it.[43] Earlier poets had rarely treated subjects such as volcanic eruptions, and Hallgrímsson was among the first to depict the violent, destructive side of Icelandic nature and its landscape.[44] This darker side of his output fascinated Leifs, who found the ideal vehicle for his own aesthetic of the "Icelandic sublime" in the volcanic poem *Víti* (set in the choral songs op. 28 as well as partly in *Hekla*). But Hallgrímsson's output is far more varied than Leifs's use of it suggests. He has been described as "the poet of vegetation, summer, and sunshine," and in his poems the land is gentle and fertile, a place where "herds of cattle graze, lakes are full of fish, and pink fields abound."[45] Only one work by Leifs is inspired by this carefree and playful side of Hallgrímsson's oeuvre, the *Spring Song* from 1958.

Einar Benediktsson (1864–1940) was a much younger poet—roughly the same generation as Leifs's father—and a devoted supporter of Leifs and his folk-inspired style (see chap. 3). His works are epic in both style and subject matter, which includes ancient heroes as well as nature. Again, Benediktsson's enthusiasm for the Icelandic language, history, and landscape was ideally suited to Leifs. Benediktsson had little regard for modernism, and his poems are essentially late Romantic. His style has been described as inflated and heavy-handed; he was fond of long poetic lines that lend his work a certain gravitas. Few composers have set Benediktsson's texts to music, and none with such determination as Leifs, who drew on his depictions of a waterfall and ice drift in *Dettifoss* and *Hafís* and also employed other lyrics in six smaller works.

Benediktsson became a "national poet" in the early decades of the twentieth century, not least because of three very successful volumes published between 1906 and 1921. He was a distinctive, forceful personality who encouraged his countrymen to step boldly into the new century and was actively involved in a brand of nationalist politics that envisaged the economic and industrial development of an independent Iceland.[46] Benediktsson was also admired for his business acumen; he dreamed of hydroelectric plants that could harness Iceland's waterfalls and make the country competitive with nations rich in coal.[47] He lived abroad in considerable style until 1932, when he retired, exhausted and penniless, at a remote property on the southwestern coast of Iceland. By that time he had fallen out of favor with his countrymen, as became painfully apparent at the 1930 Alþingi festival (see chap. 5). There, his prize-winning poem was not recited as the jury had suggested, nor was he invited to the government's official reception. On the opening day he was seen roaming the festival grounds alone.[48]

Benediktsson was the leading poet of Icelandic nationalism in the early twentieth century, and his poetry often seems larger than life. Like Leifs, he was a visionary, often far ahead of his own time. His dreams of progress were intertwined with what one scholar has called his "sincere but unfounded belief in the spiritual leadership role of Icelanders in matters concerning the world."[49] It was precisely this questionable notion of Iceland's superiority that Leifs adopted from Benediktsson and other nationalist writers of his generation.

NATURE AND LANDSCAPE

The Icelandic landscape was a constant source of inspiration for Leifs. His musical commemoration of specific locations is most obvious in his tone poems, the "place pieces" that celebrate key sites and phenomena: *Geysir* (geyser), *Hekla* (volcano), *Dettifoss* (waterfall), and *Hafís* (drift ice).[50] Yet much of Leifs's other music also suggests specific nature scenes: the open sea and vision of land in *Landfall*; Þingvellir in the *Iceland Cantata*; the atmospheric depictions of sky, sun, sea, and wind in *Edda I*; sky and cliffs in *Trois peintures abstraites*; the lulling sea and a peaceful summer night in the *Requiem*. Also, in a more general sense, the slowly unfolding open-fifth sonorities of Leifs's music project a vision of wide expanse that corresponds to the lava fields and tundra of the Icelandic landscape. Leifs himself actively sought to associate his music with nature, seeing in the country's glaciers, waterfalls, and volcanoes not only a valuable *natural* resource but a *cultural* one. When given sound through music or other artistic expression, it could sustain claims for Iceland's nationhood.

As Icelanders fashioned their own cultural self-image in the early decades of the twentieth century, nature claimed a prominent part in the discourse. Until the country's Act of Union with Denmark in 1918, the main justification for its independence had been its language and literature.[51] But already in 1919, speaking at the opening of the first public arts exhibit in Reykjavík, university professor Guðmundur Finnbogason encouraged artists to become more mindful of Iceland's natural beauty, to bring "this treasure into the nation's permanent ownership, capturing its peculiarity and beauty on canvas or shaping it into metal and stone."[52] By drawing on the landscape's exotic features as well as its beauty, he argued, artists could bring about a "new and higher co-existence of landscape and nation." Landscape painting in a Romantic-Expressionist vein was a favorite motif of Icelandic painters, but even more influential in developing an Icelandic self-image in the visual arts was the eclectic and personal style of Jóhannes Kjarval. His favorite motifs were moss, mountains, and lava formations (see fig. 4.1.), though his unpredictable art also often includes fantastical creatures and elements from Icelandic folktales. By portraying the rugged beauty of the Icelandic landscape, Kjarval (who was fourteen years Leifs's senior) embodied the national style of a newly independent Iceland. In the words of a leading Icelandic politician of the time, native art should "correspond with the character and beauty of the country" rather than attempting to imitate artists in more southerly climes.[53] Leifs's music was received in similar terms from early on. In 1932, a local critic remarked that his *Hymns* op. 12a had "both power and severity, which reminds one of the basalt columns in an Icelandic mountain. To judge these songs by the aesthetic standards of

Figure 4.1. Jóhannes S. Kjarval, 1957, *Frá Þingvöllum* (From Þingvellir). © Jóhannes S. Kjarval / Myndstef 2018.

'classical' music is as absurd as to judge the Icelandic wilderness by the standards of French formal gardens."[54]

The reference to basalt columns is not incidental. The sturdy columns are found throughout Iceland and are formed by the slow cooling of lava, creating systematic vertical fractures, typically hexagonal in shape. The rugged vertical form of basalt columns provided a potent national symbol in the art of Leifs's contemporaries, including Guðjón Samúelsson, Iceland's leading architect in the early twentieth century. Many of his most famous works show its influence, such as the ceiling of the National Theater (drawn ca. 1930) and the tower and side wings of Hallgrímskirkja, Reykjavík's main church and a major landmark (ca. 1937, see fig. 4.2). In creating a "national school" of architecture, Samúelsson also drew on other distinctly Icelandic elements: his design of the boarding school at Laugarvatn (1928) employs the triangular roof shapes of Icelandic sod farms, and the National Theater's exterior was inspired

Figure 4.2. The façade of Guðjón Samúelsson's Hallgrímskirkja, Reykjavík. Shutterstock.

by Icelandic folktales of "elves' palaces."[55] It is no coincidence that the creation of such nationalist, folk- and nature-inspired art, encouraged by public intellectuals and politicians alike, should have occurred at the time Leifs was himself developing his musical language.

Leifs rarely discussed his music in technical terms. More often, his descriptions evoke the landscape in a broad sense: he considered the parallel fifths of tvísöngur to be "a unique attempt by the nation to capture in tones the colorful and awe-inspiring Icelandic nature" while rímur melodies were "brazen and strong like the basalt columns of Icelandic mountains."[56] The influence of nature may be heard in the predominantly vertical quality of his music: it moves from one "harmonic pillar" to another. This has various parallels in the Icelandic landscape, not only basalt columns but also the vertically gushing water and fire that is the subject of *Geysir*, *Hekla*, and *Dettifoss*.

Other elements of Leifs's style are also relevant to the expression of nature through music. Like other composers before and since, he inherited the idea that music could represent nature through a repertoire of specific musical devices, understood by musicians and audiences alike.[57] Although they should not be reduced to simply a mimetic relationship, a mere depiction of nature, Leifs frequently employed conventional musical signs. For example, he creates a sense of space and distance through slow-moving sonorities built on perfect fourths and fifths, which imbues his music with a kind of timelessness. The open-fifth pedal, suggesting the immutability of nature, has been described by Julian Johnson as "one of the most deeply rooted and ubiquitous symbols of the pastoral in Western music."[58] The gradual opening out of the total registral space, found at the opening of many of Leifs's orchestral works and particularly those referencing nature, suggests a metaphor of spatial expansion: low to high, dark to light.[59] Furthermore, Leifs's use of actual "natural" material, such as large and small rocks in his orchestral works, can be viewed as an attempt to evoke something that lies at the fringes of musical tone, a kind of primal sound of nature. For Leifs, landscape is not only concerned with pictorial evocation but is a defining element of his "ideology or culture of sound."[60]

In Leifs's aesthetic, nature and landscape were inextricably linked to Iceland's ancient history. He claimed that the "landscape background" was a crucial element of Old Icelandic literature, one that had to be understood in order to fully appreciate the sagas and Eddic poetry. He found the saga characters to be shaped by their relationship to the physical landscape in its "bareness and severity, openness and spaciousness, in the solid shapes of the mountains and glaciers, in the storms that suddenly break into hurricanes, in the intimate colors of the summer dusk, the uncanny chill of the winter nights with northern lights that suddenly appear, the astonishing natural forces of fire and ice, calm and storm,—and often radiant sky."[61] He also found the opposite to be true: the landscape was made great not only by its ruggedness or its magnificent contrasts but because it was once inhabited by the great heroes of the sagas. The intertwining of music, landscape, and literature was a constant feature of Leifs's aesthetic and defines virtually his entire output, from the *Three Verses from Hávamál* in 1924 to the *Edda* oratorio that remained unfinished at his death in 1968.

Leifs also drew inspiration from nature in that he preferred to work in isolation surrounded by an idyllic landscape. In Iceland, his ideal spot for composing was Þingvellir, with its picturesque views of surrounding mountains and a lake, and far enough away from habitation to prevent any unwanted disturbance. In the late 1930s, he was drawn to idyllic or adventurous vistas both at home and on the continent. In summer 1938 the family holidayed in Štrbské Pleso in the Slovakian Tatra mountains, where he worked on the *Edda* oratorio; the following summer they took a rare journey into the Icelandic wilderness, and they celebrated Christmas 1939 in the Alpine village of Turracher Höhe. Summer 1940 was spent in Frýdlant at the foot of the Moravian-Silesian Beskids mountain range, but the following year the family returned to the Austrian Alps (Bad Gastein). Although Leifs enjoyed modest hikes, he was not an avid mountaineer like Webern; he seems to have been drawn to the abovementioned sites largely for the fresh air and picturesque mountain views. The ocean also fascinated Leifs, and he enjoyed taking sea baths when possible—for example, while living in Norderney (North Sea) and Travemünde (Baltic Sea). When the family took a holiday on the Danish isle of Møn in summer 1933, they all swam in the sea each day.[62]

STYLE AND COMPOSITIONAL METHOD

The division of a composer's career into three distinct periods is a commonplace of music historiography and often challenged, but this model is nevertheless apt in the case of Leifs. His early years as a composer (1919–30) were a time of searching for his own voice and style. He took a new approach in virtually every work: the terse and atonal *Three Verses from Hávamál* are far removed from the contrapuntal rigor of the choral *Kyrie*, the folkloric primitivism of the *Iceland Overture*, or the dense, dissonant web of the Organ Concerto. Nevertheless, these works share a common attempt to bring a new Icelandic element into an up-to-date musical language—what Guy Rickards has described, with reference to the *Galdra-Loftr* incidental music, as a "broadly Central European manner incorporating Icelandic colouristic elements."[63] In some cases, the influence of specific composers can be heard, including Bach (*Prelude and Fughetta* op. 3 and Organ Concerto), Beethoven (*Variazioni Pastorali*), and Reger (Organ Concerto).

Leifs's second period ranges from ca. 1930–52 and is largely taken up by four large compositional projects: *Edda I*, the *Saga Symphony*, *Baldr*, and the four "Requiem works" written in 1947–52. Here the three main elements of his music have already been established: parallel fifths and irregular meter (see chap. 2) as well as root-position chords, generally major triads. In Leifs's final period, which can be said to span roughly the last sixteen years of his life (1952–68), these basic elements are sometimes used with less variety than before. Yet in his more inspired works of this period—such as *Edda III* and the tetralogy of place-inspired pieces—Leifs found ways to expand his vocabulary in terms of harmony and overall approach. Some of his late works were, for him, singular experimental ventures: for example, his exploration of the pastoral mode (*Night*) and quasi serialism (*Scherzo concreto*).

Overall, Leifs's harmonic palette is quite traditional, consisting largely of consonant triads, but he achieved his unorthodox sound by consciously avoiding the cadential resources of classical tonality, such as fifth-related roots; instead his chords progress predominantly by tritones, thirds, or seconds. An analysis of works from different periods of his career suggests a predilection for tritone relations. Somewhat less prevalent are progressions up or down major thirds or minor seconds while progressions of minor thirds and major seconds are less frequent still.[64]

As unique as Leifs's triadic universe may seem, it nevertheless has clear historical antecedents. Mediant chord progressions—whereby one root-position chord proceeds to another a third above or below—were particularly common in nineteenth-century music and were described by theorist Hugo Riemann as "admittedly audacious but effective and euphonious."[65] Such relationships often served a special function and are of particular importance for the present study. As Julian Johnson has noted, they were "one of the means by which nature was depicted musically as the site of transcendence."[66] In his detailed study of the phenomenon, Richard Cohn notes that progressions such as these confounded expectations regarding triadic behavior and were often explicitly affiliated with altered or heightened realities: Wagner's magic sleep, Rimsky-Korsakov's magic and exotic kingdoms, Liszt's mountaintop meditations.[67] Other scholars have associated the device of mediant progressions with "increasing brightness," and Leifs's employment of euphonious triads related by thirds or tritones seems to take this idea to its extreme, lending his music a shimmering radiance that one might possibly relate to the illumination found at far northern latitudes.[68] His use of such progressions is more radical than that of earlier composers, who generally used it only as a fleeting, coloristic device. Still, their prevalence demonstrates yet again his reliance on a vocabulary of gestures derived from nineteenth-century music, where the device was used—as it also is in his works—to evoke the strange, exotic, and sublime.

While root-position triads are among the most prevalent features of Leifs's style, he employs other elements to stave off monotony. For example, he occasionally creates more extensive quintal harmonies than the simple fifths of the Icelandic tvísöngur. In the opening measures of *Song of Dorrud*, he layers two or three fifths on the root of the chord, creating an ominous, aggressive quality that suits the text (see example 4.1).

Leifs employs minor triads far less often than major, and these have a tendency to "resolve" to a major triad built on the same root. An oscillation between major and minor forms of the same triad is a feature of many of his works, particularly those expressing innocence tinged with regret, such as the *Lullaby* and the *Requiem*.

Example 4.1. Leifs, *Song of Dorrud* op. 60, choral part, mm. 3–7. © Iceland Music Information Center.

Passages consisting of unrelenting minor chords are rare and always serve an expressive purpose, such as in *Mors et vita*, *Night* from *Edda I*, *Torrek* op. 33a, and *Dance of Sorrow* from the *Elegies* op. 35. Half-diminished and fully diminished harmonies occur even less frequently and are generally reserved for depicting catastrophic events, such as in *Baldr* and *Hekla* (volcanic eruptions) and *Edda III* (the end of the world). As a whole, the harmonic framework of Leifs's mature compositions offers a peculiarly compelling exploration of degrees of luminosity created by relatively simple means.

As noted above, Leifs did not comment extensively on his own compositional method. The only such document is an unpublished report titled "How do I compose" (*Hvernig sem ég tónsmíðar*), written in Norway in 1960:

> At first I conceive a kind of scheme for the work that I wish to compose, not so much a tonal or harmonic scheme, but rather a scheme of the spiritual state and psychological tension,—the release or relief that the work should reveal. Chords, notes, and rhythms are certainly included in this scheme, but they are not essential, and these notes and chords have to be thoroughly sifted and revised if they are to strengthen and ripen to the supreme degree that they can serve the work's aesthetic aim—the content, as it may perhaps be called....
>
> My first and ultimate goal when composing is to be true and to be myself, —not to allow into my music the foreign influence of others, no affectation, no emergency solutions of skillfulness and style.... It is even better and guarantees better aesthetic results to learn less and know less than to be untrue.[69]

Here Leifs describes a key element of his approach: the conscious negation of facility and fluency in favor of a less "learned," more "primitive" sound. In a sense, he managed in this regard to turn his own lack of formal compositional training into a virtue in itself. He fashioned himself as a composer not influenced by works of his colleagues or predecessors, offering unreserved praise for Beethoven only. Late in his life he also expressed admiration for Palestrina and Handel, whose "majestic" music reminded him of the Icelandic landscape. (The fact that these composers also exerted an influence on Beethoven in his later years is probably not coincidental.) He found Mozart's Requiem magnificent but insisted that much of that composer's output was overestimated.[70] Such declarations, often made in newspaper or radio interviews, must be taken with a grain of salt. Leifs was thoroughly familiar with a considerable repertoire: he had conducted works by virtually all the major classic-Romantic composers and frequently attended international festivals, such as ISCM and the biannual Nordic Music Days, as well as (for example) the Edinburgh festival in 1953. Still, he may have found that his ideology, with its emphasis on cultivating a unique and primitive Nordic sound, as well as what he saw as the northern characteristic of not succumbing easily to the influence of others, necessitated a repudiation—at least officially—of large swaths of the traditional repertoire.

Leifs's sketches elucidate his compositional method. He would frequently draft a melodic outline along with letters suggesting the underlying chords, such as (in a sketch for *Landfall*): C F♯ B D (see fig. 4.3.). He often specified pitches that were to be added to the basic triad, such as: A♭ $^{9-6}$ F♯ $^{7-6}$ D; sometimes he also sketched harmonic progressions on blank paper without any notation, in which case the added numbers may suggest the melodic direction of a phrase. When it came to fleshing out his harmonic sketches, Leifs wrote directly into the full score, starting at the top staff and working his way down, one vertical harmony at a time. Often, he drafted the outline of a movement in terms of main events and dynamic shape and notated specific rhythmic gestures without indicating pitch. For some of his programmatic works, he would

Figure 4.3. Leifs's sketch for mm. 251–54 of *Landfall* op. 41. The melodic material consists largely of piccolo and bassoon (marked *Blech*) while the capital letters indicate a harmonic outline. © Leifs Archives, National and University Library, Reykjavík.

sketch a verbal outline of main events with corresponding musical depiction (see fig. 4.4.).

Much of the drama inherent in Leifs's orchestral music is generated by a specific type of rhythmic *accelerando*. He often builds momentum by establishing a steady quarter-note motion that

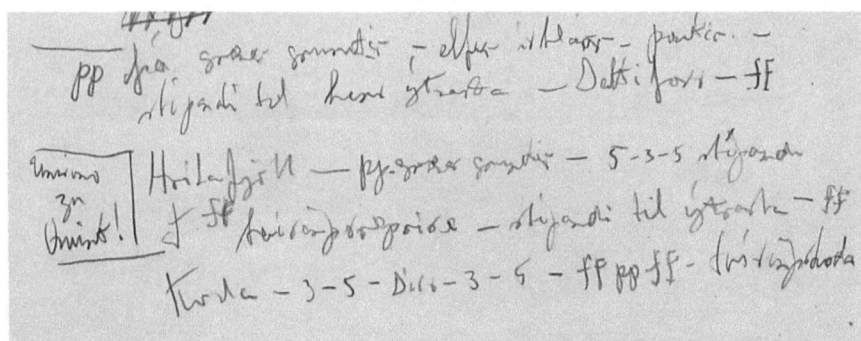

Figure 4.4. Verbal sketch (partial) for *Landfall* op. 41. The outline includes the words "Green meadows—Ice-blue rivers—Extreme upsurge—Dettifoss—Terrifying mountains—rising to *ff* tvísöngur reprise." © Leifs Archives, National and University Library, Reykjavík.

eventually yields to eighth notes, then sixteenths, and so on, followed by a gradual slowing down. This rhythmic strategy is found in the battle movements of the *Saga Symphony*, in roughly half the movements of *Baldr*, and in each of his single-movement "place pieces"—to name but a few. John Pickard has noted that Leifs's approach to harmony has quite a different effect when the rate of harmonic change is significantly accelerated, as it is at the culminating moments of these works. At slow speed the music has an unearthly calm, devoid as it is of the usual tensions of functional tonal harmony. With a faster rate of change (and often with added percussion), the effect seems highly dissonant.[71]

The gradual increase in volume and rhythmic activity that Leifs frequently employed is also reminiscent of other twentieth-century works, particularly Arthur Honegger's *Pacific 231*, which famously depicts a steam locomotive. It seems not coincidental that Honegger was one of the few contemporary composers for whom Leifs publicly expressed admiration. They had become acquainted in 1952 at a meeting in Amsterdam of CISAC (*Confédération Internationale des Sociétes d'Auteurs et Compositeurs*), an organization over which Honegger presided, and Leifs also attended a production of his oratorio *Jeanne d'Arc au bûcher* in Copenhagen in the mid-'50s.

On his death in 1955, Leifs penned two memorial tributes—one for the newspaper *Morgunblaðið*, the other for the art journal *Birtingur*—proclaiming him "the greatest of all contemporary composers, both as person and artist" and particularly admiring how he had "channeled the powers of nature."[72] Although Leifs did not specifically mention *Pacific 231* in his writings, the resemblance of its overall progression to that of *Geysir, Hekla,* and *Dettifoss* is striking.

This in turn draws attention to a remarkable feature of Leifs's output: in depicting medieval battles and violent natural phenomena, he employed sounds and structures that, for other composers, evoked the modern age of the machine. Subject matter aside, echoes of loud and percussion-heavy "city" or "factory" music from the 1920s—such as Edgard Varèse's *Amériques* or Alexander Mosolov's *Iron Foundry*—can be heard in the harsh and rhythmically stringent *Saga Symphony* and *Hekla*. Thus, Leifs's output can be viewed from three different perspectives. He shared certain modernist elements with composers of city and machine scores; he was a nationalist/primitivist in his use of vernacular music and affection for the Icelandic "golden age" of the sagas; and he was a programmatic "nature composer" influenced by Romanticism, determined to supply Iceland with its own *Moldau* or *Alpensinfonie*. It is precisely the interaction and tension between these competing musical discourses—the modernist, nationalist, primitivist, and programmatic—that make Leifs such a complex and challenging historical figure.[73]

NOTES

1. Jóhann Páll Árnason, "Icelandic Anomalies," in *Nordic Paths to Modernity*, ed. Jóhann Páll Árnason and Björn Wittrock (New York: Berghahn, 2012), 239.

2. Gunnar Karlsson, *The History of Iceland* (Minneapolis: University of Minnesota Press, 2000), 365, quoted in Jóhann Páll Árnason, "Icelandic Anomalies," in *Nordic Paths to Modernity*, 240.

3. Guðmundur Hálfdanarson, "Hugmyndir Herders um þjóðina og endalok menningarlegrar þjóðar," http://www.visindavefur.is/article.php?id=38.

4. For a detailed account of the restitution of the Icelandic manuscripts, see Jeanette Greenfield, *The Return of Cultural Treasures*, 3rd ed. (Cambridge: Cambridge University Press, 2007), 13–40.

5. Leifs, *Islands künstlerische Anregung*, 76.

6. Leifs, *Islands künstlerische Anregung*, 68.

7. Leifs, "Kveðja," *Iðunn* 17 (1933): 103, quoted in Guðmundur Hálfdanarson and Ólafur Rastrick, "Culture and the Construction of the Icelander in the 20th Century," in *Power and Culture: Hegemony, Interaction and Dissent*, ed. Jonathan Osmond and Ausa Cimdina (Pisa: Plus, Pisa University Press, 2006), 109.

8. Robert Kellogg, "Introduction," in *The Complete Sagas of Icelanders*, vol. 1, ed. Viðar Hreinsson (Reykjavík: Leifur Eiríksson Publishing, 1997), xxxii–xxxiii. The contents of this paragraph are largely derived from Kellogg's excellent introduction, which is recommended for anyone wishing to read further on the subject.

9. For a more thorough examination of Eddic verse and meter, see *The Poetic Edda*, 2nd edition, trans. Lee M. Hollander (Austin: University of Texas Press, 1962), ix–xxix; see also Dick Ringler, *Bard of Iceland: Jónas Hallgrímsson, Poet and Scientist* (Madison: University of Wisconsin Press, 2002), 363–70.

10. *The Poetic Edda*, 2.

11. Ruth L. Magnússon, translation for *Jón Leifs: Söngvar/Complete Songs*, Finnur Bjarnason and Örn Magnússon, Smekkleysa SMK 20, 2001, compact disc.

12. Keneva Kunz, translation for *Jón Leifs: Söngvar/Complete Songs*.

13. Leifs, *Islands künstlerische Anregung*, 32.

14. Leifs, *Islands künstlerische Anregung*, 16, 33.

15. Leifs, *Islands künstlerische Anregung*, 15.

16. Leifs, *Islands künstlerische Anregung*, 14.

17. Vésteinn Ólason, quoted in Jón Karl Helgason, *Hetjan og höfundurinn: Brot úr íslenskri menningarsögu* (Reykjavík: Heimskringla, 1998), 25.

18. Halldór Kiljan Laxness, "Minnisgreinar um fornsögur," *Tímarit Máls og menningar* 8 (1945): 55.

19. Jón Laxdal, *Sönglög I* (Reykjavík: Prentsmiðjan Gutenberg, 1916).

20. Pétur A. Jónsson (Copenhagen: Concert Record "Gramophone," 1920), X 920. Árni Thorsteinson, *Einsöngslög* (Reykjavík: Þorsteinn Gíslason, 1922/1923). Around the same time, Sveinbjörn Sveinbjörnsson arranged one

of the very few Icelandic folk melodies to a saga text, *Stóðum tvö í túni*, in his *Íslenzk þjóðlög* (Edinburgh: R. W. Pentland, 1923).

21. Scott Burnham, *Beethoven Hero* (Princeton: Princeton University Press, 1995), xv–xvi.

22. David B. Dennis, *Beethoven in German Politics, 1870–1989* (New Haven: Yale University Press, 1996), 67.

23. Hans Joachim Moser and Walther Rauschenberger, quoted in Dennis, *Beethoven in German Politics, 1870–1989*, 146, 149.

24. Leifs, "Der nordische Beethoven," *Rheinisch-Westfälische Zeitung*, March 13, 1927; see also Leifs, "Erfðaskrá Beethovens," *Eimreiðin* 33 (1927): 264–67.

25. Leifs, manuscript to a radio broadcast of Beethoven's music, broadcast July 29, 1934.

26. Leifs, *Islands künstlerische Anregung*, 59.

27. Leifs, *Islands künstlerische Anregung*, 59, 64.

28. Emil Thoroddsen, "Fyrstu hljómleikar Hamburger philharmonischen Orkesters," *Vörður*, June 5, 1926.

29. Leifs's conducting scores are in the collection of the Reykjavík College of Music (Menntaskóli í tónlist).

30. Leifs, "Erfðaskrá Beethovens," 265.

31. Leifs, manuscript to a radio broadcast of Beethoven's music, broadcast July 29, 1934.

32. Leifs, "Tveir draumar," *Morgunn: Tímarit um andleg mál* 40 (1959): 45–47. See also Árni Heimir Ingólfsson, "Beethoven í Tjarnargötunni: Um Jón Leifs og áhrif meistarans," *Ritmennt* 4 (1999): 94–98.

33. Leifs, "Trygging íslensks sjálfstæðis," *Vörður*, December 10, 1927, 2–4.

34. Ringler, *Bard of Iceland*, 3.

35. Leifs, "Verðlaun? Opið bréf til útvarpsins frá Jóni Leifs," *Morgunblaðið*, September 13, 1958.

36. Peter Hallberg, *Halldór Laxness*, trans. Rory McTurk (New York: Twayne, 1971), 61.

37. Sveinn Yngvi Egilsson, *Náttúra ljóðsins. Umhverfi íslenskra skálda* (Reykjavík: Háskólaútáfan, 2014), 57.

38. See Þórir Óskarsson, "From Romanticism to Realism," in *A History of Icelandic Literature*, ed. Daisy Neijmann (Lincoln: University of Nebraska Press, 2006), 252; *Fjölnir* was not published in 1840–42.

39. Óskarsson, "From Romanticism to Realism," 266.

40. *Fjölnir, árs-rit handa Íslendingum* 1 (1835): 2–3.

41. For a discussion and translation, see Ringler, *Bard of Iceland*, 102.

42. Ringler, *Bard of Iceland*, 101.

43. Egilsson, *Náttúra ljóðsins*, 42
44. Egilsson, *Náttúra ljóðsins*, 22.
45. Óskarsson, "From Romanticism to Realism," 271.
46. Heimir Pálsson, "Einar Benediktsson," in Stevens, *Icelandic Writers*, 32.
47. Elísson, "From Realism to Neoromanticism," 336.
48. Silja Aðalsteinsdóttir, *Íslensk bókmenntasaga*, vol. 3 (Reykjavík: Mál og menning, 1996), 906.
49. Elísson, "From Realism to Neoromanticism," 337–38.
50. The term "place piece" is borrowed from Denise Von Glahn; see, for example, *The Sounds of Place: Music and the American Cultural Landscape* (Boston: Northeastern University Press, 2003), 2.
51. Æsa Sigurjónsdóttir, in *Íslensk listasaga frá síðari hluta 19. aldar til upphafs 21. aldar*, vol. 2 (Reykjavík: Forlagið/Listasafn Íslands, 2011), 54.
52. Guðmundur Finnbogason, quoted in Ólafur Rastrick, *Háborgin: Menning, fagurfræði og pólitík í upphafi tuttugustu aldar* (Reykjavík: Háskólaútgáfan, 2011), 164.
53. Jónas Jónsson, quoted in Rastrick, *Háborgin*, 209.
54. Áskell Snorrason, "Eggert Stefánsson," *Dagur*, June 9, 1932.
55. Pétur H. Ármannsson, "Húsameistarinn frá Hunkubökkum," *Dynskógar* 11 (2008): 13–16.
56. Leifs, "Íslenskt tónlistareðli," *Skírnir* 96 (1922): 139; Leifs, *Islands künstlerische Anregung*, 25.
57. My discussion here is much indebted to Julian Johnson's magisterial analysis in *Webern and the Transformation of Nature* (Cambridge: Cambridge University Press, 1999), 38–78 and passim.
58. Johnson, *Webern*, 52.
59. Johnson, *Webern*, 65.
60. W. Dean Sutcliffe, quoted in Grimley, *Grieg*, 8.
61. Leifs, *Islands künstlerische Anregung*, 37–38.
62. Leifs to Þórey Þorleifsdóttir, July 15, 1933.
63. Guy Rickards, "Icelandic Orchestral Music," *Tempo*, New Series, no. 189 (June 1994): 55.
64. An analysis of Leifs's harmonic practice is Finnur Karlsson, "Greining á köflum V og VI í *Eddu II* eftir Jón Leifs," BM thesis, Iceland Academy of the Arts, 2011.
65. Hugo Riemann, "Tonalität," *Musik-Lexicon*, 1909, cited in Richard Cohn, *Audacious Euphony: Chromaticism and the Triad's Second Nature* (New York: Oxford University Press, 2012), ix.
66. Johnson, *Webern*, 54–55.
67. Cohn, *Audacious Euphony*, x.
68. Johnson, *Webern*, 55.

69. Leifs, "Hvernig sem ég tónsmíðar," quoted in Hjálmar H. Ragnarsson, "Jón Leifs, Icelandic Composer: Historical Background, Biography, Analysis of Selected Works" (MFA thesis, Cornell University, 1980), 203, 206.

70. Leifs, in an interview with Þorkell Sigurbjörnsson, "Tónskáld mánaðarins," February 1968, DB-567-1; Matthías Johannessen, "Lögmálin í hrúgunni. Spjallað við Jón Leifs," *Morgunblaðið*, May 5, 1959. For Leifs's comments on Mozart, see Leifur Þórarinsson, "Stefnum hærra, miklu hærra," *Vísir*, April 30, 1964.

71. John Pickard, "Jón Leifs (1899–1968)," *Tempo*, New Series, no. 208 (April 1999): 12.

72. Leifs, "Arthur Honegger—minning," *Morgunblaðið*, December 28, 1955; Leifs, "Arthur Honegger. Tónskáld náttúruaflanna," *Birtingur* 2 (1956): 10–11.

73. Cf. Daniel M. Grimley's analysis of Grieg's music in his *Grieg*, ix.

FIVE

ICELANDIC NATION-BUILDING AND THE 1930 ALÞINGI FESTIVAL (1929–33)

WHILE ICELAND'S LITERARY HERITAGE WAS central to its nationalist cause, other art forms were initially considered less relevant. Only after the turn of the twentieth century did politicians and public intellectuals recognize the role of music and visual arts in reinforcing the national and cultural identity of Icelanders. The establishment of a Cultural Council (*Menningarráð*) and Culture Fund (*Menningarsjóður*) in 1928 and the National Radio in 1930 are examples of increasing government interest in the arts during this period. Yet no specific event proved as significant in the cultural shaping of the country as the Alþingi festival (*Alþingishátíðin*), held at Þingvellir in summer 1930 to celebrate the one-thousand-year anniversary of the Icelandic parliament. This national festival was seen as symbolically marking Iceland's entry into the modern world, providing a platform for the nation to display its cultural uniqueness within the Danish realm but also to assert its modernity and legitimacy as a potential independent nation-state.[1] Although 1930 was a watershed year for culture building in Iceland, Leifs largely followed these events as an outsider, much to his chagrin. Nonetheless, it also proved to be a crucial year for him, with the completion of two large-scale works that announced his arrival as a mature, unique composer: the *Iceland Cantata* and the Organ Concerto.

LEIFS'S ICELAND CANTATA AND THE ALÞINGI FESTIVAL

National festivals have a special role in nation building. They are intended to cultivate a sense of solidarity, a common heritage and values. The first such festival in Iceland was the settlement festival of 1874, celebrating the millennium of the earliest Norwegian settlement; this was followed by the Alþingi festival in 1930. Several national festivals have been held since—the last in the year 2000 to celebrate a millennium of Christianity—and all have taken place at Þingvellir, the Assembly Plains where Alþingi convened for almost nine centuries, located in lava fields about a day's horse ride (thirty miles) to the northeast from Reykjavík. Þingvellir, the site of the rift valley that marks the crest of the mid-Atlantic ridge, is a place of exceptional natural beauty. The continental drift can be clearly seen in the cracks that traverse the region, including the largest one, Almannagjá, which is a veritable canyon (see fig. 5.1.). Þingvellir is also the site of Þingvallavatn, the largest natural lake in Iceland. The area has been described as "the *lieu de mémoire par excellence* in Iceland," and it is in many ways an ideal location for a national symbol.[2] A national park since 1928, it is the collective property of the Icelandic nation, and it is neutral in the sense that no one group of Icelanders can claim more right to it than another.[3]

Preparations for the Alþingi festival began in 1926, and it was intended from the outset to be a major event. Ambition was fueled by both external and internal factors. On the one hand, Icelanders sought international recognition; they wished to demonstrate to the outside world that theirs was a land of culture, prepared to take its place among other nation-states. One cabinet member remarked in a speech to parliament that while Iceland did not have the means to dazzle its guests with extravagant display, "at least we can convince them that here lives a nation already on the road to cultural maturity."[4] On the other hand, the celebrations should enhance the local population's self-image by persuading them of the country's intrinsic worth.[5] A prominent local philosopher encouraged all members of Icelandic society to set themselves particular goals

Figure 5.1. Almannagjá at Þingvellir. Shutterstock.

to be realized in time for the festival, prophesying that "1930 *will be* the day of judgement for our nation."[6] Like other nationalist intellectuals, Leifs was a fervent proponent of the upcoming festival. In a newspaper article, he proposed that the year 1930 be designated a "year of culture" during which everything possible should be done to stimulate progress in the arts, since the festival's impression on the international guests and media might have a "determining impact on our independence."[7] While he somewhat overstated the connection between the Alþingi festival and the politics of Iceland's autonomy, Leifs was in agreement with leading public intellectuals that the festival should mark the dawn of a new age.

It was decided early on that music should be prominent at the Þingvellir festivities and that it should involve both a mixed chorus and an orchestra, although both had to be essentially created for the event—a sign of the importance attached to demonstrating the nation's progress in the field of symphonic and choral art music. An organizational committee of high-ranking officials, including the prime minister, was formed in 1926, and it appointed Páll Ísólfsson its main advisor in musical matters. The composer-organist Sigfús Einarsson was appointed the festival's music director while

Ísólfsson and Jón Halldórsson—the largely self-taught director of the local YMCA (or KFUM) chorus—were chosen to conduct the festival's orchestra and choir concerts.

All this rankled Leifs, who hoped that the festival would provide a platform for himself as conductor and composer. As early as 1927, he offered to repeat the previous year's success with the Hamburg Philharmonic by arranging for a seventy-member German orchestra to travel around Iceland as part of the 1930 festivities and even contacted the Vienna Philharmonic in an attempt to spark their interest.[8] His ultimate fantasy was to perform Beethoven's Ninth for the first time on the island. He envisioned the construction in Reykjavík of a new building that could seat an audience of up to two thousand and suggested, in an unusual gesture of practicality, that after the festival it could be converted into a fish packhouse or storage building.[9] Leifs applied for funding from the city of Reykjavík but was denied on the grounds that a foreign orchestra could never be the main music event at an Icelandic national festival. The festival's music committee (which included Ísólfsson) concurred, noting in a reply to Leifs that importing a foreign orchestra was "neither feasible nor necessary."[10] In a leading newspaper, one anonymous writer voiced his relief that such "begging by foreigners" had been rejected, asserting that the Alþingi festival should be "completely and uniquely for Iceland and Icelanders" to display everything that was "the most national, cordial, and noble, that still remains of our ancestors' legacy."[11] An irate Leifs replied that it was hypocritical to let patriotism stand in the way of a foreign orchestra with "truly national Icelandic music" (i.e., his own compositions, which he would of course conduct) when the citizens of Reykjavík had for decades preferred "gramophone records, bad films, and rubbish foreign ditties" to native folk music.[12]

Plans for music at the Alþingi festival were announced in autumn 1928, and the high point would be the premiere of a festival cantata expressly composed for the occasion. A competition would be held for a cycle of poems; the winning libretto would then be set by Icelandic composers and these works evaluated by a second jury.

Leifs was deeply mistrustful of this plan. In a letter to Ísólfsson he expressed his concern that the deadline for composers would be too narrow (it was roughly eight months, though it might have been shorter had Leifs not complained), and he disapproved of composers being required to set the chosen text "regardless of whether it is suitable for a work of art."[13] Leifs's critique was based on his conviction that the winning cantata should become a "national work"— a lasting masterpiece. Here he misjudged the entire point of the competition, which was simply to provide an occasional piece for a one-time event.

Leifs was particularly vexed at Ísólfsson's extensive role in organizing the festival. Apart from serving on the general music committee, he was employed as one of the conductors and was also—somewhat questionably, given that he was sure to participate in the competition—a member of the jury in charge of selecting the libretto. This committee announced its results in December 1928: two poets, Davíð Stefánsson and Einar Benediktsson, shared first prize, but it was recommended that Stefánsson's poem be set to music while Benediktsson's would be recited at the festival.[14] This further aggravated Leifs, since the epic force of Benediktsson's writing was more to his taste than the wistful neo-Romanticism of Stefánsson, one of Iceland's most celebrated poets in the 1920s and '30s.[15] Stefánsson, on the other hand, already had a solid working relationship with Ísólfsson; many of the latter's best known songs are settings of the former's texts.

Leifs requested and received a copy of the cantata libretto, but in January 1929 he wrote Ísólfsson that it was "very unlikely" that he would take part in the competition.[16] Yet he found himself drawn to Stefánsson's poetry, perhaps in part as a way of coming to terms with the loss of his father. The cantata would be performed at Þingvellir, which had been his family's favorite location for camping trips in his youth. Decades later, when asked if he had been happy in Iceland, Leifs remarked, "I was happy for a few days at Þingvellir with my father, when I was a child. I have never had peace here since."[17] Writing to his sister in 1930, he suggested that his cantata was a kind of a *Requiem*, and its title page bears the inscription "To the forefathers" (*Helgist forfeðrunum*).[18] This suggests both a more general dedication to the founders of the Icelandic parliament in the tenth century and, obliquely, to the memory of Leifs's father. Leifs also announced his intention to his mother, expressing the hope that his grief might eventually lead him to self-improvement: "Now, as before, I feel that sorrow cleanses me of all vanity and many of the evils that reside in every man. I try to soften my grief by taking Dad as a model, for I cannot imagine a kinder person than he was. I am determined to try to also be good—like he was. This intention alone relieves my sorrow and tempers it.... At the same time, I have resolved to use all my talent to create for Dad a secular monument, a magnificent, Icelandic work of art."[19]

As the summer passed, it became less likely that Leifs would complete his work in time for the deadline of October 1. In mid-September, he wrote to the jury—which consisted of Sigfús Einarsson, the pianist Haraldur Sigurðsson, and Carl Nielsen—explaining that he would be able to submit only a few movements in full score by the deadline but that these should "give some idea of the work's style and artistic value."[20] The jury accepted Leifs's request to submit only his completed movements and asked that he send them directly to the Icelandic embassy in Copenhagen, where the jury would meet to deliberate.[21] But Leifs never did, and it seems that the deciding factor was Ísólfsson's discouraging reaction to his music when the two met in Lübeck shortly before the deadline. Their old friendship had faded, and Leifs suspected Ísólfsson of undermining his reputation and career prospects at home. According to Leifs's description of their meeting in a letter to his mother, he had brought along a copy of his recently published *25 Icelandic Folk Songs* for piano as well as the completed cantata movements to show Ísólfsson. The latter declared his folk song collection "rubbish" (*svínarí*, cf. the German *Schweinerei*) and, after examining the cantata movements, declared that he would "never want to rehearse this work."[22] Although we have only Leifs's account of their conversation, it seems plausible; their views on new music differed widely, and the written correspondence suggests that Ísólfsson was an honest and outspoken critic of Leifs's music. Leifs seems at this point to have realized that his work would never win, and he did not complete the cantata until January 22, 1930, nearly four months after the competition deadline and two months after the results were announced.

Ísólfsson had a point: Leifs's cantata made far greater demands on both orchestra and chorus than could be met by Icelandic amateur musicians in 1930. Leifs's autograph sketches imply that while he was mindful of the local resources early on in the composing process, he later decided against compromising his artistic vision. The cantata is scored for small orchestra: piccolo; flute; oboe; English horn; two each of clarinets, bassoons, horns, and trumpets; and percussion and strings. The earliest full draft for the opening movement shows that Leifs intended a small non-*obbligato* ensemble of brass and keyboards (two horns, two trumpets, three trombones, tuba, harmonium, and piano) to support the chorus, presumably on the assumption that the Icelandic singers might not be able to master his demanding music. He later changed his mind, and such a group does not appear in drafts for the later movements, nor in the autograph full score. Also, Leifs calls for a boys' choir in movements 4 and 5. At no point were there plans for a boys' choir to sing at the Þingvellir festival, and indeed there was no such ensemble in all Iceland that could have taken the part.

In the end, seven cantatas were submitted, and Ísólfsson's won first prize. Like the other music performed at the festival, his work is in what locals regarded as a "respectable" style—a tonal, conservative late-nineteenth-century idiom indebted to German models and thus the ideal illustration of Iceland's progress in adapting the tradition of "art music." It was performed to great acclaim at the Þingvellir festivities and remained a staple of the Icelandic choral repertoire for decades. Although one of its movements (*Burn, Ye Beacons*) is still frequently performed by male choirs, the cantata's overall status has diminished in recent years, as the event itself has receded from living memory.

Leifs's doubts regarding the competence of the Icelandic musicians proved well founded. The Reykjavík Orchestra (*Hljómsveit Reykjavíkur*) had received funding to hire a training conductor from abroad, and in late 1929 an Austrian, Franz Mixa, arrived to rehearse the group. He made considerable progress, and the orchestra performed several public concerts in the months leading up to the festival. It was planned from the start that five members of the Royal Chapel orchestra (*Kongelige kapel*) in Copenhagen would join the Icelandic ensemble: flute, oboe, bassoon, viola, and double bass. The two native members of the cantata jury had good connections in Copenhagen—Einarsson was married to a Danish singer, and Sigurðsson was professor of piano at the Royal Conservatory—and they could easily procure the players needed. As summer neared it became obvious that, despite the conservative style and reasonable demands of Ísólfsson's work, further reinforcements were necessary. In May 1930 it was decided to recruit four additional players from the Royal Chapel orchestra: two violinists, a violist, and a trumpetist.[23] The ultimate irony was that Iceland, now proudly celebrating its first national festival as a sovereign state (although still in personal union with the Danish king), should have to rely on nine musicians from Denmark's royal orchestra as well as an Austrian rehearsal conductor. After all, Leifs's proposal of a German or Austrian orchestra tour in 1930 had been dismissed on the grounds that "Icelanders and only Icelanders" should perform at the Alþingi festival, a goal that had proved unattainable.[24]

The Alþingi festival took place on June 26–28, attended by foreign dignitaries, including King Christian X, as well as two hundred foreign reporters and other guests. Like the Icelanders themselves had hoped, it made news around the world.[25] Aside from the cantata premiere, the Þingvellir festival program included three choral concerts featuring a mixed chorus—the one-hundred-member Þingvellir choir that had been specially formed for the occasion, the largest choir in Icelandic history thus far—and the all-male YMCA chorus. Apart from concerts, the program was heavily nationalistic, focusing on the ancient history of the parliament.

This included a historical representation of the first sitting of the medieval assembly: professors from the University of Iceland had devised a theatrical reconstruction that featured thirty-seven men in colorful, Viking-looking costumes, with long beards glued on their chins. The intent was "in all earnest," as one modern historian has noted, "to link together the sitting of the modern Alþingi and its glorified ancient precursor at the 'sacred site.'"[26]

Unlike the seven official contestants, Leifs did not give his work the self-evident title *Alþingi Festival Cantata* (*Alþingishátíðarkantata*). Instead, he called it *Þjóðhvöt*, which draws on Eddic models and may be translated as *Iceland's Whetting*. Informally, Leifs also referred to the work as the "Þingvellir cantata," suggesting that the place of its intended premiere, and the history it represents, influenced his vision of the work as a whole. His preferred German title was simply *Island-Kantate*, and thus it has generally been known as *Iceland Cantata* in English.

Despite Leifs's reservations on the format of the festival competition, his response to Stefánsson's poetry was genuinely inspired. The *Iceland Cantata* is his first large-scale masterpiece and one of the finest works of his entire career. It contains all the elements of his mature style, but here they are treated with more flexibility than in many of his later works. Although parallel fifths predominate in the first movement, the rapid harmonic rhythm and varied texture contribute to the force and excitement of the score. It can only have pleased Leifs that Stefánsson's poetry occasionally harkens back to the prosody of Old Icelandic verse. The opening poem, for example, begins with a direct quote from the Eddic *Völuspá* ("Hark I bid all / hallowed beings") and employs the ancient meter of fornyrðislag.

The *Iceland Cantata* is also indebted to older musical traditions that Leifs otherwise rarely acknowledged. The third movement is an archaic fugue, unusual for Leifs, who generally avoided polyphonic part writing. The fifth movement, sung by a boys' choir in unison, has the character of a chorale, its haunting melody hovering between major and minor over a tonic pedal—a direct offshoot of the *Lullaby* op. 14a. In the cantata's final movement, *Burn, Ye*

Beacons (*Brennið þið, vitar*), the composer summons his full expressive powers. The poem directly addresses the beacons along the country's coastline, beseeching them to shine brightly so that the "sturdy heroes" may sail their ships safely in the darkest night. Leifs depicts danger at sea, hinting at fear and despair beneath an alarming stillness. Following a hesitant prayer of unison female voices, the men proceed tentatively in parallel fifths, with bells tolling in the distance. Only in the final bars do calming major triads appear, giving the listener the sense of having arrived at the port at last. Leifs suggested that this poem could be understood in various ways. Aside from the literal interpretation (which clearly inspired Ísólfsson's muscular male-choir setting), he found that it brought to mind "the soul that yearns to return home from this earthly life; and the outlaw, who longs for his native land."[27] Such a reading allowed him to view the movement as signifying both his deceased father and his expatriate self.

Leifs did not set Stefánsson's cantata libretto in full. It consists of thirteen parts, but Leifs chose only seven, emphasizing the poet's evocation of the ancient parliament, paganism, and heroism but notably avoiding any mention of Christianity (poems 2, 5, and 12 in Stefánsson's cycle). Stefánsson had also prescribed the scoring of each movement: reciter with or without orchestral accompaniment; mixed choir; male chorus; or vocal soloist (of an unspecified voice type) with orchestra. Given the strength of Iceland's male choir tradition, his idea of assigning several movements to a male chorus was eminently practical; the mixed Þingvellir choir could reasonably be expected to learn the five movements consigned to it. In virtually every case, Leifs went against the poet's instructions. His movements 1 and 4 are for full chorus (not recitation, as specified), movement 5 is for boys' choir (not soloist), movements 2, 6, and 7 are for mixed choir (not men's choir). Ísólfsson, on the other hand, followed the poet's specifications in virtually every movement of his winning cantata.

The premiere of the *Iceland Cantata* took place in Germany and drew Leifs's ire no less than the competition itself. Greifswald

University was—and still is—home to a large Scandinavian department, and in November 1930 it organized an Iceland festival to honor the Alþingi millennium. Leifs had high hopes for this event and even entertained the improbable notion that the university would award him an honorary doctorate for his work.[28] But the cantata proved to be a challenge even for a fine amateur chorus in Germany. Rudolf Ewald Zingel, conductor of the Greifswalder Singverein, decided to leave out two movements and also dispensed with the original Icelandic text in favor of Leifs's own loose German translation, which was never intended for performance. Leifs was outraged and canceled his plans to attend the concert. He even dispatched a formal complaint to the German Ministry of Culture, demanding an apology for the apparent slight, but received only a perfunctory reply.[29] Despite this last-minute disturbance, newspaper reports and reviews suggest that the cantata's premiere was a considerable success.[30]

A CONCERTO AND VARIATIONS

Having completed the *Iceland Cantata*, Leifs returned to two long-term projects dating back to his student years in Leipzig: the Organ Concerto op. 7 and the *Variations on a Theme by Beethoven* op. 8. The Organ Concerto, by far the more ambitious of the two works, consists of an introduction, a passacaglia theme with thirty variations, and a finale. Leifs's earliest sketches for a passacaglia date from ca. 1917, and although they do not specify the organ, it seems reasonable to assume that they were intended for the instrument, given his models for the theme itself (discussed below). Only around 1925–26 does Leifs seem to have decided to develop his fragmentary sketches into a larger work for organ and orchestra. He made some adjustments to the theme and heavily recomposed the first twelve variations before continuing the work in its orchestral guise. Judging from the sketches, the introduction and finale were added late in compositional process, probably not until 1929–30, and these are the work's most typically Leifsian sections in terms of style.

The Organ Concerto owes much to the encouragement of Páll Ísólfsson. In 1923, while planning a concert tour of the United States, he asked Leifs for "a powerful passacaglia on Icelandic themes for me to play."[31] The tour did not materialize, but in 1928 Leifs, having returned to his youthful sketches, assured Ísólfsson that his passacaglia-in-progress would be one of his finest works yet: "This work will give you a chance, which you otherwise would not have, to represent Iceland in your art."[32] Later, Ísólfsson suggested performing it at a concert in Reykjavík in connection with the 1930 Alþingi festival, but the work was still not ready and in any case would have been impossible to perform in Iceland given the limited local resources. As the relationship between the two musicians soured, Leifs expressed doubt as to whether Ísólfsson's interest in his new work was genuine. In June 1930 he wrote to his mother, "I am completing a concerto for organ and orchestra, something for Páll Ísólfsson to play, if he should want to."[33] In the end, Ísólfsson never performed the work, and its Icelandic première was given only in 1999. The only performances of the concerto during the composer's lifetime were given by Kurt Utz in Wiesbaden and Berlin (see chap. 6 and 7).

At the time of its completion, the concerto was Leifs's most ambitious composition. At roughly twenty minutes, it is one of his largest single-movement structures and without doubt his most contrapuntally dense score. It is more strikingly dissonant than most of his other works, as he vigorously embraced the more radical language that he had until then employed only on a smaller scale. Progression of root-position triads by seconds, thirds, and tritones is prevalent, particularly in the introduction and finale, but this is only one component of Leifs's diverse musical vocabulary.

The main thematic material consists of three independent strands: an ostinato theme, the Icelandic funeral hymn *Allt eins og blómstrið eina*, and original melodies composed by Leifs in a vernacular style. The structure of the four-phrase ostinato theme clearly harks back to the passacaglia tradition. In particular, Leifs was influenced by the themes of two works, Bach's *Passacaglia and*

Example 5.1. Passacaglia themes by (a) J. S. Bach, *Passacaglia and Fugue* in C minor BWV 582; (b) Max Reger, *Introduction and Passacaglia* in F minor op. 63; (c) Leifs, Organ Concerto op. 7.

Example 5.2. Leifs, Organ Concerto op. 7, mm. 23–27, organ part. © Iceland Music Information Center.

Fugue in C minor BWV 582 and Reger's *Introduction and Passacaglia* in F minor op. 63, both of which were part of Ísólfsson's repertoire in the 1920s. Leifs's theme is so chromatic as to largely obscure tonal functionality—it employs all twelve pitches of the chromatic scale—but its opening and closing gestures nevertheless suggest F minor (see example 5.1). The powerful initial statement of the theme occurs in the solo organ during the introduction, where it appears in the treble register and is supported by a series of major triads (see example 5.2).

Another key thematic strand is the funeral chorale *Allt eins og blómstrið eina*, which Leifs had already employed in several smaller works (see chap. 3). It appears in its typical unadorned form in the 25 *Icelandic Folk Songs* for piano and the incidental music to

Galdra-Loftr, and it would later appear in the *Organ Prelude* op. 16 no. 3 and the *Alþýðusöngvar* (*Songs of the People*, op. 32 no. 2). An ornamented version of the tune, which Leifs recorded in Reykjavík in 1926, appears in his *Hymns* op. 12a (1929), and this also inspired variations 12–13 of the Organ Concerto. Here, the embellishment is even more florid than in op. 12a; when combined with a dense, chromatic harmonization, it all but conceals the theme's origin. Variations 12–13 are in turn foreshadowed by a quiet passage during the introduction (*moderato, quasi adagio*) in which the organ vaguely implies the chorale tune.

The funeral chorale gradually comes into focus as the work progresses. In variations 24 and 26, disjointed fragments of the theme appear in trumpets, trombones, and horns. The climax of the passacaglia proper (variations 27–29) is the simultaneous rendering of the ostinato theme and the chorale, now stated in its complete, unembellished form. During this episode, the two themes gradually pull apart. Leifs requests a slower tempo for the ostinato theme in each variation (*poco meno mosso* in var. 28, *più meno mosso* in var. 29) but notates the hymn tune in gradually faster values (half notes, dotted quarters, quarters) to compensate for the tempo change. In performance, the effect should be a gradual slowing down of the ostinato theme while the chorale—the concerto's teleological goal—unfolds at an unwavering speed.

Melodies reminiscent of Icelandic folk song constitute yet another thematic strand. Both tvísöngur- and rímur-like tunes of Leifs's own invention are superimposed on the ostinato theme (in variations 9 and 17), creating a dense polyphonic texture. In variation 9, a tvísöngur and a rímur tune occur simultaneously, each suggesting its own key and mode; the result is a kind of contrapuntal bimodality over the chromatically inflected passacaglia theme.

While the disparate thematic strands are crucial to Leifs's conception of the work, a more immediately striking feature is the amount of arresting dissonance. Often this is produced through remarkably simple means. In the introduction, Leifs creates a cluster-like sonority by superimposing two fully diminished seventh chords

Example 5.3. Leifs, Organ Concerto op. 7, opening. © Iceland Music Information Center.

(see example 5.3). One of the three possible permutations—superimposed chords on C and C-sharp—recurs more often than the others and becomes something of a referential sonority in the work. This type of dissonance disappears for most of the passacaglia proper, suggesting that the idea came late in the compositional process. Toward the work's conclusion (variation 30 and Finale), the diminished seventh chords return, as do the rows of major triads that appeared briefly during the introduction. These moments, when dense chromatic part writing yields to the granitic movement of block major chords, are particularly noteworthy in light of the development of Leifs's style. Although he had employed series of major triads before—for example in the *25 Icelandic Folk Songs* for piano—this was the first time that they made a distinctive appearance in a large-scale work. From then on, they would constitute one of the main components of his musical language.

The Organ Concerto's percussive element is also not likely to go unnoticed. The timpani are prominent from the beginning, rupturing the organ's dissonances with *fortissimo* blows. No less conspicuous is the *legno grande* (Leifs's term in the score, although *martello* is more common), a giant wooden hammer, the use of which was presumably inspired by Mahler's Sixth Symphony. Leifs employs it only in the introduction and variation 30 / finale, largely in conjunction with the diminished-seventh-chord clusters described above, but it would henceforth have a permanent place in his instrumentarium, appearing in several of his large orchestral scores. Last but not least, the solo part demands feats of acrobatic virtuosity, with an array of dazzling figuration, trills, tremolos, and sweeping glissandos up and down the keyboard.

The Organ Concerto brought to a close the thirty-one-year-old Leifs's first decade as a composer and can be regarded as a summary of his musical development. It is the culmination of his period of dissonant modernism while the appearance in the introduction and finale of chains of major triads related by seconds and thirds points forward to his later style. In terms of folk song quotation, the concerto also marked a turning point. From then on, Leifs would not employ actual folk melodies in his larger works but instead construct his own.

Leifs immediately turned to another orchestral work he had been planning for a decade. It was as if his newly found confidence as a composer led him to revisit his older sketches, a kind of creative housecleaning before devising new projects. The *Variazioni Pastorali on a Theme by Beethoven* op. 8 were conceived during a bout of illness in 1920, when he was allowed to leave the Leipzig hospital to hear the Adolf Busch Quartet in concert. Leifs's work consists of ten variations on a theme from the third movement of Beethoven's Serenade for string trio op. 8—the identical opus numbers were no coincidence. Even more than the Organ Concerto, the *Variazioni Pastorali* are akin to a time lapse of Leifs's development as a composer. His style seems tentative in the opening variations (the earliest to be sketched), with modest elaborations on the original theme. The work becomes more characteristically Leifsian as it progresses, and the appearance of open fifths in variation 3 heralds a major stylistic change. In later variations, Leifs systematically explores the vernacular styles as well as his own newly established harmonic trait: shifting meters (variation 5, marked *quasi rímur* in one of Leifs's sketches), third-related harmonies (variation 6), and parallel fifths (variation 7). The slithering chromatic string lines of variation 9 (*quasi grave*) are alleviated by the finale, in which Beethoven's theme is transformed into a bright, lyrical D major.

As a respite from composing, Leifs attended Arturo Toscanini's concerts in Berlin in May 1930, where he conducted the New York

Philharmonic to great acclaim. Leifs, for one, did not concur and penned an article for *Allgemeine Musikzeitung* voicing his displeasure. He found the Italian maestro's interpretation of Beethoven's *Eroica* nothing less than disastrous, an "artistic disappointment such as I have not felt for years," and even went so far as to liken it to the ill-fated 1928 North Pole expedition by the Italian aviator Umberto Nobile, which cost several participants their lives. To Leifs, who had promulgated the existence of "northern" and "southern" artistic personalities, the concert proved that the gap between them could not be bridged: "As an Italian, Toscanini has never fully understood Beethoven and will never fully understand him."[34]

It was through the article on Toscanini that Wilhelm Furtwängler—himself no admirer of the Italian's conducting—became familiar with Leifs's name.[35] The following year, he invited Leifs to meet in person at his home in Berlin and asked to retain several of his scores for further perusal. Although Furtwängler expressed "sincere interest" in performing the Organ Concerto with the renowned virtuoso Alfred Sittard, this proved impossible to realize; the conductor preferred not to give new works in Berlin without trying them out elsewhere first, and a Hamburg premiere was out of the question due to an inadequate instrument.[36] Still, Leifs was encouraged by Furtwängler's praise: "The few works of yours that I know have greatly awakened my interest, and your entire musical personality has appeared to me as independent and completely unique within contemporary music."[37]

HOPES AND FAILURES

As noted above, 1930 was an important year for culture building in Iceland. Besides the Alþingi festival, a new music school was founded (*Tónlistarskólinn í Reykjavík*, or the Reykjavík School of Music) that for the first time offered a well-structured music curriculum, with Ísólfsson as principal. In December, the National Radio Broadcasting Service (*Ríkisútvarpið*) began its transmission. Leifs had high hopes for the enterprise and was convinced that it could be used as a tool for raising the arts and culture in Iceland to a higher level. He also saw it as a feasible career path for himself. In 1928, Leifs had already been working covertly to guarantee his appointment there, preferably as director. Initially, he had the support of politicians in various parties, and even the prime minister seemed for a while to favor his candidacy. Yet Leifs's dream did not come to fruition. Ten applied for the position of director, but behind the scenes the government had already decided to appoint Jónas Þorbergsson, the politically minded editor of a daily newspaper. The official nomination made by the five-member "radio council"—of which Ísólfsson was a member—was perfunctory, and the appointment was widely criticized as political cronyism. The parliamentarian Jón Jónsson, who was Leifs's relative, wrote to him that the prime minister himself was "very saddened" by his inability to mediate on Leifs's behalf in the matter.[38]

When it became clear that Leifs would not become radio director, he offered instead to establish an orchestra or chamber ensemble in affiliation with the National Radio. The suggestion had wide support at the beginning. Numerous members of parliament, as well as influential musicians such as Ísólfsson and Sigfús Einarsson, signed an appeal for the government to hire Leifs for the post, but doubts lingered regarding his interpersonal skills. In the end, the National Radio accepted an offer from the Reykjavík Orchestra, which had already appointed its own permanent conductor: Franz Mixa, the Austrian who trained the group in the months leading up to the Alþingi festival. Attempting to compensate for this, the radio director offered Leifs the position of speaker, which had nothing to do with music and to which he reacted with skepticism. Leifs suspected that the idea had come from Ísólfsson, who had himself recently been appointed to a string of coveted posts—including principal of the Reykjavík School of Music and board member at the radio—and whom Leifs regarded with increasing animosity. He felt forced to choose the lesser of two evils: "Either I would reply with insults and anger ... or I would accept the position to avoid starvation. Thus I and my art would be ruined, for all paths would be closed for my work abroad, and Icelanders would lose all respect for an artist who abandoned his calling for a post of no artistic value, far beneath Páll [Ísólfsson], the 'great artist.' I want neither."[39]

Nothing in the surviving documentation suggests that Ísólfsson's intentions were less than gracious, but Leifs had become mistrustful of his former friend and colleague. He suspected Ísólfsson of disparaging him in Reykjavík, an accusation that Ísólfsson vehemently denied, although he admitted that he often found Leifs arrogant and conceited.[40] There was certainly an element of rivalry, and it irked Leifs that Ísólfsson had been appointed to posts to which he also aspired. But Ísólfsson was bound to be the more popular figure in Icelandic cultural life: he was an outstanding performer, composed music in a lyrical, conventional style, and was an outwardly good-humored and affable personality. Leifs cautiously expressed interest in the National Radio offer and suggested a trial period once he had carried out a conducting engagement in Sweden in late January 1931. Yet in the end nothing came of the speaker position, for the director had a change of heart and withdrew his offer on the grounds that any collaboration with the ill-tempered Leifs was bound to fail.[41]

The concert in Sweden turned out to be yet another catastrophe. Leifs had been invited to conduct the Gothenburg Symphony Orchestra in Tchaikovsky's Fourth Symphony, Beethoven's *Egmont* overture, and a selection of his own works. This was his first time conducting Tchaikovsky's Fourth, and his approach did not inspire confidence among the players. After the first rehearsal, the orchestra management suggested to Leifs that he should focus on his own music but leave the rest of the program to Tor Mann, the orchestra's chief conductor. Leifs was furious, and after a heated quarrel with his replacement, he took the first available train out of town.[42] The *Iceland Overture* remained on the program, but Mann, having seen the composer's most unpleasant side, can hardly have been a sympathetic interpreter. One Gothenburg critic found the work's raw material more attractive than the composition itself while another described it as "horribly monotonous, cold, and quite frankly unpleasant."[43]

Although Leifs had been content living in Travemünde, he now yearned for the opportunities a metropolis could afford. In April 1931 he and Annie rented a seven-room, two-story wooden house with a large garden at Moltkestrasse 9 (now Liselotte-Herrmann-Strasse 9) in Rehbrücke, a small town near Potsdam, a location he found ideal. He had enough peace and quiet to compose, but Berlin was less than an hour away by train. After a decade of relocating every year or two, the family's nomadic lifestyle was now at an end, for they would remain in Rehbrücke for more than a decade. It was also the first time they furnished their own home. Annie received a Blüthner grand piano from her parents, and Leifs obtained an upright piano, so they could now work at home simultaneously for the first time in their ten-year marriage.

Shortly after moving to Rehbrücke, Leifs once again wrote for the organ, this time as a kind of peace offering to Ísólfsson after the turmoil regarding both the cantata competition and the National Radio post. Ísólfsson had occasionally performed Leifs's organ prelude op. 5 and had repeatedly asked for more works in a similar vein. He was scheduled to give a recital at an organ festival in Lübeck in October 1931, and in August Leifs tossed off *Three Icelandic Chorale Preludes* op. 16 in a span of only five days. Each takes as its subject an old hymn tune. The first is based on a Danish melody also common in Iceland (*Den lyse dag forgangen er / Gone Is the Bright Day*); the second is a traditional Icelandic hymn tune sung to a text originally by C. F. Gellert (*Meine Lebenszeit verstreicht / My Life Is Passing Quickly*); the third is a setting of Leifs's beloved chorale *Allt eins og blómstrið eina*, which receives a particularly dense, dissonant chordal treatment, perhaps inspired by the Organ Concerto of the previous year.[44] The chorale preludes were in fact not heard in Lübeck, for Ísólfsson canceled his appearance there on short notice, and once again Leifs felt like he had played him for a fool. They were premiered instead in Strasbourg in 1933 by the twenty-year-old Ernest Bour, later a noted conductor of contemporary music such as Ligeti's *Atmosphères* and Berio's *Sinfonia*.

Leifs's *Three Icelandic Hymns for Church Use* (*Þrjú íslenzk sálmalög til kirkjusöngs*) op. 17b, for SATB chorus with organ accompaniment, were also written at Ísólfsson's request. In Iceland, the latter was planning a new volume of hymns in simple arrangements that could be sung or played on piano. Back in 1927 he had invited Leifs to contribute, and Leifs presumably penned his undated settings ca. 1931. They were not included in Ísólfsson's volume, published five years later, and it is not even certain that Leifs ever sent him the score.[45] Still, his intention to cater to an Icelandic amateur audience explains the modest technical demands of these arrangements. The choral writing is homophonic throughout and is far less adventurous harmonically than other works by Leifs.

Success finally came in the form of Leifs's four *Icelandic Dances* (*Rímnadanslög*) op. 11, written in Baden-Baden in 1929, in which a few folk tunes were strung together in piano arrangements of moderate technical difficulty. Some of the melodies came from Þorsteinsson's volume of folk songs, but Leifs had collected others himself, for example the B-section to the first dance, which a thirty-year-old woman from northern Iceland had sung for him in 1926.[46] In his preface, Leifs stated that the music was intended as *Gebrauchsmusik* and that the different sections of each dance could be repeated and combined at will. They could also be sung to any rímur poems that fit the meter. The *Icelandic Dances* were Leifs's most accessible work and gained some popularity; for example, they were performed in radio concerts in Hamburg, Berlin, and Leipzig as well as on the BBC and Swedish Radio.[47] Before long they could also be heard live at Berlin cafés and at the Tivoli in Copenhagen. The sheet music—piano solo as well as arrangements for salon orchestra and small symphony orchestra—sold reasonably well, but a recording made by the Trocadero Ensemble and issued on the Homocord label in 1931 was not the hoped-for success.[48] Leifs himself was only moderately pleased with the result; he complained about lack of rehearsal time and resented not having been asked to direct the performance himself.[49]

Leifs had long been vexed by the lack of enthusiasm for his music in Iceland. "What I find most regrettable in all my artistic endeavor is that I have no empathy and no support among my own people," he wrote to his cousin in 1931.[50] Now he finally had reason to be more optimistic in this regard. A group of friends and family members, including his sister Þórey and his longtime supporter Kristján Albertsson, had organized a Jón Leifs Society whose objective was to support the composer financially. In spring 1932, two Reykjavík newspapers published a declaration of support signed by forty-one founding members, all leading figures in Icelandic cultural and political life. Some were even among those Leifs considered his adversaries, including Ísólfsson and Emil Thoroddsen, but the list also included Iceland's prime minister as well as its leading visual artist, Jóhannes Kjarval.[51] The Leifs Society also had a German section. This was run mostly by Irmgard Kroner, who was enrolled in Nordic studies at Humboldt University and whose husband, Klaus, a physician, also admired all things Icelandic. The couple settled in Iceland in 1938, having been forced to leave Germany due to Klaus's Jewish ancestry.[52]

The founding of the Leifs Society was related to another positive development. While Leifs completed his Organ Concerto in Travemünde in summer 1930, Annie had traveled to Leipzig to meet with publishers who might be interested in bringing out some of her husband's scores. While Ernst Eulenburg was indifferent, the brothers Carl and Richard Linnemann, who ran the Kistner & Siegel publishing house, proved sympathetic toward Leifs's music.[53] Richard had himself studied with Teichmüller in his youth and had heard praise of the Icelander's music from Paul Graener, Leifs's former composition teacher. The Linnemanns already had several Scandinavian composers on their roster and were willing to add Leifs as long as he could subsidize the publication costs. This was the Leifs Society's main goal: membership guaranteed a numbered copy of each new score, specially printed on high-quality paper, and although the number of subscribers did not in the end suffice to fully underwrite the costs, their support was crucial. After a decade of virtually relentless trials and tribulations, it seemed like Leifs was now on the verge of a major breakthrough—just as the entire world was on the brink of being transformed.

NOTES

1. Kimberly Cannady and Kristín Loftsdóttir, "'A Nation without Music?': Symphonic Music and Nation-Building," 28.

2. Guðmundur Hálfdanarson, "Icelandic Modernity and the Role of Nationalism," in *Nordic Paths to Modernity*, eds. Jóhann Páll Árnason and Björn Wittrock (New York: Berghahn, 2012), 256.

3. On the role of Þingvellir in national festivals, see Guðmundur Hálfdanarson, "Þingvellir. An Icelandic 'Lieu de Mémoire,'" *History & Memory* 12 (2000): 4–29.

4. Jónas Jónsson, quoted in Guðmundur Hálfdanarson and Ólafur Rastrick, "Culture and the Construction of the Icelander in the 20th Century," in *Power and Culture: Hegemony, Interaction and Dissent*, eds. Jonathan Osmond and Ausma Cimdiņa (Pisa: Edizioni Plus, Pisa University Press, 2006), 107.

5. Ragnheiður Kristjánsdóttir, "1930—ár fagnaðar?," in *Kvennaslóðir. Rit til heiðurs Sigríði Th. Erlendsdóttur sagnfræðingi* (Reykjavík: Kvennasögusafn Íslands, 2001), 430, cited in Hálfdanarson and Rastrick, "Culture," 105.

6. Guðmundur Finnbogason, quoted in Rastrick, *Háborgin*, 235; cf. Hálfdanarson and Rastrick, "Culture," 106.

7. Leifs, "Ríkisafmælið 1930," *Lesbók Morgunblaðsins*, June 17, 1928.

8. Leifs to his parents, July 26, 1927; Anton Weiss (on behalf of the Vienna Philharmonic) to Leifs, September 9, 1927.

9. Leifs to Páll Ísólfsson, November 25, 1927.

10. See Leifs's article "Tónlist 1930," *Vísir*, December 15, 1927.

11. "V.G.," "Satt má sökum segja," *Morgunblaðið*, August 31, 1927.

12. Leifs, "Þjóðerni og tónlist," *Morgunblaðið*, October 4, 1927.

13. Leifs to Páll Ísólfsson, November 25, 1927.

14. See my article on the Alþingi cantata competition, "Hetjur styrkar standa," *Saga* 40/2 (2002): 178–96.

15. Jón Yngvi Jóhannsson, "Realism and Revolt," in *A History of Icelandic Literature*, ed. Daisy Neijmann, 392.

16. Leifs to Páll Ísólfsson, January 9, 1929.

17. Matthías Johannessen, "Lögmálin í hrúgunni. Spjallað við Jón Leifs," *Morgunblaðið*, May 5, 1959.

18. Leifs to Þórey Þorleifsdóttir, January 26, 1930.
19. Leifs to Ragnheiður Bjarnadóttir, April 11, 1929.
20. Leifs to the preparatory committee of the Alþingi festival, September 13, 1929, Sigfús Einarsson letters (E. 101.8), National Archives of Iceland, Reykjavík.
21. Sigfús Einarsson, notebook for the Alþingi Festival, Alþingi Festival Papers (box 7), National Archives of Iceland, Reykjavík.
22. Leifs to Ragnheiður Bjarnadóttir, November 26, 1930.
23. Sigfús Einarsson, notebook for the Alþingi Festival, Alþingi Festival Papers (box 7), National Archives of Iceland, Reykjavík.
24. "V.G.," "Satt má sökum segja."
25. Hálfdanarson and Rastrick, "Culture," 108–9.
26. Hálfdanarson and Rastrick, "Culture," 108.
27. Leifs to Þórey Þorleifsdóttir, January 26, 1930.
28. Leifs to Annie Leifs, June 5, 1930.
29. Cf. letters from Preussisches Ministerium für Wissenschaft (Kunst und Volksbildung) to Leifs, January 20 and February 16, 1931.
30. "Jahrtausendfeier Islands in Greifswald," *Hamburger Fremdenblatt*, November 12, 1930.
31. Páll Ísólfsson to Leifs, August 8, 1923.
32. Leifs to Páll Ísólfsson, May 30, 1928.
33. Leifs to Ragnheiður Bjarnadóttir, June 19, 1930.
34. Leifs, "Nachdenkliches zum Toscanini-Besuch," *Allgemeine Musikzeitung* 57 (1930): 681–82.
35. Leifs to Eggert Stefánsson, September 25, 1931. On Furtwängler's opinion of Toscanini, see Harvey Sachs, *Toscanini, Musician of Conscience* (New York: Liverlight, 2017), 481–82; Wilhelm Furtwängler, *Notebooks 1924–1954*, trans. Shaun Whiteside, ed. Michael Tanner (London: Quartet Books, 1989), 39–46.
36. Wilhelm Furtwängler to Leifs, April 22, 1931; Leifs to Furtwängler, May 26, 1931.
37. Furtwängler to Leifs, June 28, 1932.
38. Jón Jónsson to Leifs, August 24, 1931.
39. Leifs to Ragnheiður Bjarnadóttir, November 19, 1930.
40. Páll Ísólfsson to Leifs, December 28, 1927 and May 15, 1928.
41. Jónas Þorbergsson to Leifs, March 3, 1931.
42. Leifs to Annie Leifs, January 26, 1931; Leifs to Tor Mann, February 3, 1931.
43. G.J-n, "Teater och Musik," *Göteborgs Handels- och Sjöfarts-tidning*, January 29, 1931; F.L., "Symfonikonserten," *Vestsvenska dagbladet*, January 29, 1931.
44. The melody to *Mín lífstíð er á fleygiferð* comes from the Danish hymnal of 1569, *Herre Gud, mær mig mit Endeligt*; cf. Páll Eggert Ólason, *Upptök*

sálma og sálmalaga, 193. Its adaptation to Gellert's poem seems to have originated in Iceland.

45. *Sálmasöngsbók til kirkju- og heimasöngs*, ed. Páll Ísólfsson and Sigfús Einarsson (Reykjavík: Bókaverslun Sigfúsar Eymundssonar, 1936).

46. Íslenzk rímnadanslög, sketches.

47. Hermon Ould to Leifs, December 31, 1931.

48. Homophon-Company GmbH to Kistner & Siegel, November 19, 1931.

49. Leifs to Björn Kristjánsson, October 8, 1931.

50. Leifs to Jón Kaldal, April 6, 1931.

51. "Ávarp," *Morgunblaðið*, April 17, 1932.

52. More detailed information on the Kroners and their sojourn in Iceland can be found in Snorri G. Bergsson, *Erlendur landshornalýður—Flóttamenn og framandi útlendingar á Íslandi, 1853–1940* (Reykjavík: Almenna bókafélagið, 2017), 240–43.

53. Annie Leifs to Leifs, June 2 and 3, 1930.

SIX

"THIS MUSIC BELONGS TO US"
(1933–37)

ON MARCH 21, 1933, LEIFS arrived by ship in Reykjavík, his first visit there in four and a half years. The main purpose of his journey was to raise additional funds to underwrite the publication of his scores by Kistner & Siegel in Leipzig. According to Leifs's calculations, he needed 10,000 krónur—the equivalent of 6,500 marks—which in Iceland was a royal sum, equal to the yearly salary of a well-paid official. He initially hoped for government support, but when this failed to materialize, his mother took out a personal loan to fund the enterprise.[1] On returning to Berlin in May, Leifs deposited the money and took the first available train to Leipzig, where he signed a publishing contract with the Linnemann brothers.[2]

Leifs returned to a changed Germany. A few days before his departure to Iceland, the Reichstag had been set on fire, and during his absence the Nazis gained majority in parliament. In Leifs's letters to his family after his return, he assumed a cautious political stance. In May, he wrote that he and Annie hoped "everything goes well here regarding the political situation, but I'm not too sure of it; I think that given the circumstances it would be best for Germany to become a monarchy again and many prominent people here agree, but it's impossible to know what will happen."[3] Two months later he struck a more pessimistic tone, noting that he was considering moving north of the Danish border in case a civil war broke out.[4] By September he had decided to remain but also declared that he would not take full advantage of the situation by joining the Nazi party. He wanted his music to be judged on its own merit: "If I were to conform to this political wave, it is quite possible that everything would go smoothly in terms of my career, but I don't want to. They'll have to appreciate my works and play them in spite of this, or not at all!"[5]

While Leifs's private stance appears unambiguous, his public line was vaguer. He was not averse to playing up to the Nazis' sympathy to the cause of Nordic music and even made appeals to high-ranking officials for increased cultural relations. Thilo von Trotha was a former music student who had risen to prominence within the Nazi party, holding the post of private secretary to Alfred Rosenberg, the leading party ideologue. Shortly after the Nazis came to power, he received a letter from Leifs, voicing his disappointment that the "Nordic awakening" implied by both Hitler and Rosenberg had thus far failed to materialize and encouraging him to take a "Nordic-Germanic" stance in the future.[6]

Like many other artists both German and foreign, Leifs was willing to seek accommodation with the Nazi regime. He did not manage to sustain the image of the unpolitical composer that Sibelius cultivated in dealing with the Third Reich; instead, he seems often to have disregarded the political implications of his actions.[7] He ostensibly had no qualms about publishing articles in Nazi-oriented journals like the *Nationalsozialistische Lehrerzeitung* or *Deutsche Militär-Musiker-Zeitung*, the music journal of the German Wehrmacht.[8] As Jonathan Petropoulos has noted, several factors entered into the thinking of artists who sought accommodation with the new regime: first, a misunderstanding of the Nazi leaders and their goals; second, an unchecked ego and sense of self-importance; third, a highly developed survival instinct combined with a more garden-variety opportunism.[9] All these ring true in the case of Leifs. Yet, even though his artistic vision had certain points of convergence with Nazi interest in the North, he was primarily an

Icelandic nationalist, driven by an obsessive pursuit of the outside world's recognition of Iceland as a free, independent nation. This was certainly not shared by Nazi leaders, who sought to bring the Nordic countries into their fold.

None of the evidence suggests that Leifs was personally attracted to the Nazi party or its goals, apart from their fascination with the *völkisch* and *nordisch* categories of art that he promulgated in his work. The sculptor Ludwig Gies was a friend of the Leifses and was himself among the artists labeled "degenerate." He was forced out of the Prussian Academy of the Arts for his loyalty to dissident and Jewish students, and his crucifix in Lübeck's Cathedral was displayed at the 1937 exhibition of "degenerate art" and subsequently destroyed. After the war, Gies declared that he had never heard Leifs claim affinity for Nazism: "He was very critical of the situation and voiced his opinion clearly."[10] Other acquaintances left similar testimony.[11] Leifs had no contact or affiliation with the small group of Nazi followers in Iceland during his frequent sojourns there in the 1930s, nor did he make any public political statements.[12] Although Leifs's works did receive a handful of prominent performances during the early Nazi era, from 1937 onward his position deteriorated rapidly. During World War II, he wrote several works in which he expressed his opposition to the war and to the Nazi appropriation of the Nordic ideal—for example, the string quartet *Mors et vita*, the *Saga Symphony*, and the ballet score *Baldr*.

Leifs's position in Germany was made considerably more complicated by the fact that, as he discovered only in the early 1930s, his wife was of full Jewish descent—a *Volljüdin*. It appears that ever since her baptism at age nineteen, Annie had suppressed her Jewish heritage. She found the issue trivial, a common attitude among assimilated Jews who tended to view the matter not in racial terms but rather as a subject of faith and culture. In the aftermath of World War II, Leifs and his (by then former) sister-in-law Marie exchanged letters in which they discussed—with much resentment on both sides—the Riethofs' attitude to their heritage. Leifs reminded Marie that it was only after years of marriage that he had become aware of his in-laws' Jewish roots, citing an early encounter during his student years in Leipzig:

> Perhaps you recall that Páll Ísólfsson and I once asked the two of you, in Gottschedstrasse in 1918, if you were Jewish, and you both replied that you weren't. This was the end of the matter as far as I was concerned. There were no Jews in Iceland and I didn't have a clear notion of what the term implied, either for or against. Prior to our marriage, Annie hinted that there was "Jewish blood" in the family. When I asked her on which side of the family this was, she evaded giving an answer. At our marriage, she presented a baptismal certificate dated 1916 and claimed that this was a clerical error, that it should read 1906. I wasn't interested in this and probably wouldn't even have noticed it.... Surely you know that this hang-up of hers pre-dates our relationship.[13]

That Leifs and Ísólfsson should have asked the Riethof sisters directly, not long after making their acquaintance, suggests that they were not completely unwitting. Still, if Annie refused to discuss the matter, Leifs may have concluded that it was of no importance. When he finally did discover his wife's racial situation, Jews were about to lose their civil rights in Germany. Non-Jews married to Jews were classified as half Jews, and the notorious Nuremberg laws, passed in 1935, banned all marriages between non-Jews and Jews, although these were not always followed to the full extent. It seems perplexing that the Leifs family should have chosen to stay in Germany for as long as they did. After the war, Leifs claimed that it was Annie who refused to leave while they still had the chance, choosing to remain on the grounds that "she wasn't Jewish, the Hitler period would soon pass, etc. etc."[14]

"ONE OF THE PUREST SOURCES..."

For an opportunist such as Leifs, the growing fascination with Nordic culture was difficult to resist. In October 1931, he lectured on his music and played the recent recording of his *Icelandic Dances* for around two hundred members of the Nazi-affiliated *Nordischer*

Ring, reporting back to Reykjavík that "they liked it well."[15] Critics were also more lavish in their praise than he had experienced before. In December 1932, the *Zeitschrift für Musik* ran a review of the *Iceland Overture,* by Fritz Tutenberg, an opera director at the Hamburg State Theater who was fascinated by Nordic culture and had enrolled in the Nazi party the previous year. Here, for the first time, a new kind of rhetoric greeted Leifs's work in print. To this critic, the overture expressed "the quintessence of new Icelandic music, with its flourishing health, strong and austere splendor, and—its absolute refusal to make concessions towards the southern European listener. . . . This music belongs to us. With greater justification than the music of the exotic peoples, which is now being presented to us in a Europeanized fashion."[16]

Four months later, the *Zeitschrift für Musik* published a "Nordic issue" that included a feature on Leifs's 25 *Icelandic Folk Songs* by Paul Treutler, a song composer and teacher who was active in the NS-Lehrerbund in Hamburg. He also endorsed Icelandic music's "pure" racial properties, contrasting its "health" with the sickness and decay of the jazz-influenced German music scene and encouraging German composers to appropriate the "vigorous" elements of Leifs's style:

> It is really not necessary to seek refuge in Negro music and to look there for artistic renewal; no, everything of which we are in need, healthy, masculine sensitivity, rhythmic individuality, etc., all this we find in a manner related to us, in delightful, young freshness in the folk music of Iceland. . . .
>
> We must create out of the foundations of these songs for our sickly modern music. Here runs one of the purest sources. Here, and not in Africa, will we find what we require: healthy sensitivity and masculine power.[17]

Here Treutler echoes the notion, asserted by Nazi ideologues since the 1920s but particularly pervasive during the first months of Hitler's Reich, that German culture was in need of "cleansing" of destructive foreign influences.[18] Two years later, Treutler again claimed a racial and aesthetic link between Nazi ideology and

Icelandic folk music, describing the latter as "blood of our blood" as well as embodying the category of the "steel-hard Romantic" (*Stählerne Romantik*)—a term borrowed directly from a speech by Propaganda Minister Joseph Goebbels in which he postulated a new, "national-heroic" age of German art.[19]

The belief that Nordic culture, including music, could serve as a regenerating force for the new Germany was already widespread by the time of the Third Reich, and it had implications for its reception there. The second half of the nineteenth century saw the rise of an ideology that postulated the existence of a Nordic race whose members were more or less solely responsible for creating all that was valuable in European culture. Fueled by growing nationalism and a combination of anti-liberalism, racism, and cultural pessimism, this ideology formed the backbone of the racial theories put forth by Count Arthur de Gobineau and later by Houston Stewart Chamberlain. In 1918, this pessimistic outlook would find its most famous expression in Oswald Spengler's *Der Untergang des Abendlandes*, where he proclaimed the impending death throes of Western civilization. Leifs had devoured this volume during his student years in Leipzig, but Spengler was also held in high regard in Iceland, where his influence can be traced in the writings of leading cultural figures in the 1920s. For Icelandic nationalists, Spengler's view of cultures as organisms in various stages of budding, flowering, and withering—with Western culture in its final stage—did not justify pessimism per se. Rather, it encouraged a sense of "enraptured faith in the future of Iceland," as this nation was only now awakening and therefore had the potential to revitalize European culture as a whole—a view that also underpins Leifs's artistic ideology.[20]

This local nationalist reading of Spengler among Icelandic intellectuals needs to be distinguished from the far more consequential influence of his work on German writers, who saw the cultivation of the Nordic race as the only means of avoiding total cultural collapse. This view was supported by the classification of racial typologies most famously expounded in the 1925 volume

Der nordische Gedanke unter den Deutschen by Hans F. K. Günther, the most widely read and influential author on racial matters in Nazi Germany.[21] In Günther's view, the Nordic movement should counteract the pessimism of Spengler's prophecy with the "victorious rebirth of the mainly Nordic people within the German population."[22] For Germany, such a racial rehabilitation—for which Günther coined the term *Aufnordung*, re-Nordicizing—would be made possible only by an increasing awareness of "the importance of the Nordic race."[23] Günther postulated the existence of a handful of distinct racial categories (*nordisch, ostisch, dinarisch*, etc.), and according to his ideology, an awareness of these racial types would be essential in the process of "purifying" the German *Volk*. This racial classification system served as the basis for all subsequent discussion on race and music in the Third Reich.

An awareness of such racial typology can be seen in many of Leifs's writings, even ones published prior to Günther's influential volumes. The earliest appearance comes in Leifs's article "Icelandic Folk Music and the German Manner of Feeling," published in *Die Musik* in 1923, where he distinguishes between "northern" and "southern" music and lists the characteristics of each in tabular form. According to Leifs, southern music was sentimental, gentle, and verbose while that of the Nordic race was clear, harsh, and terse and did not succumb easily to the influence of others.[24] These main components of what, to Leifs, constituted the Nordic style formed the basis of his style and ideology throughout his career. He expressed similar notions in several articles published in Germany throughout the 1920s and early 1930s, including his critique of Toscanini as well as an essay praising the Nordic elements of Busoni's style. In 1934, Leifs was taken to task by one writer for having suggested that Verdi was more Nordic than Wagner, which Leifs contended was true, while he admitted to being a mere "amateur in race studies."[25] He was at least aware of the increasing prominence of a racial direction in Nazi scholarship at this time, including the 1932 book *Music and Race* (*Musik und Rasse*) by SS officer Richard Eichenauer.[26] Still, in his writings Leifs rarely ventured beyond the northern-southern dichotomy of his 1923 article, which later resurfaced in his manifesto, the monograph *Islands künstlerische Anregung*, written during World War II but published only in 1950. That Leifs should have considered this manuscript suitable for publication in the postwar era shows how oblivious he was to the implications of promoting the questionable science of Günther's racial anthropology.

German interest in the exotic, unknown, and mysterious north had a long history by the time the Nazis came to power, having been awakened decades earlier by Emperor Wilhelm II's frequent and much-reported travels to Norway. Societies devoted to Nordic culture flourished, the most influential being the Nordic Society, *Nordische Gesellschaft,* founded in Lübeck in 1921. Once the Nazis took power it came under the spell of party ideologue Alfred Rosenberg, and its main goal became to further awareness of the cultural superiority of the Nordic race.[27] Thousands attended the society's festivals, the so-called *Reichstagungen* held annually from 1934 to 1939. Two of the Nazis' leading music critics, Fritz Stege and Herbert Gerigk, were partial to the cause and spoke highly of Nordic music in their writings. Following the Nordische Gesellschaft festival in Lübeck in 1935, Gerigk wrote that the "ideological awakening that now spreads through Germany and all of Europe has sharpened our appreciation for the art of the Nordic spirit. At last, it seems as if the primacy of southern music has been broken once and for all."[28]

At around the same time, an up-and-coming Nazi member, Hermann Killer, praised Nordic music in *Völkischer Beobachter,* the Nazis' official broadsheet. Killer was the *VB*'s leading music critic and would eventually work his way to a top position at Rosenberg's *Kulturpolitisches Archiv.* In his review of a 1935 Nordic concert by the Berlin Philharmonic, at which Leifs's *Iceland Overture* was performed alongside works by Grieg and Sibelius, Killer proclaimed that nowhere was the national essence clearer than in Nordic music: "Here flows the living blood-stream from its source in primeval folk music and all the way to the present, and reveals the eternal continuity of blood, earth, and race [*Blut, Boden und Rasse*], even in different styles and the most diverse schools and personalities."[29] Killer was in no doubt over who was the "clearest and most unique" example of a Nordic personality in music. His name was Jón Leifs.

While the overall importance of the Nazis' glorification of Nordic culture should not be overestimated, it did have some impact on German musical life. Scandinavian music was performed more frequently than before, and local composers drew inspiration from Nordic themes—whether in music, text, or subject matter. Interest was most strongly felt among post-Wagnerian opera composers, although Wagner's version of the Nordic mythology in the *Ring Cycle* was so all-encompassing as to largely discourage further elaboration.[30] Later composers instead mined the ancient Icelandic sagas—in works such as Paul von Klenau's *Kjartan und Gudrun* (1917), a reworking of *Laxdæla saga*—or invented new stories inspired by the saga literature. An example of a newly fashioned Viking age opera is *Island-Saga* (1924), by Georg Vollerthun, which received several productions in Germany during the Nazi era.[31] Paul Winter, a former student of Hans Pfitzner in Berlin, drew on ancient Eddic poetry for his *Das Lied von Helge dem Hundingstöter* in 1936 (to a text that Leifs later set in his own *Lay of Helgi the Hunding-Slayer*), and the same year Max Drischner penned a powerful organ work titled *Nordic Toccata and Fugue*. Still another sign of the Nazi fascination with Iceland was the popular song "Wer will mit uns nach Island ziehn," originally a Flemish folk tune, which appeared in dozens of printed songbooks during the Third Reich, including those of the *Hitlerjugend*.[32]

Such a climate was of course conducive to the general promotion of Leifs's music, as can be seen from the rather alarming coincidence that he should finalize an extensive publishing contract just as the Nazis took power.[33] A total of seventeen works were published in 1933, including his largest compositions to date: *Galdra-Loftr*, the *Iceland Cantata*, and the Organ Concerto. During the next few years, hardly a month went by without Leifs receiving mention in prominent German music periodicals, most often through the review of a score or a concert performance. Given his cultivation of the vernacular within a novel musical language, Leifs fit well into the mold of the Nordic "exotic-original national composer."[34] While reviews of his music in the Third Reich were often mixed, aspects of his modernist style that were not easily reconciled with Nazi aesthetics were often described in multivalent terms such as *eigenartig*—peculiar, strange, odd—that left room for interpretation on behalf of the reader. Discussion of Leifs's works in newspapers and music journals largely consisted of oft-repeated clichés about Nordic nature and landscape rather than perceptive analytical commentary. In her study of Sibelius reception in Nazi Germany, Ruth-Maria Gleißner notes that Leifs and Sibelius were unique in this regard: the music of other Nordic composers did not evoke the topoi of landscape and nature in critics' minds to the same extent.[35] Yet in the case of Leifs, such Nordic exoticism had influenced the reception of his music prior to the Third Reich, and it was by no means limited to German critics or Nazi sympathizers. For example, the Nobel laureate and musicologist Romain Rolland was delighted by the songs that Leifs sent to him in Switzerland in November 1933, remarking that they exuded a "masculine originality" that reminded him of the deep roar of the ocean: "I salute the great island that sings through your voice."[36]

Leifs also benefited from his friendship with a high-ranking Nazi officer, Ernst Züchner, who became the head of the Nordic division of Goebbels's Ministry of Public Enlightenment and Propaganda (RMVP) in autumn 1933. The two had struck up a friendship in 1925, when Züchner worked at the Berlin music magazine *Echo*, which published some of Leifs's articles. Züchner was a devoted Scandophile who had made his home in Oslo for a while and journeyed to Iceland in 1924; he had translated novels into German from the Norwegian and Icelandic and belonged to the Friends of Iceland society in Berlin. Writing to Leifs at the start of their acquaintance, he expressed his hope that "we Germans can once again have a solid connection to those who are of a related race. May the new co-operation be richly fruitful!"[37] Züchner had joined the Nazi party in 1927 and received his first post at Goebbels's ministry only a few months into the regime, eventually being assigned tasks at the top level. It was Züchner who took notes, seated behind a curtain, at Hitler's disastrous meeting with the Norwegian author Knut Hamsun in 1943. There, at the sumptuous Berghof villa in the Bavarian Alps, Hamsun protested the Nazis' occupation policy with such fervor that he unleashed the Führer's fury, and the meeting came to a premature end.[38]

The sincerity of Züchner's Nazi convictions is difficult to ascertain. Historian Þór Whitehead, who has researched his career in the Third Reich, concludes that he was thoroughly unpredictable.[39] Züchner later claimed that he had often spoken up against Hitler, and he certainly got into trouble for openly accusing Rosenberg of wishing to usurp the Propaganda Ministry's Nordic division. For this, Züchner was reprimanded by Goebbels himself, and this delayed his advancement for the next few years.[40] Züchner was highly regarded among Icelanders in Berlin and was honored with the Icelandic Order of the Falcon in 1938 for "advancing Icelandic culture in Germany."[41] For all his questionable politics, Züchner proved a valuable friend to Leifs, promoting his work and later assisting the family in their departure from Germany at the eleventh hour.

LEIFS AND THE PERMANENT COUNCIL FOR INTERNATIONAL COOPERATION AMONG COMPOSERS

Despite the Nazis' interest in Nordic music, Leifs still had difficulty procuring performances of his works, and money was always scarce. At the start of 1934, he ran out of funds yet again and had to cancel a trip to Aachen, where the cathedral choir premiered his *Kyrie* on January 5. "It's like a curse on me, that I don't get to hear my own works," he lamented to his sister in Iceland.[42] Reviews were decidedly mixed. One critic said the *Kyrie* had left a "dark, painful effect" while another praised the "unusual modern work, full of Germanic feeling."[43]

More felicitous tidings seemed to come later that spring. Leifs was invited, as Iceland's representative, to become a founding member of a new organization to promote international cultural exchange as well as composers' moral right (*droit moral*), the legal ability to assert control over the way their works were used.[44] The *Ständiger Rat für die internationale Zusammenarbeit der Komponisten* (Permanent Council for International Cooperation among Composers) was founded by Richard Strauss, with Goebbels's support, and operated under the wing of the *Reichsmusikkammer*, the Nazi music council. This was the Nazi regime's response to the liberal, cosmopolitan values of the ISCM (International Society for Contemporary Music), a powerful force in European music since its founding in 1922. The ISCM's promotion of composers such as Schoenberg, Stravinsky, and Webern had led to Germany's secession from the society, denouncing its activities as "cultural bolshevism."[45] The Permanent Council was an instrument of Nazi cultural propaganda, offering an ultraconservative, nationalist vision of cultural cooperation while at the same time displaying to its foreign delegates the image of a peaceful and tolerant Germany.[46] Its first meeting took place in Wiesbaden in June 1934, and thirteen countries were represented: Germany, Austria, Sweden, Denmark, Iceland, Finland, Poland, Czechoslovakia, France, Belgium, England, Italy, and Switzerland. By the time of its final meeting, in 1942, another eleven countries had joined.[47] The council's main activity was to sponsor one or two international music festivals annually—these took place in Venice, Hamburg, Vichy, Stockholm, Dresden, Stuttgart, and Frankfurt—where the music was mostly reactionary, neoclassic, or neo-Romantic or exhibited a folklike influence.

Leifs's participation in a society largely made up of composers thought to be partial to the Nazi cause was of course politically dubious, and involvement would later cast a shadow on all those who lent it their name. Like Leifs, most of the members were not only composers but also representatives of composers' organizations in their home countries.[48] The Permanent Council's minutes suggest that Leifs mostly saw the enterprise as a vehicle for self-promotion as well as a logical consequence of his earlier efforts at cultural exchange between Iceland and Germany, such as the Hamburg Philharmonic tour.[49] He was the Permanent Council's youngest member and claimed—after the war—to have been the group's "black sheep."[50] He certainly did not share the traditionalist stylistic tendencies of most of its members, and the council's antiliberal goals conflicted with his own ideals of broad international cooperation regardless of ideology. For example, Leifs himself had a hand in arranging Iceland's entry into the ISCM, backed by musicologist Edward Dent (ISCM's president); he was also instrumental in founding the Icelandic division of the literary PEN Club, another association whose liberal goals were anathema to the Nazi regime.[51] At the very least, membership in the Nazi's Permanent Council gave Leifs a chance to hobnob with highly regarded musicians such as Richard Strauss, Emil Nikolaus von Reznicek, and Siegmund von Hausegger; the latter two were both members of the esteemed Prussian Academy of the Arts. Others were unimpressed. From Dent, Leifs heard that his former mentor, the left-wing conductor Hermann Scherchen, was "furious" at him for lending his name to such a questionable enterprise.[52]

Kurt Atterberg and Yrjö Kilpinen represented Sweden and Finland, respectively. For them, participation seems to have encouraged wider performance of their music, since few Nordic composers were performed as frequently in Hitler's Germany as they were (with the exception of Sibelius). Leifs and Atterberg had been adversaries ever since participating in a Nordic week in Kiel in the summer of 1929. Among the works performed there was Atterberg's Sixth Symphony, which had just won the $10,000 first prize in a competition sponsored by the Columbia Gramophone Company, for a work inspired by Schubert's *Unfinished*. Atterberg's work was more coolly received than Leifs's *Iceland Overture*, but the Swedish composer got his revenge with a scathing review of Leifs's work in a Stockholm newspaper: "Does this man have any talent at all, or is this work the result of some kind of musical experimentation? This is the question that lingered after hearing his patriotic overture. It can only be answered after hearing other works by the same author. Then we shall find out whether Jón Leifs is a fumbling experimenter, doggedly stubborn, or whether he is simply completely lacking in skill and talent."[53] Leifs, who also disliked Atterberg's music, was unlikely to forget such a bashing.[54] Yet he presumably found it wise to bury the hatchet, since his participation in the Permanent Council made personal contact between them unavoidable.

Leifs was delighted by the results of the first meeting, writing to Annie that he had experienced "all kinds of interesting and useful things."[55] He waited until his return to tell her that in Wiesbaden he had fallen in love with another woman: the twenty-seven-year old harpist Ursula Lentrodt (see fig. 6.1.). She had recently taken a position with the Berlin *Deutschlandsender* orchestra and later joined the Bavarian Radio Symphony, but most of her career was devoted to teaching; she held a professorship at the Munich Conservatory and was for decades among Germany's most esteemed harp pedagogues.[56] The Leifses' marriage had been unraveling, and the imbalance in their relationship became even more pronounced after Annie abandoned her career as pianist—such as it was. The earliest signs of trouble are found in letters from the summer of 1930, when Leifs was in Travemünde completing the Organ Concerto while Annie traveled to Leipzig to gather interest in her husband's music among local publishers. In one of his letters, Leifs admitted to having kissed a certain Fräulein Boldt from Berlin.[57] He told his indignant wife that he could not help flirting with other women and showed no sense of remorse: "I am a completely ordinary man, with the best of masculine inclinations, and can under these circumstances not have the least sense of guilt."[58] Annie reacted by continually putting her husband's needs above all else. She had mastered the art of self-sacrifice, admitting to Leifs that she found it "beautiful to live for making others happy."[59]

As it happened, Ursula Lentrodt scorned Leifs's advances, for she was in the midst of an affair with Carl Schuricht, the well-known

Figure 6.1. Harpist Ursula Lentrodt in 1937. © ullstein bild / GRANGER—All rights reserved.

conductor of the Wiesbaden orchestra.[60] Even the solo work that Leifs wrote for her later that year, a *Nocturne* for harp op. 19a, failed to melt her heart, and she never performed it in public. It is not among Leifs's most successful works, but then the delicate sounds of the harp were never an integral part of his dynamic soundscape. He employed the instrument only briefly, for coloristic effect, in two of his mature orchestral scores (*Edda I* and *Baldr*).

SUCCESS IN GERMANY, ANXIETY IN ICELAND

After the Wiesbaden meeting of the Permanent Council, Leifs sailed to Iceland, where he stayed until September. His main assignment there was to organize a Beethoven week at the National Radio, which included his own hour-long broadcast on the master's music each evening. The programs met with success and seem to have convinced the radio executives that Leifs might be a valuable addition to their staff after all. In mid-August, Ísólfsson, who had served as the National Radio's part-time music advisor, stepped down voluntarily in order to facilitate Leifs's appointment as a full-time music director.[61] As Leifs remarked to his sister, Annie was vexed by this turn of events: "She thinks it will decisively impair my future as a composer. She seems perhaps to be mostly concerned about fame, whereas you worry mostly about money, and of course you are both right to a certain degree. But still, in the deepest depths of my soul, I don't care about either if only I am able to work on the compositions that others cannot create, and can accomplish in my lifetime the musical work that remains mine alone."[62]

Leifs was back in Iceland in February 1935, now officially in the post of music director at the National Radio—his first full-time position. Ever since radio broadcasts began in Iceland in 1930, classical music had formed a substantial but fiercely contested part of the program. There were numerous complaints about what was sometimes referred to as "symphonic noise" (*symfóníugaul*), even demands that classical music be eliminated completely.[63] Instead, the ambitious Leifs was determined to make music a still more integral part of the broadcasting schedule.[64] He had plans to restructure the National Radio's live concerts, since he found the musicians currently employed—a pianist and violinist who occasionally were joined by a chamber ensemble—to be grossly inadequate.[65] Instead, he suggested broadcasting live music in a concert setting from Reykjavík's churches or theaters.[66] He also dreamed of organizing a music festival with first-rate foreign artists, to be held in Reykjavík in May and June each year—something along

Figure 6.2. Jón Leifs at the National Radio in Reykjavík, 1934. Photograph: Willem van de Poll. National Archives of the Netherlands, public domain.

the lines of the Reykjavík Arts Festival, which was established only after his death.[67] These were splendid ideas, but the board remained unimpressed, and most of them never came to fruition.

Leifs's relations with the National Radio's executive director, Jónas Þorbergsson, who had previously declared that Leifs would never be employed there under his leadership, were strained from the start. The main cause for their discord was the terms of Leifs's contract. He refused to report to work on a daily basis, insisting that he had made a verbal agreement with the board that his daily presence would not be required. Much to the director's chagrin, he spent only a couple of days each week at the radio headquarters in Reykjavík before heading out of town to compose.

Leifs hoped that his appointment at the National Radio would give him increased leverage in organizing cultural exchange between Iceland and Germany. In order to achieve his goals, he may even have inflated his job title, at least informally, since German newspapers and periodicals in those years occasionally refer to him as *Staatsmusikdirektor*, which he certainly was not.[68] As soon as Leifs returned to Germany in April 1935, he met with officials at the Danish Embassy in Berlin to present to them his ambitious plans for cultural exchange, in particular "what can be done on the German side for Icelandic literature, art and science." His ideas met with little enthusiasm. Reporting back to Copenhagen, the embassy's chargé d'affaires noted that Leifs in no way represented the Icelandic government and therefore was in no position to do anything "except to suggest his own compositions for cultural-exchange concerts."[69] The deputy for Icelandic affairs in the Danish Foreign Ministry took a similar line, advising caution since Leifs seemed to foster "ambitions towards being a kind of cultural ambassador for Iceland in general" but was not up to the task. Furthermore, according to the deputy, locals in Reykjavík were predicting that Leifs would last no more than a year in the radio job, "since he is known for being troublesome when working with others."[70]

On his return from Iceland in April 1935, Leifs stayed only a few days in Rehbrücke before heading to Wiesbaden, where his Organ Concerto was premiered at a Nordic music festival organized by the Nordische Gesellschaft. The organist Kurt Utz, a former Leipzig Conservatory student and newly appointed to Wiesbaden Cathedral, was an enthusiastic performer of new music and had written to Leifs asking to premiere the concerto.[71] The conductor, Helmuth Thierfelder, was no less impressed, declaring the work "colossal."[72]

The concerto began the festival's opening concert, at the Kurhaus on April 26, which also included works by Jean Sibelius, Knudåge

Riisager, and Johan Halvorsen. The critical reception was generally favorable, although some noted that German audiences were not accustomed to music of such force, like a "hurricane or powerful ocean wave."[73] One critic remarked that Leifs's concerto was "the most controversial work at the festival, but perhaps the most memorable" and likened it to a savage ocean storm on a Nordic coast.[74] A critic of the Nazi *Nassauer Volksblatt* declared it to be the evening's most impressive piece but admitted that it had probably disappointed those who expected "delirious excess of emotions . . . On the other hand, those who opened their mind and heart for a language that depicts the wild and raw landscape of Iceland through deep feeling for nature were deeply moved."[75] In *Zeitschrift für Musik*, the pianist-critic Grete Altstadt-Schütze, who led the Wiesbaden music division of *Kampfbund für deutsche Kultur*, praised the music for being strongly rooted in nature and being "so far from all the degeneration of culture that it captures you mercilessly with its power and harshness."[76] Only one critic truly panned the concerto. Herbert Gerigk claimed that it "drowned in noise" because of the "horrifying number of percussion instruments."[77] Although Gerigk was a minority voice, he was a powerful adversary, an up-and-coming Nazi member, and an official in Alfred Rosenberg's music division. Two years later, he became editor of the Nazi music journal *Die Musik*, and his slanderous *Lexikon der Juden in der Musik* appeared in multiple editions during the war.[78]

Meanwhile, Annie was busy trying to arrange a "Leifs evening" with the Berlin Philharmonic, convinced that a successful performance by Germany's leading orchestra would cement his reputation both there and in Iceland. The couple's interest was understandable given the Philharmonic's prestige, yet they must have been aware that such a performance would carry political undertones. In 1933 the orchestra had become Nazi Germany's "flagship cultural ambassador," operating under the direct authority of Goebbels' Propaganda Ministry.[79] To realize their ambitious plan, Leifs and Annie pursued a two-pronged strategy. Within the ministry they could count on their friend Züchner's advocacy, but Annie also frequently took the train into Berlin for meetings at the Philharmonic, where they had the support of an insider. Fritz Peppermüller, the violinist who had concertized in Reykjavík in 1923–24 with Leifs's help, had joined the Philharmonic shortly after his return to Germany and was active in the orchestra's organization. Although he only joined its *Fünferrat* (the five-member players' committee) after the war, he was presumably in a position to promote Leifs's music at the top level. The program was to include one large work by Leifs— either the Organ Concerto or *Iceland Cantata*—as well as several smaller ones.[80] Finding a conductor proved problematic; neither Furtwängler nor Erich Kleiber was in Berlin, and all other leading conductors had left Germany. Peppermüller suggested Eugen Jochum, and for a while it seemed that Paul Graener, Leifs's former composition professor, who had since ascended to the top of the Nazi bureaucracy, would be on the podium.[81]

As it happened, nothing came of the Leifs evening, but the Berlin Philharmonic did perform the *Iceland Overture* on May 23, 1935, at a Nordic concert led by Hermann Stange (see fig. 6.3). He had recently been voted the orchestra's principal conductor, replacing Furtwängler, whose objection to the Nazi ban on Hindemith's opera *Mathis der Maler* led him to resign all his posts and threaten to leave the country. Stange was a mediocre talent who had found support in the Nazi party and the Nazi-sponsored Kampfbund für deutsche Kultur, both of which he joined in 1932.[82] The orchestra is said to have adopted a "decidedly negative attitude" toward him, and perhaps a more inspired conductor would have obtained a better result. In any case, the *Iceland Overture* was less enthusiastically received than the Organ Concerto had been in Wiesbaden.[83] Some critics found it "interesting and unique," but others complained of monotony and gloom. Fritz Stege, one of Nazi Germany's most influential critics, found it "not very enjoyable."[84] Reports are also contradictory with regard to the audience's reception; one critic remarked that the ovation had been lively while another mentions "hesitant applause."[85] Still, the conductor, Stange, was pleased with the results, and plans were soon set into motion for a more substantial presentation of Leifs's works at the Philharmonie.[86]

Figure 6.3. Leifs with soprano Antonietta Toini and conductor Hermann Stange following the concert at the Berlin Philharmonie, May 23, 1935. © Leifs Archives, National and University Library, Reykjavík.

Overall, 1935 had been Leifs's most successful year as a composer thus far, and there were still further performances that summer. Through the advocacy of Richard Strauss, four of Leifs's songs (including the two op. 14a and *Ríma* op. 18a) were performed at the Permanent Council's music festival in Hamburg in June. While a minority of critics found fault with Leifs's "austere" and "lugubrious" style, the songs were generally praised for their "uncommonly memorable emotional intensity," as was soprano Adalheid Armhold's expressive and finely judged performance.[87] Even Gerigk, who had recently disparaged the Organ Concerto, found the songs to be "among the most lasting impressions" of the entire festival, thus demonstrating the ambivalence of Nazi critics toward Leifs's music overall.[88]

Leifs returned to Iceland in June to continue his work at the National Radio. Shortly after taking up his position there, he commenced a work that had been in the planning stage for at least seven years, an oratorio titled *Edda* for soloists, choir, and orchestra. When he'd first begun contemplating the work in 1928, he had intended to set only *Völuspá (Sybil's Prophecy)*, which is one of the great Eddic poems, a monologue of roughly sixty stanzas in which a seeress describes a vision of the world's beginning and collapse—the apocalyptic carnage of *ragnarök*, in which many of the gods die and the world is submerged in water. Still, destruction is followed by re-creation: the earth rises from the sea again, and a new generation of gods takes over.[89] The dimensions of the work far outgrew Leifs's initial plan. By 1930, he was referring to an "Edda oratorio" and had begun to assemble its libretto from various Eddic sources.[90] When the oratorio text was complete in May 1933, it consisted of 350 stanzas and ran to 86 typewritten pages. The work was to be divided into four individual parts: *The Creation of the World* (Sköpun heimsins), *The Lives of the Gods* (Líf guðanna), *Twilight of the Gods* (Ragnarökr), and *Resurrection* (Endurreisn). By using the Norse myths as a basis of a tetralogy, Leifs was of course inviting comparisons with Wagner's *Ring of the Nibelung*, with which he was well acquainted—Muck's conducting of *Siegfried* at the 1920 Munich Summer Festival had left a strong impression, and he had studied the score during his years at the Leipzig Conservatory. But he found Wagner's approach too romantic and sentimental for the subject matter and claimed to have written many of his own works, including the *Edda* oratorio and the *Saga Symphony*, as "a protest against Wagner, who misunderstood the Nordic character and Nordic artistic heritage so terribly."[91]

Leifs was enraptured by his concept of the *Edda* oratorio, and even the text alone had a profound effect on him, as he remarked to his sister: "parts of [the libretto] are so magnificent that they leave me breathless."[92] Yet he was daunted by the vast scale of his undertaking, admitting that it would be "quite pointless for me to embark on such a composition unless I can work at it without interruption for 2–3 years, that is, without having to worry about putting food on the table."[93] From 1930 to 1935, Leifs wrote only works of small scope—the *Icelandic Dances* for piano, organ preludes, hymn arrangements, and songs with piano—as if consciously avoiding large projects that might delay his magnum opus even further. Although Leifs set the original text, a performance in Iceland was out of the question given the work's difficulty and the large forces required. His hopes for a German premiere were fueled by the growing popularity there of the Old Icelandic poetry and sagas, available in a twenty-four-volume translation under the title *Sammlung Thule* (1911–30), which Leifs knew and praised as a "major achievement."[94]

In pursuit of solitude to compose *Edda I*, Leifs rented a room in Viðey, a small island just off the coast of Reykjavík, and traveled there by boat for sojourns of two to three days at a time. Although the island had around a hundred inhabitants at the turn of the century, by the 1930s the entire population had resettled on the mainland. Only two buildings were left standing, a church and a larger residential building, both from the mid-eighteenth century. Leifs arranged for a small organ to be moved from the church into the house, where he composed and slept in spartan surroundings: "a folding bed, a table and chair, that's all."[95] In the autumn, he worked on the oratorio at Þingvellir, reading Icelandic sagas for inspiration when he needed a break from composing.

Simultaneously, at the National Radio, things were coming to a head. Þorbergsson, the director, had only grudgingly given Leifs a two-month leave to attend the music festivals in Wiesbaden and Hamburg.[96] Now that Leifs resumed his habit of disappearing for days at a time, the director retaliated by insisting that he "appear at once, and every day, here at the radio."[97] When Leifs ignored this, the radio board deemed him to have violated his contract. Still, board members noted that his work there had been "very useful," and although Leifs was essentially fired, they created a new part-time post for him instead, consisting of three months' work a year.[98] Ísólfsson returned to the radio as part-time music advisor—the very position he had vacated earlier in order to make room for Leifs.[99] Despite all the vexation, the general consensus was that Leifs's work had been successful and that the radio's music programming had improved considerably under his direction.

It was now clear that Leifs would not, for the time being, have a full-time career in Iceland. He had complained of Reykjavík being stifling and insular, but his return to Rehbrücke proved no less of a trial. He had difficulty finding enough peace and quiet to continue work on the oratorio and finally rented a hotel room in nearby Neubabelsberg, the headquarters of the German film industry. When money ran out, as it was bound to, he returned to Rehbrücke and rented a small office not far from his and Annie's home.

Despite marital tensions, Leifs had hoped that Annie and the girls would accompany him to Iceland for his post at the National Radio. Surprising as it may seem, it was Annie who refused to leave Germany, believing that the Nazi regime could not last for long. "What a relief that we didn't all move to Reykjavík in January," she wrote in August 1935, as the radio situation was becoming intolerable. She was convinced that the Germans would eventually learn to appreciate her husband's work while Iceland had little to offer him as a full-time composer. "If you continue living [in Iceland], your creativity will never flourish," she wrote.[100] A week later she added, "The Icelanders don't realize what they have in you—a genius and patriot—it's all the same to them. Your time there has not yet come."[101]

TRIUMPH AT THE PHILHARMONIC

Leifs's moment of triumph at the Berlin Philharmonic finally arrived on March 15, 1936. While his violinist friend Peppermüller had been unable to convince the orchestra to devote an entire concert to his music, the program was instead divided between two composers: Jón Leifs and Richard Wagner. For Leifs, who was constantly vexed by Wagner's "appropriation of the Nordic," this was hardly the ideal context for his work, but the orchestra's programming reflects a certain zeitgeist: one of Hitler's favorite composers coupled with an "authentic" voice from the North. The program contained three works by Leifs: *Trilogia piccola*, three *Icelandic Dances* arranged for orchestra, and the *Iceland Cantata* performed by the Berliner Volkschor along with 50 boys, a total of 180 singers.[102] At the helm was Leo Borchard, a Russian maestro who had fled to Germany after the revolution. He enjoyed success there for a while and proved willing to compromise by directing several concerts on behalf of the Permanent Council, which is presumably how he came into contact with Leifs.[103] Nevertheless, the Nazis were suspicious of him and saw to it that from 1937—a year after the Leifs/Wagner concert—he received no further offers to conduct in Germany. Remaining in Berlin, he devoted his energies to an underground resistance movement that saved countless Jews and supported families of those persecuted for their political convictions. After the war, Borchard's spotless reputation served him well, and he was chosen to conduct the revived Berlin Philharmonic's inaugural concert only a few weeks after the city surrendered. Borchard was appointed its principal conductor shortly thereafter, but his career came to a tragic end when he was accidentally shot and killed by a US soldier in autumn 1945.[104]

Never before had Leifs's music received such publicity, and the reception was overwhelmingly positive. "It was a great success, probably the greatest my works have yet received," an ecstatic Leifs wrote to his sister.[105] The press was nearly unanimous in its praise, and the reviews were primarily devoted to Leifs, not Wagner—the headline in *B.Z. am Mittag* read, "Triumph for Jón Leifs at the Philharmonie."[106] One critic was delighted by his "interesting compositions and personal musical language"; another praised this "Nordic Bartók" for his "incomparably charming musical personality, which the Philharmonic audience greeted with uncommonly lively applause."[107] Yet, as always, a few critics were reluctant to accept Leifs's style. Friedrich Herzfeld, who later became the Berlin Philharmonic's press secretary, admitted that "the doors to Leifs's music are closed to us. One can neither approve nor dismiss it, only declare that it is completely foreign."[108]

While the Berlin Philharmonic concert was the highlight of the season for Leifs, his music was becoming increasingly prominent in other German cities. In December 1935, the Hamburg Philharmonic had given a concert of Nordic music in honor of Sibelius's seventieth birthday, which included the first outing of Leifs's *Three Verses from Hávamál* op. 4 in an orchestral guise, performed by tenor Hans Grahl under the baton of Hans Schmidt-Isserstedt. This time, critics much preferred the "youthful force" of Leifs's laconic settings to the "tender and sentimental" tones of Grieg and Atterberg, whose music was also on the program. One critic remarked that Leifs's setting demonstrated true Nordic character: not "feeble feelings, but heroism."[109] Also, in spring 1936, the Jón Leifs Society organized a "musical soirée" featuring his songs at the Hotel Kaiserhof in Berlin, which was lauded by former Hindemith pupil Konrad Noetel as "one of the more remarkable small-scale events of the concert season."[110]

In May 1936, Leifs traveled to Iceland to continue his part-time work at the National Radio. This time, he brought along with him the renowned Prague Quartet, whose acquaintance he had made through the Czech ambassador in Copenhagen. It was probably for this tour that Leifs arranged his *Variazioni Pastorali* for string quartet, although the work appears not to have made it onto their programs in the end. Leifs had initially proposed that a residency for the quartet should be funded by the radio, but when his request was denied (most likely due to the director's antipathy toward any ideas from Leifs), the Reykjavík Music Society (*Tónlistarfélagið í Reykjavík*) reacted quickly and engaged them to give six concerts in the capital. They were given a resounding reception, and Ísólfsson enthused in a review that their visit was the "most remarkable event in our musical life since the Hamburg orchestra was here."[111] Although Leifs's persistent advocacy for cultural exchange had its skeptics, it continued to provide Reykjavík with performances of a caliber it might otherwise not have experienced.

Having fulfilled his duties at the radio, Leifs was able to devote himself to the *Edda* oratorio during a two-week stay at Þingvellir in September 1936. He kept Annie updated on what he found to be a slow and laborious process: "You cannot imagine what a massive undertaking this is. Once I sat for three whole hours just writing three measures; this was no exception,—and it is mostly not

Figure 6.4. The Leifs family in Reykjavík, summer 1936. © Leifs Archives, National and University Library, Reykjavík.

the actual compositional work, but only writing down.—Since I arrived in Iceland I have progressed from page 76 to page 86; that is all."[112] Although Leifs was an astoundingly prolific letter writer, he did not compose with speed. By November 1937 he still had reached only page 151 of the full score but expressed his delight that many things in it were "indescribably beautiful!"[113]

The marriage was faring better than before, if only temporarily. Leifs and Annie attended a Nordic music festival in Stockholm in February 1936 and also took the girls to Reykjavík that summer. This was the first time that the family of four had been in Iceland together, and they seem to have enjoyed a carefree holiday in the company of friends and relatives (see fig. 6.4). The daughters were quite different in character. Snót was the more pensive and cerebral of the two; she excelled at school and was intent on university studies in languages and literature. Líf was more energetic and outgoing. Having taken piano lessons from her mother at an early age, she had turned to the violin and was a promising young musician.

Leifs returned to Germany via London, where he tried to promote his music without success. The director of the Globe Theater on Shaftesbury Avenue had no interest in *Galdra-Loftr*; Adrian Boult, music director of the BBC Symphony Orchestra, was indifferent to his works; John Barbirolli was out of town.[114] On his return to Rehbrücke in October, the family moved from the wooden house at Moltkestrasse to a flat at Am Wiesengrund 2, only a few streets away. There, Leifs had an office in the attic and woke at 7:30 a.m. each day to compose.[115]

In May 1937, the Permanent Council for International Cooperation among Composers sponsored a music festival in Dresden, which Leifs and Annie attended at the expense of the German government. The festival was organized by Emil von Reznicek, the council's German representative, who had selected the *Iceland Cantata* for the program, judging it to be a "very interesting work."[116] The performers at the Gewerbehaus concert on May 28, 1937, were first-rate: the Dresden Philharmonic; the choir of the *Dresdner Lehrergesangverein*; and the boys' choir of the Wettiner School, led by Paul van Kempen, the orchestra's Dutch-born principal conductor (who later became Herbert von Karajan's successor in Aachen). Despite Kempen's best efforts, the choir was unable to learn the entire work in time for the concert. Only four movements of seven were performed, this time in a splendid translation by Wolfgang Mohr, one of Germany's leading experts in Old Norse.[117] Leifs was displeased with the concert, and judging from reviews it seems that the remainder of the program—a *Marien-Kantate* by his former teacher Paul Graener, and *Sången* by his old nemesis Kurt Atterberg—elicited a stronger audience response. Still, a few critics praised the "considerable triumph" of his cantata and were impressed by the music's alternation of a "dream-like, veiled horizon, and sparkling light."[118]

Back in Berlin, Leifs was among the guests of honor at a grand though politically suspect social event. Two of the largest Nordic organizations in Germany, *Nordische Gesellschaft* and *Nordische Verbindungsstelle*, joined to celebrate the three Nordic composers in attendance at the Dresden festival: Leifs, Yrjö Kilpinen, and

Figure 6.5. The Nordic composers Christian Sinding (*far left*), Leifs, and Yrjö Kilpinen listen to the Hitler Youth perform Nordic folk songs at a reception by Nordische Verbindungsstelle in Berlin, May 31, 1937. © Leifs Archives, National and University Library, Reykjavík.

Christian Sinding (see fig. 6.5). Leifs had on occasion been invited to receptions hosted by the Nordische Verbindungsstelle, but this was the only occasion at which he was a guest of honor. It is unclear whether he was fully aware of the implications of appearing alongside Kilpinen and Sinding, both of whom were overtly supportive of the Nazi regime. He may have found himself drawn to the event out of duty, as the only one of the three composers based in Berlin, or perhaps he mistakenly hoped that his attendance would facilitate further performances of his works. But while Leifs's presence was suspect, it seems no less remarkable that representatives of the Propaganda Ministry, the Foreign Ministry, *Reichsmusikkammer*, and the Prussian Academy of the Arts should have been willing to raise their glasses in his honor at this occasion.[119] By summer 1937, Leifs's position in the Third Reich had become uncertain at best, and his career was about to begin its downward spiral.

NOTES

1. Bond signed by Ragnheiður Bjarnadóttir, April 4, 1933.
2. Leifs to Ragnheiður Bjarnadóttir, May 9, 1933.
3. Leifs to Ragnheiður Bjarnadóttir, May 19, 1933.
4. Leifs to Þórey Þorleifsdóttir, July 30, 1933.
5. Leifs to Þórey Þorleifsdóttir, September 15, 1933.
6. Leifs to Thilo von Trotha, November 23, 1933, Bundesarchiv, Berlin, Nordische Gesellschaft NS 8/221. See also Ásgeir Guðmundsson, *Berlínarblús: Íslenskir meðreiðarsveinar og fórnarlömb þýskra nasista*, 1st edition (Reykjavík: Skjaldborg, 1996), 285–86.
7. Ruth-Maria Gleißner, *Der unpolitische Komponist als Politikum* (Frankfurt am Main: Peter Lang, 2002); Lesley A. Sprout, *The Musical Legacy of Wartime France* (Berkeley: University of California Press, 2013). For a more critical (and contentious) view of Sibelius's interaction with the Nazi regime, see Timothy Jackson, "Sibelius the Political," in *Sibelius in the Old and New World: Aspects of His Music, Its Interpretation, and Reception*, eds. Timothy L. Jackson, Veijo Murtomäki, Colin Davis, and Timo Virtanen, Interdisziplinäre Studien zur Musik, eds. Tomi Mäkelä and Tobias R. Klein, vol. 6 (Frankfurt am Main: Peter Lang, 2010), 69–123.
8. Leifs, "Dichtung von Mund zu Mund. Das künstlerische Erleben der Isländer-Sagas," *Nationalsozialistische Lehrerzeitung* 3 (1935): 17.
9. Jonathan Petropoulos, *Artists under Hitler: Collaboration and Survival in Nazi Germany* (New Haven: Yale University Press, 2014), 3.
10. Testimony signed by Ludwig Gies, Cologne, December 2, 1960.
11. Testimonies by Helgi Briem, Kristján Albertsson, and Jón Helgason are preserved in the National Archives of Iceland, Reykjavík (Icelandic Foreign Ministry 1996-B/484).
12. For a survey of Nazism in Iceland, see Hrafn Jökulsson and Illugi Jökulsson, *Nasistar á Íslandi* (Reykjavík: Tákn, 1988).
13. Leifs to Marie Müller, March 20, 1946.
14. Leifs to Berta Geissmar, June 22, 1946.
15. Leifs to Þórey Þorleifsdóttir, October 7, 1931.
16. Fritz Tutenberg, "Jón Leifs: Island-Ouvertüre op. 9," *Zeitschrift für Musik* 99 (1932): 1087.
17. Paul Treutler, "Islandische Volkslieder," *Zeitschrift für Musik* 100 (1933): 329, 333. See also Karen Painter, "Polyphony and Racial Identity: Schoenberg, Heinrich Berl, and Richard Eichenauer," *Music and Politics* 5, no 2 (2011): 13n49.

18. Pamela M. Potter, *Art of Suppression: Confronting the Nazi Past in Histories of the Visual and Performing Arts* (Oakland: University of California Press, 2016), 20.

19. Paul Treutler, "Stählerne Romantik—Über die Musik Alt-Islands," *Die Sonne, Zeitschrift für nordische Weltanschauung* 12 (1935): 176–79.

20. Hallberg, *Halldór Laxness*, 61–62; see also Rastrick, *Háborgin*, 118. For Leifs's endorsement of Spengler see *Islands künstlerische Anregung*, 98, 108.

21. Hans-Jürgen Lutzhöft, *Der Nordische Gedanke in Deutschland 1920–1940* [Stuttgart: Ernst Klett Verlag, 1971 (Kieler Historische Studien 14)], 32.

22. Hans F. K. Günther, *Der Nordische Gedanke unter den Deutschen*, 2nd ed. (Munich: J. F. Lehmanns, 1927), 25.

23. Günther, *Der Nordische Gedanke*, 39.

24. Leifs, "Isländische Volksmusik und germanische Empfindungsart," *Die Musik* 16 (1923): 43–52.

25. Leifs, "Mißdeutung der Rasse," *Allgemeine Musikzeitung*, July 13, 1934; the article leading to Leifs's rebuttal was Lothar Gottlieb Tirala, "Musik und Rassenseele," *Die Sonne* 11 (1934): 103–15.

26. Potter, *Most German of the Arts*, 177–80. Leifs cites Eichenauer in his article "Mißdeutung der Rasse," see n. 25, above.

27. See Birgitta Almgren, Jan Hecker-Stampehl, and Ernst Piper, "Alfred Rosenberg und die Nordische Gesellschaft: Der 'Nordische Gedanke' in Theorie und Praxis," *NORDEUROPAforum* 11, no 2 (2008): 7–51.

28. Herbert Gerigk, "Triumph nordischer Musik," *Die Musik* 27 (1935): 733.

29. Hermann Killer, "Nordischer Abend in der Philharmonie," *Völkischer Beobachter*, May 25, 1935.

30. For an account of German operas based on Nordic mythology in the late nineteenth and early twentieth centuries, see Barbara Eichner, *History in Mighty Sounds: Musical Constructions of German National Identity 1848–1914* (Woodbridge: Boydell, 2012), 117–162 and passim.

31. Fred K. Prieberg, *Handbuch Deutsche Musiker* (Kiel, 2005), CD-ROM.

32. Prieberg, *Handbuch Deutsche Musiker*. The original tune ("Alle, die wollen naer Island gaen") is printed in Charles E. H. de Coussemaker, *Chants populairs des Flamands de France* (Gent, 1856).

33. This was indeed a coincidence, since Leifs had been trying to secure a deal with Kistner & Siegel since 1927. See Kistner & Siegel to Leifs, September 17, 1927.

34. Gleißner, *Der unpolitische Komponist als Politikum*, 49.

35. Gleißner, *Der unpolitische Komponist als Politikum*, 362.

36. Romain Rolland to Leifs, December 1, 1933; also cited in Kristján Albertsson's eulogy for Leifs, *Lesbók Morgunblaðsins*, May 11, 1969, reprinted in *Menn og málavextir* (Reykjavík: Almenna bókafélagið, 1988), 94.

37. Ernst Züchner to Leifs, February 28, 1925.

38. Ingar Sletten Kolloen, *Hamsun—Erobreren* (Oslo: Gyldendal, 2004), 280–86; Tore Rem, *Knut Hamsun: Reisen til Hitler* (Oslo: Cappelen Damm, 2014), 277–81.

39. Þór Whitehead, *Milli vonar og ótta* (Reykjavík: Almenna bókafélagið, 1995), 116.

40. Åhlén, *Jón Leifs*, 206–7.

41. Ásgeir Guðmundsson, *Berlínar-blús: Íslenskir meðreiðarsveinar og fórnarlömb þýskra nasista*, 2nd edition (Reykjavík: Skrudda, 2009), 345.

42. Leifs to Þórey Þorleifsdóttir, January 9, 1934.

43. Albert Schneider, "Zweite internationale Tagung für kath. Kirchenmusik," *Kölnische Volkszeitung*, January 8, 1934; *Gelsenkirchener Zeitung*, January 8, 1934. Two reviewers mentioned that no applause was forthcoming after the dissonant concluding chord; see, for example, W. Kemp, "Neue katholische Kirchenmusik," *Kölnische Zeitung*, January 6, 1934.

44. Benjamin G. Martin, *The Nazi-Fascist New Order for European Culture* (Cambridge, MA: Harvard University Press, 2016), 21.

45. Anton Haefeli and Reinhard Oehlschlägel, "International Society for Contemporary Music," *The New Grove Dictionary of Music and Musicians*, eds. Stanley Sadie and John Tyrell (London: Macmillan, 2001), volume 12, 496–97.

46. Petra Garberding, "Musik, Moral und Politik: Richard Strauss, Kurt Atterberg und der Ständige Rat für die internationale Zusammenarbeit der Komponisten," in *Richard Strauss im Europäischen Kontext: Richard Strauss-Jahrbuch 2011* (Vienna: Richard Strauss-Gesellschaft, 2011), 243.

47. The countries were Norway, Holland, Bulgaria, Yugoslavia, Hungary, Greece, Croatia, Spain, Slovakia, Portugal, and Romania. Japan requested to join the Ständiger Rat in 1942.

48. Martin, *The Nazi-Fascist New Order*, 24.

49. Michael H. Kater, *Composers of the Nazi Era: Eight Portraits* (Oxford: Oxford University Press, 2002), 92.

50. Leifs to Berta Geissmar, June 22, 1946.

51. Leifs to Berta Geissmar, June 22, 1946; Martin, *The Nazi-Fascist New Order*, 13.

52. Leifs to Albert Einstein, November 4, 1935, Alfred Einstein Papers, Jean Gray Hargrove Music Library, University of California, Berkeley. Interestingly, Leifs's draft of the letter (in the Leifs Collection, Reykjavík) contains the following sentence that has been crossed out by Annie and does not appear in the final version (which was sent from Rehbrücke): "Unfortunately the circumstances hinder me in expressing myself as explicitly as I would like." At least this proves that Leifs was aware of Nazi censorship, and

it suggests that he believed his views on certain aspects of his participation would not be to the authorities' liking.

53. Kurt Atterberg, "Tysk-nordisk musikfest i Kiel," *Stockholms-tidningen*, June 26, 1929.

54. See, for example, Leifs to Kristján Albertsson, October 13, 1932.

55. Leifs to Annie Leifs, June 7, 1934.

56. Åhlén, *Jón Leifs*, 178.

57. Leifs to Annie Leifs, June 3, 1930.

58. Leifs to Annie Leifs, June 5, 1930.

59. Annie Leifs to Leifs, October 5, 1935.

60. Leifs's Swedish biographer, Carl-Gunnar Åhlén, tracked Lentrodt down in Berlin in 1998 and persuaded her to tell her side of the story; see Åhlén, *Jón Leifs*, 183.

61. Leifs to Annie Leifs, August 19, 1934. Leifs was hired with a contract valid from January 1, 1935, to September 30, 1936, for a monthly salary of 600 krónur. See also Gunnar Stefánsson, *Útvarp Reykjavík: Saga Ríkisútvarpsins 1930–1960* (Reykjavík: Sögufélag, 1997), 98–100.

62. Leifs to Þórey Þorleifsdóttir, October 24, 1934.

63. See, for example, Björgvin Guðmundsson, "Hugvekja," *Heimir, söngmálablað* 2 (1936): 12; "Umræðuefni dagsins," *Alþýðublaðið*, January 9, 1939; Sveinn Bjarman, "Tónmenntir," *Stígandi* 2 (1944): 193.

64. Bjarki Sveinbjörnsson, "Tónlistin á Íslandi, með sérstakri áherslu á upphaf og þróun elektrónískrar tónlistar á árunum 1960–1990" (PhD diss., Aalborg University, 1997), 62.

65. Leifs, *Útvarp og tónment: opinber skýrsla* (Reykjavík: Tónlistarvinir í Reykjavík, 1938), 6.

66. Leifs, *Útvarp og tónment*, 5–6.

67. Marianne Langewiesche, "Kunst und Runfunk in Island," interview with Leifs in *National-Zeitung Essen*, February 2, 1935.

68. See, for example, A-B., "Philharmonie und Beethovensaal: Musik aus Island und Polen," *Nachtausgabe* Berlin, May 24, 1935.

69. Rigsarkivet Copenhagen, Herluf Zahle to Jon Krabbe, October 15, 1934 (Rigsarkivet, Udenrigsministeriet, Gruppeordnede sager 1909–1945, 9.U.7).

70. Rigsarkivet Copenhagen, Jon Krabbe to Herluf Zahle, October 18, 1934 (Rigsarkivet, Udenrigsministeriet, Gruppeordnede sager 1909–1945, 9.U.7).

71. Erwin Althaus and Peter Brusius, *Kurt Utz 1901–1974—Universitätsmusikdirektor der Philipps-Universität Marburg 1949–1966* (Marburg: Rathaus-Verlag, 1996), 89–90.

72. Helmuth Thierfelder to Leifs, April 13, 1935. On Thierfelder's advocacy for Nordic music, and that of Sibelius in particular, see Gleißner, *Der unpolitische Komponist als Politikum*, 141–42.

73. Theodor Obermann, "Nordische Musik in Wiesbaden," *National-Sozialistische Zeitung Rheinfront*, May 13, 1935.

74. Hans Piroth, "Nordische Musiktage," *Germania*, May 4, 1935.

75. *Nassauer Volksblatt*, April 28, 1935.

76. Grete Altstadt-Schütze, "'Nordische Musiktage' im Kurhaus Wiesbaden," *Zeitschrift für Musik* 102 (1935): 688.

77. Herbert Gerigk, "Nordische Musik in Wiesbaden," *Die Musik* 27 (1935): 686.

78. Pamela M. Potter, "Herbert Gerigk," *The New Grove Dictionary of Music and Musicians*, volume 9, 699; Jonathan Petropoulos, *Artists Under Hitler*, 93.

79. Misha Aster, *The Reich's Orchestra: The Berlin Philharmonic, 1933–1945* (Oakville: Mosaic, 2012), iii.

80. Kistner & Siegel to Leifs, April 17, 1935.

81. Annie Leifs to Leifs, February 7, 1935; Leifs to Þórey Þorleifsdóttir, November 24, 1935.

82. Aster, *The Reich's Orchestra*, 26.

83. Aster, *The Reich's Orchestra*, 28.

84. Wohlfart, *Deutsche Allgemeine Zeitung*, May 24, 1935 ("Eine bewußte Monotonie"); W. Sachse, *Steglitzer Anzeiger*, May 24, 1935 ("die in ihrer Dumpfheit und Unerlöstheit wenig befriedigt"); Walter Hirschberg, *Signale für die musikalische Welt*, May 29, 1935 ("interessantes und eigenartiges"); Fritz Stege, "Berliner Musikbrief," *Der Mitteldeutsche* (Dessau), June 1, 1935 ("die wenig erfreuliche Island-Ouvertüre von Jon Leifs").

85. Walter Hirschberg, *Signale für die musikalische Welt*, May 29, 1935 ("für dessen lebhaften Erfolg der anwesende Autor persönlich danken konnte"); G. H., "Nordischer Abend des Philharmonischen Orchesters," *Berliner Börsenzeitung*, May 24, 1935 ("Ihr galt auch wohl zumeist der zögernde Beifall der Hörer.").

86. Hermann Stange to Leifs, May 31, 1935.

87. Emanuel Kretschmer, "Internationales Tonkünstlerfest in Hamburg," *Deutsche Militär-Musiker-Zeitung*, June 22, 1935; Wilhelm Matthes, "Das Hamburger Tonkünstlerfest," *Schlesische Zeitung* (Breslau), June 8, 1935.

88. Herbert Gerigk, "Das Tonkünstlerfest in Hamburg," *Völkischer Beobachter*, July 14, 1935.

89. Vésteinn Ólason, "Old Icelandic Poetry," in *A History of Icelandic Literature*, ed. Daisy Neijmann, 10–11.

90. Leifs to Rudolf Ewald Zingel, April 7, 1930.

91. Leifs, "Ég mótmæli—Ég ákæri, Orðsending frá tónskáldi mánaðarins," typewritten document, March 1, 1968. Leifs found both Wagner's music and his poetry, in particular the *Stabreim* employed in the *Ring Cycle*, too feeble and rhythmically ineffective. He only professed a liking for the *Flying Dutchman* overture, which is hardly surprising given its emphasis on the interval of the fifth and its depiction of a raging storm; see Leifs, *Islands künstlerische Anregung*, 23, 36.

92. Leifs to Þórey Þorleifsdóttir, May 29, 1932.

93. Leifs to Þórey Þorleifsdóttir, April 9, 1932.

94. Leifs, "Dichtung von Mund zu Mund. Das künstlerische Erleben der Isländer-Sagas," *Rheinisch-Westfälische Zeitung*, December 1, 1933; *Der Tag* (Berlin), December 2, 1933. There is substantial literature on the reception of Old Icelandic literature in nineteenth- and early twentieth-century Germany; see for example Julia Zernack, "Old Norse-Icelandic Literature and German Culture," in *Iceland and Images of the North*, ed. Sumarliði R. Ísleifsson with the collaboration of Daniel Chartier (Québec: Presses de l'Université du Québec and Reykjavík: ReykjavíkurAkademían, 2011), 157–86; Zernack, "Nordische Mythen und Edda-Zitate im Dienst von Politik und Propaganda," in *Eddische Götter und Helden, Milieus und Medien ihrer Rezeption*, ed. Katja Schulz (Heidelberg: Universitätsverlag Winter, 2011), 143–86.

95. Leifs to Annie Leifs, June 28, 1935. See also Leifs to Annie Leifs, June 24, 1935; Annie Leifs to Leifs, July 9, 1935.

96. Leifs to Jónas Þorbergsson, March 21, 1935.

97. Jónas Þorbergsson to Leifs, July 3, 1935.

98. Minutes of Iceland National Radio board meeting, August 21, 1935.

99. Jónas Þorbergsson to Leifs, August 23 and 30, 1935; Ministry of Justice to Leifs, September 4, 1935; Sigfús Sigurhjartarson to Leifs, November 22, 1935.

100. Annie Leifs to Leifs, August 11, 1935.

101. Annie Leifs to Leifs, August 19, 1935.

102. Kistner & Siegel to Leifs, February 12, 1936.

103. Matthias Sträßner, *Der Dirigent, der nicht mitspielte: Leo Borchard 1899–1945* (Berlin: Lukas Verlag, 2017), 170.

104. Matthias Sträßner, *Der Dirigent*, 172–73, 365–96.

105. Leifs to Þórey Þorleifsdóttir, March 20, 1936.

106. M., "Jon Leifs' Erfolg in der Philharmonie," *B.Z. am Mittag*, March 16, 1936.

107. R.W., "Isländische Tonschöpfungen," *Berliner Lokalanzeiger*, March 19, 1936; J. Rfr., "Musik aus Island," *Berliner Morgenpost*, March 17, 1936.

108. Friedrich Herzfeld, "Aus dem Berliner Musikleben," *Allgemeine Musik-Zeitung*, March 28, 1936. See also F.H., "Musik aus Nord, aus West und aus

dem Himmel," *Wochenschau Berlin*, March 19, 1936 ("We stand before Leifs's Icelandic music as if before a kingdom that is closed to us.").

109. Siegfried Scheffler, "Konzert der Nordischen Gesellschaft," *Hamburger Nachrichten*, December 9, 1935.

110. K. F. Noetel, review in *Die Musikpflege* (Leipzig), July 1936.

111. Páll Ísólfsson, "Fyrstu tónleikar Prag-kvartettsins," *Morgunblaðið*, June 7, 1936.

112. Leifs to Annie Leifs, September 20, 1936.

113. Leifs to Annie Leifs, November 9, 1937.

114. Romland Kenney (Foreign Office) to Leifs, November 8, 1935; M. Gibilaw (Barbirolli's secretary) to Leifs, October 11, 1936; H. M. Tennent to Leifs, November 5, 1936; Leifs to Adolf Aber, November 17, 1936.

115. Leifs to Ragnheiður Bjarnadóttir, December 6, 1936.

116. Emil von Reznicek to Leifs, February 4, 1937.

117. Hallgrímur Helgason, "Jón Leifs," in *Tónskáld og tónmenntir*, 100.

118. A. R., "Internationales Musikfest in Dresden," *Deutsche Musik-Zeitung*, June 5, 1937; Günther Haußwald, "Musik im Spiegel der Nationen," *Leipziger Neueste Nachrichten*, May 31, 1937.

119. "Nordische Komponisten in Berlin," *Völkischer Beobachter*, June 1, 1937; "Nachmittags-Empfang zu Ehren nordischer Komponisten," *Berliner Börsen-Zeitung*, June 1, 1937. Among those present were Dr. Richard Wienstein from the *Reichskanzlei*, Ministerialrat Ott from the Propaganda Ministry, Hans Sellschopp from the foreign division of the *Reichsmusikkammer*, and Georg Schumann from the Prussian Academy of the Arts.

SEVEN

DINOSAURS IN BERLIN (1937–44)

LEIFS SPENT THE SECOND HALF of 1937 in Iceland. He stayed at Þingvellir for a few weeks, composing the seventh and eighth movements of *Edda I*, before taking up residence at Hótel Borg in Reykjavík. While there, he made plans for an arts exhibit organized by the Federation of Icelandic Artists and attended to his duties at the National Radio—for the last time, since the director terminated his part-time contract in November.[1] Never easily deterred, Leifs wrote and published at his own expense an apologia, *Radio and Music Education* (*Útvarp og tónment*), in which he vented his frustration regarding the entire situation with the National Radio.[2]

Meanwhile, Annie felt increasingly despondent and forlorn in Rehbrücke. "What will the future hold? As far as I am concerned, the good times are over!" she wrote to her husband in July.[3] Her pleas for Leifs's return grew ever more desperate: "Have you really no idea how hard it is for me to keep things going here? I've been alone now for almost five months! And you plan to stay at least until the end of November! This constant waiting is dreadful."[4] She knew the precarious state of their marriage and feared the outcome of such an extended separation: "Are we even still married? Short marital breaks are fine, but this long?"[5] Leifs gave a frigid response: "It has been long since our marriage gave spiritual or physical satisfaction, for you as well as for me. I wish the situation were different. I haven't found a replacement. Have you?"[6]

While Leifs was certainly not idle during his stay in Reykjavík, it is easy to view his protracted absence as an escape from both the marital and political situations awaiting him in Germany, where hostility toward Jews was hitting ever closer to home. In 1937, Leifs's friend Ludwig Gies was forced out of the Prussian Academy of the Arts, and Annie's brother-in-law, Hans Alexander Müller, was dismissed from his professor's post at the Leipzig Academy for Graphic Arts. Müller and his wife, Marie, sailed with their sons to New York, where he taught for two decades at Columbia University and made a name for himself as an illustrator for major publishers such as Doubleday and Random House.[7] Nonetheless, Annie kept firm to her resolve to stay put in Germany.[8] She had some security through her Icelandic citizenship, which she had achieved through marriage in 1921; both daughters also held Icelandic passports. The Nazis were ruthless when it came to German Jews, but a foreign citizen was less likely to be harassed or arrested within German borders.[9] Still, it was a distressing situation and may have been the only thing holding the marriage together. In Leifs's postwar report on his activities in Germany, he suggested that Annie chose to remain there as long as she did, knowing that he would "not dissolve the marriage as long as she and the children were living in an anti-Semitic Germany."[10] It seems remarkable that Leifs should place all the blame on his wife when the truth is clearly more complex. He certainly embraced whatever opportunities came his way in Germany while also hoping for a permanent position in Iceland.

Leifs's modest success evaporated quickly. Carl Linnemann of Kistner & Siegel had contacted various German orchestras in an attempt to procure performances in the 1937–38 season, but the scores to Leifs's works were all returned, and Linnemann suspected government interference.[11] Radio stations showed no interest; an unnamed conductor at one of the *Reichssender* orchestras informed Leifs with some alarm that his music could not be performed, on orders from the conductor's superior.[12] In February 1937, Leifs

Figure 7.1. Ink drawing of Leifs by his brother-in-law, Hans Alexander Müller, made in Leipzig in September 1932. © Leifs Archives, National and University Library, Reykjavík.

wrote to the Propaganda Ministry claiming to have proof that his works had been banned but was told that no restrictions were in place. Yet Leifs's information came from a source within the Propaganda Ministry itself, his old acquaintance Ernst Züchner. After the war, Züchner declared under oath that Leifs's music had encountered "strong opposition" from Nazi officialdom "as early as 1933 from the Party office of Rosenberg, later from the Reich Music Office and finally during the war also from the Foreign Office. . . .

From 1937, Mr. Jón Leifs's name was on the black list of the Reich Music Office. After that, I took steps from time to time to obtain 'special permissions' for his works and to obtain for him and his family easier formalities concerning their stay in Germany, with reference to his earlier friendly attitude to Germany."[13] Züchner was in a position to know the truth of the matter, and his testimony seems credible. Still, it should be noted that it was given in Leifs's presence and at his request, at the Icelandic embassy in Stockholm in 1951.

Scholars agree that official bans on music during the Third Reich were relatively rare. Mostly these were directed at American songwriters such as Irving Berlin, Jewish composers such as Kurt Weill, or composers who wrote in an undesirable style, such as the non-Jewish Austrian Ernst Krenek. Listings of banned music appeared in the *Reichsmusikkammer*'s newsletter, but these include no mention of Leifs, and it thus seems most likely that the ban on his works was unofficial.[14] Since he was only a minor figure and of no use to the authorities, they gave him the cold shoulder instead of openly working against him.

After the war, Leifs claimed to have obtained exemptions from the 1937 Nazi ban "two or three times, until the year 1941."[15] This must be a deliberate understatement, for the number was considerably higher. He conducted the Leipzig Radio Orchestra in the *Iceland Overture* in 1938, and a year later the *Iceland Cantata* was presented at the Permanent Council's festival in Frankfurt. The Organ Concerto was performed in Berlin in March 1941 and the *Variazioni Pastorali* in Gelsenkirchen in December that same year—although both were poorly received.[16] Leifs's songs were heard at a Nordic week in Hamburg in October 1938, and a month later the *Iceland Overture* was performed in Remscheid by a massive chorus of 110 adult singers and 70 children.[17] Contralto Else Lehmann performed his songs at the Goethe-Haus in Hamburg in February 1939, the tenor Eggert Stefánsson sang Leifs on Berlin Radio the following month, the *Icelandic Dances* were programmed by Reichssender Hamburg in August that year, and an Icelandic soprano sang the *Lullaby* at the Nordic Morning Festival in Hamburg in 1942.[18] German periodicals accepted Leifs's writings until 1941, including a cover piece in the *Deutsche Militär-Musiker-Zeitung* and two articles in *Zeitschrift für Musik*.[19] Kistner & Siegel even published three of his scores after the alleged ban came into effect, *Torrek* and the *Prelude and Fughetta* op. 3 in 1938, and the *Nocturne* for harp in 1943. Even counting only performances, and leaving aside a handful of published articles and scores, there were at least ten exceptions to the "ban" on Leifs's music between 1937 and 1941.[20]

It has been noted that the regime in Nazi Germany gradually grew more intolerant of modernism in the arts.[21] This may be one reason Leifs's works were more often than not favorably received in the early years of Nazi rule, while the period from 1937 to 1941 brought fewer performances and generally negative reviews. There was also a noticeable lack of a coherent policy on music in Nazi Germany. It could be haphazard and contradictory, with inconsistencies between purported ideals and actual artistic endeavors.[22] Pamela Potter has observed that to the degree that Nazi music censorship did exist, it was not very well organized, so that the fates of musicians were determined less by ideology and far more by cronyism and sheer luck.[23] Nazi actions regarding modernism were often without any apparent logic; an artist praised in one city could find his works banned and politically suspect in another.[24] Different organizations within the Nazi system could also have contradictory attitudes, as is made clear by a request to the already suspect Jón Leifs Society in February 1943 for copies of his *25 Icelandic Folk Songs* for piano "for urgent use" by the school division of the SS-Hauptamt.[25] It seems that his simple arrangements were still considered useful for educational purposes, even as other Nazi organizations regarded Leifs with disapproval.

The political situation in Iceland, particularly as it concerned the now imminent secession from the union with the Danish king, seems to have clouded Leifs's perception of European politics and incited his involvement in bizarre political dealings. In 1937, he wrote an article in the Icelandic journal *Iðunn* expressing his concerns about the impending declaration of full independence. Leifs regarded the arts as fundamentally an aristocratic venture and presumed that they could never thrive unless supported by wealth.[26] The main hindrance to the arts in Iceland was that the country had no politicians who grasped the value of culture for the nation's independence. He found it absurd that Iceland should abolish royalty altogether and concluded that the best solution would be for the country to have its own king, a foreigner "who would become Icelandic and live with his country through good times and bad."[27]

While Leifs's general idea was not without precedent—Norway had elected a Danish prince to become its king in 1905—the way in which he himself pursued it was nothing short of outlandish. In spring 1938, he arrived at the Prinz-Leopold-Palais, the eighteenth-century palace that housed Goebbels's Propaganda Ministry, along with two other Icelanders: the author Guðmundur Kamban and Leifs's old friend Kristján Albertsson, who had held the position of lecturer in Icelandic at the Berlin University since 1935.[28] They had arranged a meeting with a Nazi official, Friedrich Christian Prince of Schaumburg-Lippe, to offer him the kingdom of Iceland. Schaumburg-Lippe was an unwavering Nazi, having joined the party in 1929. More importantly as far as the Icelandic trio was concerned, he was of aristocratic birth and a godson of the Danish king. The Icelandic visitors were successful in convincing the prince that he could plausibly claim sovereignty over Iceland, and he accepted on the condition that his superiors assented to the plan. According to Schaumburg-Lippe's 1952 autobiography, Goebbels favored the idea—although he advised him "not to breathe a word about National Socialism" in Iceland—but foreign minister Joachim von Ribbentrop wouldn't hear a word of it.[29] In the end, Schaumburg-Lippe met a different fate. He fell out of favor with the Nazis in 1944 and was relieved of all duties; at the end of the war he was interned for three years. In his old age, he inquired whether the Icelandic government might grant him some kind of official title, such as Graf von Reykjavík, and even visited the country in 1973.[30] He died ten years later, never having obtained any recognition from the country he had once believed wanted him as its rightful ruler. This truly absurd episode makes plain how naive, illogical, and self-absorbed Leifs's ideas were on politics and the arts. He obviously had no mandate to offer the kingdom of Iceland to anyone, let alone to an official in the Nazi Propaganda Ministry. What propelled him to act as he did was his conviction that Iceland's political independence depended on its cultural legitimacy and that this would be best nurtured by an absolute monarchy, preferably one in which he could enjoy star status as the country's national composer.

Buoyed by the success of the Prague Quartet's visit to Iceland, Leifs continued his attempts to bring high-level cultural events to Iceland. In 1938, he nearly managed to get a chamber orchestra made up of members of the Berlin Philharmonic to visit Reykjavík, although in the end the orchestra's schedule proved too busy. Leifs's dealings with the Philharmonic led to a harsh exchange between him and Reznicek, who was incensed at Leifs for having implied during negotiations that the tour would take place under the auspices of the Permanent Council, without Reznicek's consent.[31] As late as summer 1939, Leifs tried to arrange a tour of Iceland by the Leipzig Thomanerchor, but this came to nothing with the outbreak of war.[32] Meanwhile, Leifs's efforts at cultural exchange were being regarded with increasing skepticism in Iceland. In July 1937, the left-leaning newspaper *Þjóðviljinn* called him a "most obsequious Goebbels-disciple" who assiduously tried to convince his countrymen that the Nazis were "so passionate in their desire for friendly relations with other nations" that they had an entire propaganda system devoted solely to this particular goal.[33]

The Nazis were themselves skeptical of Leifs's dealings, not least when he claimed to be acting on behalf of the Council for Cultural Exchange, a society that he himself had founded in Reykjavík in autumn 1937, with the support of several local cultural associations. The council was intended to encourage Iceland's participation in international art exhibitions, to support the publication of books and articles about Iceland, and to "attempt to rectify false accounts of Iceland abroad and of foreign countries in Iceland."[34] But the council had no guaranteed funding, and with Leifs spending most of his time abroad it never fulfilled its promise. The German consul in Reykjavík, Werner Gerlach, advised the Nazi authorities against any collaboration with Leifs or the council, noting that it existed only to promote the "tactless and importunate" composer who presided over it.[35] Still, it should be noted that Leifs did not only focus on procuring artists from or sympathetic to the Third Reich. In 1938, he met in London with the outspoken Nazi opponent Adolf Busch in an attempt to organize a tour on behalf of the Reykjavík Music Society. Busch would eventually perform in Iceland in 1945 and again (with Rudolf Serkin) a year later, in what were regarded as outstandingly successful visits.[36]

In September 1938, Copenhagen hosted a weeklong Nordic music festival. Leifs had long pleaded for Iceland's inclusion, recalling its omission at a similar festival that he had attended nineteen years earlier. This time, Iceland, like the other Nordic countries, was given its own concert. In a symbolic welcoming gesture, the gala opening night on September 3 went to Iceland, and the crown prince and princess of Denmark were among the attendees in the large hall of the Oddfellow Palace. Never before had an entire orchestra concert been devoted to Icelandic music, and the program's first half consisted only of Leifs's works. He conducted the *Trilogia piccola* and movements from the music to *Galdra-Loftr*, some of which were heard for the first time. Svend Methling, a well-known actor from the Danish Royal Theater, took the role of the sorcerer. The program's second half contained more traditional fare. Ísólfsson conducted smaller, late-Romantic works by Sigurður Þórðarson, Karl Runólfsson, and Sigfús Einarsson as well as his own *Passacaglia* for organ, newly arranged for orchestra.

The concert made headlines in the Nordic press, and it was generally agreed that it demonstrated Iceland's awakening as a nation of music. Reaction to the works themselves was mixed. Some critics found Leifs's music sublime and captivating, judging the other composers to be "completely devoid of personality."[37] Yet a majority of writers applauded the program's more conservative second half, finding fault with the "exaggerated modernism" of Leifs's "unbelievably loud and pretentious" music; the Norwegian composer

Geirr Tveitt found the *Galdra-Loftr* score (the overture excluded) to be "completely without character."[38] Leifs's competence as a conductor was also called into question. "If one can call Jón Leifs a conductor at all, then he is at any rate a very bad one," wrote the critic of the Danish *Social-Demokraten*, and the Swedish composer Sten Broman found his beat to have been "rather amateur-like."[39] Still, another critic praised him as a "moving, lively" conductor of his own works.[40] Leifs himself was displeased with the overall result, complaining that insufficient rehearsal time—a total of two hours on nonconsecutive days—had jeopardized the artistic results.[41]

In the late 1930s, Leifs became convinced that the Nazis were planning atrocities against his homeland, that they might easily "evacuate all Icelanders from the country and thus exterminate the Icelandic nation."[42] Much to Leifs's frustration, German newspapers had largely ignored the twenty-year anniversary of Icelandic sovereignty in December 1938. This strengthened his suspicion that the Nazi government held no good intentions toward his native land and that the goal of German military presence in the North Sea might be to transport all Icelanders to the continent, which would be for them "only a fairly small procedure—perhaps a three-week operation."[43] He wrote a harsh letter to Züchner expressing his dismay that the anniversary had been largely ignored, but he also demanded a clarification of his own situation:

> If we are to succeed in our common goal, it is necessary that there be a change and clarification of where things stand. I have worked for Germany for 22 years and have nearly exclusively suffered financial damage because of it—my countrymen call me a "Goebbels disciple" and anti-German papers in Denmark attack me for "Neudeutscherei," as you know. My attitude towards Germany is today firmer than ever before and I am prepared to display this in action. But it is necessary for the New Germany to finally take a clear position towards me, because I am now treated with increasing suspicion, performances of my works are cancelled, etc.[44]

Even allowing for Leifs's political naiveté and opportunism, this letter is a stunning attempt to gain ground with the Nazis by pledging faith to Germany. At that point, he seems to have been prepared to do virtually anything to get his music performed, even renouncing his political convictions—such as they were.

This letter should also be considered in the context of Leifs's creative work. A month later, in January 1939, he finally completed the first installment of the *Edda* oratorio, which had occupied him for eight years. He hoped that he might be able to procure a performance, but this proved impossible with Europe on the brink of war. In March 1939, a meeting with Heinz Drewes, head of the Propaganda Ministry's music division, was unfruitful; the chief of the radio orchestra in Cologne, Rudolf Schultz-Dornburg, seemed encouraging, but when Leifs pressed for a decision a few months later he learned that Dornburg had been drafted into the German air force.[45] As for publishers, neither Peters nor Eulenburg nor Kistner & Siegel was willing to take a risk on such a large and expensive score.[46] That Leifs would even consider showing the full score of *Edda I* to one of the highest-ranking Nazi music officials and press for its publication in Germany again demonstrates his opportunistic streak as well as the ambiguity of his situation as late as 1939.

EDDA I: THE CREATION OF THE WORLD

Many composers have attempted to describe the world's beginnings through music. In *The Creation*, Joseph Haydn tests the boundaries of tonality as he depicts chaos taking form; in Wagner's *Das Rheingold*, the primal sounds of creation transform into a depiction of the gently flowing Rhine. Leifs's thirteen-movement oratorio *Edda I*, which describes the creation myth as related in Nordic sources, also begins with infinite nothingness, a slowly unfolding *creatio ex nihilo* such as would become typical of Leifs's later works. A low *pianissimo* emerges in the double basses, to which violins add a shimmering flageolet a fifth (and many octaves) higher. This open fifth of the Icelandic tvísöngur is among the foundations of Leifs's soundscape, and large sections of *Edda I* are derived from it, whether in the slowly unfolding pedal points in the strings or bass and tenor duets in parallel fifths.

The orchestra was Leifs's largest to date and includes a somewhat extended percussion section (including rocks struck with hammers) as well as his first use of what would become his signature Nordic *lurs*, long natural horns cast in bronze, dating to the Late Bronze Age (ca. 1000 BC). A substantial number of lurs have been discovered in Denmark, where they are usually found in symmetrical pairs, with identical tunings. When Leifs wrote for lurs, in *Edda* as well as in the *Saga Symphony* and *Baldr*, he also employed them in pairs. In the eighth movement of *Edda I*, an ocarina and bagpipes also make a brief appearance; the "unpolished" sounds of such instruments add a primeval flavor to Leifs's creation story. The addition of the lurs and other primitive instruments can be seen as an attempt to reconcile the worlds of ancient and modern—the dialectical forces of his entire output—within the orchestra itself. Leifs also coaxes an unusual, primitive sound out of the more traditional instruments of the orchestra—not unlike Stravinsky in the famous bassoon solo that opens *The Rite of Spring*—for example by giving prominent solos to the piccolo in an extremely low register.

While the music carries all the hallmarks of Leifs's mature style, it is, like the earlier *Iceland Cantata*, considerably more varied than many of his later works. For example, this would be the last time that he wrote extended passages of imitative polyphony. In the second movement, a soprano theme ("Out of Elivagar sprang poison-drops," m. 26) is taken up in imitation by tenor and bass and later becomes a loose unison canon between all voices. The third movement also contains a loosely fugal texture, as does movement 7, where a sprightly bass theme to the text *Dagr átti Þóru drengja móður* ("Dag married Thora, mother of champions") is taken up in turn by the tenor, alto, and soprano (example 7.1a) and becomes a close *stretto* passage. The theme later appears in inversion (example 7.1b), and Leifs even presents both original and inverted forms simultaneously. Such fugal procedures are unique in Leifs's output and may partly explain the slow progress of his work on the oratorio.

Example 7.1. Leifs, *Edda I* op. 20, movement 7, (a) mm. 152–57; (b) mm. 253–55. © Iceland Music Information Center.

The climax of the seventh movement is one of Leifs's great achievements in *Edda I*: shimmering woodwind sixteenth-note triplets punctuate the sumptuous harmonies of the choir, providing a brilliant closure to the work's first half. The eighth movement, *Night, Morning*, is a marked change. Leifs has until this point employed mostly major triads—with added notes—but here gives the music a brooding, nocturnal quality by using only minor triads virtually from beginning to end. This can be seen as a first attempt at the bleak minor style that he would later cultivate in the string quartet *Mors and vita* and the choral *Dance of Sorrow* op. 35 no. 2.

In *Edda I*, Leifs appears for the first time as a composer explicitly concerned with evoking nature. He grouped the Eddic texts according to subject matter, drawing largely on texts describing natural phenomena, as the headings of many of the individual movements suggest: *Sea* (movement 5); *Earth* (6); *Sky, Sun, Day* (7); *Night, Morning* (8); *Winter and Wind* (12). He also strove to find appropriately descriptive orchestral gestures for many of the elements described in the libretto. In the fourth movement, a xylophone enters at the mention of the icy rime that formed the cow Auðhumla, herself depicted through low trombone glissandi. The killing of the giant Ýmir that effectively creates the world is depicted with a huge crashing sound: tutti *fff* with organ and *legno grande* (movement 5). Harp arpeggios evoke the dew that falls from the bit of Night's horse, Frost-mane, (movement 8) while the flames of Surt's fire are suggested by rapid sixteenth- and thirty-second-note flourishes in choir and orchestra (movement 13).

The choral writing is merciless. Leifs frequently requires his singers to navigate intervals of tritones or sevenths, while the demands of extreme tessitura include soprano high Cs and an occasional bass low C. Most outrageous is the tenth movement, a scherzo marked *Allegro vivace*, where the choir is made to enunciate the names of various dwarves of Norse mythology in a giddy whirlwind of *staccato* thirty-second notes. The challenge of Leifs's choral writing is no doubt the main reason why *Edda I* had to wait nearly seventy years for its première. Two movements were heard at the Nordic Music Days in Copenhagen in 1952 (see chap. 8), and another three were performed by the Reykjavík Polyphonic Choir in 1982, but a complete performance and recording took place only in 2006.

Edda I is a powerful rendering of the Nordic creation myth and surely ranks as one of Leifs's grandest achievements. At the time of its completion, the 254-page, 75-minute score was the longest, most ambitious, and most demanding work ever created by an Icelandic composer. Still, it was only the first installment of a tetralogy whose dimensions were truly overwhelming. While composing *Edda I*, Leifs often remarked on his fear of dying before achieving his life's goals as an artist. In 1932, the death and funeral in Leipzig of the poet Jóhann Jónsson had a profound effect on him, and he confessed to his sister his terror of "meeting the same fate, before I complete my main works."[47] A year later, a premature death was still on his mind: "My main concern is that I will not live to complete the works I must finish, and that no one else can accomplish. Everything else seems to me trivial in comparison."[48] It is almost as if he sensed his own fate, for while Leifs did not die young, his epic *Edda* project was doomed to remain incomplete.

DEATH AND LIFE

Having eschewed the two previous festivals of the Permanent Council for International Cooperation among Composers, Leifs attended the one in Frankfurt am Main in June 1939. The council minutes reveal his pugnacious attitude; this time, presumably bothered by the absence of Icelandic music at the 1938 event in Stuttgart, he complained that the council had neglected Iceland at its festivals. The council's main secretary, the Belgian Emiel Hullebroeck, retorted that no composer had been so well promoted at the council's festivals as Leifs himself.[49] Since Leifs refused to withdraw his complaint, the issue was brought to the general meeting, which concluded that his allegations were not merely unfounded but out of place in an organization promoting friendship among nations.[50] With this in mind, it is hardly surprising that Leifs's proposal for Iceland to host the Permanent Council's festival in autumn 1941 was summarily dismissed.[51]

Leifs's censure must have seemed particularly ludicrous since the *Iceland Cantata*, already performed in part at the Dresden festival two years before, was again on the program in 1939. Scheduling a work already heard at a previous festival was without precedent, but this was a goodwill gesture intended to atone for the last-minute omission of three movements at the Dresden concert.[52] Performed by the local radio orchestra and the Frankfurter Singakademie chorus, the cantata was well received; one critic praised its "powerful simplicity and succinct grandeur," and even those who quibbled with its "foreign-sounding harmony and rhythm" judged the performance a success.[53] But Leifs remained an outsider at the Frankfurt festival, even more than usual. At each inaugural session of a Permanent Council meeting, it was customary to send a telegram to Hitler and Goebbels, thanking them for their support via the Reichsmusikkammer. Now Leifs declared his objection to this procedure—his only demonstrable act of public protest to Hitler's regime—but he had the support of only one colleague, the Danish composer Peder Gram, and the telegram was dispatched as usual.[54]

The Leifs family sailed to Iceland in June 1939. Leifs had to secure a new term as president of the Federation of Icelandic Artists, but once this was settled the family went hiking in the wilderness. They explored Kerlingafjöll, a mountain ridge with a spectacular variety

Figure 7.2. Snót and Líf Leifs in Hveravellir, Iceland, summer 1939.
© Leifs Archives, National and University Library, Reykjavík.

of landscape and nature, with a predominantly red hue due to the volcanic rhyolite stone, as well as Hveravellir, a geothermal belt with bubbling, sulfur-spewing holes in the earth, some of which are suitable for bathing. The photographs in the Leifs family album depict a relaxed, cheerful family foursome enjoying their last holiday together in a world at peace (see fig. 7.2). They returned to Rehbrücke in August, a few days before German troops invaded Poland. Leifs's astounding lack of political acumen is again evident in his prognosis to his sister in Iceland: "For the time being, it seems like this won't be as dangerous as many had predicted."[55]

Leifs must have soon grasped the gravity of the situation, for he began writing a dark and brooding string quartet, *Mors et vita* (*Death and Life*), which he completed on December 30. With the exception of his quartet arrangement of the *Variazioni Pastorali*, this was his first foray into chamber music. It was also a new departure for Leifs in terms of musical content. Typically, his works consist of a fairly rigid chord structure in which major and minor triads alternate, with a preponderance of major chords. This quartet is primarily made up of minor triads and also exhibits a far more fluid approach to counterpoint. The single-movement work moves at a funereal pace, although twice interrupted by frenzied passages in a quicker tempo. Toward its conclusion, the viola quotes a bleak Icelandic folk song, *Húmar að mitt hinsta kvöld*, which Leifs had first employed in his folk song volume for piano fourteen years earlier. In his manuscript of the quartet, Leifs also copied the original text, in which the nineteenth-century poet Hjálmar Jónsson visualized death approaching:

Húmar að mitt hinsta kvöld,	It looms, the dusk of my last eve,
horfi eg fram á veginn;	I look ahead along the path;
gröfin móti gapir köld;	the gaping grave is cold and wide;
gref ég á minn vonarskjöld	on the shield of my hopes I carve
rúnir þær, sem ráðast hinumegin.	runes to be read on the other side.[56]

Describing Leifs's choral arrangement of this folk song, the novelist Halldór Laxness wrote that it embodied the "gravity of an Icelandic funeral on a cold winter's day, with much hard-frozen snow."[57] The same can be said for the quartet, which seems caught in a perpetual state of gloom and anxiety.

The authorities had begun investigating Annie's racial origins. In January 1940, Leifs hired an amanuensis, Wolfgang Dubois, who was the son of a Cologne music agent and had been exempted from war service due to a heart condition.[58] He did his best to advise them when inquiries began arriving by mail. The Reichsmusikkammer sent a questionnaire regarding details of their Aryan origins—which seems to have gone unanswered; next came a letter from *Deutsche Arbeitsfront* (The German Labor Front), the Nazi trade union organization.[59] Dubois advised Leifs to try to suppress the matter by demonstrating that he was a foreigner and of verifiably Aryan origin. Yet even Dubois did not immediately grasp the situation: "How difficult is it for your wife to procure the certificate? If the Jewish blood is farther back than the grandparents' generation, this can be overlooked completely."[60] When he discovered that Annie was a full Jew, the gravity of the matter became clear: "Your wife's case is of course extremely difficult. It is very unfortunate that the issue has been raised at all. As a foreigner, who has without doubt been of service for the German cause, I would have objected to any investigation from the start. Some adversary of yours must have leaked this information?"[61]

Dubois's theory was that some foe within the Reichsmusikkammer had informed Gerigk, the anti-Semitic music critic who was Rosenberg's influential right-hand man.[62] While this remains conjecture, Gerigk was certainly no admirer of Leifs's music; he gave the Organ Concerto a trashing at the Wiesbaden premiere in 1935, reacted negatively to the Berlin Philharmonic concert in 1936, and found the piano pieces op. 2 to be "less than enjoyable" at the 1938 Permanent Council festival in Brussels.[63] Züchner's claim that Leifs's music had met with opposition from the Rosenberg office as early as 1933 (see above) may be relevant in this context. It is also possible that the information on Annie had been leaked from Reykjavík, where news and gossip could spread fast. In an internal memorandum written sometime between December 1939 and May 1940, the German consul in Reykjavík noted that Leifs was married to a "woman of Jewish descent."[64] Whatever the source, once the Nazi authorities were on their trail, Leifs's acquaintances in *Kraft durch Freude* and the Propaganda Ministry were helpless to assist.

The situation intensified in April 1940, when the Reichsmusikkammer requested a complete list of members of the Jón Leifs Society.[65] Dubois in turn asked that the Foreign Ministry officially endorse the society, hoping that this could be seen as a validation of Leifs and his music. In his letter to the ministry, Dubois again emphasized Leifs's efforts at cultural exchange—he specifically noted the Hamburg Philharmonic tour—and even suggested that Leifs might be of "valuable service" in the future.[66] Assurances of this kind were of course useless, and the official stance is clear from a memorandum by a Foreign Ministry bureaucrat:

> Based on the report at hand, it does not seem appropriate to endorse the Jón Leifs Society. Furthermore, Mrs. Leifs, according to the society's spokesman, Mr. Dubois, is not fully Aryan.
>
> However, Dr. Klein at *Nordische Verbindungsstelle*, while remaining skeptical towards Jón Leifs personally, emphasized that Leifs has done much for the promotion of German music in Iceland and so he cannot be completely disowned.
>
> The best solution seems to be to perform Jón Leifs's music on the radio now and then, but otherwise to ignore him and wait until the political situation becomes clear.[67]

This is as close to a decisive position on Leifs as Nazi documents allow, and it suggests indifference rather than full censorship, at least as far as the Foreign Ministry was concerned.

On the eve of April 9, 1940, Nazi troops invaded Denmark and Norway. Leifs was by that time deeply anxious over the fate of his own native country, and he followed the events with trepidation. The danger of a German takeover in Iceland lasted only a month, for on May 10 the British Royal Marines landed in Reykjavík. The local government, while providing the invading force with de facto cooperation, formally maintained a position of neutrality. Leifs would later regard the Icelandic protest of the occupation as having saved his life in Germany, since he could claim to be a neutral foreigner.[68] By the time of Iceland's occupation, he had nearly completed a new work inspired by the turn of events in Scandinavia: a setting of the Eddic poem *The Lay of Guðrún* (*Guðrúnarkviða*). He symbolically finished the work on Norway's National Day, May 17, dedicating it to the memory of the "unknown Norwegian soldier."[69]

Leifs already had ample experience in constructing his own textual collage from the *Poetic Edda*. In *The Lay of Guðrún* he drew on four different poems that tell the story of Guðrún Gjúkadóttir after the death of her husband, Sigurður, whom her brothers have murdered. (These characters are better known to opera lovers as Gutrune and Siegfried from Wagner's *Ring Cycle*.) Guðrún sits, grief-stricken, by Sigurður's body, and she remains silent for the first half of the ten-minute work. The initial narrative portion, sung by tenor and bass soloists, sets the scene and concludes with a description of how Guðrún's sister pulls the veil from the deceased husband's face. This deed in turn unleashes the widow's own emotions, and the remainder of the work is her monologue, sung by a contralto, declaring love for her slain husband. Most of the music itself has a narrative character, and the orchestral accompaniment is restrained, except at key points such as Guðrún's initial entrance. Here, a tutti outbreak of *fortissimo* sixteenth notes signals the surge of emotion that prompts her to speak.

It is telling that Leifs, who had intended to set *The Lay of Guðrún* since the early 1920s, should turn to the text at precisely this moment. While the poem is a poignant expression of grief, it also explores, through the plight of a woman whose brothers have slain her husband, the theme of conflicting loyalties. Although Leifs never explicitly made a connection between his choice of text and the political situation, he intended *The Lay of Guðrún* as an expression of dismay at Germany's takeover of Denmark and Norway, which could also be seen as a kind of fratricide. The inference here is presumably that Leifs took a position with the Nordic countries—the violated terrain in the geopolitical maneuvers of spring 1940—and that Guðrún's sorrow was also his own.

Leifs regarded Guðrún as an archetype of Nordic heroism, not least through her deliberate self-control. Even as she bids final farewell to her husband, only a single tear runs down her cheek:

Þá hné Guðrún	Then Guðrún knelt,
höll við bolstri,	leaning on the cushion,
haddr losnaði,	her hair came loose,
hlýr roðnaði,	and her cheeks grew red,
regns dropi	a drop like rain
rann niðr um kné.	ran down over her knees.[70]

Leifs remarked that such "stiffened sorrow" was a sign of the "ancient Nordic laws of the soul" and "the constitution of a heroic spirit."[71] In the larger context of his output, *The Lay of Guðrún* provides a link between two larger works: it fuses the Eddic poetry of *Edda I* and the image of the laconic Nordic hero that Leifs would memorialize on a larger scale in the *Saga Symphony* a year later.

Besides *The Lay of Guðrún*, the year 1940 was rather unproductive. In September, Leifs arranged the *Lullaby* op. 14a for mixed chorus, sending a copy to the renowned Bavarian choir of boys and young men *Regensburger Domspatzen*—but he apparently never received a reply.[72] Apart from this, most of his time was spent elucidating his artistic ideology in book form. The first draft, written in summer 1940, was titled *The Consummation of the North* (*Die Vollendung des Nordens*), but he was dissatisfied with the outcome and decided in December to rewrite it. The revised version was called *Iceland as a Signpost for the Development of the Arts* (*Island als Wegweiser der Kunstentfaltung*), but another decade would pass before Leifs published the volume under yet another title (see chap. 8). In a preface to the original 1940 draft, he acknowledged the interest shown to his music by *nordisch* and *völkisch* circles in Germany since the early 1930s but deplored that it had gotten "mired in the daily babble of party politics, without its fundamentals ever having been fully grasped"—something he now declared had been "one of the greatest disappointments of [his] life."[73]

SCANDAL AT THE SINGAKADEMIE

For several years, Leifs had entertained the hope that Emil von Reznicek, the German delegate of the Permanent Council, might endorse his music for the Prussian Academy of the Arts' annual concert series.[74] A venerable institution dating back to the 1690s, the academy had been appropriated by Nazi authorities in 1933 and its Jewish members discharged, including Arnold Schoenberg. Among those still in the fold were Reznicek and Graener, Leifs's former composition teacher, but in general the academy's members seem to have been skeptical of Leifs's talent. In 1934, his application for membership in the academy was rejected and his compositions declared "quite mediocre." Instead, it was suggested that a selection of his songs with piano accompaniment might be performed at one of the academy's concerts, although this never materialized.[75] It was only in early 1941 that another academy member and acquaintance of Leifs's, the composer Gerhard von Keussler, secured a performance of the Organ Concerto at a concert on March 10.[76]

The academy's concerts took place at the Singakademie, the neoclassical hall where, more than a century earlier, Felix Mendelssohn had directed the first performance of Bach's *Saint Matthew Passion* since the composer's own time. The Berlin Philharmonic was to perform under the direction of Georg Schumann, the academy's president and director of the Singakademie. The decision to include Leifs on the program was made only in early February, leaving the soloist, Kurt Utz, with merely a month to relearn the fiendishly difficult organ part. Keussler's decision to press for a performance on such short notice may have been deliberate, since it seems that Leifs did not have to procure a *Gutachten*, or official consent, otherwise required for composers whose works were performed at the academy's concerts.[77]

It was Leifs himself who suggested the Organ Concerto, certainly his most ambitious orchestral composition to date and the only major work (apart from *Edda I*) that had not yet been performed in Berlin.[78] In light of its considerable amount of wrenching dissonance, this was a terribly misguided choice.[79] After the first orchestra rehearsal, Leifs received a phone call from a distressed Keussler, informing him that Schumann refused to conduct the work and that Leifs would have to step in. The seventy-four-year-old Schumann was himself a late-Romantic composer and presumably had little sympathy for Leifs's modernism. His last-minute decision to bow out suggests that he sensed an impending catastrophe and wished to keep his hands clean. The next morning, Leifs found himself on the podium facing the Berlin Philharmonic. He complained of insufficient rehearsal time but was enthralled by the orchestra's reaction to "the smallest gesture, even that of the pinky!"[80] According to one account (probably derived from the composer), Utz attempted to kindle the Philharmonic players' enthusiasm for the concerto by evoking natural phenomena, already standard fare when describing Leifs's music: "Magnificent! An iceberg crashes into a volcano!"[81]

The concert on March 10 began at 6:00 p.m., and Leifs's Organ Concerto was last on the program, preceded by a Divertimento by Otto Besch, a Viola Concerto by Walter Abendroth, and a Concertino for piano and orchestra by Kurt Rasch (see fig. 7.3). All three wrote eminently "acceptable" music in an accessible style. Abendroth was better known as a leading Nazi music critic; Rasch was a composer and recording engineer whose career in postwar Germany was compromised because of his perceived pro-Nazi sympathies.[82] One reviewer noted that his concertino was so "clean and accomplished" that the audience burst into applause after each of its four movements.[83]

The contrast with Leifs's concerto could not have been more pronounced. Kristján Albertsson, Leifs's longtime friend and a lecturer at Berlin University, was in the audience and later gave the following description:

> I was sitting up in the balcony and didn't see the floor below, didn't see that people were leaving throughout the performance, so that in the end only a few were left in the hall. I found Leifs's work magnificent, and expected the hall to tremble with jubilation after the

Preußische Akademie der Künste
Abteilung für Musik

Fünftes Konzert

am Montag, dem 10. März 1941, abends 6 Uhr
im Saale der Singakademie

Das Berliner Philharmonische Orchester
Solisten: Hans Beltz (Klavier)
Fritz Lang (Bratsche)
Kurt Utz (Orgel)
Leitung: Georg Schumann

Divertimento für kleines Orchester (Uraufführung) . . . . . . Otto Besch
    1. Lebhaft und mit Humor   geb. 1885
    2. Intermezzo. In ruhiger Bewegung
    3. Variationen über ein Kinderlied

Konzert für Bratsche und Orchester (f-moll) in einem Satz op. 9 . . . Walter Abendroth
    Solist: Fritz Lang (Bratsche)   geb. 1896

Concertino für Klavier und Orchester op. 30 . . . . Kurt Rasch
    1. Allegro vivace   geb. 1902
    2. Andante espressivo
    3. Scherzo
    4. Con fuoco
    Solist: Hans Beltz (Klavier)
    Leitung: Der Komponist

Konzert für Orgel und Orchester op. 7 . . . . Jón Leifs
    Introduzione (Allegro moderato)   geb. 1899
    Passacaglia (Tempo moderato)
    Finale
    Solist: Kurt Utz (Orgel)

C/1439   Konzertflügel Steinway & Sons, Hamburg-Berlin

Figure 7.3. Program from the Prussian Academy concert at the Singakademie, March 10, 1941. The program had already gone to print when it was decided that Leifs would conduct the Organ Concerto himself. © Archiv Stiftung Akademie der Künste, Berlin.

performance. But we were in fact fewer than twenty who applauded, and at far distances from each other in the large, nearly empty hall. Jón Leifs turned and bowed with a smile, and all twenty of us kept applauding for a long time, and he kept on bowing, to the right and to the left and up to the balcony, his face beaming with satisfaction as if this were a singular achievement, as if one could hardly attain more sincere recognition from a small, impartial, and highly qualified audience. Perhaps this is the final hour of Leifs's music in Germany, I thought—a well organized execution.[84]

Leifs's own account of the event survives in a letter he wrote after the war to Bertha Geissmar, Furtwängler's Jewish secretary at the Berlin Philharmonic, who had left the orchestra in spring 1935. According to Leifs, the unrest spread from where the critics were seated—a notion perhaps corroborated by one of the reviews, which claims the uproar was initiated by "a number of men who are far from unknown in German musical life."[85] Leifs was convinced that the ruckus was organized by the Nazis, and one hypothetical scenario involves Rosenberg's *Kulturpolitisches Archiv*. Leifs and his amanuensis Dubois already suspected its director, Gerigk, of having launched an investigation into Annie's racial origins a year before. Gerigk's closest coworker at the *Kulturpolitisches Archiv* was Hermann Killer, who was present at the Singakademie concert; he had praised Leifs's *Iceland Overture* in 1935 but now gave the concerto a scathing review. If the Rosenberg faction wished to create a stir, Killer would have been the ideal instigator. In any case, the commotion was on par with some of the great scandals of twentieth-century music history. In Leifs's telling, some yelled, "Stop it!" "Outrageous!" and "Shameless!" while yet another cried, "This is worse than Hindemith!"[86] If his account is accurate, the brawl can hardly have escaped Albertsson's attention in the balcony. One critic noted that, as the concerto reached its end, "in lieu of applause there resounded the roaring laughter of those still remaining."[87] Yet Leifs stood firm. "I have never been as certain of my own calling," he later declared.[88]

The amount of dissonance made the Organ Concerto an easy mark for Nazi critics, despite its Nordic origins. In 1935

Altstadt-Schütze had stressed the work's "affinity with nature" and emphasized its distance from "decadent" stylistic trends, but by 1941 critics unanimously denounced the work as degenerate. To Killer, the concerto placed "unbearable demands on normal musical sensitivity," turning the organ into an "instrument of noise."[89] Ernst Krienitz, who had praised the *Iceland Cantata* at its premiere in Greifswald, bluntly called it "a renewed attempt at a musical style, which the efforts at purification since 1933 should basically have eliminated."[90] Goebbels's leading music critic, Fritz Stege, echoed the view that such a work had no place in Nazi Germany. He also registered his surprise that the concerto had been well received at its 1935 premiere, given the "agonizingly narrow-minded intellectual world revealed in this piece, a world that renounces free creative impulse and engenders apathy and displeasure in the form of a colossal passacaglia. Was it Jón Leifs's intention to present Icelandic prehistory in music, when streams of lava were still flowing and dinosaurs made the earth tremble with their weighty steps? Because the extravagant use of percussion cannot be otherwise explained, with four timpanis roaring and a man trashing the floor with malicious persistence."[91] In Stege's review, the familiar Nordic topoi of landscape and nature are effectively turned on their head. No longer a paradise of idyllic landscapes and long summer nights, inhabited by blond, blue-eyed Aryans, Iceland has become a prehistoric lava land, a dinosaur-infested nightmare—hell on earth.

Nor was the venom limited to music critics. Both Leifs and the Prussian Academy received letters from at least one outraged audience member, a Berlin engineer who aptly called the piece a "musical deathblow."[92] A local newspaper demanded an explanation from the academy and interviewed the chairman of its music division, the composer Kurt von Wolfurt, who expressed his regret at the incident but blamed the acoustics of the Singakademie, a fairly small hall in which even normal orchestral works could sound uncomfortably loud. "When Leifs let loose his percussion-stuffed *fortissimo*-piece with all its fury, it was bound to become absolutely unbearable."[93] Wolfurt did have a point—even Leifs admitted the work was an "acoustic problem"—although the properties of the Singakademie were clearly not the only cause of the scandal.[94] In any case, the academy was determined to wash its hands of the whole affair. On May 26, when little more than two months had passed, all twenty-one Leifs scores that belonged to the academy's music library were returned to the publishers Kistner & Siegel.[95]

A SYMPHONY OF HEROES

At least the disaster prompted Leifs to begin composing again. He had written nothing since the previous spring, but now he sought stimulation in the medieval sagas, with their robust heroes who remain fearless in the face of adversity. He later described his immediate reaction on returning home to Rehbrücke after the Berlin concert: "I stayed up the whole night and read Icelandic sagas. Thus was born my intention to compose a symphony called *Saga Heroes*, and to base its movements on the characters who bore the strongest characteristics of our forefathers, who were individualists and completely different from the collectivists of the Nazi era."[96]

He began drafting the first movement in April, and *Symphony I, Saga Heroes*—which Leifs usually referred to as the *Saga Symphony*—was complete in July 1942. Two decades later, Leifs introduced the work in a radio broadcast, shedding invaluable light on his objectives and elucidating the symphony's descriptive content. He remarked that he intended the work as a protest against Nazi ideology and its misappropriation of the Nordic spirit while also wishing to breathe new life into the symphonic genre, which he felt had lost its power of expression after Bruckner and Brahms.[97]

Each of the symphony's five movements depicts a specific character from the Icelandic sagas. Its basic aesthetic premise is that of the nineteenth-century program symphony; it can be regarded as the Nordic version of Liszt's *Faust Symphony*, fused with hero worship in turn influenced by both the medieval sagas and a Romanticized image of Beethoven. In particular, its two outer movements depict moments of quintessential saga heroism, which Theodore

Andersson defined as an act of laconic but supreme bravery on the part of a doomed man just before he is slain. This is usually some flamboyant and memorable gesture of endurance, a "last flash of spiritual as well as martial grandeur" but often also "improbably and theatrically heroic."[98] In this light, Leifs's attitude at the conclusion of the Singakademie concert itself becomes an act of hero posturing—perhaps influenced by his familiarity with the Icelandic sagas but also becoming the impetus for an immediate rereading of them, thus inspiring his creation of the new work.

The opening movement, *Skarphéðinn*, depicts the fearless character of the well-known *Saga of Burnt Njáll*, or *Njáls saga*. The music begins defiantly, with a two-part texture of long notes in string and wind instruments punctuated by irregularly placed *fortissimo* chords in brass and timpani (see example 7.2). Leifs himself acknowledged that he had modeled this music directly on the opening measures of Beethoven's *Coriolan* overture, where long notes are similarly shattered by dark, ominous chords. Leifs went further than to acknowledge the purely musical correlation. In his radio introduction, he specifically claimed the same heroic stature for the two characters thus depicted, the Icelandic warrior Skarphéðinn and the Roman general Coriolanus: both were brave, proud men who had no fear of death.[99]

Judging from Leifs's remarks, he viewed Skarphéðinn as a sympathetic hero, noting that the music was intended to depict "the man and his life, his appearance, battles, poetry, and reactions."[100] Still, Skarphéðinn's killings of key characters trigger a chain of events leading to the catastrophic inferno of Njálsbrenna, the burning of the family farmhouse by his enemies, in which the hero meets his end along with his parents. Skarphéðinn's character is suggested in the music by sturdy rímur tunes, while a contrasting *tranquillo* section is sporadically interrupted by loud intrusions of brass and percussion. Here Leifs said the music was meant to suggest "the preparations of Skarphéðinn's enemies, their slander and cowardice, the treachery that later is magnified into the Njálsbrenna fire."[101] The movement's climax occurs as the farmhouse is

Example 7.2. Leifs, *Saga Symphony* op. 26, first movement (Skarphéðinn), opening. © Iceland Music Information Center.

ablaze and Skarphéðinn attempts to stamp down the fire until the whole roof collapses with a crash, here provided by a *legno grande* in full force.

The second movement is Leifs's only depiction of a female saga character: Guðrún Ósvífursdóttir from *The Saga of the People of Laxárdal* (or *Laxdæla saga*). At the heart of this family saga is a love triangle, as two close friends fight for the affections of "the most beautiful of women ever born in Iceland."[102] Leifs claimed that "for every woman, love is the strongest power" yet also insisted that his music depicted "not the cloying flames of love as in Wagner's *Tristan and Isolde*, but grandeur of spirit, as befits Nordic people."[103] The main theme is associated with Guðrún and returns throughout the movement in various guises. Roughly midmovement, it receives an unexpected accompaniment: the noise of armor (muted brass) to depict the murder of Kjartan—the man she loved the most—at the hands of her husband while she sits at home and keeps her feelings in check by spinning yarn. Guðrún later became the first nun in Iceland, and Leifs suggested that the movement's tranquil conclusion was intended to evoke her Christian faith and humility.

The third movement, *Björn behind Kári* (*Björn að baki Kára*), provides comic relief. It is based on another scene from *The Saga of Burnt Njáll*, where the warrior Kári heads off to avenge Njáll's murder and is accompanied by the cowardly Björn. While the battle rages, Björn hides behind Kári, but when victory is won he brags about his bravery. Leifs here illustrates the extremes of heroism and cowardice; brass fanfares suggest Kári's bravery while the strings portray a fumbling Björn. In his radio introduction, Leifs again suggested a parallel to Beethoven's output, in this case the vivacious rondo for piano *Rage over a Lost Penny*. Whereas Beethoven in his setting mocks his own rage over a missing coin, Leifs pokes fun at Björn, who "searches for his honor and bravery, which do not exist."[104]

Leifs originally planned the *Saga Symphony* in four movements but suspected that the battle music of the final two movements might be too unrelenting.[105] He therefore added a slow intermezzo, *Grettir and Glámur*, based on *The Saga of Grettir the Strong* (*Grettis saga*). Grettir Ásmundarson (997–1031) was an outlaw and a villain whose main weakness was his fear of the dark. Here Leifs created a movement of substantial psychological tension. It begins slowly and quietly as Grettir awaits his destiny in the dark. Suddenly a ferocious noise erupts in the percussion as the ghost Glámur springs forth; the clatter of xylophones suggests a skeletal danse macabre, and the attack concludes with the mighty blow of a wooden hammer. "Grettir attacks Glámur," reads one of Leifs's sketches, a demonstration of his keen sense of the pictorial/narrative as he composed.[106] Eventually, the ghost is killed, and the music calms down again, with slow, heartbeat-like punctuations. Leifs remarked that the conclusion was meant to suggest Grettir's fear and solitude. Here he claimed to have been guided by his own experience of the air raids in Berlin, "when people sat and waited underground for hours while bombs fell, and the helplessness of humanity against a mightier force seemed so evident. Thus Grettir awaited the ghost Glámur."[107]

The *Saga Symphony*'s final movement depicts Þormóður Kolbrúnarskáld (or Kolbrún's Poet), the hero of the *Saga of the Sworn Brothers* (*Fóstbræðra saga*), which takes place in the eleventh century. Leifs described Þormóður as a "poet and ladies' man, an actor and fighter who was constantly embroiled in adventures and predicaments."[108] The movement begins with a vigorous theme in rímur style, but it quickly moves to a depiction of the Battle of Stiklestad (1030), where Þormóður fought for King Olaf of Norway and where both lost their lives. Here Leifs employs, for the first time, the vastly expanded percussion section that would become his trademark; iron shields and whips, anvils, stones, hammers and bells bring to life this battle scene of thousands of men clad in medieval armory. In midbattle there is sudden silence—a deep bell tolls to mark the death of King Olaf. The fighting resumes for a while, but the bell tolls again, this time for Þormóður. The saga relates how he valiantly tore an arrow from his own heart, proclaiming that the king "has nourished us well. The roots of this man's heart are white." He then expired "standing by the wicker wall and fell not to the ground until he was dead."[109] In Leifs's score, forceful chords mark his final demise, followed by a pair of soft *pizzicati* in the strings.

The irony of the *Saga Symphony* is that although it was written *against* the Nazis—and in no way pandered to their musical taste—it nevertheless shares fundamental points with their aesthetic principles. With the symphony, Leifs claimed for himself what had seemed to be part of an ideological common ground: the steely and unsentimental, the heroic and sublime.[110] Rosenberg and other national socialist ideologues had singled out "heroism" as a particular attribute of "racially healthy" Nordic individuals and praised the "heroic world-view of the North."[111] Moreover, *the heroic* was one of two key terms employed over and over again by Nazi writers on music in evoking the sublime—the other being *the monumental*, with an emphasis on large instrumental forms.[112] In the *Saga Symphony*, Leifs fuses the sublime genre of the symphony—one that, according to many Germans, only German musicians could fully master—with Nordic heroism as it is depicted in Old Icelandic literature.[113] Yet this work, as Leifs himself noted, fundamentally differs from Nazi aesthetics in that it rejects the collective will—the *Gemeinschaft*—in favor of the subjective individual factor that the National Socialist sublime sought to eradicate. It is a hero symphony with an anti-Nazi message.

The Icelandic sagas contain a substantial amount of poetry, and as a side project to his symphony Leifs composed two song cycles: *Three Songs from Icelandic Sagas* op. 24 and *Songs of the Saga*

Symphony op. 25. These are somewhat akin to preparatory sketches for the larger work, not in terms of the musical material but of grasping the dramatic characters and deriving a general musical style from the rhythms and flow of the medieval language. The settings are heroic in every sense of the word, and they require a robust *Heldentenor* who can project through the piano's dense and forceful chords. Leifs worked on the songs and symphony concurrently. In April 1941 he set *Skarphéðinn's Song from the Fire* from *The Saga of Burnt Njáll* at the same time as he portrayed Skarphéðinn in the symphony; a year later, *Þormóður's Death Song* was a compendium to the symphony's last movement. Another related side project (though slightly later, from November 1944 until January 1945) was a setting of three *Skaldic Verses* op. 31 for tenor and piano.

BERLIN RADIO INTERLUDE

The furor unleashed by the Organ Concerto emboldened Nazi critics to continue bashing Leifs in the few reviews of his music published after March 1941. The fiercely difficult violin *Prelude and Fughetta* op. 3 had been published three years previously, in an edition by Willibald Schweyda, the Prague Quartet's first violinist, who adjusted some of the composer's more awkward passages. The volume had received little attention at its publication, but now Ernst Krienitz, editor of *Die Musikwoche*, who had been ruthless in his review of the concerto, struck again. He liked nothing about the piece except the opening measures, in which he discerned some melodic character.

> But then, already in the fourth staff, obstinate chords sneak in, quickly and without hindrance glide into atonality, and from the fifth staff they run wild for quite a while. "My kingdom for a pure octave," cries the tormented violinist, but his plea echoes unheard. To an E-flat is added an E, to an F-sharp is added F in the upper octave, and so these poor creatures are dragged on like the sinners in Dante's Purgatory.... Hypocrisy, artificiality, snobbishness, and vehemence have their part in these chords, which to the violinist signify the twilight of the violin [*Götterdämmerung der Geige*].[114]

Leifs's career as a composer in Nazi Germany had effectively come to an end; this review, with its echoes of Shakespeare, Dante, and Wagner, was only the final nail in the coffin. From now on, his relations with the authorities took a turn for the worse, even in day-to-day situations. Leifs's personal identity card reveals that on May 29, 1941, the security police noted "haughty" behavior on the part of Leifs and his wife as they refused to contribute to a Nazi charity drive—presumably the *Winterhilfswerk*—on the grounds that they were foreigners.[115] Nazi authorities routinely kept track of donations and included this information on reports concerning political reliability. Leifs's response shows that he was now more mindful than ever to emphasize the family's Icelandic citizenship when dealing with the authorities.

Despite all this, the Nazis actively sought Leifs out for collaboration as they commenced propaganda radio broadcasts to Iceland. Ludwig Lienhard, the head of the Foreign Office's radio division responsible for broadcasts to Scandinavia, had suggested in summer 1940 that broadcasts to Iceland in the Icelandic language might be necessary to stem the tide of Allied influence, given the British occupation.[116] Nothing came of his plans at the time, but in spring 1941, shortly before German military authorities declared an embargo south and southwest of Iceland, he brought up the matter again. To supervise the broadcasts, Lienhard contacted four Icelanders residing in or near Berlin: Leifs, Kristján Albertsson, Gunnar Böðvarsson (an engineering student at the technical university), and the composer Þórarinn Jónsson. All but the last were skeptical of the whole enterprise, but Leifs and Albertsson briefly attempted to use their position as leverage to ensure the safety of Icelanders at sea; after all, over one hundred Icelandic sailors had already been killed by German submarine attacks. At a meeting with Werner von Grundherr, head of the Foreign Office's Scandinavian department, they were bold enough to demand that in exchange for their services, the navy must declare that all Icelandic ships would be spared from German raids. Even more astonishing was Leifs's assertion that no one knew how the war would end and that in case of German defeat he might be unable to get to either Iceland or England. Outraged by the remark, Grundherr swiftly called the meeting to an end and concluded that the attitude of Leifs, Albertsson, and Böðvarsson precluded their participation in the broadcasts.[117] In any case, Albertsson, speaking on behalf of the Icelandic troika, informed the authorities in May 1941 that they would not collaborate. The Nazi radio broadcasts to Iceland began on June 17 that year, supervised by Jónsson, and continued until the end of the war.

Despite his initial resistance, Leifs did occasionally lecture on German radio. For example, in January 1942 he read a speech he had earlier given to the Icelandic Students' Association in Copenhagen, which was intended to "prepare my countrymen for a German invasion."[118] Leifs had for several years expressed his growing concern that a foreign nation might at some point "destroy our nationhood in short order."[119] With the outbreak and development of the war, his concerns grew. In the Copenhagen lecture, titled "Can the Icelandic Nation Perish?" he argued that the country's very existence was in grave danger, since it was "easier to destroy the nationhood of Iceland than of any other country." The audience of Icelandic expatriates were incensed by many of his claims, such as that Germany had "shown great understanding to our nationhood," and the inappropriate tone of Leifs's talk would later come back to haunt him.[120] In August 1945, as the Allied forces were investigating Leifs's case as a purported Nazi sympathizer, the Icelandic Foreign Ministry requested a transcript of his talk from the embassy in Copenhagen.[121] Leifs asserted that his radio talks had been given of his own volition and that he had only expressed a "neutral and Icelandic point of view," but it would prove difficult to convince the Allies of this once the war had run its course.[122]

TWILIGHT IN PRAGUE

In October 1938, Nazi forces annexed Sudetenland, and the persecution of Jews became more rigorous than before. Annie's parents,

Edwin and Gabriele Riethof, had left their apartment in Teplitz, initially planning to sail to New York City, where they would be welcomed by their daughter Marie. But they had qualms about the long journey and settled instead in Prague, Gabriele's city of birth. It proved to be a grave miscalculation. In March 1939, Hitler founded the so-called protectorate of Bohemia and Moravia, annexing the region as an autonomous Nazi-ruled territory. Two years later, Reinhard Heydrich, one of the Nazis' most cruel executioners, became its protector, leading to a new surge in the execution of Jews. By that time, Leifs and Annie were traveling frequently to and from Prague to try to ensure the safety and comfort of her parents, who were able to transfer money, jewelry, and antique furniture to Leifs's name—a matter of increasing urgency as the Nazis were confiscating Jewish possessions—under the pretext that Riethof had never paid his daughter's rightful dowry.[123] It seems that the Riethof family fortune was their main source of income during that period, although Leifs also received money from his mother in Reykjavík as well as a yearly artist's stipend from the Icelandic government. Although he often griped about being misunderstood in Iceland, Leifs was among those who received the highest such bursaries during the war.[124]

Edwin Riethof died of natural causes on February 12, 1942, and Gabriele chose to remain in Prague.[125] In June, she was arrested and taken to Terezín (Theresienstadt) in northern Bohemia, where the Nazis had established a prison camp earlier that year. The Terezín camp was unique in that inmates were encouraged to participate in artistic pursuits—concerts, poetry readings, and art exhibits—which the Nazis in turn employed as propaganda.[126] In autumn 1942, the older generation of Terezín prisoners was sent to Treblinka, one of the more notorious Nazi extermination camps, northeast of Warsaw. There, it was possible to murder 300 people in two hours; an estimated 850,000 people were killed at the camp before it was shut down in October 1943.[127] Gabriele was dispatched on October 22, a month before her seventy-first birthday. Other members of the Riethof family also perished in

Figure 7.4. Gabriele Riethof, in a painting presumably made by her husband, Edwin, who was an amateur painter. Private collection of the author.

the Holocaust. Sofie, Edwins's sister-in-law, died in Terezín along with her daughter; Viktor Rode, Edwin's nephew, took his own life in Prague in 1942.[128]

News of the atrocities began to filter out among the German population only over the course of 1942. Had Leifs and Annie realized the imminent danger, they would no doubt have encouraged the Riethofs to act more decisively. Back in Iceland after the war, Leifs recalled how they had discovered Gabriele's fate:

> For a long time, we knew nothing about whether my mother-in-law was dead or alive. And we had no means of finding out, because the prison camps were a closed realm to anyone in the outside world. We began to suspect that the genocide was not a lie but a horrible reality, and we were advised to try to find out whether she was alive or dead by dispatching a letter along with some cash, addressed to her, to the prison camp where we knew she had been last. We were told that if

the letter was returned to us, this meant she had been transported to the place of death and was no longer alive.

The envelope came back, opened and empty. It bore a stamp: "Departed." We needed no further proof.[129]

This exchange must have occurred in February 1943, when Leifs also wrote the following entry in his diary: "I have decided to no longer appear in public in Germany, now that the fate of my mother-in-law has been confirmed."[130] By appearing in public he presumably meant attendance at any kind of public event, the avoidance of which now led him into a kind of "inner emigration." The Leifs family was still protected through their Icelandic passports, since the Nazi regime was careful to avoid situations where anti-Jewish measures might lead to negative consequences for Germany's foreign policy and strategic position. Still, there were few hard and fast rules in such cases. At least four Icelandic nationals were incarcerated in Nazi camps; one of them died in Sachsenhausen in 1944, but others survived, including the tenor Sigurður Skagfield, who was arrested by the Gestapo for refusing to work at an ammunition factory. He spent two months at a subcamp of Buchenwald, until US forces liberated it in April 1945.[131]

SINK TO THY REST...

All around him, Leifs's world was about to crumble. The final meeting of the Permanent Council for International Exchange among Composers took place in Berlin in June 1942. Its activities had been suspended since the outbreak of the war, but now the Propaganda Ministry hoped to restart and intensify the council's work as part of what has been described as a "Nazi-fascist cultural project"—a vision of a nationally rooted European culture led by institutions under Italian-German leadership.[132] The lavish program included a gala dinner at Hotel Kaiserhof and a performance of Strauss's *Guntram* at the Staatsoper in the presence of the composer, whose fall from grace with the Nazi leadership had not affected his role in the council.[133] The meeting itself was the one time Leifs saw the Nazis' master of propaganda in the flesh. According to Leifs's account, Goebbels gave a thundering speech to the assembly while Strauss flushed with shame and anger.[134]

Between June and September 1942, the family stayed in Taarbæk, near Copenhagen, where Leifs worked on the final movement of the *Saga Symphony*. It was still a year until Nazis began demanding the arrest of Danish Jews, and therefore Copenhagen seemed like a safer place than Rehbrücke. Leifs wished to move there, and Líf even began attending a German high school in Copenhagen in August, but a few weeks later they all took the train back to Germany. It seems it was Annie who pressed for their return, presumably in the hope that she might be able to assist her mother, who by that time was already in Terezín.[135]

With the *Saga Symphony* completed, Leifs devoted most of his "inner emigration" to an ambitious project that would take him four years to complete: a vast "choreographic drama" based on the mythological story of Baldr (see chap. 8). Apart from this work, Leifs focused his energies on writing choral music intended for his countrymen. The *Three Patriotic Songs* for male chorus op. 27 are original works to Icelandic poems; although Leifs's settings are brief, his style was anathema to the traditionally minded male choir tradition, and they remain unperformed to this day. In 1943 he also wrote three more ambitious choral settings: *Three Verses by Jónas Hallgrímsson* for mixed chorus op. 28 and two sets of *Poems of Icelanders*, opp. 29 and 30, for male and mixed voices, respectively.

Of the works Leifs composed during this fateful year, perhaps the most remarkable is *A Hymn to the Setting Sun* (*Sólsetursljóð*) from the choral songs op. 28. It is unique in Leifs's output in that it sets a text by a foreign author, although Jónas Hallgrímsson's Icelandic rendering of the poem—originally from George Payne Rainsford James's 1837 novel *Attila*—is not so much a translation as a rewriting, in the ancient Eddic meter of *fornyrðislag*.[136] The opening is a tender duet for men's voices, employing the oscillating major/minor thirds characteristic of Leifs's wistful, lyrical mood. As the setting progresses, the nocturnal atmosphere gives way to majestic major triads. The poem may have appealed to Leifs not only for its vivid depiction of a sunset but also for expressing hope of a bright new day emerging out of darkness:

> Vonin vonblíða,
> vonin ylfrjóva
> drjúpi sem dögg
> af dýrðarhönd þinni,
> döpur mannhjörtu
> í dimmu sofandi
> veki, sem vallblómin
> vekur þú á morgni.

> Warm hopes drop like dews from thy life-giving hand,
> Teaching hearts closed in darkness like flowers to expand;
> Dreams wake into joys when first touch'd by thy light,
> As glow the dim waves of the sea at thy sight.[137]

The last of the three choral settings op. 28 is also notable, since it is Leifs's first foray into the volcanic. It may come as a surprise that this should occur not with large orchestral forces (as in the later *Baldr* and *Hekla*) but in a piece for unaccompanied chorus. Here, Leifs sets Hallgrímsson's poem *Víti* (Hell), after the eponymous crater near the volcano Krafla, in northern Iceland. The poet depicts, in the ancient Icelandic *dróttkvætt* meter, the danger and brutality associated with the volcanic region:

Bar mig á brendum auri	On the burnt ground
breiðar um funa leiðir	the black horse carried me along
blakkr að Vítis bakka....	paths of fire, to the edge of Víti....
Krafla með kynja afli	Krafla with fierce power
klauf fjall og rauf hjalla.	cleaved the mountain and reaved the sheds.

Leifs's setting is rapid and unswaying, with a far greater emphasis on dissonances (sevenths and ninths) than is his custom. He later also set the concluding quatrain from this poem in his orchestral/choral work *Hekla* (see chap. 9).

The family's day-to-day life was becoming increasingly difficult. Their request for permission to travel to Switzerland had been denied, but in summer 1943 they obtained entry permits for

Sweden through the assistance of Züchner at the Propaganda Ministry. Travel permits and currency transfers from the Nazi government were more difficult to procure, and this is why the family remained in Germany for another six months. In October, Leifs noted in his diary that they were experiencing "severe food shortage," and toward the end of the year he wrote, "The year 1943 was physically the most difficult year of my life."[138] Air raids by Allied forces were becoming more frequent. After one raid on Berlin, on November 22, 1943, Leifs's copyist salvaged one of his manuscripts (the songs for male chorus, op. 29) from the ravaging fire. In a massive raid on Leipzig on December 4, the office and storeroom of Kistner & Siegel burned to the ground. Their entire back catalogue of Leifs scores went up in flames, but the autograph manuscripts were safe—some in Rehbrücke, others in a bank vault in Prague.

The family left Rehbrücke for Nazi-occupied Copenhagen on February 27, 1944 and continued their journey to Stockholm two days later. They brought only their vital belongings, leaving behind most of their clothes and furniture, as well as Leifs's manuscripts, printed scores, letters, and books.[139] Their arrival in Sweden marked a new beginning, but Leifs, like so many musicians who lived and worked in the Third Reich, emerged from his life there severely tainted. For Leifs, who had to rebuild his reputation in the face of continued personal and professional hardship, there was no zero hour. His tragedy, in terms of his career, was that while he maintained his innocence in dealing with the Nazi authorities, he continued to single-mindedly advance his dogmatic vision of a Nordic Renaissance. In the years that followed, it often seemed as though Leifs failed to grasp how his deeply held ideals might already have been compromised beyond repair.

NOTES

1. Annie Leifs to Leifs, August 26, 1937.
2. Leifs, *Útvarp og tónment* (Reykjavík: Tónlistarvinir í Reykjavík, 1938), also published in *Alþýðublaðið*, November 1–4, 1937.
3. Annie Leifs to Leifs, July 15, 1937.
4. Annie Leifs to Leifs, November 1, 1937.

5. Annie Leifs to Leifs, September 23, 1937.
6. Leifs to Annie Leifs, October 5, 1937.
7. The definitive work on Müller is Uli Eichhorn and Ronald Salter, *Hans Alexander Müller, Das buchkünstlerische Werk* (Rudolstadt: Burgart-Presse, 1997).
8. Cf. a report by Leifs's Swedish advocate, L. Janssen, March 21, 1946.
9. This was on the basis of Icelandic laws no. 64/1935, retroactive to December 1, 1918, which stated that when a male Icelandic citizen married a foreign national, the wife automatically became an Icelandic citizen, as did their underage children.
10. Leifs, "Rapport," undated (autumn 1950), Foreign Ministry Papers 30L5, National Archives of Iceland, Reykjavík.
11. Leifs to Propaganda Ministry, January 3, 1937.
12. Leifs to Propaganda Ministry, March 23, 1937.
13. A written declaration by Ernst Züchner, made at the Icelandic embassy in Stockholm, January 17, 1951.
14. See the *Amtliche Mitteilungen der Reichsmusikkammer*, published in 1934–43. The first list of unwanted music was printed in September 1938; see also Albrecht Dümling and Peter Girth, *Entartete Musik, Dokumentation und Kommentar zur Düsseldorfer Ausstellung von 1938* (Düsseldorf: dkv—der Kleine Verlag, 1993).
15. "Ætluðu Þjóðverjar að flytja íslensku þjóðina af landi burt?," *Morgunblaðið*, November 23, 1946.
16. See K. W. Niemöller, "Nordische Musik neben Anton Bruckner," *Gelsenkirchener Allgemeine Zeitung*, December 6, 1941.
17. Letter from unnamed conductor to Leifs, October 27, 1938.
18. Gerhard Schwarz, "Nordische Komponisten," *Offenbacher Nachrichten*, February 16, 1939; letter from an unnamed conductor to Leifs, October 27, 1938; *Morgunblaðið*, March 21, 1939; "Nordische Morgenfeier" program sheet, April 12, 1942, with handwritten comment: "Grosser Erfolg". The *Zeitschrift für Musik* announced plans for a Leifs festival in Düsseldorf in winter 1938, but this came to nothing; see *Zeitschrift für Musik* 105 (1938): 681.
19. "Musik in Island," *Zeitschrift für Musik* 107 (1940): 266–68; "Erinnerungen an Karl Muck," *Zeitschrift für Musik* 107 (1940): 289–91, repr. in *Hamburger Fremdenblatt*, April 18, 1940; "Musisches Island," *Frankfurter Zeitung*, January 11, 1940; "Die altnordischen Luren," *Deutsche Militär-Musiker-Zeitung*, March 23, 1940.
20. The last such *Sondergenehmigung* seems to have come, rather remarkably, in May 1941—two months after the Singakademie scandal, when Leifs was allowed to do "further work within the scope of the Reichsmusikkammer" (Reichsministerium für Volksaufklärung und Propaganda to Leifs,

May 23, 1941; Der Präsident der Reichsmusikkammer/Seeger to Leifs, May 29, 1941).

21. Jonathan Petropoulos, *Artists Under Hitler: Collaboration and Survival in Nazi Germany* (New Haven: Yale University Press, 2014), 4.

22. Petropoulos, *Artists Under Hitler*, 92; Pamela Potter, "The Arts in Nazi Germany: A Silent Debate," *Contemporary European History* 15 (2006): 587.

23. Potter, quoted in Petropoulos, *Artists Under Hitler*, 200; Potter, "The Arts in Nazi Germany," 587.

24. Petropoulos, *Artists under Hitler*, 53.

25. D. Hegel, SS-Sturmbannführer to the Jón Leifs Society, February 1, 1943.

26. Matthías Johannessen, "Lögmálin í hrúgunni. Spjallað við Jón Leifs," *Morgunblaðið*, May 5, 1959; Leifs, "Listir og stjórnmál," *Alþýðublaðið*, March 9, 1960.

27. Leifs, "Ísland frá erlendu sjónarmiði," *Iðunn* 20 (1937): 69–70; see also Örn Helgason, *Kóng við viljum hafa! Áform um stofnun konungdæmis á Íslandi* (Reykjavík: Skjaldborg, 1992), 23–24, which contains a comprehensive account of the Schaumburg-Lippe affair.

28. Helgason, *Kóng við viljum hafa!*, 105–10.

29. Friedrich Christian Prinz zu Schaumburg-Lippe, *Zwischen Krone und Kerker* (Wiesbaden: Limes Verlag, 1952), 260–63.

30. A letter survives from Friedrich Christian Prinz zu Schaumburg-Lippe to Leifs (dated May 10, 1956) in which he expresses his wish to resume contact with the composer.

31. Emil von Reznicek to Leifs, January 3, 1938.

32. Berlin Philharmonic to Leifs, January 15, 1938; Baron Emil von Reznicek to Leifs, January 3, 1938; Curt Hoffmann, Konzertdirektion Leipzig, to Leifs, July 6, 1939. The Berlin Philharmonic group (known as *Kammerorchester der Berliner Philharmoniker*) focused on German music of the seventeenth and eighteenth centuries and was viewed by its organizer, Hans von Benda, as a "useful tool for propaganda abroad"; see Aster, *The Reich's Orchestra*, 33.

33. "Hugleiðingar Örvarodds," *Þjóðviljinn*, July 13, 1937.

34. "Nýr fjelagsskapur: Íslenskt menningarráð alþjóðaviðskifta," *Morgunblaðið*, July 28, 1945.

35. Þór Whitehead, *Milli vonar og ótta*, 53–54.

36. "Fiðlusnillingurinn Adolf Busch heimsækir Ísland," *Morgunblaðið*, July 25, 1945. See also Tully Potter, *Adolf Busch: The Life of an Honest Musician* (London: Toccata Press, 2010), 786–87.

37. K. R-n., *Svenska Dagbladet*, September 4, 1938; K.Bo., *Arbejderbladet*, September 6, 1938.

38. K. B., "Den 8. nordiske Musikfest i København," *Social-Demokraten*, September 4, 1938; H. S., *Politiken*, September 4, 1938; *Nationaltidende*, September 4, 1938; Geirr Tveitt, "Den 8de nordiske musikfesten," *Ragnarok*, Oslo, October 1938.

39. K. B., "Den 8. nordiske Musikfest i København," *Social-Demokraten*, September 4, 1938; Sten Broman, *Svenska Dagbladet*, September 4, 1938.

40. William Behrend, *Berlingske Tidende*, September 4, 1938.

41. Leifs to Björn Kristjánsson, October 29, 1938. Björn Kristjánsson collection, National and University Library, Reykjavík.

42. "Ætluðu Þjóðverjar að flytja íslensku þjóðina af landi burt?," *Morgunblaðið*, November 23, 1946.

43. "Ætluðu Þjóðverjar að flytja íslensku þjóðina af landi burt?," *Morgunblaðið*, November 23, 1946.

44. Leifs to Ernst Züchner, December 2, 1938.

45. Heinz Drewes to Leifs, March 17, 1939; Schultz-Dornburg's secretary to Leifs, September 25, 1939.

46. Johannes Petschull (C. F. Peters) to Leifs, April 18, 1940; C. F. Peters to Leifs, April 29, 1940; Eulenburg to Leifs, May 24, 1940. On March 5, 1941, the *Signale für die musikalische Welt* announced that Kistner & Siegel were publishing *Edda I* as a study score. While no documentation survives to support this report, it is possible that the catastrophe at the Berlin Singakademie a few days later led to the cancellation of this project. At any rate, the score to *Edda I* was located in Kistner & Siegel's bank vault when Leifs left Germany (Kistner & Siegel to Leifs, August 25, 1944).

47. Leifs to Þórey Þorleifsdóttir, January 13, 1933.

48. Leifs to Þórey Þorleifsdóttir, January 24, 1934.

49. Emile Hullebroeck to Leifs, May 4, 1939.

50. *Ständiger Rat* minutes, Frankfurt, June 19, 1939.

51. *Ständiger Rat* minutes, Frankfurt, June 21, 1939.

52. The Organ Concerto had intially been suggested for performance at the 1937 and 1939 Permanent Council festivals. The choice, instead, of the *Iceland Cantata* demonstrates the conservative nature of the festivals' programs (see Carl Linnemann to Leifs, February 6, 1937; Emil von Reznicek to Leifs, January 20, 1939).

53. Walter Jacobs, "Internationales Musikfest in Frankfurt," *Kölnische Zeitung*, June 23, 1939; Dr. Hendel, "Musik der Temperamente," *Mittelschlesische Gebirgszeitung*, June 23, 1939.

54. Leifs to Peder Gram, April 4, 1946.

55. Leifs to Þórey Þorleifsdóttir, September 21, 1939.

56. Bernard Scudder, translation for *Tvísöngur*, Smekkleysa SMK 35, 2004, compact disc.

57. Halldór Laxness, "Um þjóðlega tónlist," *Dagleið á fjöllum* (Reykjavík: Heimskringla, 1937), 179.
58. Wolfgang Dubois, undated "Lebenslauf."
59. "Erklärung betreffend arische Abstammung," Der Präsident der Reichsmusikkammer to Leifs, November 26, 1937.
60. Wolfgang Dubois to Leifs, March 16, 1940.
61. Wolfgang Dubois to Leifs, March 29, 1940.
62. Wolfgang Dubois to Leifs, May 24, 1940.
63. Herbert Gerigk, "Europäische Musikschau in Konzertsälen—Abschlußbericht von den Brüsseler Musiktagen," *Völkischer Beobachter*, December 6, 1938. See also Gerigk's review in *Völkischer Beobachter*, March 19, 1936. A 1940 memorandum on Leifs from the *Kulturpolitisches Archiv*, signed by "Dr. Gk." (presumably Gerigk), also survives. Leifs had offered to give a public lecture under the auspices of the *Amt Deutsches Volksbildungswerk*, the department of adult education that was part of the *Kraft durch Freude* movement, presumably to attest his own standing vis-à-vis the authorities. The memo states that Leifs was not to be hired since he was married to a *Volljüdin* and since his proposed lecture topic—presumably of a geopolitical nature—was considered "completely unfeasible given the present circumstances." Yet Gerigk noted that "it would be a different matter if he wanted to speak about Icelandic music sometime," especially since he had in earlier years worked on behalf of the German cause (Hauptstelle Kulturpolitisches Archiv to Amt Deutsches Volksbildungswerk, April 23, 1940, Bundesarchiv Berlin: NS 15/30). Once again, even though Annie's Jewish origin did, strictly speaking, work against Leifs, his position as a Nordic composer who had facilitated German-Icelandic cultural relations still seemed capable of repairing some of the damage.
64. Werner Gerlach, memorandum on Iceland. National Archives of Iceland, Reykjavík (1993–71, Ministry of Finance, Gerlach Papers).
65. President of Reichsmusikkammer to the Jón Leifs Society, April 6, 1940; Jón Leifs Society to Herr Sieger, April 9, 1940.
66. Auswärtiges Amt, Kult. Gen. 819, Wolfgang Dubois to Legationssekretär Lohmann, April 11, 1940.
67. Auswärtiges Amt, Kult. Gen. 819.
68. Njörður P. Njarðvík, "Ekki margt—heldur mikið," *Vísir*, December 22, 1962.
69. Leifs, introduction to *The Lay of Guðrún*, Icelandic National Radio Archives, DB-637.
70. *The Poetic Edda*, trans. Carolyne Larrington (Oxford: Oxford University Press, 1999), 179.
71. Leifs, introduction to *The Lay of Guðrún*, Icelandic National Radio Archives, DB-637.

72. Letters from Wolfgang Dubois to Leifs (September 9 and October 22, 1940) suggest that Theobald Schrems, the conductor of Regensburger Domspatzen, had enquired about shorter a cappella works and that Leifs consequently made this arrangement. It does not seem as though the Regensburg choir ever performed *Lullaby*. Leifs also made an arrangement for male chorus, which was printed in an Icelandic music journal (*Tónlistin*) in 1946.

73. Draft of *Die Vollendung des Nordens* (summer 1940), 9.

74. Cf. letters from Emil von Reznicek to Leifs, December 27, 1937 and January 10, 1938. On the political implications of the Prussian Academy, see Hildegard Brenner, *Ende einer bürgerlichen Kunst-Institution: Die politische Formulierung der Preußischen Akademie der Künste ab 1933* (Stuttgart: Deutsche Verlags-Anstalt, 1972).

75. Minutes of the Prussian Academy of the Arts, December 17, 1934, Stiftung Archiv der Akademie der Künste, Berlin.

76. Minutes of the Prussian Academy of the Arts, January 31, 1941, Stiftung Archiv der Akademie der Künste, Berlin. Keussler had been aware of Leifs ever since reading his 1923 article on Icelandic folk music in *Die Musik* (Keussler to Leifs, 23 December 1923).

77. See letters and minutes in the Stiftung Archiv der Akademie der Künste, Berlin, AdK 2.1/059.

78. Leifs to Berta Geissmar, June 22, 1946.

79. Mark R. Taylor, record review of the Organ Concerto (BIS CD-930), *Tempo*, New Series, no. 213 (July 2000): 55.

80. Leifs to Berta Geissmar, June 22, 1946.

81. Quoted in Hallgrímur Helgason, *Íslands lag—þættir sex tónmenntafrömuða* (Reykjavík: Leiftur, 1973), 100. Helgason does not provide a source for this anecdote, but it presumably came from Leifs himself.

82. See Wolfram Huschke, *Zukunft Musik: eine Geschichte der Hochschule für Musik Franz Liszt in Weimar* (Köln, Böhlau Verlag, 2006), 337–39.

83. Ernst Krienitz, "Es geht um die Musik," *Die Musikwoche* 9 (1941): 112.

84. Kristján Albertsson, "Sextugur í dag: Jón Leifs tónskáld," *Morgunblaðið*, May 1, 1959.

85. Krienitz, "Es geht um die Musik."

86. Leifs to Berta Geissmar, June 22, 1946.

87. Fritz Stege, "Berliner Musik," *Zeitschrift für Musik* 108 (1941): 240.

88. Leifs, introduction to the *Saga Symphony*, Icelandic National Radio Archives, TD-248.

89. Hermann Killer, "Berliner Konzerte," *Die Musik* 33 (1941): 324.

90. Krienitz, "Es geht um die Musik."

91. Fritz Stege, "Berliner Musik," *Zeitschrift für Musik* 108 (1941): 240. Until 1941, Stege had seldom discussed Leifs's music in his monthly reviews.

Yet it is clear from his occasional remarks, such as his description of the *Iceland Overture* (at the Berlin Philharmonic concert in 1935) as "wenig erfreulich," that he had never been a great admirer. See Stege, "Die Berliner Kunstwochen," *Zeitschrift für Musik* 102 (1935): 763.

92. Theodor Becker to Leifs, March 12, 1941; Stiftung Archiv der Akademie der Künste, Berlin.

93. Walter Steinhauer, "Kann gute Musik heute durchfallen," *B.Z. am Mittag*, March 12, 1941.

94. Leifs to Berta Geissmar, June 22, 1946.

95. Preußische Akademie der Künste (Abteilung für Musik) to Kistner & Siegel, Berlin May 26, 1941. Stiftung Archiv der Akademie der Künste, Berlin.

96. Leifs, introduction to the *Saga Symphony*.

97. Leifs, introduction to the *Saga Symphony*.

98. Theodore M. Andersson, *The Icelandic Family Saga: An Analytic Reading*. Harvard Studies in Comparative Literature 28 (Cambridge, MA: Harvard University Press, 1967), 62.

99. Leifs, introduction to the *Saga Symphony*.

100. Leifs, introduction to the *Saga Symphony*.

101. Leifs, introduction to the *Saga Symphony*.

102. *The Complete Sagas of Icelanders*, ed. Viðar Hreinsson, vol. 5, The Saga of the People of Laxárdal, trans. Keneva Kunz, 1.

103. Leifs, introduction to the *Saga Symphony*.

104. Leifs, introduction to the *Saga Symphony*.

105. Leifs, introduction to the *Saga Symphony*.

106. "Various sketches" (Ónotaðar skissur frá ýmsum tímum), Leifs collection.

107. Leifs, introduction to the *Saga Symphony*.

108. Leifs, introduction to the *Saga Symphony*.

109. *The Complete Sagas of Icelanders*, ed. Viðar Hreinsson, vol. 2, 402.

110. Cf. Petropoulos, *Artists under Hitler*, 73.

111. Gleißner, *Der unpolitische Komponist als Politikum*, 105, 154, 365.

112. Reinhold Brinkmann, "The Distorted Sublime: Music and National Socialist Ideology—A Sketch," in *Music and Nazism: Art Under Tyranny, 1933–1945*, ed. Michael H. Kater and Albrecht Riethmüller (Laaber: Laaber-Verlag, 2003), 49; see also Pamela M. Potter, "What is "Nazi Music"?," *The Musical Quarterly* 88 (2005): 437.

113. Michael H. Kater, "Introduction," *Music and Nazism*, 9.

114. Ernst Krienitz, "An der Grenze des Violinklanges," *Die Musikwoche* 9 (1941): 116.

115. Leifs's personal record card (Bundesarchiv/Document Center) is printed in Åhlén, *Jón Leifs*, x.

116. Guðmundsson, *Berlínar-blús*, 2nd edition, 167.
117. Guðmundsson, *Berlínar-blús*, 2nd edition, 343–45.
118. Leifs to the US embassy, November 28, 1947.
119. Leifs, "Ísland frá erlendu sjónarmiði," *Iðunn* 20 (1937): 61.
120. Copy of the minutes of the Icelandic Students' Association, Copenhagen, January 8, 1942, National Archives of Iceland, Reykjavík (Icelandic Foreign Ministry 1996-B/484).
121. Icelandic Foreign Ministry to Icelandic Embassy, Copenhagen, August 19, 1945, National Archives of Iceland, Reykjavík (Icelandic Foreign Ministry 1996-B/484).
122. See Leifs, "Declaration of Neutrality" ("*Greinargerð fyrir hlutleysi*"), March 7, 1944, typescript, Leifs collection.
123. Leifs to *Reichsstelle für Devisenbewirtschaftung*, February 20 and March 16, 1939.
124. "Aldrei meiri ástæða en nú að hlynna að góðri tónlist," *Þjóðviljinn*, March 31, 1943; "Úthlutun fjár til íslenzkra tónlistarmanna," *Þjóðviljinn*, February 13, 1944.
125. Leifs to Berta Geissmar, June 22, 1946; Annie Leifs to Marie Müller, March 18, 1942.
126. Saul Friedländer, *The Years of Extermination, Nazi Germany and the Jews 1939–1945* (New York: HarperPerennial, 1998), 354.
127. Friedländer, *The Years of Extermination*, 431.
128. See the Riethof family genealogy at http://freepages.genealogy.rootsweb.ancestry.com/~prohel/names/pollakmorawetz/rindskopf.html, accessed December 7, 2008.
129. "Ætluðu Þjóðverjar að flytja íslensku þjóðina af landi burt?," *Morgunblaðið*, November 23, 1946.
130. Leifs diary, February 1943. See also Leifs to Björn Kristjánsson, April 23, 1943. Björn Kristjánsson collection, National and University Library, Reykjavík.
131. Guðmundsson, *Berlínar-blús*, 2nd edition, 271–75, 279–93.
132. Martin, *The Nazi-Fascist New Order*, 270 (see also 213–21); Richard Strauss to Leifs, April 30, 1942.
133. Martin, *The Nazi-Fascist New Order*, 38.
134. Leifs to Berta Geissmar, June 22, 1946.
135. Deutsche St. Petri-Schule to Leifs, July 16, 1942; Leifs to Þórey Þorleifsdóttir, March 8, 1944.
136. *Ritverk Jónasar Hallgrímssonar*, eds. Haukur Hannesson, Páll Valsson, and Sveinn Yngvi Egilsson (Reykjavík: Svart á hvítu, 1989), vol. 4, 163.
137. George Payne Rainsford James, *Attila: A Romance* (London, 1837), 7–8.

138. Leifs diary, December 1943.

139. The manuscripts were returned to Iceland only in 1949 (through Moscow, since Rehbrücke was part of East Germany); Icelandic Embassy (Stockholm) to Foreign Ministry (Reykjavík), May 12, 1949.

EIGHT

GUILT AND RETRIBUTION
(1944–55)

THE LEIFS FAMILY'S NEW LIFE was fraught with uncertainty. They were virtually penniless on their arrival in Stockholm, then as now among Europe's most expensive cities, and Leifs was forced to borrow cash from the Icelandic embassy there. Even after he was able to access the bank account into which he had transferred funds from his deceased parents-in-law, money was in short supply. "Immense fatigue," Leifs wrote in his notebook, adding in a letter to his sister that after arriving in Stockholm they often slept for twelve hours at a time.[1]

Leifs found lodgings for all four of them at a hostel in the seaside resort town of Saltsjöbaden, southeast of Stockholm, but the marriage was beyond repair. In August he moved out and expressed his intention to seek divorce. Annie, who opposed the process, rented a small apartment for herself and their daughters in the Stockholm suburb of Solna. "Everything is beyond sad—but Jón insists on having it this way," she wrote to Leifs's sister.[2] His relationship with Snót and Líf was also fraught with tension. In December 1944 he asked to meet with each of them separately once a week, but they declined. "The friction seems irreparable," he wrote in his notebook, but he was somewhat heartened when they agreed to spend a few hours with him on New Year's Eve.[3]

In summer 1944 Leifs resumed work on a score he had begun in Rehbrücke the previous year. He had been contemplating a piece based on the Norse mythological tale of the "white god" Baldr since 1926, but not until fourteen years later did he complete a draft synopsis for a *"Baldr-Ballade,* pantomime with music in one act."[4] In the end, *Baldr* became a two-act "choreographic drama without words"—although Leifs's description on the title page is strictly speaking inaccurate, for the work contains a smattering of sung verses from the Prose and Poetic Eddas. The Prose Edda provides the crux of the story: the battle between the divine Baldr, Óðinn's son and the fairest of the gods, and Loki, the personification of evil. (Óðinn and Loki are familiar to music lovers as Wotan and Loge from Wagner's *Ring Cycle.*) Leifs's reworking of the material is fundamentally different from the text-driven and largely nondramatic *Edda I;* in *Baldr* he dispenses almost entirely with text and relies on physical gestures to propel the story. Leifs's avoidance of the term "ballet" in the title is understandable, for the gestures prescribed by his score are more akin to pantomime. He even suggested that his vision of the staging was comparable to that of Richard Strauss's 1914 pantomime-ballet *Josephslegende.*[5]

Leifs's version of the legend focuses on two key elements: Baldr's love for the fair maiden Nanna and his death, plotted by the scheming Loki. Act I begins in primordial darkness, as the primitive creatures of the earth gradually fill the stage and work themselves into a bestial frenzy. The voice of Óðinn, accompanied by Viking lurs, calms the tumult, and Baldr appears, casting light over the stage and motioning to the creatures to become human. The graceful Nanna enters and begins a dance with Baldr, during which Loki's jealous advances become more insistent. Baldr intervenes and throws him down; in revenge, Loki transforms himself into an eagle and conjures up a hurricane to destroy Baldr and Nanna. When the storm subsides, it reveals the serene Iðavellir, home of the gods, and Baldr announces that he will take Nanna for his wife. As the bridal march commences, the gods call on all humans to join the feast, and the curtain falls on a newly established harmony between heaven and earth.

In the second act, everything goes awry. Óðinn declares that in order to prevent Baldr's death, all things, living and dead, must swear not to bring about his downfall. First, all diseases and poisons take the oath, then fire, water, metals, and wood. The innocent-looking mistletoe, whose part is danced by a child, attempts to join in the oathtaking but is gently brushed aside. Eager to demonstrate the oath's efficacy, the gods play with Baldr's life, throwing in his direction all the things that cannot harm him. Tricked by Loki, the blind god Höður unwittingly throws the mistletoe at Baldr, who is mortally wounded and dies in Nanna's arms. Overcome with grief, she seizes a spear and lets herself fall on its point; her body is placed next to Baldr's on the funeral pyre. The gods vow to avenge Baldr's death, which has sent the universe into convulsions: a violent earthquake is followed by a volcanic eruption. Loki is captured and chained to a cliff, and a reptile is placed over his head to spout poison on him. In the end, the voice of Óðinn rings forth with the prophecy that Baldr will return.

Leifs asserted that, like the *Saga Symphony*, he had conceived *Baldr* as a "protest against the abuse of the northern tradition in recent years."[6] His claim is to some extent supported by the sketch material, which demonstrates how his ideas developed over a fifteen-year period. In the earliest draft synopsis, penned in 1926, the love story between Baldr and Nanna was the focal point of the entire plot. As Leifs returned to the work in 1940–42, the character of Loki gained in prominence, and the symbolic struggle between good and evil became a driving force. In the final version, it is tempting to see Loki as signifying Germany herself. According to Leifs's stage directions, after Loki conjures up a hurricane in act I (scene 4), he transforms himself into the Prussian eagle, which during World War II could easily be seen as a symbol of German military power.

Baldr was Leifs's first essay in explicitly depicting the violent forces of nature through an orchestral score, and as such it points the way to his later tone poems evoking natural phenomena. The work includes both a hurricane in act I and a volcanic eruption in the cathartic final scene, the latter inspired by the eruption of Mount Hekla in March 1947, the longest and most powerful of its five eruptions in the twentieth century. The timing was propitious, for Leifs, who had by then returned to Iceland, was just about to begin composing the final scene. Fascinated by the enormity of the outbreak, he drove to the farm nearest to Hekla in order to view the spewing volcano and hear the rumble of explosions in the distance.[7] According to legend (cited by composer Jón Ásgeirsson in a concert review decades later), locals were terrified when Leifs ventured much closer to the flowing lava than was considered safe.[8]

The forces of hurricane and volcanic disaster are mostly achieved by rhythmic acceleration and by a huge assembly of percussion. In the eruption that concludes the work, Leifs calls for eighteen percussionists employing traditional instruments (cymbals, side drum, tamtam, triangle, giant ratchet, two sets each of timpani and bass drums) as well as large and small rocks, gun and cannon shots, iron chains, a pair of anvils, large bells, and two Mahlerian giant hammers. To complete the instrumentarium, an organ lends weight to the diminished-seventh harmonies that spell out the most intense scenes of spewing lava—harking back to the Organ Concerto as well as forward to *Hekla*, a score that outdoes *Baldr* in terms of percussionists required (a total of nineteen).[9]

In his stage directions for *Baldr*, Leifs describes the natural surroundings of the gods in meticulous, realistic detail that seems nearly impossible to realize. In the act I hurricane scene, he calls for gusts of wind and beating rain, with "flurries of snow and dense hail" sweeping the stage at a forty-five-degree diagonal, the slant of the hail and snow gradually increasing until it sweeps "horizontally across the stage." As the storm subsides, Leifs calls for "colors of Icelandic landscape" with "preferably a river and a waterfall, a landscape of glaciers with light green patches of spring grass." Perhaps his detailed vision of nature in its many forms might best be fulfilled through video projections or even full-blown cinematic treatment. His stage directions also frequently underline the score's programmatic aspect—for example, when the thunder god Þór seals the oaths with his massive hammer (the Mahlerian *martello* once again) or when Baldr's ship is set on fire as tremolos spread throughout the orchestra.[10]

Despite Leifs's eagerness to procure a performance of *Baldr*, he never heard a note of the score. It was Iceland's entry to a competition held in conjunction with the 1948 London Olympics, where it received honorable mention but not a prize (the Polish composer Zbigniew Turski won with an *Olympic Symphony*).[11] Leifs even entertained the notion that a leading opera house might stage the work and sent enquiries to the Metropolitan Opera, Covent Garden, the Paris Opera, and the Royal Theater in Copenhagen. In 1960 he submitted *Baldr* to the Prince Rainier III competition in Monaco—once again, without success.[12] A single movement from the score was performed by the Iceland Symphony Orchestra at a memorial concert for Leifs in 1969, but *Baldr* had to wait until 1991 for its first full concert performance, by the Icelandic Youth Orchestra under the baton of Paul Zukofsky. A staged dance performance followed in 2000, in a joint production by Reykjavík, Bergen, and Helsinki—three of that year's European Cities of Culture.

A DISMAL HOMECOMING

As soon as peace was restored in 1945, Leifs made plans to travel from Sweden to Iceland. His initial request for transportation by an American aircraft was rejected by the US embassy after a monthlong investigation, presumably on the grounds that his political status was still uncertain. In the end he made the journey on the Icelandic ocean liner *Esja*, which departed Gothenburg harbor on July 4, 1945. The ship had been provided by the Icelandic government to facilitate the homeward journey of 304 citizens who had been residing on the continent at the outbreak of the war. British and US authorities had given their permission for the journey, with the proviso of a close inspection of passengers and cargo before setting sail.

For Leifs, this would prove to be a fateful journey. The ship was under the supervision of a Danish American commanding officer, Niels Knudsen, assisted by four armed British soldiers. By the time Leifs boarded the ship, tension was already mounting between Knudsen and the Icelandic passengers. One traveler noted that the officer's stern behavior made the passengers feel "as if they were all suspects and therefore more or less prisoners on the Icelandic state's vessel."[13] Having been denied air travel, Leifs was himself ill at ease and wary of the Allied officers. All passengers were to relinquish their passports at boarding, but Leifs refused, insisting that he was aboard an "Icelandic vessel in a neutral country and therefore not subject to orders by soldiers of nations at war." His argument with the soldiers escalated into a full-out brawl, and Knudsen ordered him to be placed under cabin arrest. It was only after the ship's (Icelandic) captain and several passengers had intervened—protesting that an American officer had no right to make an arrest on board an Icelandic ship in a Swedish harbor—that Knudsen relented and allowed Leifs to leave his cabin, although he was ordered to keep his conversations with other passengers to a minimum.[14]

The penultimate day of the journey, July 8, was the first day that Leifs enjoyed full freedom to move about the ship. He had expressed to Knudsen his wish to see Iceland emerge from the distance, since he hoped to use the experience as the basis for a composition. The orchestral overture *Landfall* (*Landsýn*), for male chorus and orchestra, came into being only a decade later. As Leifs noted on the title page, it was written "under the influence of my imprisonment on the Esja on July 4, 1945, and my journey on the ship to Iceland."[15] In the work, he depicts the sensation of gradually seeing his homeland emerge from afar and drew inspiration from a stanza of a poem by Jónas Hallgrímsson, which is not sung but appears as a preface to the score:

Ó, að þú mættir	Oh, if only
augum leiða	Your eyes could behold
landið loftháva	The land—sky-vaulted

og ljósbeltaða,	And girt with light—
þar sem um grænar	Where ice-blue streams
grundir líða	Make their way
elfur ísbláar	Out to the ocean
að ægi fram.	Over green meadows.[16]

In typical Leifs style, *Landfall* begins with low, grumbling pitches and gradually builds toward more distinct melodic shapes. It is a work of dramatic contrasts, alternating soft and loud passages. In one of his sketches, Leifs noted that the music should depict "green meadows (*p*) and terrifying mountains (*f*)," culminating in the resounding roar of a waterfall: "Dettifoss—*ff*"; the last presumably refers to a thundering C-major chord (m. 129).[17] As Iceland at last comes into view, the male chorus sings a majestic paean to the homeland and to the future that Leifs dreamed of building there. The text here is by Einar Benediktsson and depicts how Iceland—likened to a queen with a "firm, clear, glacial look" and a "snow-tiara above her noble brow"—emerges from the distance. In this work, more than any other in his output, Leifs projects a vision of landscape as home, a space in which he is restored to his true self, while also conveying a vision of a distant, nearly utopian reality.[18]

It is understandable that it should have taken Leifs a full decade to shape his idyllic reconstruction of a memory that was far more painful than the music suggests, for his homecoming in 1945 was utterly humiliating. A crowd had assembled on the Reykjavík pier to greet the ship's arrival, the city was bedecked with flags, local choirs performed patriotic songs, and, after a speech from a government minister, the entire throng joined in singing the national anthem. Leifs heard only a faint echo of these proceedings from his cabin, as he was still under ship's arrest. During the journey, Knudsen had implied that the order to arrest Leifs had come from Major General Dewing, head of the Allied SHAEF mission in Denmark, and now Leifs feared that he might be sent as a prisoner to Denmark or Britain.[19] He was fortunate in that the two US military intelligence officers who interrogated him in Reykjavík were both native Icelanders and sympathetic to his situation; one of them, Ragnar

H. Ragnar, was a musician and the father of Hjálmar H. Ragnarsson, who would later become a leading proponent of Leifs's music. The officers released him under supervision and pledged a speedy investigation. Still, the entire affair cast an unfortunate shadow over Leifs's return and made it even more arduous to rebuild his reputation in Iceland.

Leifs's attempts to clear his name from purported Nazi collaboration now began in earnest, and they consumed much of his time and energy for more than a decade. He claimed to have proof that his works were banned in England and applied for a visa to attend the 1946 ISCM festival in London, hoping that this would at least clarify the official line toward him. His application was granted, although not until August, by which time the festival had ended.[20] When the Icelandic Foreign Ministry, at his behest, requested that the US legation share any knowledge of Leifs rendering political aid to Germany during the war, the US officials replied only that it was "generally and widely known ... that Mr. Leifs participated in Germany's wartime broadcasts to Iceland."[21] Leifs countered that he had spoken only on matters of "national interest," that the German Foreign Office had considered his broadcasts opposed to their political agenda, and that in any case the content of his talks had been poorly translated for the Allied forces.[22] Six months later, the Icelandic Foreign Ministry completed its investigation of the *Esja* incident, declaring that no evidence had been found to corroborate rumors that Leifs had been a Nazi sympathizer.[23]

The forty-six-year-old Leifs had not visited Iceland for six years, and his prospects for establishing a career there were uncertain at best. Páll Ísólfsson, whom Leifs considered an adversary, was in charge of the Reykjavík School of Music as well as the National Radio's music division. Concert activities were largely organized by the Reykjavík Music Society under the leadership of Ragnar Jónsson, a wealthy cultural patron who had made his fortune from a margarine manufacturing company and who was a friend of Ísólfsson's. Three outstanding musicians who had fled Germany and Austria in the 1930s had established promising careers in Reykjavík: the music educator Heinz Edelstein and conductors Victor Urbancic and Robert Abraham (the latter the son of a noted Berlin ethnomusicologist and coworker of Hornbostel's at the Berlin Phonograph Archive). Any hopes Leifs may have had of making his mark as a conductor, educator, or concert organizer or at the National Radio were therefore unlikely to come to fruition.

He also faced the task of convincing Icelanders of his worth as a composer. Reykjavík had neither a professional orchestra nor a choir that could begin to do justice to his scores, and local taste was still overwhelmingly conservative. His larger works were completely unknown there, apart from the *Iceland Overture* (performed by the Hamburg Philharmonic in 1926) and the *Iceland Cantata*, which had been transmitted on the radio from the Berlin Philharmonic concert in 1936. Performances of Leifs's music had been infrequent during the war. At a 1942 Artists' Congress (a festival held under the auspices of the Federation of Icelandic Artists), the tenor Eggert Stefánsson sang a few of his songs, and the Reykjavík Orchestra played the *Icelandic Dances*. At a second such congress in 1945, Ísólfsson premiered a new choral work, a substantial arrangement of the tvísöngur melody *Ísland, farsælda frón* (op. 28 no. 1), the score of which Leifs had sent on microfilm from Stockholm. Still, by and large, Icelanders were both ignorant of his music and indifferent to it.

Another challenge was that Leifs returned to an Iceland that was undergoing rapid change and that was already quite transformed from the country he knew. The Anglo-American presence during the war had cultural as well as financial ramifications: Iceland's economy was flourishing and was soon to receive a further boost through a generous Marshall Aid package from the United States. This resulted in an ambitious modernization project aimed to bring the formerly backward country into the twentieth century. Leifs's nationalism reflected his vision of a country that did not exist; as modern Icelanders of the young republic looked toward America, interest in folk-derived art was even less than before.

The reception of Leifs's music was also not aided by his controversial public persona and what was seen as his uncompromising

Figure 8.1. Leifs at Þingvellir, Iceland, summer 1946. © Reykjavík Museum of Photography.

representation of STEF, the local performing rights society (see below). At times he became a kind of comic figure, spoofed in the local satirical magazine *Spegillinn* (*The Mirror*) and the popular revue *Bláa stjarnan* (*The Blue Star*). In the latter, one scene involved a group of people making an infernal noise by rattling all kinds of pots, pans, and washboards. When asked what was going on, one member of the group replied that they were performing the *Saga Symphony* by Jón Leifs. The skit, which mocked Leifs's percussion-heavy style and was presumably inspired by the *Saga Symphony*'s ill-fated premiere (see below), was received with much amusement and applause.[24]

A RELUCTANT MUSE

Leifs sojourned frequently in Sweden between 1945 and 1950, mostly for personal reasons. He had fallen in love with Thea Heintz, the proprietor of the inn in Saltsjöbaden where the Leifs family had lodged for a while after arriving in Stockholm (see fig. 8.2). It began as a clandestine affair. Shortly before New Year's Eve 1945, Leifs wrote to his sister in Iceland that "neither Annie nor the children have any inkling of my relationship with Thea," adding that he expected the two of them to be "together for the rest of our lives."[25] Her full name was Althea Maria Duzzina Heintz, and she was born in Lund, Sweden, on September 26, 1905. By the time she met Leifs she was already a double divorcee and mother to a teenage son, Klas. In April 1946 Leifs moved into the second floor of her newly expanded Grand Pensionat. Thea—whom Leifs affectionately called by the Icelandic name Þorgerður—was by all accounts a self-assured, cultured, and intelligent woman. Still, they did not see eye to eye on what mattered most to him. In general, Thea was unimpressed with Icelandic culture; her son, in a conversation with Carl-Gunnar Åhlén in the 1990s, recalled their frequent debates about Leifs's vision of a Nordic renaissance.[26] She also spurned his invitation to move to Iceland, which in her mind equaled "drawing the curtains and disappearing into the darkness."[27]

Leifs seems to have been the weaker partner in his relationship with Thea. He was in need of emotional security and companionship during this tumultuous period in his life and may also have surmised that a new relationship would make Annie accept the finality of their divorce. Thea, on the other hand, was hesitant to commit herself to Leifs. She also loathed writing letters, which did not bode well for their long-distance relationship. In February 1947, when Leifs was in Reykjavík, they had spoken only once on the telephone since that previous Christmas. When he flew to Stockholm a few weeks later, she was not at the airport to greet him, and he resumed work on *Baldr* "hesitant and disappointed" by the situation. The tug-of-war continued: in 1948 he attended meetings in Copenhagen and Oslo without hearing a word from her, and after writing numerous letters she finally replied from Paris—where she had gone without his knowledge. "Unrelenting sorrow," he wrote in his notebook, but a few weeks later she asked him to return to Saltsjöbaden, and they vowed to begin anew.[28]

Figure 8.2. Thea Leifs. © Carl-Gunnar Åhlén, private collection.

They were married in the medieval church at Gamla Uppsala in Sweden on February 3, 1950, and at Thea's suggestion they used the old wedding rings that had belonged to Leifs's parents. But even in marriage she remained elusive, and by December 1953 Leifs was on the verge of despair: "Since we first met I have not loved any woman but you. All the chaos and everything that we have gone through since would never have occurred had you really repaid in your own heart the love you elicited from me.... I haven't heard a word from you since I telephoned from Copenhagen more than two months ago, and even then I did not get to see you. Do you really find this reasonable?"[29] When Leifs heard nothing from Thea on his fifty-fifth birthday, he wrote, suggesting divorce unless the situation changed. He made one final attempt at reconciliation, inviting her to join him in Reykjavík for a meeting of the Nordic Composers' Union in June 1954. At first she agreed to come, then cancelled her flight at the last minute. Their marriage was dissolved in May 1956.

Thea, who passed away in 1977, remains an ambiguous character in Leifs's biography, and it is difficult to gauge her true emotions for him. Whereas Annie had always been prepared to put her husband's needs first, Thea was unwilling to forgo her independence. Perhaps the complexities of Leifs's personal and professional situations also proved too much for her. His self-esteem, already weakened by accusations of Nazi collaboration, was certainly further drained during his years with Thea, as was his productivity. In the nine years from 1947 to 1955, Leifs completed only nine works, one of which is dedicated to Thea: *Songs of Þorgerður* (*Þorgerðarlög*) op. 38 for men's chorus. In the first movement, *Love Verses* (*Ástarvísur*), Leifs sets his own collage of aphorisms and verses about love and marriage, including an appeal for love to thaw the bitter cold within:

Líkt og sólargeisli um sumardag	As the sun's rays on a summer's day
leysir svellið svalrar nætur,	soften a cool night's ice,
þíddu heiftar frost	thus melt the frost of anger
úr huga mér.	from my mind.

Leifs's atmospheric setting of these words is marked off from the rest of the movement; they are sung to sustained half notes in chorale style, *pianissimo* and *molto tranquillo*. An old Icelandic adage receives more expressive treatment and seems to speak directly to his situation: "Women often cause pain" ("*Oft verðr kvalræði af konum*"). In *Songs of Þorgerður*, Leifs seems to express all the conflicting emotions of his relationship with Thea—the reluctant muse.

STEF AND THE CRUSADE FOR PERFORMING RIGHTS

While Leifs's career prospects as a composer and conductor were limited in Iceland, much work lay ahead in securing performing rights and royalties for local artists. Leifs was virtually the only Icelandic musician with extensive knowledge of such matters, thanks largely to his experience from the Permanent Council, and this would prove a valuable asset both for himself and the artistic community at large. Two weeks after his return to Reykjavík in 1945, Leifs summoned four of the leading composers of his generation— Páll Ísólfsson, Sigurður Þórðarson, Karl O. Runólfsson, and Helgi Pálsson—to the founding meeting of the Icelandic Composer's Society (*Tónskáldafélag Íslands*). Leifs's proposal for the organization's statutes was accepted, and there was a palpable (though short-lived) effort at peacemaking between him and Ísólfsson, who was elected president at Leifs's suggestion and who reciprocated by nominating Leifs as his vice president.

The main short-term objective of the Composer's Society was to urge the Icelandic government to update the country's obsolete laws on performing rights, which had been written in 1905, a time when few Icelanders even considered the arts a profession. New laws were passed in 1947, and shortly thereafter Iceland ratified the Berne Convention, which was the prerequisite for establishing a separate legal entity to collect royalties. In January 1948 Leifs was the main instigator of a new organization: STEF, which is both an acronym (*Samtök tónskálda og eigenda flutningsréttar*, or Society of Composers and Owners of Performing Rights) and the Icelandic word for *theme*. Leifs was elected STEF's first president and immediately began negotiations with industry representatives in Iceland—restaurants, movie theaters, concert promoters—though with little initial success. Royalties were regarded as a bizarre, even ludicrous idea, and Leifs thus resorted to filing a number of lawsuits in the Icelandic court system to advance his case.

One of the lawsuits became an international news item. The US armed forces ran a military airbase in Keflavík as part of NATO operations from 1951 to 2006, and the broadcast of its radio station, although intended for airbase personnel only, could be picked up throughout much of western and southern Iceland. As the US armed forces had been granted special dispensation by American rights societies, STEF received no royalties for these broadcasts. STEF's counterpart in Germany had already lost a similar case against the US Army, but the ever-combative Leifs dispatched a notice to US president and commander in chief Eisenhower demanding full payment. He followed that up, in April 1955, with a court case on behalf of four foreign composers: American songwriter Jimmy McHugh for "On the Sunny Side of the Street," the Dane Jacob Gade for "Tango Jalousie," the Swiss Paul Burkhard for "Oh Mein Papa," and the estate of Giacomo Puccini for "Mi chiamano Mimì" from *La Bohéme*. The Icelandic court ruled in favor of STEF, resulting in an annual payment of $4,600 from the US armed forces and similar payments in other countries that had implemented the Berne Convention. European media followed the story, and for a while Leifs was fielding interviews from publications such as the German *Der Spiegel*, where he remarked that "we Icelanders regard culture and artistic creation as the foundation of our national existence. We have no other foundation, since we do not have an army or any material fortune."[30]

Leifs's headstrong leadership of STEF did nothing to endear him or his cause to the Icelandic public. On the contrary, it confirmed his image among locals as an irascible curmudgeon; in 1952 one composer remarked that STEF was "in all likelihood the least popular institution in our society."[31] One incident in particular made national headlines. In September 1955 Leifs had the use of a small cabin in the lava fields south of Hafnarfjörður for his composing, and he traveled there by bus. One Saturday evening, the radio was playing as passengers boarded the vehicle, and Leifs demanded that the driver turn it off since no contract was in force between STEF and the bus company. An argument ensued, during which Leifs worked himself into such a fury that he kicked the radio, breaking it into pieces. Police were summoned and took Leifs into custody, "much to the amusement of fellow passengers," according to a local news report. In a newspaper interview following his release, Leifs insisted that he had been neither drunk nor deranged but that he had simply wished to draw attention to the performing rights violation.[32]

At the very least, Leifs's work for STEF assured him, for the first time in his life, a satisfactory monthly salary. Reykjavík was still something of a cultural backwater, and locals regarded some of his more refined habits as ostentatious display. He frequently dined at local restaurants (of which there were only a few at the time), famously ordering expensive wines and returning them if the temperature was not to his satisfaction, and when traveling abroad he stayed at elegant hotels.[33] This eventually fueled rumors that Leifs himself was pocketing some of STEF's profits. A cartoon from the satirical magazine *Spegillinn* in December 1952 shows two human figures, both of whom are purportedly Leifs: one, dressed as Santa Claus, hands a present—presumably cash—to the suit-clad composer (see fig. 8.3). Two years later, *Morgunblaðið*, Iceland's leading newspaper, printed an unsigned satirical poem insinuating "dishonesty" in STEF's finances.[34] No evidence has come to light suggesting that these allegations were founded in truth. They seem to have been motivated by locals' distrust of the novel idea of royalty payments and their skepticism that a creative artist could earn a respectable salary—even if most of it was for Leifs's organizational work and not his compositions.

Leifs's duties for STEF included attending meetings in Paris, the center of performing rights' societies in Europe. He had never studied French but now began taking private lessons in Reykjavík from a young woman, Vigdís Finnbogadóttir, who had recently returned from university studies in Paris and would in 1980 be elected president of the republic. Leifs even showed an interest in

Figure 8.3. Cartoon from the satirical magazine *Spegillinn*, 1952. © National and University Library, Reykjavík.

French music, which he had previously dismissed as too "southern" for his Nordic aesthetic. At a reception hosted by the Reykjavík division of Alliance Française in 1962, he performed a selection of Debussy's piano preludes—his first public appearance as pianist since the 1920s—and remarked that his newly found appreciation for French culture had opened a "new world" to him.[35] His Francophone experience presumably explains why he gave French titles to two of his works from the 1950s: *Réminiscence du Nord* op. 40 and *Trois peintures abstraites* op. 44.

TRAGEDY IN SWEDEN: THE REQUIEM MUSIC

On July 12, 1947, as he was completing the score of *Baldr* in Reykjavík, Leifs received an urgent telegram from Stockholm. His daughter Líf, age seventeen, was reported missing after going for a swim off the coast of Hamburgsund, Sweden, where she was attending a summer course for young violinists.

Leifs's decision to separate from Annie had put immense strain on his relationship with his daughters. Snót openly accused him of abandoning them in order to salvage his career but also encouraged him to take steps toward self-improvement. Her Christmas present to him in 1945 was a copy of the Bible, and she recommended that he read Ernst Wiechert's *Totenwald*, an account of the author's incarceration at the Buchenwald concentration camp, advising that "it is necessary to know what one must do to become a good person, for everything that has happened can happen once again."[36] Líf, on the other hand, hardly ever wrote. Her few surviving letters are filled with dejection, such as the sarcastic greeting at Christmas 1946, which she was able to convey only in German: "The pathetic remains of the Leifs family thank the great master for the carnations and the Christmas telegram" ("Die kümmerlichen Überreste der Familie Leifs danken dem großen Meister für die Nelken und das Weihnachtstelegramm"). Her letter continues, "Dear Daddy! Unfortunately I could not say this in Icelandic."[37]

The early months of 1947 were also ridden with conflict and pain. In March, Leifs was in Stockholm and took Líf out to dinner and the theater, but her gloomy state of mind gave him cause for concern. He met with her violin teacher, Charles Barkel, a professor at the Royal Conservatory, who informed him that she was no longer making progress in her studies. Financially, Annie was in dire straits, and their situation was about to worsen considerably, for the Icelandic Finance Ministry ceased payments of a subsidy for Icelandic students abroad, which both Snót and Líf had received.[38] Declining her father's suggestion that she take a break from school, Líf attended Barkel's violin course in Hamburgsund for the third time that summer. Her classmates there hardly recognized her on her arrival, believing her to be a younger, skinnier sister.[39]

Hamburgsund is a fishing village on the western coast of Sweden, roughly halfway between Gothenburg and Oslo. There are

Figure 8.4. Líf Leifs in Hamburgsund, Sweden, summer 1945. © Leifs Archives, National and University Library, Reykjavík.

granite cliffs and white, sandy beaches, with views of an archipelago made up of countless small islands. During the course, Líf routinely swam a kilometer in the ocean each day, to the nearby Jakobsö (Jacob's Island) and back. On July 12, she went swimming despite a nearby fisherman warning her of the cold weather. She replied that she was an experienced swimmer and entered the sea naked; her swimming costume and shoes were later found on the beach. When Líf was discovered to be missing, Barkel telephoned Annie, who arrived with Snót the next day, "nearly deranged with sorrow," according to a memorandum written by a staff member at the Icelandic embassy in Stockholm.[40] An elaborate search was launched, but nine days would pass before a Swedish lieutenant, who was sailing in the archipelago with his family, discovered her body.

The harrowing question, and one that would remain unanswered, was whether Líf had meant to take her own life. Annie and Snót searched in vain for clues as to her mental state during her last days, but Snót reported to her father that she left "everything behind clean and in order ———"; the dashes were presumably meant to imply what could not be said.[41] On their return to Solna, Líf's final postcard awaited them, and again Snót tried to assuage her father: "One sees clearly that she was completely unknowing of her fate.... Perhaps she was too good for this life."[42] But a few weeks later Snót had adopted a harsher tone and now did not shy away from implicating her father in the undoing of the entire family: "You did not regard your own children and your wife as creatures of God, who were entrusted to you, but rather as tools for implementing your own ideas.... Everything that we had achieved in our lives was taken for granted. In the most fragile teenage years you destroyed her faith in humanity, so that she broke down emotionally much too soon."[43] Shattered by his daughter's accusations, Leifs replied, "We have all failed, but we cannot stop striving for what is good. I will try my best."[44]

Leifs's experience of bereavement immediately fed into his own creativity. Within three weeks, he had written two works in Líf's memory (*Torrek* and *Requiem*), and he would later compose two more (*Vita et mors* and *Elegies*). The urgency of his musical response reflected the extreme emotional situation at hand. Leifs had always been (and would remain) an autobiographical composer, but this impulse is nowhere stronger than in these four works. In writing them, he sought to construct some form of understanding and to mend posthumously his deeply fractured relationship with Líf. These requiem works are among his finest and most emotionally engaging. Their power lies in the music's intense grief, with

Leifs attempting to achieve consolation and forgiveness in every measure.

In creating musical monuments for Líf, Leifs had an inevitable point of departure: the quiet, understated, yet eerily foreboding *Lullaby* op. 14a, composed shortly after her birth. The *Lullaby* was certainly on Leifs's mind in July 1947. As he and Annie made preparations for Líf's body to be transported to Iceland, Annie specifically requested that it be sung at the funeral, which took place at Reykjavík Cathedral on August 13.[45]

The funeral was also the premiere of Leifs's choral *Requiem* op. 33b, completed in Reykjavík on July 31 and the most immediate descendant of the *Lullaby* among the four memorial works. Its text is not the traditional Latin; instead, Leifs assembled a collage of text fragments from Icelandic folk poetry and verses by Jónas Hallgrímsson, all of which share a similar subject. The main source is a gentle but haunting lullaby: in the stillness of a bright Icelandic summer night, each of the various species of flora and fauna has found its proper resting place. The daughter, who is twice addressed directly in the text as Leifs compiled it, is encouraged to follow nature's example:

Sofinn er fífill	The dandelion sleeps
fagr í haga,	fair in the field,
mús undir mosa,	the mouse under moss,
már á báru,	the mew on the billow,
lauf á limi,	the leaf on the twig,
ljós í lofti,	the light in the sky,
hjörtr á heiði	the heart on the hearth,
en í hafi fiskar.	the herring in the deep.
Sefr selr í sjó,	The seal on the skerry,
svanr á báru,	the swan on the moat,
már í hólmi,	the newt in the pond,
manngi þau svæfir.	with no one to lull them.
Sofa manna börn	The children of men sleep
í mjúku rúmi,	in a soft bed,
bía og kveða	lulling and singing
en babbi þau svæfir.	and daddy lulls them to sleep.

Sof þú nú sæl og sigrgefin.	Sleep now, content and victorious.
Sofðu, eg unni þér.	Sleep, I love you.

The depiction of nature in Leifs's *Requiem* differs from other representations of landscape in his music, which tend toward external drama with powerful, even violent forces of nature. Here nature is portrayed as a calm, comforting element, yet this music carries its own kind of tragedy. As Guy Rickards has observed, it has the character of a lullaby, "only the child is dead and beneath the song, never stated but almost corporeally tangible, is a raw howl of anguish of numbing intensity."[46]

In the *Requiem*, Leifs takes even further the simplicity of the earlier *Lullaby*. The interval of the fifth is all-pervasive, and large stretches of the work are built on the tonic harmony, oscillating between A-major and A-minor triads (see example 8.1).

Requiem consists of two contrasting elements: outer sections grounded in tonic harmony (A major/minor) and a central section in which nontonic harmonies (subdominant and dominant) appear, if only fleetingly. The central section also strikes a note of gloom and foreboding. It consists of two parts; in the first, the text moves from dormant nature to the internal grief of the bereaved father:

Blæju yfir bæ	Over the weary
búanda lúins	workman's cottage
dimmra drauma	night has drawn a veil
dró nótt úr sjó.	of dark dreams from the sea.

Here the male voices sing alone, in harmonies darker and more dissonant than any of the preceding music. When the female voices enter again, their reassuring text seems to address the father as much as the child:

Við skulum gleyma gráti og sorg	Let us forget tears and sorrow,
gott er heim að snúa.	it is good to return home.
Láttu þig dreyma bjarta borg	Let yourself dream of a bright place
búna þeim, er trúa.	made for those who believe.

The third line of this stanza provides the work's harmonic and emotional climax, when Leifs dramatically withholds the sopranos' F-sharp, employing an F-natural for only the second time in the

Example 8.1. Leifs, *Requiem* op. 33b, mm. 1–13. © Iceland Music Information Center.

entire work. This mournful clouding over hints at the darker emotional world already laid bare by the preceding passage for male voices, but here it is short-lived, and the music leads directly to a shortened repeat of the opening section.

Leifs compiled the text to his *Requiem* from five sources. Most of the lyrics (the A-section) are taken from three folk poems, all of which were published in a widely read anthology in 1898–1903.[47] For the opening "the dandelion sleeps" quatrain as well as "over the weary workman's cottage," Leifs turned to Jónas Hallgrímsson's *The Lay of Magnús* (*Magnúsarkviða*), an elegy in twenty stanzas from 1842, where the poet creates his own version of the folk poetry images.[48] The least well known of Leifs's texts for the *Requiem* is the anonymous quatrain that forms the work's climax ("let's forget sorrow and tears"). This text had appeared only once in print, in a 1916 article by the poet Theodóra Thoroddsen in the literary journal *Skírnir*.[49] Leifs was likely familiar with the publication for two reasons: the author was the mother of a childhood friend, and the topic of the article—folk poetry that was said to have originated as dream prophecies—would have been of interest to his spiritualist parents. This particular verse is embedded in a larger folk tale: a widow dies and leaves a young daughter; she later appears to the daughter in dream and comforts her with this verse. The other folk verses that form the bulk of the *Requiem* text also have supernatural connotations. They are examples of *ljúflingslög*, texts that were supposedly sung by "hidden people" (*huldufólk*) to human children, often in times of need or distress. According to the edition of these texts from 1898 to 1903, such poems were supposed to bring good fortune to the child.[50] In Leifs's *Requiem*, they instead become a funeral prayer.

Leifs composed the *Requiem* in a flurry of activity that also included *Torrek* for baritone and piano, completed three days earlier. This is a setting of verses from *Egils saga*, attributed to the Viking Age poet and warrior Egill Skallagrímsson (ca. 904–ca. 995) on the death of two of his sons. After burying his second son, Egill returns home and locks the door to his bed chamber and takes neither food nor drink, intending to starve himself to death. His daughter cunningly convinces him to instead compose a poem about his grief, and thus he conceives the twenty-five-stanza *Sonatorrek* (*Sons' Elegy*), parts of which Leifs set:

Mjök hefr Rán	The sea goddess
ryskt um mik,	has ruffled me,
em ek ofsnauðr	stripped me bare
at ástvinum;	of my loved ones:
sleit marr bönd	the ocean severed
minnar ættar,	my family's bonds,
snaran þátt	the tight knot
af sjálfum mér.	that ties me down.[51]

Both *Requiem* and *Torrek* convey intense emotion through simple means, but musically they could hardly be more different. Leifs's sparse setting of *Torrek* is at times almost violent, a barely contained cry against the injustice of fate. The piano part is essentially derived from only five minor triads (on G-sharp, A-sharp, C, D, and E), which appear in the right hand while the left is firmly grounded on an open fifth for large stretches of the song (see example 8.2). The simplicity of means is somewhat concealed by

Example. 8.2. Leifs, *Torrek* op. 33a, mm. 1–7. © Iceland Music Information Center.

the pungent dissonances while the near-exclusive use of minor triads only enhances *Torrek*'s bleak emotional world. Leifs pointedly omits the poem's last half stanza, where the author declares he will remain "glad and with good will" until death claims him. Instead, the musical setting reaches a desolate, exhausted conclusion.

Together, *Torrek* and *Requiem* cover a wide emotional range, but they did not exhaust Leifs's need to work through his grief by composing. In the three years that followed, he completed two further works in Líf's memory, both on a considerably larger scale and both including strikingly narrative elements: *Elegies* for male chorus (1947) and the string quartet *Vita et mors* (*Life and Death*, 1948–51). The three-movement quartet was meant to suggest Líf's life, death, and afterlife. Its title is an inversion of Leifs's previous quartet (*Mors et vita*) but also a reflection both on Líf's name and her fate. The first movement (*Childhood*) was completed on August 19, 1948, and Leifs wrote in his score that it was a "birthday present for Líf," who would have celebrated her nineteenth birthday a week earlier. It begins with a premonition: a grim, descending chromatic phrase, played *sul ponticello*, over an F-minor harmony—not unlike a shiver running down one's spine. The movement gains momentum through gradual rhythmic acceleration, from cautious quarter notes to exhilarated dotted sixteenths by the end, presumably meant to suggest Líf's development from an infant to a child of strong character.

Example 8.3. Leifs, *Vita et mors* op. 36, mm. 199–205. © Iceland Music Information Center.

The second movement (*Youth*) has a darker quality, with particular emphasis on minor harmonies. Its climax is both sudden and stunning: a mournful *espressivo* gesture in the viola is shattered by a *ff sf* chord, promptly followed by a cry in the first violin marked *quasi desperato* and a shorter gesture marked *quasi morendo* (see example 8.3). This moment is a striking example of Leifs's penchant for programmatic music, as it seems to echo Líf's anguished final moment. Although the music is shocking, the material itself is familiar. The descending scale is a variant of the ominous *ponticello* opening gesture while the harmony is the third bar of *Torrek* transposed down a whole step.

The finale, *Requiem and Eternity*, is a kind of fantasy on the main idea of the choral *Requiem*. The first thirty-eight bars are firmly grounded on A, the key of the *Requiem*, and Leifs cites specific passages of that work, such as the opening "the dandelion sleeps" (mm. 9–10 and 162–64), "mouse under moss" (mm. 17–18), and, most extensively, the entire refrain "sleep now, content and victorious / Sleep, I love you" (mm. 28–33). As the work reaches its serene conclusion, the focus is still on the first violin, which eventually soars to stratospheric heights, marked *morendo*.

This was not the first time Leifs had been almost pathologically drawn to re-creating his daughter's death. His *Elegies* (*Erfiljóð*) op. 35, composed between October 22 and November 15, 1947, consists of three movements for male chorus. The first, *Grief* (*Söknuður*), is once again a reworking of the *Requiem* idea but with a more varied harmonic palette. The second movement, *Dance of Sorrow* (*Sorgardans*), is a bleak danse macabre to an eclectic collage of Icelandic folk verses and adages on the subject of death. The harmonies are dark, with F minor as a tonal center, and there is an overwhelming sense of heavy grief. While large stretches of the movement are homorhythmic, Leifs adds gravitas and urgency through his polytextual setting; the tenors and basses sing different texts throughout.

The third and final movement, titled *Sea Poem* (*Sjávarljóð*), is also the longest at thirteen minutes and, from narrative and psychological standpoints, the most remarkable. Here Leifs expands the emotional and tonal range by adding a solo violin and mezzo-soprano to the ensemble. Through the texts and the musical context, he creates a kind of operatic scena inhabited by several characters. The mezzo-soprano sings verses that frequently suggest a divine presence, sometimes comforting ("God bless the children, both big and small") and sometimes enticing, like a magical *huldukona* or "hidden woman" from Icelandic folk tales ("swim in the sea, should you wish to"). Most chillingly, she also seems to take on the role of Líf herself, in her postmortem state, such as in the following verse:

Eg er á floti út við sker	Out by the skerries I am afloat,
öll er þrotin vörnin.	my resistance is at an end.
Báran vota vaggar mér,	The watery wave rocks me,
veistu nú hve notalegt það er.	now you know how soothing that is.

The solo violin again seems to suggest Líf herself. The violin part begins calmly, but a sudden change occurs at m. 107, when the chorus sings, "The weather soon changes in the sky." There ensues what can easily be heard as a depiction of her final battle, the violin part becoming increasingly agitated with loud *sforzandos* in an accelerating tempo. It is a brief but exhausting fight for life; by m. 148 the mezzo-soprano sings a well-known children's verse (*o moon, take me up to the clouds*), and the music takes on the character of the *Requiem* with oscillating major/minor triads. Through a recurring tonal move from F up to A major/minor, Leifs even revisits the *Requiem* in terms of both its music and its key.

Through the dramatic gestures of *Vita et mors* and *Elegies*, Leifs seems to have confronted the situation in a way that was otherwise not available to him. By composing his daughter's death, he rejected his status as a helpless bystander, attempting to regain the control he so desperately sought. In the face of their deteriorating relationship, one senses in this music an almost palpable sense of guilt, a desperate attempt for a personal *Wiedergutmachung*. As is so often the case with Leifs, composition and biography are inseparably intertwined.

Leifs's method of devising the texts to the *Requiem*, and to the second and third *Elegies*, is characteristic of his vocal music in the 1940s and '50s. During that time he compiled a vast assortment of Icelandic folk verses, aphorisms, sayings, and other short texts that he arranged thematically by subject; his archives contain countless typewritten sheets with verses on love, summer, winter, horses, trolls, etc. The earlier libretto to the *Edda* oratorio had also been a kind of collage, but now Leifs gathered texts from a far wider variety of sources, and the snippets are shorter than in the *Edda*, often only a line or two.[52] Presumably he sensed in such texts a national element that derived directly from the anonymous common folk, unlike the high literary tradition of the Eddas or skaldic poetry. Leifs's first settings of such collage texts are his two sets of *Poems of Icelanders* opp. 29 and 30 (1943). He employed the same method in opp. 37, 38, and 43 as well as his arrangement for men's chorus of the *Icelandic Dances* op. 11—done in 1948 and the only one of his choral works to become truly popular in Iceland during his lifetime.

ANNIE AND SNÓT

Annie wished to live near her daughter's final resting place and moved to Iceland after Líf's death. Her new life there was increasingly occupied with an improbable project: to raise enough money, in Líf's memory, to found a Roman Catholic monastery in Iceland that would also serve as a cultural center. Coming from a Jewish-born German Protestant, this was certainly a surprising idea, but Annie had sought solace in the Catholic faith after her divorce, and a Jesuit priest in Stockholm had become her spiritual mentor and confidant.[53] Plans for an Icelandic convent gave new purpose to her solitary life, but perhaps she also saw it as absolution for Líf's death, in the event that she had taken her own life and thus violated the divine law.

Annie brought to this project the same sense of idealism and commitment with which she had once promoted her husband's career. Reykjavík was a small city, and she had easy access to leading intellectuals and politicians: the foreign minister discussed the matter informally with cabinet members and suggested that if the Vatican agreed, the government might donate land to the project.[54] Annie corresponded with Bernard Kaelin, Abbot Primate of the Benedictine Confederation, who journeyed to Iceland to discuss the matter with local authorities. She even managed to arrange, in October 1948, an audience in Castel Gandolfo with Pope Pius XII, but this was not the success she had hoped for. The pope proved unwilling to commit funds or resources to an Icelandic monastery, and in any case the Catholic Bishop of Iceland was also skeptical of the idea.[55] For five years, Annie's travels on behalf of this project took up most of her time and money. She spent the winter of 1948–49 in Switzerland, where she unsuccessfully petitioned Benedictine monasteries to supply her foundation with monks.[56] From there, she flew to New York to visit her sister and brother-in-law, whom she had not seen since 1937 and who pleaded with her to move to the United States.[57] In one of her plane trips, her right hand got caught while descending a mobile staircase, and two fingers suffered permanent nerve damage. While she had not performed in public since Salle Pleyel in 1928, this signaled the official end of her career as a pianist.[58]

Meanwhile, Snót returned to Germany. She resumed her doctoral studies in German literature at the University of Hamburg, a city still reeling from the destruction caused by the war, and completed her

Figure 8.5. Snót Leifs, ca. 1950. © Leifs Archives, National and University Library, Reykjavík.

dissertation in 1949. It was Leifs, always the controlling father, who suggested the topic of her study: rhyme and rhythm in Nietzsche's *Also sprach Zarathustra* and how the "principles of rhythm in prose writing must be taken into consideration when translating ancient Icelandic literature."[59] Once her dissertation was complete, Snót returned to Iceland, where she and her mother moved into a small basement flat near the Reykjavík harbor. Annie made a modest living as a piano teacher, and Snót obtained an office job at the French embassy, though she lasted only a few months. She had become increasingly quiet and withdrawn, and eventually she was diagnosed as schizophrenic. In 1953, Leifs took her to Denmark to seek a cure, and she stayed there for a year undergoing various tests and treatments.[60] On her return, Leifs seems to have made a genuine attempt to mend their fractured relationship. When not away on business, he accompanied her on daily walks and did what he could to make her life more comfortable, always hoping that her condition might improve. Annie lived in Reykjavík until her death in 1970; Snót never recovered from her illness and passed away in 2011.

In February 1955, Leifs jotted down in his notebook a discussion he had had with the leading Icelandic psychiatrist of the time, Helgi Tómasson, who informed him that Snót's condition was most likely hereditary and that he also displayed signs of schizoid personality disorder. Leifs had read widely on the subject during Snót's illness, and he seems to have resigned himself calmly to the diagnosis: "I think back to my youth and childhood and realize that he is right; I read about Strindberg, van Gogh, and others . . . and find many things in common, try to improve my mental health and at the same time try to help Snót, whom I understand better now."[61]

Although Leifs's reaction can seem conceited—he comes to terms with his illness by equating himself with geniuses such as Strindberg and van Gogh—his composure suggests that he already suspected the root of his own mental instability. According to psychology, the symptoms of schizoid personality disorder include detachment from social relationships, difficulty expressing emotions, lack of desire for intimacy, and emotional coldness. Most of Leifs's contemporaries agreed that he could be "rough and ruthless" and "lacking the ability to see and respect the views of others."[62] Leifs committed himself single-mindedly to his artistic mission. To him, his uncongenial and narcissistic attitude was justified by the greater cause, even if it meant ignoring the needs of those closest to him. "I am determined to live and die for my ideals, without being more considerate of my surroundings and my fellow men than is necessary for the advancement of my goals," he wrote to his parents in 1927.[63]

It must also be noted that coldness and emotional detachment were precisely the personality traits that Leifs extolled as Nordic and valorized in his works—for example, the *Saga Symphony* and *The Lay of Guðrún*. It is difficult to judge the extent to which this was Leifs's way of rationalizing his own character. In his letters he occasionally admits his weaknesses in this regard while remaining seemingly unperturbed by them. He wrote to Ísólfsson that he derived "no pleasure from hurting people and making enemies; I am instead sensitive to it, although I can be rough on the exterior."[64] To his sister, he confessed that he was "too selfish to try to understand others, for I have enough trouble with myself."[65] Leifs seems to have become, in general, less confrontational in his interpersonal dealings later in life (see also chap. 9). His widow described him as cheerful but "extremely shy"; the author Sigurður A. Magnússon, who knew him in the 1950s and '60s, remarked that although he could be "more stubborn than the devil," he also had an amiable and charming side.[66] To what extent his newly found equanimity was a result of a more probing attitude toward his own mental health, or whether it simply came with aging, cannot be inferred from surviving sources.

ILL-FATED PREMIÈRES

Another of Leifs's projects after returning to Iceland was to found a publishing firm, called Islandia Edition, that would focus on music by native composers. Through Islandia Edition, Leifs published several of his own works as well as a series of solo and chamber works by other Icelandic composers, but due to currency restrictions and limited capital, it never became the influential publishing house Leifs hoped for. Among Islandia Edition's first publications was *Iceland's Artistic Impulse* (*Islands künstlerische Anregung*), the manifesto that Leifs had been writing intermittently for more than a decade.[67] Leifs felt that his vision for the global potential of Icelandic culture had always been misunderstood and that in part he himself was to blame for not communicating his ideas properly. In the 110-page book, he expounded his belief that the ancient Nordic culture preserved in Iceland might, in the next few centuries, spawn a new artistic renaissance.

Islands künstlerische Anregung was essentially a vanity publication, intended to clear Leifs's name as a Nazi sympathizer. He sent signed copies of the book to friends and colleagues with clout on the international scene, such as émigré German musicologists Adolf Aber and Alfred Einstein (who had published Leifs's report on his folk song gathering trips in the *Zeitschrift für Musikwissenschaft*), and Henry Goddard Leach, president of the American-Scandinavian Foundation.[68] Still, the book was largely derided by German critics, who found it an "embarrassing reminder of certain spiritual products whose origin lies in National Socialism."[69] The only positive reviews came from authors whose credentials had already been blemished during the Nazi era. The Scandophile opera director (and former Nazi) Fritz Tutenberg penned a review for *Zeitschrift für Musik* and found the book's main strength to be "an honest, unshakeable conviction; self-confidence without arrogance"; Carl Orff, to whom Leifs sent a copy, replied with a letter declaring it a "confirmation and a gold-mine."[70] Of course, such acclaim was hardly conducive to Leifs's cause.

In March 1950 the Iceland Symphony Orchestra gave its first concert under that name, and its founding was considered a milestone in Icelandic musical life. Leifs, who had more or less initiated the whole idea of serious symphonic music in Iceland, conducted the ensemble for the first time on April 29 (*Iceland Overture*) and the following day in the funeral march from *Galdra-Loftr*, both in the newly consecrated National Theater. The reception was altogether positive, and a local critic remarked that it was a sign of the times that audiences were hardly perturbed by Leifs's unusual works while at their previous outing in Reykjavík, with the Hamburg Philharmonic in 1926, "no one seemed to find words strong enough to describe what utter nonsense this music was."[71]

The *Saga Symphony* received its premiere in autumn 1950, at a Nordic music festival in Helsinki. The Nordic Composers' Council (*Nordisk komponistråd*) had been founded four years earlier, as a venue for cooperation and promotion of new works throughout the Nordic countries. The council took over the music festivals that had been held intermittently since 1888 and made them biannual events, hosted by each of the Nordic capitals in turn. The *Saga Symphony* premiere took place in the Helsinki University Aula on September 18 and was broadcast live throughout the Nordic countries. The Helsinki Theater Orchestra had procured copies of authentic lurs from the Danish National Museum, and the conductor was Jussi Jalas, Sibelius's son-in-law, who proved an enthusiastic interpreter.[72] Sibelius himself listened to the radio broadcast and later told Jalas that he was impressed by the work, in which he discerned "the real roots of the sagas, with their hard surface and their power."[73] Yet, while one reviewer, the Swedish composer Bengt Hambræus, lauded the "strongly personal, mainly atonal and rhythmically pregnant language" that reminded him of Messiaen and Varèse, the remainder of the critics took a different view.[74] Norwegian composer Klaus Egge wrote that the symphony was "the most devilish pandemonium that I have ever heard one orchestra produce at once.... The audience was highly amused, although one assumes this wasn't the composer's intention."[75] The Finnish Väinö Pesola noted that some audience members had "shaken their heads and smiled when it was over" while the influential Swedish critic Sten Broman fulminated that the work was such a "blown-out, excessive, and unwittingly risible concoction that it makes one laugh to have had the chance to hear something so unbelievably stupid."[76]

Some critics even invoked the negative nature imagery of Fritz Stege's review of the Organ Concerto in 1941. According to Egge,

"The work's formal construction was like hardened lava," but Pesola went still further: "The main work of the festival was a symphony by one of Iceland's leading musicians, Jón Leifs.... On hearing it, one thought: Do dwarf-like ogres inhabit every lava fissure and giant phantoms fill every mountain ravine? And does Hekla constantly roar with explosions? Do the percussionists have life insurance? The work's monstrous formation encouraged the imagination to travel even further; it almost reminded one of a mammoth from Eastern Siberia."[77]

For Leifs, perhaps the most devastating comment came from the Swedish critic of *Dagens Nyheter*, who noted that all the noise had the effect of "considerably lessening the public's interest in the Icelandic sagas."[78] Leifs had devoted his entire career to preparing a global renaissance based on his country's medieval heritage, but now it all seemed to have been in vain.

In the wake of the Helsinki fiasco, an influential critic once again made insinuations about Leifs's career in Nazi Germany. Bo Wallner, the music editor of Sweden's *Expressen*, found the *Saga Symphony* "tiresome in its monotony" and noted that Leifs's intended riposte against Nazism did not fit well with "another rumor about the composer—one that is less convenient for himself."[79] In a private letter to the composer, Wallner asserted that his works would never get performed at major festivals until the Nazi rumor was dismissed once and for all.[80] It was in the aftermath of the Helsinki concert that Leifs began to petition for de-Nazification, although that official program run by the occupying powers had already run its course. Leifs believed that if he received a travel visa from the US embassy in Reykjavík, this would be regarded as a declaration of innocence. The embassy was reluctant, not least because of lingering doubts regarding Leifs's wartime radio speeches, but in March 1951 he finally received a visa allowing him to travel to the United States. He immediately dispatched copies of the document to the Icelandic Foreign Ministry, requesting that they be forwarded to the Icelandic Embassies in Copenhagen, London, and Paris, should they receive enquiries about his political past.[81]

Figure 8.6. Jón Leifs conducts his "symphony of noise"—a cartoon from the satirical magazine *Spegillinn*, November 1950, shortly after the premiere of the *Saga Symphony* in Helsinki. © National and University Library, Reykjavík.

In Iceland, Leifs had assumed presidency of the Composers' Society, and one of his main goals was to ensure the regular programming of Icelandic music on the National Radio, as this would guarantee a steady royalty income for local composers. His ideas were met with resistance by the radio's two music administrators, both of whom were growing increasingly unsympathetic toward Leifs: his former schoolmate Ísólfsson and the younger Jón Þórarinsson, who had studied composition with Hindemith at Yale University and had recently returned to the island. Besides his position at the radio, Þórarinsson was the head of the theory division at the Reykjavík School of Music, and he and Leifs had had an adversarial relationship from the start. Leifs found Hindemith's method of composition to be "completely dead" while Þórarinsson delighted in recounting that Hindemith, when asked if he was familiar with Leifs's works, had replied, "Yes, if you call that music."[82]

Things came to a head in spring 1950, with a takeover in the two societies formerly under Leifs's leadership: Ísólfsson became president of the Icelandic Composers' Society and Þórarinsson president of STEF. Furious at this turn of events, Leifs tried to depose the new boards of both organizations, without success. Although much of his anger stemmed from a bruised ego, he also felt—rightly—that in negotiating royalty payments Ísólfsson and Þórarinsson were guilty of conflict of interest, since they represented both the National Radio and local composers. There was also the lingering question of whether Leifs's music had been actively suppressed at the radio, for example through the mark "do not broadcast," found on a 1948 live recording of *The Lay of Guðrún*, from the Nordic Music Days in Oslo where the work was premiered. Leifs published an open letter in two Reykjavík newspapers complaining that his work had never been put on the air. Þórarinsson replied that the instruction had come from the composer himself, who had been dissatisfied with both the live performance and the quality of the recording.[83]

In the end, Ísólfsson resigned his presidency of the Composers' Society and withdrew from the organization shortly thereafter.

In 1953, his dispute with Leifs reached the pages of *Morgunblaðið*, when the generally mild-tempered organist wrote a vehement article in which he professed that the reason for his resignation had been to "not need to have unnecessary contact with Mr. Jón Leifs" and that it was "well known that the better one gets to know this man, the more exasperating he becomes."[84] Leifs retaliated a few months later by writing, on the eve of Ísólfsson's sixtieth birthday, a remarkably insolent article in the form of a "birthday greeting." It was no such thing. "His longing for sympathy and harmony is nearly pathological," Leifs wrote. "It is precisely this that has won him popularity and recognition, both of which are as vital for him as the air he breathes."[85] After thirty years of a strained relationship, Leifs's bruised feelings had finally come to the surface. Feeling misunderstood, he contended that all the ungrateful tasks of creating a financially viable future for Icelandic composers had fallen on his shoulders while Ísólfsson garnered only admiration and respect.[86]

The 1952 Nordic Music Days, held in Copenhagen, were a box office disaster. A total of 198 tickets were sold for the festival's five concerts, and even with complimentary attendance for the composers themselves, Copenhagen's concert venues were half full at best.[87] Leifs had hoped for two of his works to be performed at the festival—movements from the never before heard *Edda* oratorio and the string quartet *Mors et vita*, which had been premiered in Iceland the previous year—but only the former found favor with the program committee. Two movements from *Edda I* were performed, alongside music by Swedish and Finnish composers, at the final concert on May 24 in the Danish Radio concert hall, with Launy Grøndahl conducting the radio's orchestra and choir.

Grøndahl, himself a well-known composer, expressed his pleasure with Leifs's work, but the younger generation of Scandinavian composers jeered at it. Perhaps these movements from *Edda* were not, on their own, ideal samples of Leifs's unheard magnum opus; for example, despite its memorable depiction of nocturnal chill, the eighth movement (*Night, Morning*) certainly has its longueurs. Following the performance there was only faint applause in the half-empty hall. Leifs rose from his seat, but rather than walk to the stage he headed straight for the lobby. His colleague, the younger composer Jón Nordal, who was sitting next to him at the concert, followed him into the hallway, but Leifs proved unwilling to reenter the hall. "That was no proper applause," he muttered despondently.[88]

This was the third time in little more than a decade that an ambitious work by Jón Leifs had been greeted with indignation. One critic wrote that the oratorio was "monotonous and heavy"; another claimed that it failed to "awaken one's interest, let alone maintain it."[89] It all proved too much, even for the resolute and intractable Leifs. The years since 1945 had been taxing in every respect: his marriage with Thea was foundering, Snót's illness caused him distress, his work on behalf of STEF provoked severe antipathy in Iceland. Devastating as it was, Líf's death had provided a temporary way out of a compositional cul-de-sac, but now he found himself unable to continue. Leifs had already begun the six-movement *Edda II: Lives of the Gods* in December 1951, and by the time he departed for the Copenhagen festival in spring 1952 he had completed forty-eight pages of the first movement, a majestic depiction of Óðinn, the greatest of the Norse gods. From Copenhagen he traveled to Saltsjöbaden, where he intended to immerse himself in work, but his inspiration lasted for only two pages. He returned to the score again a decade later. A remark on page fifty-one reads, "Here I commenced work on this composition again, July 11, 1962."

Instead, Leifs devoted still more of his time to administrative matters. In summer 1954 Iceland hosted for the first time the Nordic Music Days, a challenging test for the small and still underdeveloped musical community. Unlike the larger Nordic capitals, Reykjavík had only one symphony orchestra and one professional chamber ensemble (the Radio String Quartet), so this festival was out of necessity on a smaller scale than the previous ones. As the hosts, Icelandic composers relinquished their share of the performances so that only works by Danish, Swedish, Norwegian, and Finnish composers were heard.[90]

Leifs attached particular importance to one event at the 1954 festival. He had invited representatives from several non-Nordic countries to Iceland to participate in the founding of the International Council of Composers (*Conseil International des Compositeurs*, or CIC), an organization intended to foster international cultural relations and serve as a forum for dialogue regarding performing rights. Ten representatives made the trip to Iceland specifically for this purpose. The French composer Henri Dutilleux was elected as one of five board members; other composers from outside Scandinavia were Salvatore Allegra (Italy), Karl Höller (West Germany, deputy for Werner Egk), Oskar Wagner (Austria), and Guy Warrack (Great Britain). The meetings took place in the hall of the Icelandic parliament building on June 13–17, and the council was formally established on the final day, which was also the tenth anniversary of the Republic of Iceland. While Dutilleux was fascinated by the island's lunar landscape, with "huge expanses of lava, crevasses, volcanoes, and rivers of hot and sulphurous water," he found the results of the meeting disappointingly meager.[91] He and Leifs nevertheless got along splendidly, and decades later the French composer still retained a "captivating memory" of the Icelander's music, which he considered "just the opposite of an academic art ... an art sometimes marked with violence, but anyway of a great variety of colors."[92]

The charter of Leifs's International Council of Composers reads uncomfortably like that of the old Permanent Council of the Nazi years.[93] The CIC was meant to serve a smaller circle of serious composers than the larger performing rights organizations (such as GEMA in Germany), but it had no financial support, and composers themselves saw little need for yet another association. Leifs organized five annual meetings of CIC, but they were poorly attended, with representatives only from the Nordic countries, West Germany, and Great Britain. The council was quietly discontinued in 1963, but Leifs hoped until his death that he would be able to revive it in some form. He even suggested moving the organization to Paris and handing the leadership over to Dutilleux, which the latter declined. The fate of the CIC was thus typical for the late 1940s and early 1950s, a period in which Leifs's earnest efforts—whether as a composer, organizer, husband, or father—all seemed doomed to fail.

NOTES

1. Leifs, diary/notebook; Leifs to Þórey Þorleifsdóttir, March 13, 1944.
2. Annie Leifs to Þórey Þorleifsdóttir, November 17, 1945.
3. Leifs, diary/notebook.
4. Leifs, sketches for *Baldr*.
5. Leifs to Berta Geissmar, June 22, 1946.
6. Leifs, foreword to *Baldr* full score.
7. Leifs, diary/notebook, 1946–52 (*Æfiatriði Jón Leifs 1946–1952*).
8. Jón Ásgeirsson, "Endurskin úr norðri," *Morgunblaðið*, May 27, 1989.
9. The Iceland Symphony Orchestra, long seasoned in the performance of Leifs's scores, has assembled an unusual instrumentarium especially for such projects, including a specially built giant ratchet and rocks collected from the innermost part of Hvalfjörður, a long fjord in western Iceland, near Reykjavík. See Eggert Pálsson, "Um notkun ásláttarhljóðfæra í Baldri," *Morgunblaðið*, August 18, 2000.
10. Leifs, *Baldr*, full score.
11. "Tónverk eftir Jón Leifs á Ólympíuleikunum," *Þjóðviljinn*, March 31, 1948; Súsanna Svavarsdóttir, "Baldr var framlag til Ólympíuleika," *Morgunblaðið*, August 5, 2000.
12. Leifs, telegram to *Prix de composition musicale Prince Rainier III de Monaco*, February 1960 (undated); Archives du Palais Princier, telegram to Leifs, May 5, 1960. When asked to provide a piano score of *Baldr* for the jury, Leifs replied that he would be willing to pay for a skilled pianist to play from the full score instead.
13. S.S. to Icelandic Foreign Ministry, July 7, 1945, Foreign Ministry Papers 1996-B/484, National Archives of Iceland, Reykjavík.
14. Leifs, "Dagbók Esjuferðar," ("Diary of My Journey Aboard the *Esja*"), report to the Icelandic Foreign Ministry in Reykjavík, July 12, 1945, copy in the Leifs collection.
15. Leifs, *Landsýn*, full score.
16. Dick Ringler, translation for *Víkingasvar*, Iceland Symphony Orchestra and Hallgrímskirkja Motet Choir, BIS CD-1080, 2004, compact disc.

17. Leifs, sketches for *Landsýn*.
18. Cf. Johnson, *Webern*, 48.
19. Leifs, "Dagbók Esjuferðar."
20. Leifs to Icelandic Foreign Ministry, August 31, 1946, Foreign Ministry Papers 1996-B/484, National Archives of Iceland, Reykjavík.
21. Leifs to Einar B. Guðmundsson, August 31, 1945; British Legation to Leifs, March 15, 1946; Icelandic Embassy Copenhagen to Icelandic Foreign Ministry, November 23, 1950, Foreign Ministry Papers 1996-B/484, National Archives of Iceland, Reykjavík.
22. Leifs to Icelandic Foreign Ministry, November 8, 1946, Foreign Ministry Papers 1996-B/484, National Archives of Iceland, Reykjavík.
23. "Fangelsun Jóns Leifs á Esju," *Morgunblaðið*, October 12, 1946. A similar investigation into Kurt Atterberg's involvement with the Nazis took place in Sweden, also at the composer's request. There, the Royal Academy of Music in Stockholm found the accusations of Nazi collaboration to be unfounded (Garberding, "Musik," 248).
24. Atli Heimir Sveinsson, "Jón Leifs—Brautryðjandi á heimsvísu," *Lesbók Morgunblaðsins*, September 21, 1991.
25. Leifs to Þórey Þorleifsdóttir, December 29, 1945.
26. Leifs to Þórey Þorleifsdóttir, December 29, 1945.
27. Åhlén, *Jón Leifs*, 217.
28. Leifs, diary/notebook, 1946–52.
29. Leifs to Thea Leifs, December 15, 1953.
30. "Amerikaner sollen zahlen," *Der Spiegel*, September 26, 1956.
31. Björgvin Guðmundsson to Jón Leifs, August 28, 1952.
32. "Krafðist þess, að tækinu yrði lokað, er því var ekki hlýtt, sparkaði hann í tækið svo það þagði," *Alþýðublaðið*, September 8, 1955; "Alþjóðakrafa, að höfundarréttarmál dæmist sem lögreglumál," *Alþýðublaðið*, September 22, 1955.
33. Jóhannes Helgi, *Sigfús Halldórsson opnar hug sinn* (Hafnarfjörður: Skuggsjá, 1980), 122.
34. *Morgunblaðið*, April 15, 1954; the verse is printed in Ingólfsson, *Jón Leifs—Líf í tónum*, 270.
35. Leifs, "Frakkland og Debussy," *Morgunblaðið*, February 25, 1962.
36. Snót Leifs to Þórey Þorleifsdóttir, December 2, 1945; Snót Leifs to Leifs, October 30, 1946.
37. Líf Leifs to Leifs, December 27, 1946.
38. Icelandic Finance Ministry to Icelandic Foreign Ministry, Reykjavík, May 23, 1947, Foreign Ministry Papers 1996-B/484, National Archives of Iceland, Reykjavík.
39. Snót Leifs to Leifs, July 29, 1947 (private collection, Reykjavík).

40. Vilhjálmur Finsen to the Icelandic Foreign Ministry, July 16, 1947, Foreign Ministry 1996-B/484, National Archives of Iceland, Reykjavík.
41. Snót Leifs to Leifs, July 19, 1947.
42. Snót Leifs to Leifs, July 21 and 19, 1947.
43. Snót Leifs to Leifs, July 29, 1947.
44. Leifs to Snót Leifs, August 2, 1947.
45. Annie Leifs to Leifs, August 5, 1947.
46. Guy Rickards, "Music of Fire and Ice: A Survey of Icelandic Music on Record," *Tempo*, New Series, no. 181 (June 1992): 54.
47. *Íslenzkar þulur og þjóðkvæði*, ed. Ólafur Davíðsson (Copenhagen: Hið íslenzka bókmentafélag, 1898–1903), 255–59. The three folk verses begin "Sofi, sofi sonur minn," "Sofðu með sæmdum," and "Sofa urtu börn."
48. For the poem and commentary, see *Ritverk Jónasar Hallgrímssonar*, vol. 1, 147–54; vol. 4, 165 (Leifs uses only the second verse of twenty).
49. Theodóra Thoroddsen, "Draumljóð," *Skírnir* 90 (1916): 56. Interestingly, this same article contains the folk verse "Eg er á floti út við sker," which Leifs also set to music in Líf's memory, in *Erfiljóð*.
50. *Íslenzkar þulur og þjóðkvæði*, 254.
51. *The Complete Sagas of Icelanders*, ed. Viðar Hreinsson, vol. 2, 152–53.
52. His main sources were the four-part *Íslenzkar gátur, skemtanir, vikivakar og þulur* (*Icelandic Riddles, Entertainments, Dances, and Poems*), collected by folklorists Jón Árnason and Ólafur Davíðsson and published in 1887–1903, as well as a more concise anthology, Einar Ólafur Sveinsson's *Fagrar heyrði eg raddirnar* (Reykjavík, 1942).
53. See, for example, August Adelkamp, S.J., to Annie Leifs, August 31, 1947 (Annie Leifs Collection).
54. Bjarni Benediktsson to Annie Leifs, May 7, 1948 (Annie Leifs Collection).
55. Annie Leifs, Diary of Rome trip, 1948; Jakob David to Annie Leifs, June 15, 1949 (Annie Leifs Collection).
56. Jakob David (Apologetisches Institut, Zürich), undated letter (autumn 1948) to Dr. Krieg, Gardekaplan der Schweizergarde (Annie Leifs Collection).
57. Halldór Hansen in discussion with the author, June 23, 2003.
58. Annie recorded three short pieces for the Iceland Radio in September 1954, but here she chose repertoire that was not particularly taxing, by Chopin, C. Ph. E. Bach, and Paul Graener. The recordings were released on a CD accompanying Carl-Gunnar Åhlén's biography of Leifs, *Jón Leifs: Kompositör i motvind* (Stockholm: Atlantis, 2002).
59. Leifs to Sigurður Nordal, October 30, 1944. Snót's thesis, "Stilistische und rhythmische Untersuchungen zu Nietzsches Zarathustra," was only the third doctoral dissertation completed by an Icelandic woman.

60. See Leifs to Vagn Zahle (doctor at the Copenhagen Rigshospital), July 23, 1954.
61. Leifs, diary/notebook 1953–61 (*Æfiatriði Jóns Leifs 1953–1961*).
62. Sigurður Reynir Pétursson, *Þú skalt ekki stela. Störf og barátta STEFs í fimm áratugi til verndar og styrktar höfundarétti* (Reykjavík: STEF, 1998), 57; "Athugasemd við "greinargerð" Jóns Leifs með tillögu um vantraustsyfirlýsingu á stjórnir Tónskáldafélags Íslands og STEFs," typewritten document, April 8, 1951.
63. Leifs to his parents, October 28, 1927.
64. Leifs to Páll Ísólfsson, November 25, 1927.
65. Leifs to Þórey Þorleifsdóttir, December 29, 1934.
66. Jóhanna Kristjónsdóttir, "Hvað er bak við þessi dökku gleraugu? Síðdegisstund með Þorbjörgu Leifs," *Morgunblaðið*, November 26, 1989; Margrét Sveinbjörnsdóttir, "Nú þurfum við að snúa okkur að tónlist Jóns Leifs," *Morgunblaðið*, January 19, 1999.
67. Leifs's manuscript copy (in the Leifs collection) contains several discarded ideas for a title, some of which suggest more clearly his intention: *Islands künstlerische Aufgabe (Iceland's Artistic Mission)* or even *Islands künstlerische Weltmission (World Mission)*.
68. Aber's inscribed copy is now in the Eda Kuhn Loeb Music Library at Harvard University. Einstein's copy is at the Jean Gray Hargrove Music Library at the University of California, Berkeley; Leach's is at Princeton University Library.
69. R. D., "Nordische Mission," *Der Bund*, August 17, 1951.
70. Fritz Tutenberg, "Besprechungen," *Zeitschrift für Musik* 112 (1951): 376–77; Carl Orff to Leifs, January 12, 1952.
71. Bjarni Guðmundsson, "Hljómsveitartónleikarnir á sunnudag," *Morgunblaðið*, May 3, 1950.
72. "Frumflutti Sögusinfóníuna fyrir 22 árum," *Morgunblaðið*, June 4, 1972.
73. Jussi Jalas to Leifs, November 12, 1950; "Hvað sagði Sibelius um sinfóníu Jóns Leifs?," *Tíminn*, November 28, 1950.
74. Bengt Hambræus, "De nordiska musikdagarna i Hälsingfors. En återblick," *Tidning för Upsala stad och län*, September 26, 1950.
75. Klaus Egge, "Nordiske musikdager 1950," *Arbeiderbladet*, September 28, 1950.
76. Väinö Pesola, "Pohjoismaiset musiikkipäivät: Islantilainen konsertti," *Suomen Sosialidemokraatti*, September 20, 1950; Sten Broman, *Sydsvenska Dagbladet*, September 20, 1950.
77. Egge, "Nordiske musikdager 1950"; Pesola, "Pohjoismaiset musiikkipäivät."
78. Curt Berg, "Träklubba, stenar, hammare i ny isländsk symfoni," *Dagens Nyheter*, September 20, 1950.

79. Bo Wallner, "Individualismens triumf," *Expressen*, September 19, 1950, quoted in Åhlén, *Jón Leifs—Tónskáld í mótbyr*, 14; see also Leifs to Icelandic Foreign Ministry, March 30 and May 31, 1951, Foreign Ministry Papers 30L5, National Archives of Iceland, Reykjavík.

80. Leifs to Icelandic Foreign Ministry, Reykjavík, March 30, 1951, Foreign Ministry Papers 1996-B/484, National Archives of Iceland, Reykjavík.

81. Icelandic Foreign Ministry to Leifs, Reykjavík, January 3, 1951; Icelandic Embassy in Stockholm to Icelandic Foreign Ministry, May 7, 1951.

82. Ríkharður H. Friðriksson, "Tónskáldið sem þjóðin gleymdi," *Sagnir* 6 (1985): 49; Leifs in an interview with Þorkell Sigurbjörnsson, Tónskáld mánaðarins, Iceland National Radio Archives, DB-567-1.

83. Leifs, "Má ekki spila—Opið bréf til útvarpsráðs," *Morgunblaðið*, March 22, 1960; "Týnt verk—eða 'Má ekki spila'?," *Alþýðublaðið*, March 22, 1960; Jón Þórarinsson, "Barizt við vindmyllur," *Morgunblaðið*, March 23, 1960.

84. Páll Ísólfsson, "Svar Páls Ísólfssonar," *Morgunblaðið*, April 15, 1953.

85. Leifs, "Sextugur á morgun: Páll Ísólfsson," *Tíminn*, October 11, 1953.

86. Ísólfsson's attitude toward Leifs was also complex. In his reminiscences from 1964, he subtly criticizes Leifs without mentioning his name; see Matthías Johannessen, *Í dag skein sól* (Reykjavík: Bókfellsútgáfan, 1964), 11, 158–59. Still, two years previously he had written to the committee of the Order of the Falcon, recommending Leifs for the country's highest civilian honor "for his important work on behalf of Icelandic music." Leifs received the medal six years later (Páll Ísólfsson to Order of the Falcon committee, August 10, 1962, quoted in Sif Sigmarsdóttir, "Ómstríð hljómkviða umbótanna," BA thesis, University of Iceland, 2001, 65).

87. Åhlén, *Jón Leifs—Tónskáld í mótbyr*, 241.

88. Jón Nordal, in discussion with the author, March 3, 2006.

89. Axel Kjerulf, "Nordisk musikuges afslutningskoncert," *Politiken*, May 25, 1952; Nils Schiørring, "Afslutning paa Musikdagene," *Berlingske Tidende*, May 25, 1952.

90. Leifs, "Norrænu tónlistarhátíðirnar," *Alþýðublaðið*, June 4, 1954.

91. Henri Dutilleux, "Congrès de Reykjavík," typewritten report (Dutilleux archives, Paul Sacher Stiftung, Basel), quoted in Pierre Gervasoni, *Henri Dutilleux* (Paris: Actes Sud/Philharmonie de Paris, 2016), 520–21.

92. Henri Dutilleux to the author, September 26, 2008.

93. A copy of the charter is in the Finance Ministry Papers, 1991-B/713, National Archives of Iceland, Reykjavík.

NINE

THE FINAL YEARS (1955–68)

LEIFS'S LAST DECADE WAS ONE of relative peace and stability. He found happiness in a third marriage, and his work for STEF and the Icelandic Composers' Society ensured a comfortable lifestyle. While his music was still regarded with skepticism, and his prickly and quarrelsome personality continued to ruffle some feathers, it seems that during this period Leifs finally found comfort in his own skin. When, shortly before his sixtieth birthday, a local reporter asked him if he was emotional, he replied, "Aren't we all? But I am becoming more balanced, I think, as I get older. I'm not as easily frustrated as before and I also don't set my hopes too high."[1] Leifs could even adopt a droll stance toward his crabby public persona and controversial music. Citing a well-known quip attributed to Brahms, his final words in a 1962 front-page interview were, "If there is anyone here I have forgotten to insult, I apologize."[2] In another interview five years later, having pulled a muscle in his arm while carrying coals to the lighthouse warden's apartment at Dyrhólaey (see below), he joked that there was "no reason for people to celebrate, for despite my injury I can still compose."[3]

Virtually all of the composing projects of Leifs's final years can be divided into four groups. He depicted Iceland's natural phenomena in four tone poems (*Geysir, Hekla, Dettifoss, Hafís*); set several texts by the nineteenth-century nationalist poet Jónas Hallgrímsson;

worked on the second and third installments of the *Edda* oratorio; and composed several vocal works on a smaller scale for soloists (or, in one case, chorus) and orchestra, most of which set texts from the Eddas and sagas. His musical language remained largely unchanged, but within that relatively stable framework one senses an increasing willingness to expand his melodic and harmonic vocabulary. While a few of Leifs's works from this final period may strike the listener as formulaic, he was more often able to crystallize his musical ideas in statements as unique and powerful as anything he had previously done.

In autumn 1955 Leifs fell in love again. Þorbjörg Möller (1919–2008) was twenty years his junior and had recently moved back to Iceland from Copenhagen, where she had been employed at the Icelandic embassy during her uncle's tenure as ambassador. She and Leifs were married on July 15, 1956, and barely nine months later, on April 5, 1957, she bore a son, Leifur (see fig. 9.1). For his christening in Reykjavík Cathedral, Leifs wrote a *Baptismal Hymn* (*Skírnarsálmur*) op. 43 for baritone and organ, in which some of the poetic and musical imagery from his *Requiem* music for Líf is transformed into a prayer for the young boy's future happiness. As in *Requiem*, Leifs turned to folk poetry, including the following incantation found in a seventeenth-century manuscript and used to ward off evil spirits:

Komi þér hjálp af himni,	May you have help from heaven,
heill af jörðu,	bounty from the earth,
sælan af sólu,	happiness from the sun,
sigr af tungli,	victory from the moon,
styrkr af stjörnum,	strength from the stars,
stoð af öllum góðum öndum.[4]	succor from all good spirits.

Despite his father's benediction, Leifur was not blessed with good fortune. At age nineteen (a few years after Leifs's death), he was overtaken by mental illness and has not returned to full health.

In 1958, Leifs completed three works to texts by Jónas Hallgrímsson: *Elegies on the Death of Jónas Hallgrímsson* op. 45, *Spring Song* op. 46, and *Stand, House of Stone* op. 47a. While Leifs had always

Figure 9.1. Leifs with his wife, Þorbjörg, and son Leifur. © Leifs Archives, National and University Library, Reykjavík.

admired Hallgrímsson's poetry, the immediate incentive for these works was a competition organized by the National Radio in celebration of the 150th anniversary of the poet's birth. He set to work with abandon, writing the abovementioned works in little over a month, between March and April. Leifs's music is seldom lighthearted, but a rare exception is the cheerful *Spring Song* (*Vorvísa*) for choir and orchestra, completed on April 8, 1958. The work is a set of variations, Leifs's first since the *Variazioni Pastorali* of the 1920s, and it is based on an Icelandic folk melody that dates back to the eighteenth century—Leifs's first use of an actual vernacular tune in his works since the choral *Poems of Icelanders* (*Íslendingaljóð*) in 1943.[5] The frolicsome poem depicts the coming of spring and its effects on nature: the mountain ice melts, waterfalls become more forceful, the grass comes to life, fish and fowl reappear, children play, adults fall in love. Although the lively pace of Leifs's setting does not allow for extended tone painting of each element, one can see in its depiction of mountains and waterfalls a precursor to his four tone poems on Icelandic nature that would follow a few years later.

A week after completing *Spring Song*, Leifs also finished the smaller-scale *Stand, House of Stone* (*Stattu steinhús*) for tenor and piano. Here, inspiration presumably came from Leifs's personal situation, for he and Þorbjörg had moved into a two-story house at Freyjugata 3 in October 1957, conveniently located in central Reykjavík and a stone's throw away from the childhood home where his aging mother still lived; this would remain their home until Leifs's death. Leifs also submitted to the radio competition a handful of his older works to Hallgrímsson's poetry—of the sixty-four works submitted, eight were his. As it happened, first prize went to *A Hymn to the Setting Sun*, his as yet unperformed choral setting from 1943, which as a result duly received its premiere in a radio broadcast by the National Theater chorus.[6] Yet Leifs, ever unpredictable, was enraged by the jury's decision and refused to accept the award. He even declared, in a newspaper article, that he considered "most of the other works I submitted to the competition . . . far more important and greater works of art—yet the jury found none of them worthy of so much as second prize or special distinction."[7] Leifs insisted that *Spring Song* should have won first prize, since it was livelier and more accessible than his other submissions. Perhaps he was also vexed that yet again a competition of Icelandic music was being judged by Páll Ísólfsson, who chaired

a committee of four. Leifs's response was, in a way, laughable—
having complained about lack of recognition for decades, he flew
off the handle when he finally received his due. Despite his frustration with the results, Leifs continued to set Hallgrímsson's poetry.
In 1961 he completed his settings of *Weather Verses* (*Veðurvísur*)
op. 47b and *Jónas Hallgrímsson in memoriam* op. 48, and that same
year he employed Hallgrímsson's text for the massive *Hekla* score
(see below).

VIKING'S ANSWER

Ever since his return to Iceland in 1945, Leifs had been in search of a
suitable workplace. He required absolute stillness when composing
and had never been able to concentrate fully at his family home at
Bókhlöðustígur, where he had resided for a while in the postwar
years. Leifs would occasionally rent small huts and summer houses
near the city; these gave him the solitude he required, but he grew
increasingly tired of the primitive conditions they often entailed.
As Leifs became more comfortable financially, he began to travel
abroad often and did much of his composing in the 1960s away
from Iceland. Substantial portions of *Edda II* and *Edda III* were
written in Paris; much of *Night* was composed on the cruise ship SS
Akropolis; he began writing *Viking's Answer* in Lavandou in southern France, then continued in Paris, Versailles, and Klampenborg
near Copenhagen and completed the work in Reykjavík. When at
home, Leifs typically rose at 5:00 a.m. and composed for two to
three hours before eating breakfast; the remainder of his day was
then occupied by work for STEF and attending to his daughter
Snót. Leifs composed at a desk in a small room on the upper floor of
his home at Freyjugata, usually without an instrument although he
had close to hand a small travel harmonium that he had purchased
in Berlin decades earlier.[8]

In 1953 the Icelandic government announced a vacancy in
the post of supervisor of Þingvellir national park, and Leifs was

convinced that this would be the ideal solution to his dilemma. He was particularly fond of the site, which is historically important and holds a special place in the national psyche (see chap. 5); years earlier it had inspired him as he wrote the *Iceland Cantata*, and he had composed several movements of *Edda I* there. Leifs had long maintained that it was the state's responsibility to adequately provide for its artists, and he now wrote an op-ed article suggesting that the Þingvellir post should be given to a nationally minded artist who would, in return, "glorify the country and its culture in his works."[9] Leifs saw no need for a church at Þingvellir, since the ancient parliament had been founded before the advent of Christianity. In one interview he asked, "Can you imagine how incensed the Italians would be if someone proposed to erect a church at the Forum Romanum?"[10] Instead, he proposed a reconstruction of the ancient parliament site as well as a new building that would host exhibits of medieval manuscripts and provide facilities for scholars of Icelandic language and history.[11] Leifs did everything he could to gain support for his candidacy—even suggesting to the chairman of the selection committee that he would compose a "national opera" on the popular historical novel *Skálholt* if his application was accepted—but to no avail.[12] The position was offered to a theologian, and the post of Þingvellir park supervisor was informally linked to that of local priest until the early 2000s.

When the Þingvellir post again became vacant in 1959, Leifs applied once more, again without success. Three years later, his dismay over the snub led him to compose *Viking's Answer* (*Víkingasvar*), written, according to its title page, "while searching for a place to work and in protest at the ecclesiastical takeover of Þingvellir."[13] The instrumentation is without parallel in Leifs's output, and his choice remains something of mystery: a wind band, which included four saxophones, and a string section using violas and double basses. Still, the work's defiant tone is unmistakable. It begins with a saxophone tvísöngur, to which trumpets add a resolute rímur tune, both composed by Leifs in the vernacular style. He then added an ironic twist intended as a snub to the Icelandic church leaders. In the midst of his nationally styled music, the piccolo plays, in fragmented form and uncoordinated with the rest of the ensemble, the opening phrases of Martin Luther's well-known hymn tune "Vom Himmel hoch da komm' ich her." The rest of the ensemble reacts with abrasive chords; Leifs's sketch for this passage contains the scribbling "protest," suggesting that these are intended as a remonstrance to Luther's melody.[14] Later, as the work reaches its climax, the tuba contributes its own version of the hymn's concluding phrase. Leifs's treatment of the venerable chorale, in extreme high and low registers, verges on comedy. Still, his intention was earnest: to give a heroic riposte in true Viking manner to what he saw as the government's disregard for his artistic mission.

For all the fortitude of *Viking's Answer*, Leifs's idealistic vision of the Nordic hero was rapidly losing ground in Iceland. The country's leading novelist, Halldór Laxness, had specifically critiqued the image of the Viking hero in his 1952 novel *Gerpla* (the title is derived from *garpur*, the Old Icelandic word for hero). This is in part a historical novel based on two Icelandic sagas, *Saga of the Sworn Brothers* and *Saint Olaf's saga*, but with an ironic twist, for it parodies the idealized view of heroes espoused in the medieval literature. Laxness's work is a critique of war and the perverse hero worship it entails, an "anti-saga" of sorts, and although it takes place in the eleventh century it is widely read as the author's reckoning with World War II, drawing parallels between the atrocities of King Olaf and those of Hitler and Stalin.[15] In the words of one literary scholar, Laxness, by turning "heroic feats into acts of terror and senseless cruelty," provided a troubling inquiry into the literary tradition taken to be among the foundations of Icelandic culture.[16]

Such critique from Iceland's leading author confirmed Leifs's ideological isolation in the postwar cultural milieu. To add insult to injury, the "poet-hero" that Laxness treats so mockingly is none other than Þormóður Kolbrúnarskáld, whom Leifs had glorified in the final movement of his *Saga Symphony*. Leifs was particularly sensitive to *Gerpla*'s message and even chastised Laxness in public, accusing him of writing the novel as a direct critique of his symphony.[17] While this seems unlikely, Laxness was skeptical of Leifs's ideology and took him to task for some of the ideas expressed in *Islands künstlerische Anregung*, particularly for crediting the Vikings for establishing Icelandic culture: "It wasn't Vikings, but peaceful intellectuals, before and after the Viking age, who created the works of art: woodcarving, music, gold, and bronze, the Edda poems and particularly—the pride of all our ancient achievements—the great sagas."[18] In 1955, the Nobel Prize in Literature was awarded to Laxness, not least for his achievement in *Gerpla*, and the author was widely recognized as a national artist. Thus, Leifs's glorification of Viking Age heroism became even more marginalized than before.

Although Leifs remained a controversial figure in Iceland, his sixtieth birthday, in May 1959, was a welcome respite from the daily squabbles. This was more or less the only occasion during his lifetime that leading individuals and institutions in Iceland joined forces to celebrate his artistic achievements. He was awarded honorary membership in the Reykjavík Music Society, and local newspapers published panegyric articles by friends and colleagues. Most importantly, the Iceland Symphony Orchestra and National Radio joined forces for a gala concert at the National Theater, where the *Iceland Overture*, movements from *Galdra-Loftr*, and a movement from the *Saga Symphony* ("Grettir ok Glámur") were performed under Leifs's own direction—his last appearance on the podium. The concert also included the first Icelandic performance of the *Iceland Cantata*, by the choir of the Icelandic Workers' Union led by Hallgrímur Helgason. This was a considerable achievement, particularly as this choir was not among Iceland's finest, and the taxing choral part had presented problems even for well-trained German ensembles in the 1930s. For the Icelandic group, it required no fewer than seventy rehearsals over a period of seven weeks.[19]

Yet even this cheerful occasion was clouded by accusations of Nazi collaboration, this time from Israel. Helgason, who presided over the Icelandic Composers' Union, had contacted several concert organizations in Israel to suggest the performance there of

Figure 9.2. Leifs at his home on his sixtieth birthday, beneath a reproduction of Ferdinand Waldmüller's well-known portrait of Beethoven. © Leifs Archives, National and University Library, Reykjavík.

some of Leifs's works in celebration of his birthday. This was a bold proposition, to be sure, but one calculated to try to clear Leifs's name through an officially sanctioned performance in the Holy Land. In short, the plan backfired. In October 1959, the general director of ACUM, the Israeli performing rights association, replied that they were unable to offer any performances of Leifs's music.

He also returned the scores, which included the *Iceland Overture*, on the title page of which had been scribbled: "Nazi. Fr."[20] "Fr." was the signature of Heinz Freudenthal, formerly a violinist in the Gothenburg Symphony Orchestra—who was concertmaster in 1931, when Leifs had been released from his conducting engagement one day prior to the concert. Freudenthal had moved to Israel in 1953 and was now conductor of the Radio Symphony Orchestra in Tel Aviv. Enraged by the remark, Leifs demanded a personal meeting with the Israeli ambassador to Iceland, threatening legal action against Freudenthal to make him "responsible for his accusations."[21] Even a formal apology from the head of programming at Israeli Radio did nothing to calm his ire.[22]

Having returned to Iceland after the war, Leifs kept a deliberately low political profile. For example, he did not engage in the most bitterly contested political topic of the postwar years: Iceland's inclusion in NATO and the ensuing US military presence at Keflavík Naval Air Station. Still, Leifs could show remarkable naïveté when it came to promoting his own music in a dubious political context. In 1960, he traveled to Cologne for the ISCM festival, whose program he found "very monotonous"—it included the premières of Kagel's *Anagrama* and Stockhausen's *Kontakte*.[23] From Cologne, he continued to East Germany at the invitation of the East German government's cultural exchange department and spent a few days in East Berlin before heading to Rostock. There, the *Iceland Overture* was performed by the Volkstheater orchestra at the Ostseewoche Festival, followed by a reception in Leifs's honor. He returned home full of praise for his host country, expressing in the socialist daily newspaper *Þjóðviljinn* his view that East Germans were attempting to make "science and the arts a free enterprise. One cannot be opposed to such people."[24] The next day, the editorial of Reykjavík's leading right-wing newspaper launched a scathing attack on Leifs, and soon yet another local article alleged that he had been a "close friend of the Nazis."[25]

Leifs's acquiescence to politically questionable regimes was manifested yet again in 1967, when the Soviet Composers' Association invited him for a three-week visit to the Soviet Union. Leifs replied that due to his busy work schedule, he could make time for the trip only if the Soviets could guarantee the performance of one of his larger works; he suggested *Baldr* and sent the score to the Icelandic embassy in Moscow for perusal. The Soviets declined, under the pretext that this was a festival year (the fiftieth anniversary of the Revolution) and that all the leading music organizations had already planned their activities.[26] In his exchange of letters with the Soviet Composers' Association, Leifs appears once again as the cunning opportunist, prepared to accommodate himself politically in order to promote his works.

Around 1960, Leifs continued his series of memorial compositions with two works commemorating his sister and mother, respectively. A quintet for flute, clarinet, bassoon, viola, and cello op. 50 was written shortly after the January 1959 death of Þórey, the older of his two sisters and the sibling to which he had formed the closest connection. In September 1961, Leifs's mother, Ragnheiður, passed away in her eighty-eighth year. She had been widowed for thirty-two years and had lost all but two of her children, and at her death the ownership of the childhood home at Bókhlöðustígur passed to Leifs. Ragnheiður had been her son's most dedicated supporter throughout his life, and now he memorialized her in *Elegy* (*Hinsta kveðja*, op. 53) for string orchestra, completed on Christmas Day 1961.

The Quintet op. 50 was given its première at Reykjavík's Hótel Borg in December 1961, at a concert organized by a new Icelandic association for contemporary music, Musica Nova. This was a performers' collective, founded in 1959 by a group of young musicians who wished to create a platform for new music; its concerts generally took place in unusual locales, cafés and hotel ballrooms where one could enjoy light refreshments during the performance. One critic had particular praise for Leifs's quintet, expressing his hope that it would be heard soon again, as indeed it was, for it was one of four Icelandic works chosen for the program of the Nordic Music Days in Copenhagen in September 1962.[27]

In conservative Reykjavík, Musica Nova was a controversial enterprise—not least the infamous concert given by Fluxus artists Nam June Paik and Charlotte Moorman in 1965, in which Paik pulled down his pants and Moorman, dressed in a nightgown, dove into a giant water tank before continuing her performance on the cello.[28] Still, the society was emblematic of a growing local interest in modern music. For example, the Hótel Borg concert also included two works by Magnús Blöndal Jóhannsson, a thirty-six-year-old Juilliard graduate who was the first Icelander to write twelve-tone and electronic works. At the Reykjavík School of Music, the Yale graduate Jón Þórarinsson was a fervent proponent of Hindemith's composing method, but once his students—including Jón Nordal and Leifur Þórarinsson—went on to study abroad, they all took a turn toward serialism. Leifs was gracious toward the new generation of composers and spoke encouragingly of their works, taking on the role of elder statesman and mentor.[29] Still, as the Reykjavík music scene developed, and as younger composers took on the role of enfants terribles, Leifs became even more marginalized. The older generation of listeners still had little sympathy for his works while younger composers more or less uniformly rejected his nationalist, folk-derived style.

In 1960, Leifs wrote for solo piano for the first time since arranging the *New Icelandic Dances* in 1931. He maintained that Chopin, Liszt, and Busoni had long ago "exhausted the possibilities of the instrument," whereas writing for orchestra still allowed room for new expression.[30] The new work, *Boys' Song* (*Strákalag*), consists of a twenty-measure theme in archetypal rímur rhythm (4–3–4–2, etc.), followed by a set of four free variations. Leifs's immediate inspiration was his three-year-old son, Leifur, but he composed the work specifically for the Icelandic pianist Rögnvaldur Sigurjónsson. According to the latter, Leifs had promised to dedicate the work to him if he played it in concert, but in the end the pianist only made a studio recording at the National Radio and never performed the work in public. Leifs, furious at the perceived slight, withdrew his promise.[31] While the work makes considerable technical demands, the lyrical theme opens with a simple two-part texture in F-sharp major—with key signature, a rare occurrence in Leifs's works. It is curious that Leifs should anchor his "youthful" theme in the tonality of his earliest surviving piece, the *Reverie* from 1913. Whether consciously or not, the *Boys' Song* theme seems like a vague recollection of Leifs's own adolescent exercise at a distance of nearly half a century.

In 1960, Leifs also completed a set of brief sketches for orchestra titled *Three Abstract Paintings* (*Trois peintures abstraites*) op. 44. Although only six minutes in duration, the work was five years in the making. The first movement (eight pages in full score) took seven months to compose, after which the work took a back seat to other projects, such as the works to poems by Hallgrímsson in 1958. Perhaps the slow gestation was also caused by a larger conflict between the abstract and the extramusical in Leifs's music. In the program notes for the premiere, he remarked that he'd been inspired to write the piece after seeing works by contemporary abstract painters who, "with limited means, only a few abstract lines and blotches of color," expressed "psychological insight" in their works.[32] He seems not to have been prompted by specific works but rather to refer to a general influence of local artists such as Svavar Guðnason and Þorvaldur Skúlason, who in the 1950s were gaining recognition. In any case, the three movements of *Trois peintures abstraites* are only "abstract" in a most general sense, for Leifs provided each with a suggestive heading (*The Beauty of the Sky*, *Zig-Zag*, and *Cliffs*). Perhaps Leifs was primarily attracted to the concision and economy of these modernist works (recalling his own dislike of repetition in his music), rather than their abstraction as such. His choice of headings for the outer movements demonstrates yet again his attraction to the Icelandic landscape, in this case the contrast of heaven and earth, sky and rock. The fleeting, scherzo-like central movement, on the other hand, may correspond to geometric patterns employed by the Icelandic abstractionists; according to Leifs's program notes it is meant to suggest "wedges, being thrown like arrows against each other."[33] By employing only

Figure 9.3. Leifs composing at home in Reykjavík in October 1962. © Leifs Archives, National and University Library, Reykjavík.

a medium-size orchestra, Leifs had written a work within the means of the Iceland Symphony to perform, and its premiere in December 1961 was considered a success. Even Jón Þórarinsson, in his review for *Morgunblaðið*, somewhat grudgingly admitted that this music had been "not unpleasant to the ear."[34]

HOMELAND SOUNDSCAPES: THE "PLACE PIECES"

Between 1961 and 1964, Leifs wrote a series of four orchestral tone poems inspired by natural phenomena in and surrounding Iceland: *Geysir*, *Hekla*, *Dettifoss*, and *Hafís*. These substantial stand-alone pieces—each between ten and eighteen minutes in length—echo a longstanding tradition within the genre of the tone poem of what has been termed "homeland soundscape," with Leifs here attempting to capture the essence of Iceland through specific sites (not unlike Smetana in *Má vlast* or Albéniz in *Iberia*, though both are cycles in a way that Leifs's works are not).[35] These "place pieces" were in a certain sense a new departure for Leifs, who had never before depicted Icelandic nature so unequivocally in his works. Still, he could draw on decades of experience in depicting the "Icelandic sublime": as a teenager he had tried to evoke the Northern lights on the piano, the *Iceland Cantata* has an oblique association with Þingvellir, and *Baldr* concludes with both an earthquake and a volcanic eruption. Furthermore, discussion of his works in both Germany and Scandinavia had employed exotic nature imagery from early on. In 1927, a Berlin critic reviewing his piano pieces op. 2 was reminded of the "glissando of an Icelandic geyser" while in 1931 a Swedish reviewer heard both volcanic outbreaks and the play of geysers in his *Iceland Overture*.[36] In his own writings, particularly during his years in Germany, Leifs had also sought to capitalize on the rhetoric of Nordic exoticism. His four "place pieces" are thus a systematic working-out of ideas and elements that had been latent in his music for a long time while also perhaps influenced by the very imagery critics had employed to describe his style. Immersed in the project, Leifs expressed in an interview his wish to translate the Icelandic landscape directly into music: "There are harmonies in the landscape and the climate, the truest harmonies that exist. These are the chords I must use."[37]

Geysir came first in the series, written in March and April 1961. This hot spring in southwestern Iceland is believed to have come into existence in an earthquake in the thirteenth century; its bowl is roughly sixty feet in diameter while the hole reaching down is about sixty-five feet deep.[38] The name, from which the English term *geyser* is derived, comes from the Icelandic verb *gjósa*: to gush. Geysir has been largely dormant for the past decades, but in its prime it could spurt boiling water up to 230 feet in the air (see fig. 9.4). A smaller geyser nearby, Strokkur, continues to erupt every few minutes to this day.

As any geyser fills with water, cooler water on top presses down on the boiling water beneath until ultimately the superheated water bursts through. This is what Leifs suggests in his composition, which has the shape of a large *crescendo/decrescendo* coupled with

Figure 9.4. Geysir erupting in June 2000. Photograph © Brynjar Gauti Sveinsson / Morgunblaðið, Reykjavík.

acceleration and deceleration. This had long been Leifs's preferred method of propelling his music forward, but here it is a particularly apt and realistic portrayal of the geyser phenomenon. Leifs's "place pieces" all share this overall shape (although the details differ in each), and all begin with a *creatio ex nihilo,* the barely audible din of a "creation from nothing" as the phenomenon begins to manifest itself. In an ideal performance, the audience is unable to discern exactly when the music begins, only gradually becoming aware of a sound that has *always* been there. The models here are most likely Beethoven's Ninth and, though Leifs would have been loath to admit it, Wagner's prelude to *Das Rheingold*.[39] In *Geysir*, the opening sound is a primordial low B-flat in the contrabassoon, to which Leifs adds a tritone in the double basses. The effect is of something uncanny and remarkable forming deep underground. As the music grows in volume and rhythmic activity, it gives the sensation of barely contained, boiling energy waiting to be released. Trills and glissandos become more prominent, and Leifs gradually unleashes his large percussion section (m. 63 ff.). The eruption itself occurs at an explosive F-major climax (m. 112), with the orchestra at *fff* volume, including cymbals, triangle, tubular bells, and two sets each (on- and offstage) of timpani, bass drum, and small side drum. After roughly thirty seconds of triumphant chordal progressions in quarter and half notes, Leifs returns to the more transparent texture of the opening. The work concludes just as it began, with a low B-flat in the contrabassoon, the circularity of which reflects the phenomenon itself. As Geysir reaches its quiet repose, the process can begin all over again.

Geysir and the geothermal area of which it is part is an iconic site for Icelanders, the most famous example of the island's geothermal activity. (The name Geysir was frequently evoked in daily life in twentieth-century Iceland; it was the name of a male choir, a brand of laundry detergent, and a store for camping and fishing equipment.) Yet both the preservation and the ownership of the hot spring were often problematic. The activity of Geysir, which is reported to have erupted thrice daily in the eighteenth century, declined rapidly in the early twentieth century, and by 1916 its eruptions had all but ceased due to the buildup of silica around its bowl and hence the overload on the water column in the pipe. In 1935, a channel was dug through the rim around the edge of the geyser vent, which resulted in a lower water table and a temporary revival in activity.[40] Leifs had witnessed the "great Geysir" in action, possibly during his sojourns in 1935–37 when eruptions were rather frequent, and certainly in September 1945, when he accompanied violinist Adolf Busch to Þingvellir, Gullfoss, and Geysir.[41] Eventually, the channel again became clogged with silica, and by the time Leifs wrote his work in 1961, Geysir was inactive.

Ownership of the Geysir area had passed out of the hands of Icelanders in 1894, when a local farmer sold the area to James Craig (later Lord Craigavon), the millionaire whiskey distiller who in 1921 became the first prime minister of Northern Ireland. He initially charged an entrance fee to the site but eventually tired of the project, and in 1935 the area was purchased by an Icelander who donated it to the nation in perpetuity.[42] Leifs's choice of *Geysir* as the initial work in his tetralogy thus takes on added significance; it is both a memorialization of an iconic natural phenomenon in decline and a celebration of its return to national ownership. Geysir's status as a tourist attraction may also have fueled Leifs's hopes of an international reception of the work. His glorification of Icelandic nature was never intended for a native audience alone.

Although Leifs never heard *Geysir* performed—it was premiered only in 1984—he was pleased with the outcome and immediately began planning an even larger work. Hekla, located in southern Iceland, is one of the country's most active volcanoes. It reaches a height of 4,892 feet, and over twenty eruptions have been documented since Iceland's settlement 874; in recent times it has erupted roughly once every decade. Leifs's work can be seen as an expanded version of the volcanic outbreak at the conclusion of *Baldr*—which in turn was inspired by the actual eruption of Hekla in 1947. *Hekla* is an enormous score, its orchestra including small and large rocks, metal chains, sirens, gunshots, and anvils as well as most of the traditional percussion instrumentarium. For the first time in his composing career, Leifs resorted to the cut-and-paste method of creating staff paper in order to obtain the thirty-six staves needed for such an epic affair (see fig. 9.5).

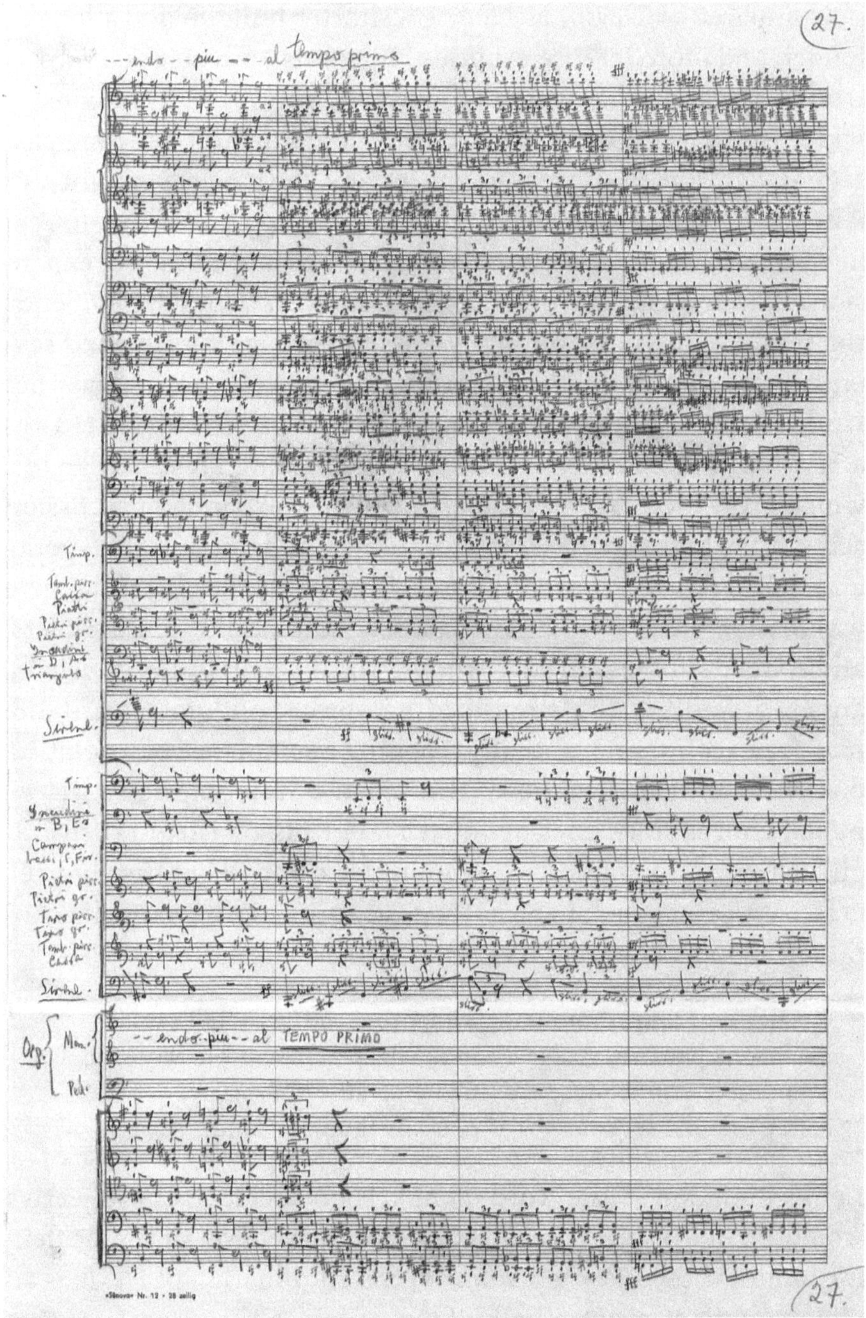

Figure 9.5. Leifs's autograph score to *Hekla*. © National and University Library, Reykjavík.

Compared to *Geysir*, *Hekla* has a shorter buildup and a longer, louder, and more intense eruption. It begins with an open fifth in trombones and tuba, which gradually expands to an immensely widely spaced F-C dyad (m. 15); Leifs noted that the opening passage was meant to suggest "quiet ice and the glacier's nobility."[43] Already in m. 26 there is a shift to a faster tempo (*Allegro molto, ma non troppo*), with explosive timpani thumps and a gradual expansion in lower winds and brass. As tension starts to build, Leifs lends the music a distinctly ominous quality through diminished seventh chords, employed here far more extensively than in his other works, and rising melodic tritones in a low register. He also creates a fascinating web of ascending and descending brass glissandos, which grow increasingly loud as the hugely expanded percussion section becomes more violent, graphically depicting the spouts and spurts of a volcano in full force. Eventually the glissandos give way to a forceful hammering of quarter notes, eighth-note triplets, and sixteenth notes (in succession). To this, Leifs adds gunshots, anvils, organ, and two sirens sliding upward and downward, the massive cacophony eventually reaching a semblance of resolution on a climactic C-major chord. Through the deafening noise, a large mixed chorus sings lines by Jónas Hallgrímsson that in their original context do not describe Mount Hekla at all but the volcanic crater Víti, and which Leifs had already used in his a cappella choral setting op. 28:

Grimm eru í djúpi dimmu	Violent are the howls of death
dauða org, þaðan er rauðir	in the deep depths; from there red
logar yfir landið [bljúga]	flames led the boiling lava
leiddu hraunið seydda.	over the [humble] land.

Leifs's omission of the word *humble* is no accident; the adjective would be out of place in such forceful music. For all the deafening loudness of a spewing volcano, the culmination of *Hekla* is an almost jubilant event. The buildup of forces is so immense that the listener is swept away in what one commentator has called a "concluding drama of volcanic celebration."[44] Unlike in *Geysir*, the eruption of Hekla does not gradually subside. Leifs retains the massive sound of eight-part chorus and full orchestra until the very end, concluding with a loud and abrupt G-major chord.

In his preface to the *Hekla* score, Leifs admitted that his demands verged on the impossible and that he entertained no hopes of hearing it performed during his lifetime.[45] As it turned out, *Hekla* was the only one of the landscape works he lived to hear, at the Nordic Music Days festival in Helsinki on October 2, 1964, performed by the Helsinki City Orchestra under the baton of Jussi Jalas. The performance was hardly ideal: there was no chorus, and some of the percussion instruments could not be procured, such as rolling chains, which Leifs, in a newspaper interview, remarked were intended to suggest flowing lava. Still, he put on a happy face, insisting that composers "never hear their works as they imagine them" and maintaining that overall, the performance had been a success.[46]

He knew better. In the context of 1960s European modernism, Leifs's style seemed hopelessly obsolete, and Finnish critics did nothing to hide their distaste. One reviewer proclaimed it "comical" that "any Nordic composer should still compose such music, that—to crown it all—is selected for the Nordic Music Days."[47] Apparently a handful of outraged audience members left the hall during the performance of *Hekla*; one critic jokingly referred to "six innocent victims" who had raced from the volcanic catastrophe.[48] For Leifs, such an incident can only have stirred unpleasant memories of a more widespread flight from another concert hall, in Berlin in 1941. The other Icelandic works at the Helsinki festival, although very different in style from one another—by the late-Romantic Páll Ísólfsson and the young serialist Leifur Þórarinsson—were far better received.

By the time of the Helsinki concert, Leifs had already completed the third tone poem in the series: *Dettifoss* for baritone, choir, and orchestra. Situated in northeastern Iceland, Dettifoss (literally, "crashing" or "falling waterfall") is reputed to be the most powerful cataract in all of Europe. Its water derives from the enormous

Vatnajökull glacier; the falls are 330 feet wide and have a drop of 150 feet. Unlike the eruption of a geyser or a volcano, a waterfall is relatively unchanging in its force—its volume discharge is more or less stable. The *crescendo/decrescendo* structure of *Geysir* is therefore not ideally suited to such a subject, but Leifs found a way to employ it nevertheless. In *Dettifoss*, he sets the first stanza of an eponymous poem by Einar Benediktsson, first published in 1906. Leifs explained, in his preface to the score, that he conceived the work as a "dialogue between the poet and the waterfall, with the poet approaching the waterfall from afar, and then departing towards the end."[49] For the first time in the tetralogy, Leifs adds a human presence to the landscape; this subjective persona (the poet/composer) conjures the waterfall to provide poetic/musical inspiration for his "lays eternal." Leifs's setting of Benediktsson's poem, with its approach to and departure from the waterfall, thus becomes a self-reflective essay on the artist's presence in nature.

While *Geysir* and *Hekla* expand upward from low tessitura, *Dettifoss* glides downward. It begins with a virtually inaudible flageolet D in the violins, to which a low C is added in double basses—a double-fifth interval that Leifs then proceeds to fill with a G in the cellos. The opening creates a sense of vast space, and the buildup here is considerably longer than in either *Geysir* or *Hekla*—over seventy measures of sustained *pppp* or *ppp* dynamics, with only a gradual *crescendo* as the winds enter with trills that begin the process of intensification.

Unlike in *Hekla*, where the choir is part of the orchestral fabric and its short text virtually inaudible through the clamor, Leifs here gives the chorus a far more substantial role. The orchestral passages occur as dramatic outbreaks between the sung material, which itself contains elements of contrast: the choral statements are often imposing and sonorous while the passages for baritone solo tend to be lyrical and reflective. This contrast is also seen in Leifs's distribution of the text. Each statement of the first-person pronoun (*I, me, my,* and surrounding text) is given to the baritone (the poet/composer) while words evoking the waterfall and its power (*Dettifoss, din, force, rocks, empowers, smite, fall-heart*) are sung only by the choir.

Chorus/solo (m. 114):

Syng, Dettifoss. Syng hátt mót himins sól.	Sing, Dettifoss, and sunward lift each tone!
Skín, hátign ljóss, á skuggans veldisstól.	Shine, lustrous light, upon the shadow's throne!
Og kný minn huga, gnýr, til ljóða, er lifa,	And mold my thoughts, thou din, to lays eternal
um leik þess mesta krafts, er fold vor ól.	About the greatest force our earth has grown!

Outbreak 1 (m. 153)
Solo/chorus (m. 160):

Lát snerta andann djúpt þinn mikla mátt,	Let touch my spirit deep thy wondrous might,
sem megnar klettinn hels af ró að bifa.	That can disturb from rest the rocks infernal.

Outbreak 2 (m. 171)
Solo/chorus (m. 175):

Ég veit, ég finn við óms þíns undraslátt	I know, I feel thy voice with music bright
má efla mannleg hjörtu.	Empowers hearts of men.
Slá þú hátt,	Thy chords now smite,
fosshjarta.	Fall-heart!

Outbreak 3 (m. 187)
Solo/chorus (m. 222):

Styrk minn hug og hönd að skrifa.	For writing give me strength supernal.

Outbreak 4 (m. 230)
Chorus (m. 235):

[Syng, Dettifoss!	Sing, Dettifoss!][50]

In this piece even more clearly than the others, Leifs's representation of nature can be understood as "a series of waves of energy," the buildup and climax of which create an overwhelming experience.[51] The third orchestral outbreak is by far the longest, and it includes a reminiscence of the dramatic harmonic world of *Hekla* with diminished seventh chords moving in chromatic stepwise motion. The

Example 9.1. Leifs, *Dettifoss* op. 57, mm. 225–30. © Iceland Music Information Center.

influence of *Hekla*'s chromaticism left a mark on Leifs's harmonic thinking, also in the characteristic passages of consecutive major triads. In the choir's penultimate (wordless) statement, Leifs writes a rising scale, first diatonic but then moving chromatically through an entire octave in the soprano part (see example 9.1). The effect, particularly as it is combined with a *molto crescendo* and leads directly into the final outbreak of percussive sixteenth-note frenzy, is of an exhilarating rush, unlike anything else in Leifs's music. After the fourth outbreak there is a rapid subsiding, so that in only twelve measures the music is reduced from a full *ff* statement of the poem's concluding word ("Dettifoss") to the calm sound of the opening's widely spaced ninth, marked *morendo*.

Leifs's choice of a cataract for his third nature piece was in many ways to be expected. Iceland boasts of countless waterfalls that are treasured by locals and tourists alike, and Dettifoss is the most imposing of them all. Leifs had presumably visited Dettifoss at least once, possibly during his folk song gathering journey in 1928. But during the 1960s, as politicians sought to make Iceland's newly achieved modernization (substantially aided by the British-American occupation during World War II and the subsequent Marshall Plan) economically viable in the long term, the fate of its rivers and waterfalls was put into question. Iceland had already begun harnessing hydroelectric power on a small scale to generate electricity in 1921, but plans for continued harnessing saw a division among politicians and the general population into camps of conservationism (i.e., using resources sparingly) versus preservationism (preserving wilderness).[52] In the 1940s the Icelandic government was planning to harness energy from Gullfoss (the "golden waterfall"), the most expansive and easily accessible of Iceland's large waterfalls. This project was ultimately jettisoned, but by 1962 plans were afoot to build a massive hydroelectric plant at another location, in tandem with a large, power-intensive factory. One option under serious discussion was harnessing Jökulsá á fjöllum, the river that forms Dettifoss. Such a plant, referred to at the time as the "Dettifoss Plant" (*Dettifossvirkjun*), would have significantly diminished the waterfall's power. This was ultimately abandoned, following a geopolitical struggle between northern and southern constituencies, in favor of another plant powered by the Þjórsá river in the south.[53] This plant, known as *Búrfellsvirkjun*, opened in May 1970, and a day later Iceland's first aluminum smelter began operating in Straumsvík, near the capital.

Leifs's views on the power plants and the increasing industrialization of Iceland are not known, but his composing of the nature pieces in the early 1960s—a period of intense debate about harnessing Iceland's wilderness for electricity—is telling. This is particularly true of Dettifoss, the only one of his sites that was being targeted for a specific hydroelectric project at that time. Ironically, Benediktsson, the poet of Leifs's text, had been one of Iceland's earliest proponents for hydroelectric power, yet harnessing Dettifoss was never part of his ambitious plans. In the poem he specifically extols its dramatic power, and potential harnessing is implied only as a spiritual/artistic endeavor—the line "*Kný minn huga ... til ljóða, er lifa*" translates literally as "Propel my mind ... to poems, that will live." Thus, Benediktsson suggests that the waterfall's force should be converted into art, not electricity. It should be noted that the question of harnessing Dettifoss's power was not fully laid to rest in 1970. The project resurfaced in the early 2000s during a period of further industrialization on a massive scale, including the construction of the Kárahnjúkar hydroelectric plant, which caused irreparable damage to the eastern highlands.[54] For Icelanders today, the negotiation between modernization, conservation, and preservation is an ongoing—and controversial—one.

The final installment in the tetralogy of "place pieces," *Hafís* (*Drift Ice*), differs in kind from the others. Geysir, Hekla, and Dettifoss are all landscapes, quintessential destinations, and critical to the country's self-identity. Drift ice, on the other hand, is not a locale but a phenomenon and one that Icelanders have, historically speaking, regarded as an adversary rather than as a national symbol. In cold winters, large sheets of drift ice from the Arctic Ocean or Eastern Greenland can lie across the Icelandic fjords. In earlier times, they could close off entire inlets for months at a time, threatening the existence of the rural communities that depended upon ships for merchandise. Ice winters were also invariably followed by chilly summers that proved disastrous for farmers. One writer has suggested that in the history of Iceland, ice played a larger and more devastating part in the nation's disasters than "most other catastrophes, even plagues and volcanic eruptions."[55] One such episode of particularly harsh winters and drift ice occurred in the years around 1880–90 and was still very much in people's memory when Leifs was a child. From 1918 until 1965, drift ice was more or less absent from the oceans around Iceland, but then a six-year period saw a dramatic increase in ice and was referred to locally as the "drift ice years." News of ice in spring 1965 provided the immediate stimulus for Leifs's work. In late April he made a trip to northern Iceland with the intention of "hearing" the ice and sketched the opening measures while there; the work was complete in August that same year.

At nearly eighteen minutes, *Hafís* is the longest of the place pieces and the one that carries the most text. As in *Dettifoss*, the lyrics are by Benediktsson, in this case three stanzas from a poem published in 1913. Leifs's frequent use of extreme choral tessitura and angular leaps in *pianissimo* dynamics makes the piece extremely challenging to perform, and indeed *Hafís* was the last of the four to be premiered—on the occasion of Leifs's centenary in 1999. The very first entry is a high soprano B-natural, and the wide, angular leaps are typical of Leifs's demands from his long-suffering choral singers (see example 9.2).

Example 9.2. Leifs, *Hafís* op. 63, mm. 92–101, soprano part. © Iceland Music Information Center.

Apart from isolated outbreaks in the orchestra, Leifs evokes in *Hafís* an eerie sense of calm, a wide expanse of ice and ocean. A notable feature is his ingenious evocation of the cracking of the large ice sheets through a simple musical device: repeated hammering eighth notes in percussion or winds/brass. His use of a ratchet also produces a loud, crisp sound that suggests breaking ice. At the work's climax, the text refers to the "bursting blockades of water dashing," and here the large percussion section is joined by a piano, Leifs's first orchestral use of the instrument since the 1927 overture to *Galdra-Loftr*.[56] He instructs the pianist to play with the elbows, perhaps a nod to Henry Cowell, whom he had met in Iceland two years previously (see below), or possibly a more general acknowledgment of the extended performing techniques now commonly employed by a younger generation of composers.

Leifs's place pieces provide the most explicit manifestation of the sublime in his output, although certain of his other works share many of the same qualities. By evoking through sound the remote and potentially deadly phenomena of nature, Leifs induces terror and awe as well as evoking power, vastness, difficulty, and magnificence. The moment of the sublime in Leifs's music is one of intense force: the annihilating eruption, the cataclysmic hurricane. As Malcolm Andrews has noted, the position of being both spectator and potential victim/participator is crucial to the full experience of the sublime; one is taken as close to disaster as is compatible with still retaining the sense that one is not actually in danger.[57] This is certainly also true of Leifs's works: they are both destabilizing and reassuring, creating a dynamic tension of terror (the subject) and safety (the concert hall experience). In his visceral, overpowering depictions of landscape, Leifs evokes a similarly gendered aesthetic as had informed his earlier "heroic" works such as the *Saga Symphony*: this is music of brutal force, capable of destroying the human being whose experience is being depicted. The strategy of the powerful climax, or musical apotheosis, that overwhelms the listener by its force and magnitude itself has roots in the Romantic orchestral works of Liszt, Bruckner, Strauss, and Mahler, and it is likewise a key element in Leifs's orchestral aesthetic of the monumental and the heroic.[58] The experience of the sublime is also one that bypasses the rational mind. Almost by definition, it subverts order, coherence, and a structured organization—and this was fully in line with Leifs's lifelong rejection of traditional formal structures.[59]

PERFORMANCES AT HOME

Throughout his life, Leifs played the part of the misunderstood genius. He was, of course, neglected as a composer: many of his largest and most important works were never performed during his lifetime. But this was also, in part, due to a combination of political circumstance (his later years in Germany) and his refusal, after his return to Iceland, to compromise his artistic vision by writing less demanding works for smaller forces. His larger works were certainly far beyond the capabilities of the Iceland Symphony Orchestra, which in the 1950s was only a fledgling ensemble of around forty players. In a 1964 interview, Leifs lamented that "only around one percent of my works, in terms of performance time, has ever been performed in this country, and then only in a very imperfect way."[60] He even implied that leading figures in Icelandic music circles, such as Ísólfsson, were working against him behind the scenes, hindering him from "creating music in this country."[61] Yet in 1964 he received one of the highest artist bursaries awarded by the Icelandic government, a total of 30,000 krónur (roughly the equivalent of US$6,000, adjusted for inflation).[62] Only a handful of artists were specially chosen by the parliament to receive a higher stipend, among them Laxness and Ísólfsson, whose higher ranking only increased Leifs's discontent.

Nevertheless, Leifs had many opportunities to introduce his art at home in the 1960s. His smaller orchestral works were performed, for instance *Réminiscence du Nord* in 1960, *Trois peintures abstraites* in 1961, and *Landfall* in 1962. In January and February 1962, the National Radio broadcast the 1950 Helsinki recording of the *Saga Symphony* as a five-part series on Sunday evenings, each movement preceded by an introduction by the composer himself. It was unusual for the radio to devote so much airtime to a single composition, and the program certainly had its critics. An anonymous newspaper columnist called it a tedious affair, noting that the saga hero Skarphéðinn had suffered a drawn-out death—"and he seemed to expire of boredom rather than burn wounds."[63] Jón Þórarinsson, Leifs's adversary who held the post of music advisor at the National Radio, was far from convinced of the work's artistic value. Somewhat unusually, he penned a review of the radio program in *Morgunblaðið* disparaging the composer's musical ideas as monotonous and the orchestration as "remarkably unvaried and heavy-handed."[64]

The year 1963 saw the Icelandic premieres of some of Leifs's earliest works. In March the Iceland Symphony performed selections from *Galdra-Loftr*, and at the same concert a newly commissioned symphony by Henry Cowell premiered, through the encouragement of the orchestra's American conductor, William Strickland, whose post there was sponsored by the US State Department.[65] Cowell, who had studied Leifs's wax cylinder recordings of Icelandic folk songs during his Guggenheim fellowship in Berlin in the 1930s, employed elements of the vernacular style in his new Symphony no. 16 ("Icelandic") but through the lens of memory. Cowell flew to Iceland to attend the premiere and met Leifs in person for the first and only time.[66] Strickland recorded both Cowell's symphony and Leifs's *Iceland Overture* for an LP release by the US-based Composers Recordings, Inc. (CRI), and this was for decades the only internationally available release of Leifs's music. Three days after the *Galdra-Loftr* concert, Leifs's *Nocturne* for harp was performed, and in July the Iceland Symphony's concertmaster,

Björn Ólafsson, gave what seems to have been the world premiere of the fiendishly difficult *Prelude and Fughetta* for violin op. 3.

Although Leifs's last years were generally peaceful, there were occasional flashes of his former curmudgeonly persona—for example, when it was his turn to assume the presidency of the Nordic Music Council, which passed between the directors of the national composers' unions every two years. In 1962, Leifs refused to take up the position, claiming that not enough had been done to promote Icelandic music at past festivals (reminiscent of his outbursts at the Permanent Council meetings in the 1930s), although then he did take on the position two years later.[67] Leifs also remained an easy object of ridicule, as when he suggested in 1965 that Breiðholt, a new suburb then under development in Reykjavík, should be designated a "quiet neighborhood" for creative artists and scientists. He had earlier made a formal request to city officials to reside in the area, claiming that he found it impossible to compose in the city due to noise, but at that time there was no running water in Breiðholt, and his application was denied.[68] He saw the request as an opportunity for officials to atone for his earlier rejection for the Þingvellir post, but the idea was roundly ridiculed in the local press, and it was not lost on his detractors that it came from a composer infamous for writing uncommonly loud music.[69]

NEW DIRECTIONS

In July 1962, Leifs picked up *Edda II* where he had left off ten years earlier, and the first movement was complete within four months. In a newspaper interview in summer 1962 he boasted about how easy it had been for him to return to it: "I have just resumed writing a piece that I abandoned *in medias res* ten years ago. I was surprised that the writing and thinking should not have changed during this time. You can't even see where I broke off ten years ago and where I now began again."[70]

Upon further reflection, Leifs may have realized that his statement was deeply problematic. His style had become routine and his reliance on third- and tritone-related harmonies and parallel fifths rather predictable and formulaic. He finished the second movement of *Edda II*, then put the work aside yet again. Leifs's next works—particularly *Scherzo concreto*, *Night*, and the string quartet *El Greco*—are fairly radical departures in terms of style and subject matter and can be seen as an attempt to escape from a certain stylistic rut as he entered the final phase of his composing career.

With the *Edda* cycle delayed even further, Leifs's fear that time would run out and that his immense opus would remain incomplete was bound to resurface. In November 1963 he wrote two short, single-movement works for orchestra, *Fine I* and *Fine II*, prescribing that were he to leave behind at his death an unfinished work, either one could be used as an ending.[71] The two *Fine* pieces are opposites in terms of tempo and character, and the intention was presumably to ensure a smooth continuation regardless of the character of the movement they were meant to conclude. The blunt and abrasive *Fine I* is a synthesis of Leifs's more aggressive, heroic style while *Fine II* is slow and subdued. The manuscript carries the inscription "Gratitude—Peace," and the work, scored only for strings and vibraphone, concludes with a luminous D-major chord that gradually dissolves into higher and higher registers—suggesting, perhaps, a soul being released from earthly constraints.

The four-minute *Scherzo concreto* (1964) is in several respects unique among Leifs's compositions, and its genesis and title have never been adequately explained. "Scherzo" suggests a humorous stance while "concreto" must refer to *musique concrète*, the term introduced by Pierre Schaeffer in 1948 for electronic music based on existing sound materials. Yet Leifs's work has nothing in common with musique concrète. It is a fanciful piece of program music for ten instruments (piccolo, flute, oboe, English horn, clarinet, bassoon, trombone, tuba, viola, and cello) and "seven characters," each of which is assigned a suggestive name in the score: The Buffoon, the Naïf, the Melancholic, the Majestic, the Boor, the Deceiver, and the Lover. The characters are not generally assigned to one specific instrument: the gentle phrases of the Naïf alternate between oboe and clarinet while the Buffoon's disjunct, atonal utterances are taken by flute and piccolo. The Majestic is depicted by *maestoso* parallel fifths in bassoon and trombone; the Boor is given low, growling notes in bassoon, trombone, or tuba. Two instruments are consistently identified with a specific personage: the Melancholic with the English horn and the Lover with the cello (its long, lyrical phrases marked *sempre espressivo* and *passionato*). In the opening measures, the music sounds vaguely reminiscent of Webern (although not serial; Leifs does not employ a specific row), and the texture often consists of only a single line moving from instrument to instrument. As the work progresses, Leifs's own voice emerges more clearly. Besides the parallel fifths of the Majestic (perhaps suggesting Leifs himself as a character in his own work), the piece includes the major/minor oscillations, rhythmic acceleration building to a climax, and third-related major triads so typical of his style.

It is striking that Leifs, who claimed to expressly avoid outside influence in his works, should in his sixties have made such an overt reference to serialism and only in a single work. In writing *Scherzo concreto*, he was influenced by the American composer Gunther Schuller, who visited Reykjavík in January 1964, conducting the Iceland Symphony Orchestra in a program that included three symphonies: Schuller's own, Webern's Symphony op. 21, and a symphony by Leifur Þórarinsson, Schuller's Icelandic student and protégé. During his trip, Schuller also lectured at the University of Iceland on "new currents in American and European music," a lecture Leifs attended. He completed *Scherzo concreto* in May, and in the program notes for its premiere that November at a Musica Nova concert, he remarked that it was "composed as a kind of response to a lecture given recently by Gunther Schuller. I leave it to the individual listener to interpret the nature of the work's basic idea, and whether it is meant to be taken seriously or as a joke."[72] If Leifs's intention was for *Scherzo concreto* to be interpreted as a kind of caricature, it must have been a good-humored one, since the Musica Nova concert at which the *Scherzo* was premiered also contained works by Schuller and Þórarinsson, who held the baton.

Another work from 1964 shows Leifs experimenting in a different direction. *Night* (*Nótt*) op. 59, for tenor, baritone, and chamber orchestra, is his only setting of a poem by the Romantic poet Þorsteinn Erlingsson (1858–1914), whose sentimental verse was popular in its day but far removed from Leifs's aesthetic. It has none of the characteristics of style or subject matter that typically commended texts to the composer's attention: archaic Eddic meters, emphasis on Iceland's heroic past, or sublime natural forces. Instead, *Night's* 30 quatrains are a reflection on nature in the pastoral mode and describe the nocturnal tryst of young, innocent lovers. Leifs's setting is appropriately (if uncharacteristically) gentle and relaxed. His choice of a tenor/baritone duet is explained by the poem's third-person narrative voice, and it is of course ideal for the parallel fifths of tvísöngur, which Leifs uses with abandon. The work's most unusual element is a brief orchestral interlude that depicts the lovers' physical consummation, with a *crescendo/accelerando* reaching an evocative climax before subsiding again. This was Leifs's first exploration in his music of such an overtly sexual theme, although the musical technique of rhythmic acceleration/deceleration had been a hallmark of his style for decades. He would also soon return to a similar erotic theme in *The Lay of Helgi the Hunding-Slayer*.

The year 1964 was a productive one for Leifs: as well as *Dettifoss*, *Scherzo concreto*, and *Night*, he completed two works to Eddic and saga texts. The first of these was *Song of Dorrud* (*Darraðarljóð*), to a poem from *Njáls saga*. The saga's final chapters take place in the Orkney Islands and Scotland and relate the bloody battle of Clontarf on Good Friday 1014, where Earl Sigurd of the Orkneys fought the Irish high king Brian Boru. The poem tells of events that were believed to have foretold the carnage. In Caithness, a man named Dorrud walked outside and saw twelve people riding together to a house and entering it. He looked through a window and saw twelve Valkyries inside and that they had set up a loom. Men's heads were used for weights, men's intestines for the weft and warp, a sword for the sword beater, and an arrow for the pin beater. While weaving their fabric, he heard the Valkyries chanting a song, through which they chose who was to be slain at the battle. The poem consists in large part of analogies between weaving on a loom and fighting on a battlefield, and it offers a grim prophecy for the ensuing combat:

Vítt er orpit	A wide warp
fyr valfalli,	warns of slaughter;
rifs reiðiský	blood rains
rignir blóði....	from the beam's cloud....
Vindum, vindum	We wind and wind
vef Darraðar,	the web of spears,
þar er vé vaða	there where the banners
vígra manna	of bold men go forth
látum eigi	we must not let
líf hans farast	his life be lost—
eiga valkyrjur	Valkyries decide
vals um kosti.	who dies or lives.[73]

Leifs had been planning to set this text for decades. A typewritten worklist from ca. 1938 contains as a projected item, along with the *Edda* oratorio and *The Lay of Guðrún*, a work for choir and orchestra titled *Walküren-Lied* to a text from *Njáls saga*. His idea for the work was presumably much older still, since he wrote in the completed score that it had been composed "according to a 50-year-old plan."[74] Although fairly short and scored for a medium-size orchestra, *Song of Dorrud* remains unperformed. The instrumentarium contains Leifs's usual percussion component—anvils, rocks, clapper, and shields—which is unleashed with full force at the work's climax. As the clamor suddenly dies down, the text tells of the terrifying sight of blood-drenched skies. Here Leifs employs the ominous sound of gloomy minor triads for a considerable stretch; the effect is reminiscent of the minor-tinged *Night, Morning* from *Edda I*.

Two short works to Eddic poems, composed in 1964–65, are arguably less successful. *The Lay of Helgi the Hunding-Slayer* (*Helga kviða Hundingsbana*) demonstrates Leifs's renewed interest in Eddic poetry as a side project to the larger *Edda* oratorio. The verses tell of the love between the hero Helgi and Sigrún, a Valkyrie. Her father has pledged her to another, but Helgi assembles an army and kills the groom-to-be as well as Sigrún's father and brother. Although the lovers are married, their conjugal bliss comes to a violent end as another of her brothers murders Helgi with Óðinn's spear. Leifs set verses from the final part of the poem, where Óðinn grants the deceased Helgi permission to revisit his burial mound so that he can share a night of passion with Sigrún before returning to Valhalla. *The Lay of Helgi the Hunding-Slayer* is delicately scored and its texture almost chamber-like, except for a remarkable orchestral interlude as Helgi and Sigrún consummate their love. At the start, strings slide delicately from one minor chord to another, marked *pppp*; then more instruments join in as the glissandos turn from minor to major triads, and these eventually yield to hammered quarter notes getting constantly louder and faster. Here, as in the earlier *Night*, Leifs's favored device of rhythmic acceleration takes on an erotic association while the musical effect of the opening glissando passage is strikingly similar to that of Benjamin Britten's introduction to the opera *A Midsummer Night's Dream*, composed in 1960. Although it seems unlikely that Leifs knew this work, it cannot be ruled out that he heard the live Aldeburgh broadcast on BBC in June 1960 or that he heard it at Covent Garden or the Edinburgh Festival in 1961 or 1962.

Leifs began composing *The Lay of Helgi the Hunding-Slayer* on September 28, 1964, during his stay in Helsinki for the Nordic Music Days. The scathing reception of *Hekla* four days later did not drain his energy: he completed the work within a month and immediately moved on to a more ambitious Eddic work, *Gróa's Spell* (*Grógaldr*), for alto, tenor, and orchestra. The poem tells of a young man who visits the grave of his mother, Gróa (a common name in old Iceland and also a word for *völva*, or seeress). He asks her to protect him, as his stepmother has put a spell on him so that he may not have peace until he finds the woman he is to marry. Gróa responds by chanting nine spells to aid him in his undertaking. Gróa is the main character in both the poem and Leifs's work; the tenor part is a lesser one, but occasionally Leifs combines the voices during her chants of magic, for a supernatural effect. It was hardly a coincidence that Leifs should be drawn to this text—about a son's attempt to contact his deceased mother, and her protection from beyond—shortly after his own mother had passed away. After all, in his spiritualist childhood home, attempts to communicate with the spirits of the dead had been everyday events.

Amid all his composing, Leifs continued his involvement in international organizations promoting cooperation between musicians. After the war, he frequently attended the ISCM's World Music Days, representing the Icelandic Composers' Society, which gave him the chance to hear new music of a kind that rarely reached Iceland, by composers such as Nono, Berio, and Stockhausen. At the 1965 World Music Days in Madrid, Leifs proposed that Iceland host the festival two years later, and while his bid was not successful, the ISCM festival did take place in Reykjavík in 1973, an event that Leifs himself did not live to witness.[75]

On Leifs's journey to Spain he encountered in situ the vivid and dramatic paintings of the sixteenth-century master El Greco, or Doménikos Theotokópoulos. Their vivid colors, elongated figures, and mystic atmosphere made a lasting impression, and shortly after returning to Iceland Leifs made plans for a string quartet titled *El Greco*. The summer of 1965 was a hectic one due to preparations for a meeting of the Nordic Council of Composers, but in August and September he was able to fully devote himself to the new work. He composed rapidly, writing the final three movements in just over a week.

Each of the five movements of *El Greco* op. 64 is inspired by a particular painting. The first and longest is "Toledo in the Midst of a Thunderstorm"; here Leifs is fully in his element depicting the wild and threatening forces of nature. The gentle second movement is inspired by El Greco's self-portrait, in which Leifs claimed to sense a kindred Nordic spirit. Several versions of "Christ Driving the Money Changers from the Temple" by El Greco exist, all of which portray Christ raising his left hand as he prepares to strike the perturbed sinners. The quartet's corresponding third movement is brief and brusque; in its more violent passages Leifs requests that the players hit the wood of their instruments with their hands. The fourth movement evokes the stunned silence of Golgotha with dark skies looming overhead, and Leifs suggests Christ's release of his final breath with exhausted downward glissandi. The finale,

Figure 9.6. Leifs with jazz legend Louis Armstrong at a reception at the US embassy in Reykjavík, February 1965. © Photographic Collection, National Museum of Iceland.

Resurrection, is the shortest movement of all. Its vigorous chords become calmer as the violins reach into the stratosphere—a musical gesture that Leifs seems on more than one occasion to have connected with the final release of the spirit, as for example in *Vita et mors* and *Fine II*.

The 1960s saw only a handful of Leifs's larger works performed outside Iceland. The *Beethoven Variations* were programmed by the Dresden Philharmonic in 1960, and the *Iceland Overture* was performed by Sixten Ehrling and the Montréal Symphony at a Nordic concert at the city's Universal and International Exposition in 1967.[76] In Iceland, some of his works were being revived after decades of neglect: the *Overture to Galdra-Loftr* was performed by the Iceland Symphony in March 1967 (its first outing since Copenhagen in 1938), and the Nordic Music Days festival in Reykjavík in September that year saw the local premiere of his choral *Kyrie* as well as a production of *Galdra-Loftr* at the National Theater—the first to include Leifs's incidental music.[77]

But Leifs still felt that his music was neglected, and even in his final year he fought fervently for what he saw as his right for recognition. In the winter of 1967–68, the National Radio promoted Icelandic music in a program called *Composer of the Month*. It was decided that February should be Leifs's month, and it was not lost on him that it was the year's shortest.[78] He kicked up a fuss, sending to the culture minister, the National Radio director, and the entire board of the radio a heated statement titled "I Protest—I Accuse," in which he demanded an independent investigation of the institution's "deplorable working methods." As if further aggravation was needed, at that same time the National Radio began a broadcast of Wagner's *Ring Cycle*, which Leifs insisted was bound to "confuse people, as many of my own works are composed expressly as a protest against Wagner."[79]

The early months of 1968 were also marked by internal discord in the Composers' Society. Four years earlier, Leifs had floated plans to found an Icelandic music center to promote Icelandic music abroad. He was familiar with similar national organizations

Jón Leifs er tónskáld útvarpsins í febrúarmánuði, og á það vel við, þar sem hann er án efa, stórbrotnasta tónskáld Íslendinga og sjaldan farið troðnar slóðir við samningu verka sinna !!!

Figure 9.7. Leifs, as "Composer of the Month," wielding a spiked club while composing. Cartoon from *Morgunblaðið*, February 11, 1968. © National and University Library, Reykjavík.

elsewhere in Europe and suggested that the local one be modeled after the Dutch center, Donemus.[80] In the end, Leifs's demands that the center be run in close cooperation with STEF, and that it should promote only works by the most accomplished of Icelandic composers, alienated his fellow members in the Composers' Society, who suspected that his intention was to focus more or less exclusively on promoting his own works.[81] The Icelandic Music Information Center (*Íslensk tónverkamiðstöð*) was founded on January 17, 1968, largely without Leifs's involvement. Although he was present as the meeting began and was even chosen to chair the proceedings, he stormed out before the discussion got underway, insisting that he could not be in the same room as his fellow composer Jón Þórarinsson.[82] Leifs was still convinced that Ísólfsson and

Þórarinsson, through their ties to the National Radio and the symphony, had hindered the performance and appreciation of his music and was unwilling to make peace with them, even though the end was approaching. By that time, he had only half a year left to live.

TWILIGHT

Leifs had made several previous attempts at *Edda II* but hit his stride only in early 1966, completing the final four movements between January and May. He had originally intended for the first movement to be titled *Gods* (*Æsir*), a portrayal of each of the male gods in turn (Óðinn, Þór, Baldr, Njörður, etc.). He later decided to divide it into two movements: the first (*Óðinn*) depicts the father of all the gods; the second enumerates his sons (*Sons of Óðinn*). The calmer third movement, *Goddesses* (*Ásynjur*), is a portrayal of the female characters: Frigg, Freyja, Sigyn, Eir, Gefjun. The oratorio's last three movements (*Valkyries*, *Norns*, and *Warriors*) are far shorter than the previous ones, perhaps an indication that Leifs suspected time was running out and that he was determined to finish the work at all cost.

In June 1966, while on holiday in Kahlenberg near Vienna, he began the next installment. *Edda III—Twilight of the Gods* (*Ragnarökr*) calls for mammoth performing forces, a decision inspired in part by hearing what he later described as "two of the most magnificent Requiems ever written"—by Berlioz and Verdi—in November that year in Paris, where he attended a CISAC meeting in the company of Icelandic novelists Gunnar Gunnarsson and Halldór Laxness.[83] On All Souls' Day, he heard the Berlioz Requiem performed at the Panthéon by the ORTF Philharmonic and the fanfare of the Garde républicaine; Verdi's Requiem was given at Saint-Roch three days later. The dramatic qualities of both works, but not least the vast resources of the former, inspired him to make the single-movement *Edda III* his most expansive work by far.

Edda III is the only truly dramatic part of the trilogy. Having portrayed the creation myth in *Edda I* and provided a character study of the gods in *Edda II*, Leifs now sets the stage for the confrontation between good and evil. Virtually no sketches exist for *Edda III*; it is as if Leifs, sensing that time was running out, wrote most of his ideas directly into the full score. And a very full score it is: he even outdid his earlier efforts in *Hekla*, this time taping together pages of score paper to reach a total of sixty staves, appropriate for the apocalyptic story. In an interview he remarked that "I've never done anything like it before. It's impossible to describe such events without employing gigantic forces."[84]

The performers are divided into three groups, a clear nod to the Berlioz Requiem with its spatial separation of performing forces. In *Edda III* a large orchestra occupies the stage along with a percussion ensemble, a mixed chorus, and two soloists: mezzo-soprano and baritone. Two separate groups are situated behind the audience: to the right, a male chorus with three trombones, two tubas, and percussion; to the left, a female chorus and tenor soloist along with four trumpets, timpani, and percussion. Leifs also employs electronic amplification for the first and only time in his output. To depict the monstrous Midgard serpent, Loki's offspring who surrounds the earth and grasps his own tail, the male chorus is instructed to sing into a microphone, with the sound projected from "every corner of the auditorium."[85]

In Leifs's last works, such as *Song of Dorrud* and *Edda III*, there is a tendency to employ more angular, chromatic lines than ever before. This was in all likelihood a consciously modernizing trait on Leifs's part, perhaps one that betrays a lingering influence from the experimental *Scherzo concreto* but also from his travels to the ISCM and Nordic festivals. A novel departure is his use of chromatic parallel fifths, particularly in ominous passages. In *Edda III*, chromatically descending parallel fifths form the sinister, recurring refrain of the seeress's prophecy in *Völuspá*: "wit ye further, or how?" (*Vituð ér enn eða hvað?*).[86] Another example of pictorial chromaticism is when the fire burning from the nostrils of the Midgard serpent is depicted through an ascending chromatic octave in the sopranos, harmonized with fully diminished seventh chords (see example 9.3).

Example 9.3. Leifs, *Edda III* op. 65, mm. 144–45, choral part. © Iceland Music Information Center.

It is fitting for such music for the end of the world to evoke fear and anxiety. In Leifs's libretto, the work was supposed to end with the image of blood-red clouds covering the sky, taken not from Eddic poetry but from the poem in *Njáls saga* that he had already mined for *Song of Dorrud*.

Despite its gruesome subject, *Edda III* was composed in part with the most serene and inspiring backdrop imaginable. Leifs had received permission to reside in the lighthouse warden's apartment at Dyrhólaey during the summer of 1967, since the lighthouse is turned off in the summertime when the days are long. Dyrhólaey is a small promontory on the south coast of Iceland, home to puffins that reside in its cliffs and with breathtaking vistas in every direction. To the north there is the Mýrdalsjökull glacier; to the east, the black lava columns of Reynisdrangar rise from the ocean; to the west, much of the southern coastline of Iceland is visible. During his stay in Dyrhólaey, Leifs also made plans for a new home in Seltjarnarnes, a neighboring town to Reykjavík, on land he had inherited at his mother's death. The house, designed by a prominent local architect, was to have been built on pillars on the waterfront, with a spacious workspace for Leifs facing the sea, surrounded by a terrace where he could breathe the fresh ocean air.

But Leifs's elegant waterfront home was never built, and the apocalyptic final scene of *Edda III* played out only in his own mind. In late April 1968, a few days after yet another dramatic confrontation

Figure 9.8. Leifs's study at his home in Reykjavík. The photograph was taken shortly after his death. The unfinished score to *Edda III* lies on the desk, above which can be seen a well-known drawing of Beethoven's study (made three days after his death) and Beethoven's autograph to the *Ode to Joy*. © Leifs Archives, National and University Library, Reykjavík.

at a Composers' Society meeting, he began vomiting blood. He was admitted to the Reykjavík City Hospital on May 14, where doctors discovered a malignant tumor. In response, Leifs briefly put aside *Edda III* to express more tender emotions in a simple, touching work for string orchestra, *Consolation* op. 66. It is his own requiem, a farewell to life and a consolation to his widow and their son. He then returned to *Edda III* once more, completing page two hundred of the full score at the hospital on June 5, 1968, the day before undergoing an operation. He managed to write twelve more pages before his powers were exhausted. *Edda III* remained incomplete and to this day has never been performed. Only a libretto draft hints at Leifs's intentions for the final installment, *Edda IV—Resurrection* (*Endurreisn*), in which a green and fair earth rises from the ocean and a new world order is established under the leadership of Baldur, the "white god."

Leifs was released from the hospital on June 16. The next day (Iceland's Independence Day) it was announced that he was among the recipients of the Icelandic Order of the Falcon, an honor bestowed by the president upon individuals for their services to Iceland.[87] This was the only official honor Leifs ever received, and it came at the last possible moment. A few weeks later his condition worsened, and he was again admitted to the hospital on July 11. He passed away at the Reykjavík City Hospital on July 30, 1968, and his funeral was held at the Reykjavík Cathedral on August 7.

NOTES

1. Matthías Johannessen, "Lögmálin í hrúgunni. Spjallað við Jón Leifs," *Morgunblaðið*, May 5, 1959.
2. Jakob Möller, "Ég biðst afsökunar hafi ég gleymt að móðga einhvern," *Vikan*, November 8, 1962, 11.
3. "Tónlistarhátíð Norðurlanda," *Morgunblaðið*, September 19, 1967.
4. The original manuscript source is AM 92 8vo (59v), quoted in Sigurður Skúlason, "Íslenzkar særingar," *Eimreiðin* 36 (1930): 352.
5. Leifs took the tune from Bjarni Þorsteinsson's folk song anthology, where it is printed to the text *Enginn falli ærugalli*, a poem by Jón Þorláksson (1744–1819) that the younger poet Hallgrímsson used as a model for his text (see *Íslenzk þjóðlög*, 542, 785).
6. Leifs won first prize for "individual work," and Jón Ásgeirsson won second prize for *Occidente sole* for voice and piano. Another category in the competition was devoted to song cycles, where Sigurður Þórðarsson won first prize, and Hallgrímur Helgason came second. See "Lög við kvæði Jónasar Hallgrímssonar," *Þjóðviljinn*, September 4, 1958; Stefánsson, *Útvarp Reykjavík*, 365.
7. Jón Leifs, "Verðlaun? Opið bréf til útvarpsins frá Jóni Leifs," *Morgunblaðið*, September 13, 1958.
8. Möller, "Ég biðst afsökunar," 10.
9. Jón Leifs, "Niðurlæging Þingvalla," *Þjóðviljinn*, December 1, 1959.
10. Möller, "Ég biðst afsökunar," 10.
11. Jón Leifs, "Þingvellir í sárum," *Morgunblaðið*, July 15, 1959.
12. Möller, "Ég biðst afsökunar," 10. The novel was Guðmundur Kamban's *Skálholt* (four volumes, 1930–32).
13. Leifs, *Víkingasvar*, full score.
14. Leifs, sketches for *Víkingasvar*.

15. Halldór Guðmundsson, *Halldór Laxness—Ævisaga* (Reykjavík: JPV, 2004), 566.
16. Ástráður Eysteinsson, "Icelandic Prose Literature, 1940–1980," in *A History of Icelandic Literature*, ed. Daisy Neijmann, 417.
17. Kristján Albertsson, "Um Brekkukotsannál og sitthvað fleira," *Morgunblaðið*, April 30, 1957.
18. Undated memorandum (probably 1951) in the hand of Halldór Laxness, Leifs collection.
19. Leifs, "Hugsjónir þakkaðar," *Morgunblaðið*, May 9, 1959.
20. Menachem Avidom, president of ACUM, to Hallgrímur Helgason, October 5, 1959.
21. Leifs to the Icelandic Foreign Ministry, November 6, 1962.
22. The apology, from Dr. Y. Shapira of Israeli Radio, is quoted in a letter from the consul general in Tel Aviv to the Icelandic Foreign Ministry, January 13, 1960.
23. S. V. F., "Það er ekki hægt að vera á móti þessum mönnum," *Þjóðviljinn*, July 2, 1960.
24. S. V. F., "Það er ekki hægt að vera á móti þessum mönnum," *Þjóðviljinn*, July 2, 1960.
25. "Ég var hylltur," *Morgunblaðið*, July 3, 1960; Benedikt Gröndal, "Um helgina," *Alþýðublaðið*, July 10, 1960; Jón Leifs, "Vinur nazista," *Þjóðviljinn*, July 13, 1960.
26. Icelandic Embassy to Icelandic Foreign Ministry, Moscow, August 24, 1967, Foreign Ministry Papers 1996-B/484, National Archives of Iceland, Reykjavík.
27. Þ. H., "Musica Nova-kvöld," *Vísir*, December 7, 1961.
28. See Árni Heimir Ingólfsson, "Clothing Irons and Whisky Bottles—Creating an Icelandic Musical Avant-Garde," in *A Cultural History of the Avant Garde in the Nordic Countries, 1950–1975*, ed. Tania Ørum and Jesper Olsson (Leiden: Brill, 2016), 285–87.
29. Following a concert of Icelandic music on April 13, 1960, Leifs led an informal discussion and gave each of the composers (including Leifur Þórarinsson, Magnús Blöndal Jóhannsson, and Þorkell Sigurbjörnsson) constructive remarks on their works; see Leifs, "Til ungra tónskálda," *Vísir*, May 6, 1960.
30. Njörður P. Njarðvík, "Ekki margt—heldur mikið," *Vísir*, December 22, 1962.
31. Interview with Rögnvaldur Sigurjónsson, November 14, 2003.
32. Leifs, Program note for *Trois peintures abstraites*, performance on December 7, 1961, Iceland Symphony Orchestra Archives, Reykjavík.
33. Leifs, Program note for *Trois peintures abstraites*.

34. Jón Þórarinsson, "Sinfóníuhljómleikar," *Morgunblaðið*, December 9, 1961.
35. Riley and Smith, *Nation and Classical Music*, 95, 99.
36. Fritz Brust, review in *Allgemeine Musikzeitung*, March 11, 1927; B. A-N, "Isländsk desillusion," *Göteborgs Posten*, January 29, 1931.
37. Möller, "Ég biðst afsökunar," 10.
38. Þorsteinn Jósepsson and Steindór Steindórsson, *Landið þitt Ísland*, vol. 1 (Reykjavík: Örn og Örlygur, 1980), 239.
39. See Warren Darcy, *Wagner's Das Rheingold* (New York: Oxford University Press, 1993), 78.
40. Helgi Torfason, "Geysir vakinn upp," *Náttúrufræðingurinn* 53 (1984): 5–6.
41. "Úr daglega lífinu," *Morgunblaðið*, September 11, 1945.
42. Helgi Torfason, *The Great Geysir*, 2nd ed. (Reykjavík: Geysir Centre, 2010), 4.
43. "Nýtt tónverk frumflutt eftir Jón Leifs," *Morgunblaðið*, January 20, 1965.
44. "Inkpot Sibelius Nutcase," review of BIS-CD 1030, http://inkpot.com/classical/leifshekla.html, accessed November 30, 2015.
45. Leifs, *Hekla*, full score.
46. "Norrænir tónlistardagar," *Morgunblaðið*, November 8, 1964; "Íslenzk tónskáld á norrænni hátíð," *Morgunblaðið*, March 25, 1964.
47. Kaj Chydenius, "Brokig nordisk konsert," *Hufvudstadsbladet*, October 4, 1964.
48. "Kuivuutta ja vulkaanisuutta: Pohjoismaiset musiikkipäivät alkoivat," *Kauppalehti*, October 5, 1964. Reviews are not consistent regarding the number of escapees, but this may be explained by the critics' placement in the hall. Seppo Heikinheimo noted that two women had left the concert; according to Tauno Karila "a few audience members" walked out ("Pohjoismaista musiikkia," *Helsingin sanomat*, October 5, 1964; "Pohjoismaiset musiikkipäivät," *Suomen Sosialidemokraatti*, October 4, 1964).
49. Leifs, *Dettifoss*, full score, ii.
50. Einar Benediktsson, *Harp of the North: Poems by Einar Benediktsson*, trans. Frederick T. Wood (Charlottesville: The University of Virginia Press, 1955), 14.
51. Johnson, *Webern*, 70.
52. The following discussion is indebted in a general sense to recent ecomusicological writings, especially Brooks Toliver, "Eco-ing in the Canyon: Ferde Grofè's *Grand Canyon Suite* and the Transformation of Wilderness," *Journal of the American Musicological Society* 57 (2004), 325–68.
53. Björn Haraldsson, "Jökulsárvirkjun—Búrfellsvirkjun," *Dagur*, October 24, 1962.

54. See, for example, an article by a former energy commissioner in which he recommends harnessing the energy of Dettifoss even if this would mean diminished water flow in the cataract: Jakob Björnsson, "Í tilefni af grein Tryggva Felixsonar," *Morgunblaðið*, August 25, 2004. An ecocritical account of the controversy surrounding the Kárahnjúkar dam project is Andri Snær Magnason, *Dreamland: A Self-Help Manual for a Frightened Nation* (London: Citizen Press, 2008).

55. Sveinn Víkingur, "Formálsorð," *Hafís við Ísland* (Akureyri: Kvöldvökuútgáfan, 1968), 10.

56. Benediktsson, *Harp of the North*, 55.

57. Malcolm Andrews, *Landscape and Western Art* (Oxford: Oxford University Press, 1999; Oxford History of Art), 134–35.

58. See Alexander Rehding, "Liszt's Musical Monuments," *19th Century Music* 26 (2002): 56–57.

59. Andrews, *Landscape and Western Art*, 132.

60. *Morgunblaðið*, January 26, 1965.

61. "Composer of the Month," Þorkell Sigurbjörnsson interviews Jón Leifs, Icelandic National Radio Archives, DB-567-1 (first broadcast February 2, 1968).

62. "Þrjár milljónir til 129 listamanna," *Alþýðublaðið*, April 12, 1964.

63. "Úr hverju dó Skarphéðinn?," *Alþýðublaðið*, January 25, 1962.

64. Jón Þórarinsson, "Íslenzk tónlist á krossgötum," *Morgunblaðið*, March 11, 1962.

65. On Strickland's work in Iceland and his ties to the US State Department, see Danielle Fossler-Lussier, *Music in America's Cold War Diplomacy* (Oakland: University of California Press, 2015), 66–68.

66. Joel Sachs, *Henry Cowell: A Man Made of Music* (New York: Oxford University Press, 2012), 483–86.

67. "Norrænir tónlistardagar," *Morgunblaðið*, November 8, 1964.

68. "Þögult hverfi," *Alþýðublaðið*, September 24, 1965; "Vilja 'þögult hverfi' lista- og vísindamanna í Reykjavík," *Tíminn*, September 24, 1965.

69. "Í paradís þagnarinnar," *Alþýðublaðið*, September 26, 1965.

70. Möller, "Ég biðst afsökunar," 10.

71. *Fine I, Fine II*, score. A draft page for *Fine I* suggests that he had even more such works in mind, such as one for string quartet and another for voices.

72. Leifs, program note for Musica Nova concert, November 29, 1964.

73. "Njal's Saga," trans. Robert Cook, *The Complete Sagas of Icelanders* vol. 3 (Reykjavík: Leifur Eiríksson, 1997), 215–16.

74. Leifs, *Darraðarljóð*, full score.

75. Minutes of the Icelandic Composers' Society, May 12, 1965.

76. "Verk eftir Jón Leifs flutt á heimssýningunni," *Morgunblaðið*, March 3, 1967.

77. Jón Þórarinsson, "Sinfóníuhljómsveitin," *Morgunblaðið*, March 11, 1967; Loftur Guðmundsson, "Galdra-Loftur," *Vísir*, September 18, 1967.

78. The decision to devote February to Leifs's music was not as spiteful as the composer himself believed. The program was launched in November with music by Páll Ísólfsson (then Iceland's oldest living composer) and continued in order of year of birth; the program went on hiatus during the Christmas season in December.

79. Jón Leifs, "Ég mótmæli—Ég ákæri, Orðsending frá tónskáldi mánaðarins," typewritten document, March 1, 1968.

80. Minutes of the Icelandic Composers' Society, January 31, 1961, quoted in Sveinbjörnsson, "Tónlistin á Íslandi," 135, where the matter is discussed in detail.

81. Interview with Þorkell Sigurbjörnsson, March 28, 2009.

82. Minutes of the Icelandic Composers' Society, January 17, 1968; see also Leifs, report on the founding of the Icelandic Music Information Center, dated March 17, 1968; Örnólfur Árnason, *Lífsins dóminó—Skúli Halldórsson: Ævisaga* (Reykjavík: Skjaldborg, 1992), 249.

83. "Alþjóðaráð höfunda," *Þjóðviljinn*, November 18, 1966. I am grateful to François-Pierre Goy at the Bibliothèque nationale de France for confirming the dates of the concerts in question.

84. "Tónskáld mánaðarins," Þorkell Sigurbjörnsson interviews Jón Leifs, Icelandic National Radio Archives, DB-567-1.

85. Leifs, *Edda III*, full score, 105.

86. *The Poetic Edda*, trans. Hollander, 10.

87. "Orðuveiting á þjóðhátíðardag," *Morgunblaðið*, June 19, 1968.

POSTLUDE: REVIVAL AND INFLUENCE

LEIFS NEVER BECAME, AS NIELSEN in Denmark or Sibelius in Finland, a beloved national figure in Iceland. His music was too modern for a community that was only gradually becoming familiar with the Western tradition of art music, yet it drew too heavily on folk traditions for a society that aspired to—but had not yet achieved—modernity. During his lifetime, Leifs was frequently dismayed at the lack of interest in his works, but he regarded this as only a temporary setback. Addressing young local composers in 1960, he specifically encouraged them not to seek praise from their contemporaries but rather to "embrace the difficulties and all kinds of disapproval as proof that you are heading in the right direction."[1] Leifs's preservation of his extensive archive of letters, manuscripts, and sketches suggests that he was convinced—or at least hopeful—of a future revival.

In the years immediately following his death, Leifs's music was rarely heard. In 1969, three weeks before what would have been his seventieth birthday, the Iceland Symphony Orchestra gave a memorial concert in Háskólabíó, the university cinema that was its home between 1961 and 2011. There, two movements of *Baldr* and the vocal and orchestral *Night* were given their first performances alongside the *Iceland Overture* and the *Galdra-Loftr* funeral march, under the direction of Róbert A. Ottósson. The sparsely attended concert was hardly a success: one critic admitted that he found Leifs's music "very tiring" and suggested that a better solution might have been to devote only half the concert to his works.[2] The performance seems to have been less than adequate, as the composer Leifur Þórarinsson lamented in his review that he had never heard the orchestra play as poorly and that he had "never left a concert in a more dejected mood."[3] In 1972, Leifs's *Trilogia piccola* was finally performed in Iceland, as was the *Saga Symphony*, which had not been heard in concert since its Helsinki premiere in 1950, but now was one of the main events of the newly established Reykjavík Arts Festival, under the direction of Jussi Jalas, who had also conducted the Helsinki performance. The symphony could not be performed with ancient lurs as planned, as the instruments borrowed from the Icelandic National Museum turned out to be woefully out of tune, but the performance was well received nevertheless.[4] Three years later, the symphony was recorded, again by the Iceland Symphony and Jalas, albeit with extensive cuts (roughly one-fifth of the score) to allow it to fit on a single LP record.

Another milestone came in 1980, when the composer Hjálmar H. Ragnarsson wrote an MFA thesis on Leifs's life and music at Cornell University. This was the first serious attempt at analyzing his compositional style, focusing on three early works: the *Three Verses from Hávamál*, the *Iceland Overture*, and the organ prelude *Allt eins og blómstrið eina* op. 16.[5] Ragnarsson has since been a tireless promoter of Leifs's music, and much of the subsequent reappraisal can be more or less directly attributed to his efforts.[6] In the wake of Ragnarsson's thesis, an ambitious plan was conceived to give the world premiere of *Edda I* with the Polyphonic Choir (*Pólýfónkórinn*) at the 1982 Reykjavík Arts Festival, but the music proved too demanding for an amateur group, and in the end only three movements were performed.[7]

Even the Organ Concerto, dormant since the catastrophic Berlin performance of 1941, began to gain interest. At the instigation of Ragnarsson and the Swedish music historian Carl-Gunnar Åhlén, the Stockholm Philharmonic performed it with soloist Gunnar

Idenstam in January 1988, and reactions were overwhelmingly positive. This concert would prove decisive. Åhlén had been in contact with Robert von Bahr, owner of the Swedish record label BIS, who became convinced that Leifs's music deserved to be better known. He began an edition of Leifs's complete works that is still in progress; at the time of this writing, thirteen volumes have been released.

In Iceland, recognition also came through the efforts of a foreign musician with a passion for Leifs's works. The American violinist Paul Zukofsky conducted the Iceland Symphony in a concert commemorating Leifs's ninetieth birthday in 1989 and, two years later, gave the world premiere of *Baldr* with the Icelandic Youth Orchestra, which he himself had founded more than a decade earlier. Critics unanimously praised Zukofsky's keen understanding of Leifs's sound world and claimed the concerts as a landmark.[8] Both performances were released on CD and were influential in making Leifs's music known outside Iceland. Three Finnish maestros also showed interest in Leifs's music in the 1990s and disseminated key works to a wider audience through their recordings. In 1990, Esa-Pekka Salonen recorded *Geysir* for a Nordic-themed Sony Classical CD; Leif Segerstam took on *Hekla* with the Helsinki Philharmonic for a 1997 Ondine release titled *Earquake: The Loudest Classical Music of All Time*, which came, appropriately enough, with a pair of earplugs. Most importantly, Osmo Vänskä and the Iceland Symphony Orchestra committed the complete *Saga Symphony* to disc for BIS in 1995.

Another major event in the reappraisal of Leifs's life and works was a fictionalized film account of his years in Germany, *Tears of Stone* (*Tár úr steini*, 1995). The film was well received both locally and internationally; it was the year's highest grossing Icelandic motion picture and won awards at festivals in Gothenburg and Prague. The screenplay, cowritten by Ragnarsson, depicted Leifs as a sincere, sympathetic artist, thus inviting a positive reappraisal of his artistic persona by local audiences. The film's success was also due to the vivid cinematography, and atmospheric scenes of

Icelandic landscape provided the visual images that Leifs's music so often suggests.[9]

Leifs's centenary in 1999 was a felicitous year for his admirers. It saw the publication in Icelandic of his first full-length biography (by Carl-Gunnar Åhlén) and two major concerts presented by the Iceland Symphony Orchestra and the Reykjavík Chamber Orchestra, including the premieres of *Hafís*, *Gróa's Spell*, and *The Lay of Helgi the Hunding-Slayer*. In 2000, a full-scale dance performance of *Baldr* was staged in Iceland, Norway, and Finland, and the complete *Edda I* was finally brought to light in 2006, both performances captured on CD by BIS. There has also been increased interest in Leifs's music internationally. The Leipzig Gewandhaus Orchestra performed the Organ Concerto in 2008 under Vänskä's direction, and three of Leifs's works have now been heard at the BBC Proms in short succession (*Hekla*, *Geysir*, and the Organ Concerto, in 2009, 2014, and 2015, respectively). At the Los Angeles Philharmonic's Reykjavík Festival in 2017, which was otherwise devoted to new music from Iceland, the Organ Concerto was particularly well received by audiences and critics alike.[10] In March 2018, the world premiere of *Edda II* by the Iceland Symphony was one of the main events celebrating the nation's one hundredth anniversary of self-rule.

While the recent Leifs revival has been successful in terms of critical response and number of performances, his status in Iceland remains ambiguous. Although he is no longer viewed, as one writer put it, as "a composer who wrote terrible works full of uncommonly silly noise and nationalist braggadocio," he is revered rather than loved.[11] Despite the Leifs renaissance, some of his key works—including *Edda III* and *The Song of Dorrud*—remain unperformed, making it difficult to fully assess his life's work as a composer.

Leifs's influence on later generations of composers has been mostly indirect. He paved the way for the nationally tinged idiom of Jórunn Viðar (1918–2017) and Jón Ásgeirsson (b. 1928), both of whom combined local traditions of folk music with a more refined, central European sensibility than Leifs generally cultivated.

Among composers of a later generation influenced by Leifs in a general sense is Áskell Másson (b. 1953), whose works often contain references to or direct quotation of Icelandic vernacular melodies. Not surprisingly, the music of Leifs scholar Hjálmar H. Ragnarsson (b. 1952) occasionally betrays his fascination with the composer in a more direct way. Ragnarsson is particularly influenced by Leifs's use of third-related harmonies, for example in his *Ave Maria* for mixed choir (1985). A more large-scale employment is Ragnarsson's Organ Concerto (1997), the first movement of which was intended specifically as an homage to Leifs's work in that genre. The bitingly dissonant chordal writing is reminiscent of Leifs while an emphasis on parallel fourths at once evokes his tvísöngur-derived sound and diverts from it.

Haukur Tómasson (b. 1960) has described Leifs's influence in terms of a general soundscape: a rough orchestral sound including contrabassoon in its low register (e.g., the opening of *Geysir*), open fifths, elaborate use of percussion, passages of harmonic stasis, and use of extreme registers.[12] The conclusion of Tómasson's orchestral work *Magma* (*Storka*, 1998) is a conscious reminiscence of a typically Leifsian sound (the opening of *Dettifoss* or *Hafís*, for example): soft, held notes at the extreme ranges of the violin and double-bass, with a growling contrabassoon—although here Tómasson adds rapid flourishes in flute and piccolo to relieve monotony. The opening of another orchestral work, *The Elements* (*Höfuðskepnur*, 2012), also conjures up a wide registral space, from bass drum to the highest notes of the piano. Yet another example of registral extremes and harmonic stasis is "Högni's Death" from Tómasson's 1996 semi-opera *Guðrún's 4th Song*, the libretto of which is based on Eddic poetry—it is the same story that informs Leifs's *The Lay of Guðrún*.

Another kind of Leifsian influence emerges in the output of Anna Þorvaldsdóttir (b. 1977), who has in recent years become one of Iceland's best-known composers; her awards include the Nordic Council Music Prize (2012) and being named the New York Philharmonic's Kravis Emerging Composer in 2015. Þorvaldsdóttir's music is strongly inspired by nature, and she has pointed to Leifs as a crucial influence in her musical development. The difference, she suggests, is that while Leifs depicts nature in a descriptive or programmatic sense, she instead chooses to "reflect on the surroundings and turn them into something *different* through reflection and therefore project my own distinct experience of nature."[13] She employs fifths as a prevalent building block, although again her method differs from Leifs's; rather than continuously moving in parallel fifths, she moves from one fifth to another by gradually overlapping them within the harmonic progression.[14] Her evocative creations echo Leifs's feeling for landscape but within a gentler, ultrarefined context of what Alex Ross has termed "cosmopolitan environmentalism."[15]

The connection of music and landscape has perhaps been more prevalent in recent Icelandic popular music, including Björk Guðmundsdóttir and Sigur Rós. In her songs and music videos, Björk frequently evokes Icelandic nature, such as the ocean (*The Anchor Song; Oceania*), volcano (*One Day*), or mountain (*Hyperballad*). A more overt use of vernacular music to emphasize locality is her use of parallel fifths to underline the "national" sentiment behind the song *Jóga* (from *Homogenic*, 1997). At the time of its release, she frequently commented on the Icelandic qualities of the album and remarked that its combination of string octet accompaniment and electronic beats was an attempt to synthesize two dominant features of Icelandic reality: the natural elements on the one hand and modern high-tech society on the other. She also remarked that *Jóga* was an attempt to create a "National anthem"—a reference to the overt nationalist expression of *Ísland, farsælda frón*, the very song prominent in Leifs's output.[16] To provide the rhythmic underpinning for the recurring parallel fifths, Björk created "volcanic beats" (literally, computer-generated beats using recordings of erupting volcanoes). The song's uniquely Icelandic character is emphasized even further by the lyrics, whose "puzzling" "emotional landscapes" refer to the craggy terrain of the singer's native land.

Despite his current status as the quintessential Icelandic national composer, then, Leifs's influence on compositional style has been limited. In a sense, he both succeeded and failed in his life's mission. He dreamed of leading musical progress in Iceland, yet his abrasive personality often made collaboration impossible, and his overall influence was largely limited to organizational work. His vision of a Nordic cultural renaissance, shaped both by Icelandic nineteenth-century nationalism and 1920s German theories on the influence of race on culture, was at best questionable and in any case remained unfulfilled. Leifs's true success was in his actual compositions. Inspired by vernacular music, literature, and landscape, they were born of a particular historical moment, as Iceland sought and acquired nationhood and its artists took on the task of defining the country in artistic terms. Leifs's music achieved just that. It is powerful, rugged, and luminous, evoking the sweeping landscapes and cultural heritage of Iceland in an intensely individual manner.

NOTES

1. Leifs, "Til ungra tónskálda," *Vísir*, May 6, 1960.
2. Stefán Edelstein, "Stuðlaberg og frumefni," *Vísir*, April 16, 1969.
3. Leifur Þórarinsson, "Minni Íslands," *Þjóðviljinn*, April 23, 1969.
4. "Frumflutti Sögusinfóníuna fyrir 22 árum," *Morgunblaðið*, June 4, 1972.
5. Hjálmar H. Ragnarsson, "Jón Leifs, Icelandic Composer: Historical Background, Biography, Analysis of Selected Works" (MFA thesis, Cornell University, 1980).
6. Ragnarsson wrote a biographical essay on Leifs published in *Andvari* 115 (1990): 5–38, and produced a four-episode radio program on Leifs and his music, broadcast on Icelandic National Radio in October 1995.
7. "Óskað eftir fólki með góða söngrödd á Listahátíð," *DV*, November 26, 1981; *Í ljósi líðandi stundar: Pólýfónkórinn 1957–1987* (Reykjavík: Pólýfónkórinn, 1987), 82–83.
8. See, for example, Jón Ásgeirsson, "Endurskin úr norðri," *Morgunblaðið*, May 27, 1989.
9. For an overview of the Leifs renaissance in Iceland until 1997, see Alda Sigmundsdóttir, "Jón Leifs: Iceland's Sanctified Son," *Scandinavian Review* 85 (1997): 64–68.

10. Mark Swed, "Iceland Shows Its Cool," *Los Angeles Times*, April 19, 2017; Alex Ross, "Nordic Fire," *The New Yorker*, May 1, 2017, 78.

11. Egill Helgason, "Úr kargaþýfinu til stjarnanna," *Helgarpósturinn*, September 21, 1995.

12. Haukur Tómasson, e-mail correspondence with the author, October 26, 2015.

13. Anna Þorvaldsdóttir, "Three Answers. Submitted for Satisfaction of the Written Portion of the Doctoral Qualifying Exam," University of California, San Diego, 2010, 9.

14. Þorvaldsdóttir, "Three Answers," 56.

15. Ross, "Nordic Fire," 79.

16. "With this song, I really had a sort of National Anthem in mind. Not the National Anthem but certain classic Icelandic songs—very romantic, very proud. Mountains, glaciers, that kind of thing" [David Hemingway, "Björk," *Record Collector* no. 276 (August 2002), 42].

APPENDIX: LIST OF JÓN LEIFS'S COMPLETED WORKS

THIS LIST CONTAINS ALL OF Leifs's completed works, arranged by opus number. Works without opus numbers are listed at the end by date of composition. Premieres (P) are noted wherever such information is available. If the first performance was a studio recording, the first live performance is also given.

op. 1   *Trilogia piccola* for orchestra (1919–24)
    1. Praeludium: Lento
    2. Intermezzo: Adagio
    3. Finale: Allegro spiritoso

  P: Karlsbader Kurorchester, cond. Robert Manzer, Großer Kurhaussaal, Karlsbad, November 28, 1925.

op. 1 nr. 2   *Torrek* (Elegy) for piano (1919)

  P: Kurt Haeser, Nýja bíó, Reykjavík, September 1, 1925.

op. 2   *Four Pieces for Piano* (Fjögur lög fyrir píanó, 1922)
    1. Valse lento
    2. Praeludium über ein Quintenlied (Ísland, farsælda frón)
    3. Isländische Ballade (Rímnalag)
    4. Isländisches Scherzo (Rímnakviða)

  P: (1, 4) Annie Leifs, Großer Saal der Stadtmission, Magdeburg, November 14, 1923; (2) Jón Leifs, Nýja bíó, Reykjavík, October 2, 1925; (1–4) Kurt Haeser, Grotrian-Steinweg Saal, Berlin, March 3, 1927.

op. 3   *Studies for solo violin* (Æfingar fyrir einleiksfiðlu, 1924)
    1. Praeludium
    2. Fughetta

P: Björn Ólafsson, Icelandic National Radio, Reykjavík, July 15, 1963 (recording); Rut Ingólfsdóttir, Kjarvalsstaðir Art Museum, Reykjavík, February 14, 1995.

op. 4   *Three Verses from Hávamál* for high voice and piano (Þrjú erindi úr Hávamálum, 1924/1926)
    1. Þagalt ok hugalt (Quiet and Thoughtful)
    2. Ungr vark forðum (I Was Young)
    3. Deyr fé (Beasts Die)

P: Andreas Kreuchauff, pianist unknown, Bayerischer Sender, München, January 1934.

Arranged for soprano or tenor and orchestra, 1935. P: Hans Grahl, Hamburg Philharmonic Orchestra, cond. Hans Schmidt-Isserstedt, Hamburg, May 1936.

op. 5   *Kyrie* for mixed choir with organ prelude (1924/1932)
    1. Choral prelude: Grátandi, kem eg nú, Guð minn, til þín (Weeping, O Lord, I Come to Thee)
    2. Drottinn, miskunna þú oss (Kyrie Eleison)

P: (1) Páll Ísólfsson, Reykjavík Cathedral, October 18, 1925; (2) Aachener Domchor and boys' chorus, cond. Theodor Bernhard Rehmann, Städtisches Konzerthaus, Aachen, January 5, 1934.

op. 6   *Loftr the Sorcerer*, incidental music to a play by Jóhann Sigurjónsson (Galdra-Loftr, 1915–25)

Act One:
    1. In modo de Rímur
    2. Andante, ma non troppo
    3. Kirkjuklukkur (Church Bells)
    4. Tvísöngur
    5. Tvísöngur
    6. Melodrama

Act Two:

    7. Praeludium
     8. In modo de Rímur
     9. Mimodrama
    10. Tempo giusto, in modo de Rímur
    11. Melodrama

Act Three:
    12. Praeludium. Marcia funèbre
    13. Melodrama
    14. Melodrama
    15. Finale

P: (9, 12) Hamburg Philharmonic Orchestra, cond. Jón Leifs, Oslo University Aula, Oslo, May 26, 1926; (selections) Svend Mathling, Danish Radio Symphony Orchestra, cond. Jón Leifs, Oddfellow Palace, Copenhagen, September 3, 1938; (complete) Iceland Symphony Orchestra, cond. Páll P. Pálsson, National Theater, Reykjavík, September 17, 1967.

op. 7   Concerto for organ and orchestra (1917–30)

P: Kurt Utz, organ, Wiesbadens Kurorchester, cond. Helmuth Thierfelder, Kurhaus, Wiesbaden, April 26, 1935.

op. 8   *Variazioni Pastorali* (Variations on a Theme by Beethoven) for orchestra (1920–30)

P: Breslau Radio Orchestra, cond. Jón Leifs, December 20, 1934.

op. 9   *Iceland Overture* for orchestra and mixed chorus *ad libitum* (Minni Íslands, 1926)

Text: Jónas Hallgrímsson and Einar Benediktsson

P: Hamburg Philharmonic Orchestra, cond. Jón Leifs, Oslo University Aula, Oslo, May 26, 1926.

op. 10   *Overture to Galdra-Loftr* for orchestra (1927)

P: Danish Radio Symphony Orchestra, cond. Jón Leifs, Oddfellow Palace, Copenhagen, September 3, 1938.

op. 11   *Icelandic Dances* for piano (Íslenzk rímnadanslög, 1929)

    1. Allegretto
    2. Tempo giusto
    3. Allegro moderato ed energico
    4. Allegro vivace

P: Jón Leifs, Deutsche Welle Königswusterhausen, June 23, 1929.

Arranged for salon orchestra, 1931. P: Tivoli Orchestra, Copenhagen, August 18, 1931.

Arranged for symphony orchestra (Leopold Weninger), 1931. P: Berlin Radio Orchestra, November 24, 1931.

Arranged for men's chorus, 1948. P: Reykjavík Men's Chorus, cond. Sigurður Þórðarson, Gamla bíó, Reykjavík, April 6, 1948.

op. 12a   *Three Hymns* for voice and piano (Þrjú íslenzk kirkjulög, 1929)

Text: Hallgrímur Pétursson
    1. Vertu, Guð faðir, faðir minn (Father God, Be My Father)
    2. Allt eins og blómstrið eina (Just as a Single Flower)
    3. Upp, upp mín sál (Up, Up, My Soul)

P: (1, 3) Eggert Stefánsson, Gunnar Sigurgeirsson, Samkomuhúsið, Akureyri, June 5, 1932; (2) unknown.

op. 12b   *Our Father* for soprano or tenor and organ (Faðir vor, 1929/1932)

Text: Matthew 6:9–13.

P: Elín Sigurvinsdóttir, Marteinn H. Friðriksson, Reykjavík Cathedral, April 28, 1985.

op. 13   *Iceland Cantata* for mixed chorus, children's chorus, and orchestra (Þjóðhvöt, 1929–30)

Text: Davíð Stefánsson
    1. Hljóðs biðk allar (Hark I Bid All)
    2. Þér landnemar, hetjur af konunga kyni (Ye Settlers, Heroes of Royal Line)
    3. Eld og orðþunga (Words of Fire)
    4. Sjá liðnar aldir líða hjá (See Ages Pass as in a Dream)

5. Sjá, dagar koma (See, Days Come)
6. Vakið. Vakið. Tímans kröfur kalla (Waken. Waken. Time's Demands Now Call)
7. Brennið þið, vitar (Burn, Ye Beacons)

P: (1–2, 4–6), Greifswalder Singverein, Männerchor Frohsinn, Städtisches Orchester, cond. Rudolf Ewald Zingel, Stadttheater Greifswald, November 8, 1930; (complete performance), Berliner Volkschor, Berlin Philharmonic Orchestra, cond. Leo Borchard, Philharmonie Berlin, March 15, 1936.

op. 14a *Two Songs* for medium voice and piano (Tvö sönglög, 1929–30)

Text: Jóhann Jónsson
1. Máninn líður (Moon Song)
2. Vögguvísa (Lullaby)

P: (1) Eggert Stefánsson, Gunnar Sigurgeirsson, Samkomuhúsið, Akureyri, June 5, 1932; (2) María Markan, Valborg Einarsson, K.R.-húsið, Reykjavík, September 8, 1930.

Arranged for medium voice and orchestra, 1936. P: Kristinn Hallsson, Iceland Symphony Orchestra, cond. Olav Kielland, ca. 1955 (recording); Ingveldur Ýr Jónsdóttir, Iceland Symphony Orchestra, cond. Anne Manson, Hallgrímskirkja, Reykjavík, May 7, 1999.

Lullaby arranged for men's chorus, ca. 1940. P: Reykjavík Men's Chorus, cond. Sigurður Þórðarson, Austurbæjarbíó, Reykjavík, March 23, 1955.

Lullaby arranged for mixed chorus, 1940. P: Hamrahlíð Choir, cond. Þorgerður Ingólfsdóttir, National Gallery of Iceland, Reykjavík, January 25, 1999.

op. 14b *New Icelandic Dances* for piano (Ný rímnadanslög, 1931)
1. Allegretto
2. Allegro

P: unknown.

op. 15a *Poems of Icelanders* for men's chorus (Íslendingaljóð, 1931)
　　1. Grafarljóð (Funeral Poem)
Text: Bólu-Hjálmar, Jónas Hallgrímsson

　　2. Drykkjuvísur (Drinking Verses)
Text: Bjarni Thorarensen

P: (1), unnamed men's chorus, Bayerischer Sender, München, January 1934; (2) unknown.

op. 15b *Sea Verses* for men's chorus (Sjávarvísur, 1931)
　　1. Titra, kvika langa leið (The Calm Sea Quakes)
Text: Einar Benediktsson

　　2. Ýfist grettin ægis kinn (The Sea Shows Its Grimace)
Text: Þorsteinn Gíslason

P: unknown.

op. 16 *Praeludiae organo* (Þrír organforleikir, 1931)
　　1. Sá ljósi dagur liðinn er (Gone Is the Bright Day)
　　2. Mín lífstíð er á fleygiferð (My Life Is Passing Quickly)
　　3. Allt eins og blómstrið eina (Just as a Single Flower)

P: Ernest Bour, Conservatoire de Musique, Strasbourg, August 8, 1933.

op. 17a *Icelandic Dance Songs* for voices and instruments (Íslenskir söngdansar, ca. 1931)
　　1. Heill þér, ylur, heill þér ljós (Hail, Warmth; Hail, Light)
Text: Hannes Hafstein

　　2. Siglir dýra súðin mín (Sailor's Verse)
Text: Einar Benediktsson

P: unknown.

op. 17b *Three Icelandic Hymns* for mixed chorus and organ (Þrjú íslensk sálmalög, ca. 1931–40)
　　1. Mín lífstíð er á fleygiferð (My Life Is Passing Quickly)
Text: Einar Jónsson

　　2. Margir upp árla rísa (Many Rise Up Early)
Text: Hallgrímur Pétursson

3. Kær Jesú Kristi (Dearest Jesus Christ)
Text: Stefán Ólafsson

P: (1–2, tenor solo and organ) Eggert Stefánsson, Páll Ísólfsson, Reykjavík Cathedral, November 17, 1937; (1–2) Nessókn Church Choir, cond. Jón Ísleifsson, Victor Urbancic (organ), Reykjavík Cathedral, July 10, 1952; (1–3) Reykjavík Cathedral Choir, cond. Páll Ísólfsson, Reykjavík Cathedral, April 28, 1957.

op. 18a *Two Songs* for high voice and piano (Tvö sönglög, 1932)
    1. Góða nótt (Good Night)
    2. Ríma (Rhyme)

Text: Einar Benediktsson

P: (1) Þórunn Guðmundsdóttir, Kristinn Örn Kristinsson, Fella- og Hólakirkja, Reykjavík, July 1995 (recording); (1) Finnur Bjarnason, Örn Magnússon, Salurinn Concert Hall, Kópavogur, January 13, 1999; (2) Adelheid Armhold, Werner Schröter, Hamburg, June 4, 1935.

Ríma arranged for baritone and orchestra, 1936. Not yet performed.

op. 18b *Love Verses from the Edda* for tenor and piano (Ástarvísur úr Eddu, 1931–32)
    1. Löng er nótt (Night Is Long)
    2. Í Gymis görðum (In Gymis Gardens)

P: (1) Ólafur Þorsteinn Jónsson, Árni Kristjánsson, Icelandic National Radio, Reykjavík, July 7, 1972 (recording); (1–2) Finnur Bjarnason, Örn Magnússon, Salurinn Concert Hall, Kópavogur, January 13, 1999.

op. 19a *Nocturne* for solo harp (Næturljóð, ca. 1934)

P: Käthe Ulrich, Icelandic National Radio, Reykjavík, June 14, 1958 (recording); Jude Mollenhauer, Hótel Saga, Reykjavík, March 24, 1963.

op. 19b *Two Icelandic Folk Songs* for mezzo-soprano and piano (ca. 1934)
    1. Sofðu, unga ástin mín (Slumber, Dearest Child of Mine)
Text: Jóhann Sigurjónsson

2. Breiðifjörður
Text: Folk poetry

P: (2) Þórunn Guðmundsdóttir, Kristinn Örn Kristinsson, Fella- og Hólakirkja, Reykjavík, July 1995 (recording); (1–2) Finnur Bjarnason, Jónas Ingimundarson, Reykjavík City Theater, August 16, 1997.

op. 20 *EDDA I—The Creation of the World*, oratorio for tenor, bass, mixed chorus, and orchestra (Sköpun heimsins, 1935–39)

Text: from the Prose Edda, Poetic Edda, et al.
1. Ár var alda (Young Were the Years)
2. Ýmir (Ymir)
3. Þursa þjóðar sjöt (The Giants' Palace)
4. Auðhumla, Óðinn ok hans bræðr (Audhumla, Odin and His Brothers)
5. Sær (Sea)
6. Jörð (Earth)
7. Himinn, sól, dagr (Sky, Sun, Day)
8. Nótt, morgunn (Night, Morning)
9. Ásgarðr, Askr ok Embla, Miðgarðr (Asgard, Ash and Embla, Midgard)
10. Scherzo. Allir menn urðut jafnspakir (All Men Aren't Equally Wise)
11. Viðr, sumar, logn (Wood, Summer, Calm)
12. Vetr ok vindr (Winter and Wind)
13. Finale. Ífing, níu heimar (Ifing, Nine Worlds)

P: (7, 8) Volmer Holbøll (tenor), Danish Radio Symphony Orchestra and Chorus, cond. Launy Grøndahl, Copenhagen, Radiohusets Koncertsal, May 24, 1952; (1, 5, 6) Jón Þorsteinsson, Kristinn Sigmundsson, Polyphonic Choir and Reykjavík Chamber Orchestra, cond. Ingólfur Guðbrandsson, Háskólabíó, Reykjavík, June 29, 1982; (complete performance) Gunnar Guðbjörnsson, Bjarni Thor Kristinsson, Schola cantorum (cond. Hörður Áskelsson), Iceland Symphony Orchestra, cond. Hermann Bäumer, Háskólabíó, Reykjavík, October 14, 2006.

op. 21 String Quartet no. 1, *Mors et vita* (1939)

P: Björn Ólafsson Quartet (Björn Ólafsson, Jósef Felzmann, Jón Sen, Einar Vigfússon), Icelandic National Radio, Reykjavík, November 15, 1951 (recording); Björn Ólafsson Quartet at Leifs's funeral, Reykjavík Cathedral, August 7, 1968.

op. 22 *The Lay of Guðrún* for mezzo-soprano, tenor, bass, and chamber orchestra (Guðrúnarkviða, 1940)

Text: from the Edda.

P: Randi Brandt Gundersen, Bjarne Buntz, Egil Nordsjø, Filharmonisk Selskaps orkester, cond. Odd Grüner-Hegge, Oslo, September 29, 1948.

op. 23 *Three Songs* for medium voice and piano (Þrjú sönglög, 1941)
    1. Þula (Verse)
Text: Sigurður Grímsson

    2. Draugadans (Dance of the Spectres)
Text: Sigurður Grímsson

    3. Vorkvæði (Spring Poem)
Text: Halldór Kiljan Laxness

P: Kristinn Sigmundsson, Jónas Ingimundarson, Nordic House, Reykjavík, February 18, 1989.

op. 24 *Three Songs from Icelandic Sagas* for tenor and piano (Þrír sögusöngvar, 1941)
    1. Þat mælti mín móðir (My Mother Wants a Price Paid)
Text: from Egils Saga

    2. Ástarvísur til Steingerðar (Love Poems to Steingerður)
Text: from Kormáks Saga

    3. Haugskviða Gunnars (Gunnar's Verse from His Mound)
Text: from Njáls Saga

P: (1, 3) Sigurður Skagfield, Fritz Weishappel, Icelandic National Radio, Reykjavík, November 25, 1949 (recording); (1–3) Finnur

Bjarnason, Örn Magnússon, Salurinn Concert Hall, Kópavogur, January 13, 1999.

op. 25 *Songs of the Saga Symphony* for tenor and piano (Söngvar Söguhljómkviðunnar, 1941)
1. Brennusöngr Skarphéðins (Skarphéðinn's Song When Burning)
2. Húskarlahvöt (Exhortations to the Farmhands)
3. Helsöngr Þormóðar (Þormóður's Death Song)

P: Sigurður Skagfield, Fritz Weishappel, Icelandic National Radio, Reykjavík, November 25, 1949 (recording); Finnur Bjarnason, Örn Magnússon, Salurinn Concert Hall, Kópavogur, January 13, 1999.

op. 26 *Saga Symphony* [Symphony I—Saga Heroes (Söguhetjur), 1941–42]
1. Skarphéðinn
2. Guðrún Ósvífrsdóttir
3. Björn at baki Kára. Scherzo (Björn behind Kári's Back)
4. Glámr ok Grettr. Intermezzo (Glámr and Grettr)
5. Þormóðr Kolbrúnarskáld

P: Helsinki Theater Orchestra, cond. Jussi Jalas, Helsinki University Aula, Helsinki, September 18, 1950.

op. 27 *Three Patriotic Songs* for men's chorus (Þrír ættjarðarsöngvar, 1943)
1. Eldgamla Ísafold (Ancient Iceland)
Text: Bjarni Thorarensen

2. Málið (The Language)
Text: Einar Benediktsson

3. Minningaland (Memory-Land)
Text: Einar Benediktsson

P: unknown.

op. 28 *Three Verses by Jónas Hallgrímsson* for mixed chorus (Þrjú kvæði eftir Jónas Hallgrímsson, 1943)
1. Ísland, farsælda frón (Iceland, Fortunate Isle)

2. Sólsetursljóð (A Hymn to the Setting Sun, after George Payne Rainsford James)
   3. Víti (Hell)

P: (1) mixed chorus, cond. Páll Ísólfsson, University of Iceland Aula, Reykjavík, May 26, 1945; (2) National Theater Choir, cond. Róbert A. Ottósson, Icelandic National Radio, Reykjavík, January 4, 1959 (recording); (2–3) Iceland University Choir, cond. Egill Gunnarsson, Seljakirkja, Reykjavík, April 19, 1998.

op. 29 *Poems of Icelanders* for men's chorus (Íslendingaljóð, 1943)
   1. Draugavísur (Ghost Verses)
   Text: from Icelandic folktales

   2. Ástarvísur (Love Verses)
   Text: Hannes Hafstein, Jónas Hallgrímsson

   3. Hestavísur (Horse Verses)
   Text: Páll Ólafsson, Matthías Jochumsson, and Eggert Ólafsson

Not yet performed.

op. 30 *Poems of Icelanders* for mixed chorus (Íslendingaljóð, 1943)
   1. Álfavísur (Elf Verses)
   Text: from Icelandic folktales

   2. Ævintýravísur (Fairy Tale Verses)
   Text: from Icelandic folktales

   3. Hestavísur (Horse Verses)
   Text: Hannes Hafstein, Þorsteinn Erlingsson, Eggert Ólafsson, Örn Arnarson, and folk poetry.

Not yet performed.

op. 31 *Old Skaldic Verses from Iceland* for tenor and piano (Forníslenskar skáldavísur, 1944–45)
   1. Höggvinsmál Þóris jökuls (Up on the Keel You Shall Climb)
   Text: from Sturlunga Saga

   2. Siglingavísa (Seafaring Verse)
   Text: Egill Skallagrímsson

3. Hrafnsmál (The Words of the Raven)
Text: Sturla Þórðarson

P: (1–2), Finnur Bjarnason, Örn Magnússon, Salurinn Concert Hall, Kópavogur, January 13, 1999; (3), Finnur Bjarnason, Örn Magnússon, Salurinn Concert Hall, Kópavogur, December 2000 (recording).

op. 32   *Three Songs of the People* for mixed chorus (Þrír alþýðusöngvar, 1945)
1. Árhvöt Íslands (Iceland's Whetting)
Text: Guðmundur Kamban

2. Allt eins og blómstrið eina (Just as a Single Flower)
Text: Hallgrímur Pétursson

3. Sorgarlausn (Sorrow's Release)
Text: from an Icelandic folk tale

P: (1) Alþýðukórinn, cond. Hallgrímur Helgason, January 12, 1961 (recording); (3) Liljukórinn, cond. Jón Ásgeirsson, April 1963 (recording); (1–3) unnamed vocal ensemble, cond. Marteinn Hunger Friðriksson, Háteigskirkja, Reykjavík, October 17, 1970.

op. 33a   *Torrek* for baritone and piano (Eulogy, 1947)

Text: Egill Skallagrímsson

P: Sigurður Skagfield, Fritz Weishappel, Icelandic National Radio, Reykjavík, November 23, 1948 (recording); Finnur Bjarnason, Örn Magnússon, Salurinn Concert Hall, Kópavogur, January 13, 1999.

op. 33b   *Requiem* for mixed chorus (1947)

Text: Jónas Hallgrímsson and from folk poetry

P: unnamed vocal ensemble at Líf Leifs's funeral, Reykjavík Cathedral, August 13, 1947; Choir of the Reykjavík Music Society, cond. Victor Urbancic, Forum, Copenhagen, June 2, 1948.

op. 34 *Baldr*, a choreographic drama in two acts (1943–47)

Act One:
1. Dans mannhrakanna (Dance of the Creatures of the Earth)
2. Sköpun mannsins (The Creation of Man)
3. Nanna
4. Fárviðri (Hurricane)
5. Einherjar (The Chosen Warriors)
6. Brúðkaup (Wedding)
7. Lokadans (Final Dance)

Act Two:
8. Draumar Baldrs (Baldr's Dreams)
9. Eiðtakan (The Oathtaking)
10. Kastleikar (Throwing Play)
11. Dauði Baldrs (Baldr's Death)
12. Bálför Baldrs (Baldr's Cremation)
13. Eldgos og friðþæging (Volcanic Eruption and Atonement)

P: (2) Iceland Symphony Orchestra, cond. Róbert A. Ottósson, Háskólabíó, Reykjavík, April 10, 1969; (complete performance) Jóhann Sigurðarson (narrator), Ólafur Kjartan Sigurðarson (Óðinn), Philharmonia Choral Society, Icelandic Youth Orchestra, cond. Paul Zukofsky, Háskólabíó, Reykjavík, March 24, 1991.

op. 35 *Elegies* for male choir, mezzo-soprano, and violin (Erfiljóð, 1947)
1. Söknuðr (Grief)
Text: Jónas Hallgrímsson

2. Sorgardans (Dance of Sorrow)
Text: Verses from Icelandic folktales, by Hjálmar Jónsson and others

3. Sjávarljóð (Sea Poem)
Text: Verses and aphorisms from folktales and by Egill Skallagrímsson, Gunnar Gunnarsson and others.

P: (1) Reykjavík Men's Chorus, cond. Sigurður Þórðarson, Austurbæjarbíó, Reykjavík, April 27, 1954; (2) unnamed men's chorus at Reykjavík Chamber Orchestra concert, cond. Bernharður Wilkinson, National Gallery of Iceland, Reykjavík, May 14, 2002;

(3) Þórunn Guðmundsdóttir (soprano), Hildigunnur Halldórsdóttir (violin), Hljómeyki, cond. Bernharður Wilkinson, Skálholt Church, July 10, 1999.

op. 36 String Quartet no. 2, *Vita et mors* (1948–51)
    1. Bernska (Childhood)
    2. Æska (Youth)
    3. Sálumessa—Eilífð (Requiem—Eternity)

P: Ludwig-Schuster-Quartett, Aula, Martin-Luther-Universität (Händel-festival), Halle, Germany, April 27, 1960.

op. 37 *Mountain Songs* for male chorus with (1) mezzo-soprano and baritone solo, (2) percussion and double bass (Fjallasöngvar, 1948)
    1. Útlagasöngr (Song of the Outlaw)
Text: Verses from Icelandic folktales and by Jón Guðmundsson, Matthías Jochumsson, and Sigurjón Friðjónsson

    2. Tröllaslagr (Song of the Trolls)
Text: Verses from Icelandic folktales and by Jón Sigurðsson Dalaskáld, Sigurjón Friðjónsson, et al.

Not yet performed.

op. 38 *Songs for Þorgerður* for male chorus (Þorgerðarlög, 1948)
    1. Ástarvísur (Love Verses)
Text: Verses from Icelandic folktales and by Sigurjón Friðjónsson and others

    2. Trúarvísur (Religious Verses)
Text: Verses from Icelandic folktales and by Hallgrímur Pétursson, Bólu-Hjálmar and others

    3. Sumarvísur (Summer Verses)
Text: Verses, adages, and aphorisms from Icelandic folktales and by Jónas Hallgrímsson, Hallgrímur Pétursson, and others

P: (1) Fóstbræður Male Chorus, cond. Ragnar Björnsson, Langholtskirkja, Reykjavík, May 3, 1989; (2–3) not yet performed.

op. 39 *Two Songs* for male chorus (Tveir söngvar, 1961/1948)
   1. Sumarmál (Early Summer)
   2. Nótt (Night)

Text: Lárus Thorarensen

Not yet performed.

op. 40 *Réminiscence du Nord* for string orchestra (Endurskin úr norðri, 1952)

P: Icelandic National Radio Orchestra, cond. Hans Antolitsch, Icelandic National Radio, Reykjavík, April 11, 1960 (recording); Iceland Symphony Orchestra, cond. Paul Zukofsky, Háskólabíó, Reykjavík, May 25, 1989.

op. 41 *Landfall*, overture for orchestra and male chorus ad libitum (Landsýn, 1955)

Text: Jónas Hallgrímsson, Einar Benediktsson

P: Iceland Symphony Orchestra, cond. Jindřich Rohan, Háskólabíó, Reykjavík, February 22, 1962; (with male chorus) Reykjavík Men's Chorus (cond. Catherine Williams), Iceland Symphony Orchestra, cond. Paul Zukofsky, Háskólabíó, Reykjavík, May 25, 1989.

op. 42 *EDDA II—The Lives of the Gods*, oratorio for mezzo-soprano, tenor, bass, mixed chorus and orchestra (Líf guðanna, 1951–66)

Text: from the Prose Edda, Poetic Edda, et al.
   1. Óðinn
   2. Synir Óðins (Sons of Óðinn)
   3. Ásynjur (Goddesses)
   4. Valkyrjur (Valkyries)
   5. Nornir (Witches)
   6. Einherjar (The Chosen Warriors)

P: Hanna Dóra Sturludóttir, Elmar Gilbertsson, Kristinn Sigmundsson, Schola cantorum (cond. Hörður Áskelsson), Iceland Symphony Orchestra, cond. Hermann Bäumer, Harpa Concert Hall, Reykjavík, March 23, 2018.

op. 43 *Baptismal Hymn* for mezzo-soprano or baritone and organ (Skírnarsálmur, 1957)

Text: Folk poetry

P: Kristinn Hallsson, Victor Urbancic, Reykjavík Cathedral, December 7, 1957.

op. 44 *Trois peintures abstraites* for orchestra (Þrjár myndir, 1955–60)
1. Fegurð himinsins (The Beauty of the Sky)
2. Víxlspor (Zigzag)
3. Klettar (Rocky Cliffs)

P: Iceland Symphony Orchestra, cond. Jindřich Rohan, Háskólabíó, Reykjavík, December 7, 1961.

op. 45 *Elegies on the Death of Jónas Hallgrímsson* for mezzo-soprano or baritone and piano (Minningarsöngvar um ævilok Jónasar Hallgrímssonar, 1958)
1. Heimþrá (Homesickness)
2. Sólhvörf (Solstice)
3. Hjörtun hefjast (Hearts Rise Up)

P: Finnur Bjarnason, Örn Magnússon, Salurinn Concert Hall, Kópavogur, January 13, 1999.

op. 46 *Spring Song* for mixed chorus and orchestra (Vorvísa, 1958)

Text: Jónas Hallgrímsson

P: Schola cantorum (cond. Hörður Áskelsson), Iceland Symphony Orchestra, cond. Hermann Bäumer, Hallgrímskirkja, Reykjavík, February 2002 (recording).

op. 47a *Stand, House of Stone* for tenor and piano (Stattu steinhús, 1958)

Text: Jónas Hallgrímsson

P: Finnur Bjarnason, Örn Magnússon, Salurinn Concert Hall, Kópavogur, January 13, 1999.

op. 47b *Weather Verses* for male chorus (Veðurvísur, 1961)

Text: Jónas Hallgrímsson

Not yet performed.

op. 48 *Jónas Hallgrímsson in Memoriam* for mixed chorus and orchestra
(Jónasar minni Hallgrímssonar, 1961)

Text: Jónas Hallgrímsson

P: Schola cantorum (cond. Hörður Áskelsson), Iceland Symphony Orchestra, cond. Hermann Bäumer, Hallgrímskirkja, Reykjavík, June 2002 (recording).

op. 49 *Boy's Song* for piano (Strákalag, 1960)

P: Rögnvaldur Sigurjónsson, Icelandic National Radio, Reykjavík, September 1961 (recording); Örn Magnússon, National Gallery of Iceland, Reykjavík, March 6, 1994.

op. 50 Quintet for flute, clarinet, bassoon, viola, and cello (1960)

P: Jósef Magnússon, Gunnar Egilson, Sigurður Markússon, Jón Sen og Einar Vigfússon, Hótel Borg, Reykjavík, December 6, 1961.

op. 51 *Geysir*, overture for orchestra (1961)

P: Iceland Symphony Orchestra, cond. Jean-Pierre Jacquillat, Háskólabíó, Reykjavík, November 1, 1984.

op. 52 *Hekla*, overture for orchestra and mixed chorus (1961)

Text: Jónas Hallgrímsson

P: Helsinki City Orchestra, cond. Jussi Jalas, Helsinki University Aula, Helsinki, October 2, 1964.

op. 53 *Elegy* for string orchestra (Hinsta kveðja, 1961)

P: Iceland Symphony Orchestra, cond. Björn Ólafsson, Icelandic National Radio, Reykjavík, July 15, 1963 (recording); Iceland Symphony Orchestra, cond. Proinnsías Ó Duinn, Háskólabíó, Reykjavík, December 5, 1963.

op. 54 *Vikings' Answer*, intermezzo for orchestra (Víkingasvar, 1962)

P: Stockholmsmusiken, Kroumata Percussion Ensemble, Stockholm Saxophone Quartet, Osmo Vänskä, Stockholm, February 18, 1990.

op. 55   *Fine I. Farewell to Earthly Life* for orchestra (Kveðja til jarðlífsins, 1963)

P: Iceland Symphony Orchestra, cond. Petri Sakari, Háskólabíó, Reykjavík, October 17, 1991.

op. 56   *Fine II. Farewell to Earthly Life* for vibraphone and string orchestra (Kveðja til jarðlífsins, 1963)

P: Iceland Symphony Orchestra, cond. Paul Zukofsky, Háskólabíó, Reykjavík, May 25, 1989.

op. 57   *Dettifoss* for baritone, mixed chorus, and orchestra (1964)

Text: Einar Benediktsson

P: Keith Reed, Iceland Symphony Orchestra and Hallgrímskirkja Motet Choir (cond. Hörður Áskelsson), cond. Petri Sakari, National Theater, Reykjavík, January 31, 1998.

op. 58   *Scherzo concreto* for 10 instruments and seven characters (1964)

P: Musica Nova, cond. Leifur Þórarinsson, Lindarbær, Reykjavík, November 29, 1964.

op. 59   *Night* for tenor, bass, and chamber orchestra (Nótt, 1964)

Text: Þorsteinn Erlingsson

P: Guðmundur Guðjónsson, Kristinn Hallsson, Iceland Symphony Orchestra, cond. Róbert A. Ottósson, Háskólabíó, Reykjavík, April 10, 1969.

op. 60   *Song of Dorrud* for mixed chorus and orchestra (Darraðarljóð, 1964)

Text: from Njáls Saga

Not yet performed.

op. 61   *The Lay of Helgi the Hunding-Slayer* for alto, bass, and chamber orchestra (Helga kviða Hundingsbana, 1964)

P: Guðrún Edda Gunnarsdóttir, Jóhann Smári Sævarsson, Reykjavík Chamber Orchestra, cond. Johann Arnell, National Theater, Reykjavík, May 1, 1999.

op. 62 *Gróa's Spell* for alto, tenor, and orchestra (Grógaldr, 1965)

Text: from the Poetic Edda

P: Jóhanna V. Þórhallsdóttir, Finnur Bjarnason, Reykjavík Chamber Orchestra, cond. Johann Arnell, National Theater, Reykjavík, May 1, 1999.

op. 63 *Drift Ice* for mixed chorus and orchestra (Hafís, 1965)

Text: Einar Benediktsson

P: Schola cantorum (cond. Hörður Áskelsson), Iceland Symphony Orchestra, cond. Anne Manson, Hallgrímskirkja, Reykjavík, May 7, 1999.

op. 64 String Quartet no. 3, *El Greco* (1965)
    1. Toledo
    2. Ímynd af sjálfsmynd af El Greco (Vision of El Greco's Self-Portrait)
    3. Jesús rekur braskarana úr musterinu (Christ Driving the Money Changers from the Temple)
    4. Krossfestingin (The Crucifixion)
    5. Upprisan (The Resurrection)

P: Björn Ólafsson Quartet, National Theater, Reykjavík, October 7, 1968.

op. 65 *EDDA III—The Twilight of the Gods* for mezzo-soprano, tenor, baritone, female chorus, male chorus, mixed chorus, and orchestra (Ragnarökr, 1966–68, incomplete)

Text: from the Prose Edda, Poetic Edda, et al.

Not yet performed.

op. 66 *Consolation*, intermezzo for string orchestra (Hughreysting, 1968)

P: Iceland Symphony Orchestra, cond. Reinhard Schwarz, Háskólabíó, Reykjavík, February 22, 1979.

WITHOUT OPUS NUMBER:

Reverie for piano (Vökudraumur, 1913)
    P: Örn Magnússon, August 1994 (recording).

Cadenza for Ludwig van Beethoven's Piano concerto no. 3 (1920)
    Not yet performed.

Allt eins og blómstrið eina, arr. for three trombones and tuba (1922)
    P: Lúðrafélagið Gígja, Reykjavík, spring 1922.

Banner Song (Rís, þú unga Íslands merki, 1922)
    Text: Einar Benediktsson
    P: Jón Leifs, Þrúðvangur (Reykjavík), September 2, 1925

25 Icelandic Folk Songs for piano (1925)
    P: Jón Leifs, Þrúðvangur (Reykjavík), September 2, 1925.

Memory-Land for voice and piano (Minningaland, 1927–28)
    Text: Einar Benediktsson
    P: Unknown
    Printed in *Alþýðublaðið*, October 11, 1936 and *Heimir* 5 (1938): 12–13.
    Arranged for orchestra, Albert Klahn
    P: Hótel Borg, Reykjavík, December 20, 1936, orchestra made up of members from the Reykjavík Town Band and Reykjavík Music School, cond. Albert Klahn

Icelandic Folk Songs for Common Singing (Íslensk þjóðlög til alþýðusöngs, 1943)
    Breiðifjörður
    Vorkvæði (Spring Verse)
    Þorravísur (Winter Verses)

Tvísöngur
Mansöngur (Love Song)
Ísland, farsælda frón (Iceland, Fortunate Isle)
Yfir kaldan eyðisand (Over the Cold Desert Sand)
Allt eins og blómstrið eina (Just as a Single Flower)

P: National Radio Choir, cond. Róbert A. Ottósson, Icelandic National Radio, Reykjavík, February 18, 1948.

Turm-Glockenspiel über Themen von Ludwig van Beethovens IX. Symphonie for carillon (1958)

Not yet performed.

Das Leben muss, trotz Allem, stets weiter gehen for carillon (1958)

Not yet performed.

Es ist ein Ros' entsprungen for mixed chorus (1958)

Arrangement of a melody by Michael Praetorius

Text: Anonymous (Germany, 16th century)

Premiere: Unknown

Published in *Morgunblaðið*, December 24, 1959.

Allt eins og blómstrið eina, arr. for alto or baritone with organ (1959)

Text: Hallgrímur Pétursson

P: Kristinn Hallsson (with unknown organist) at Þórey Þorleifsdóttir's funeral, Reykjavík Cathedral, January 13, 1959.

Health Regained for mixed chorus (Heilsuheimt, 1965)

Arrangement of third movement from String Quartet in A minor op. 132 by Ludwig van Beethoven.

Text: Þorsteinn Valdimarsson

P: Hljómeyki, cond. Bernharður Wilkinson, Skálholt Church, July 10, 1999.

SELECTED BIBLIOGRAPHY

THE BIBLIOGRAPHY LISTS ALL ARCHIVAL and unpublished sources, printed sources in languages other than Icelandic, and sources in Icelandic published after 2009. Older Icelandic sources consulted especially for this edition of the book are also included. For a complete bibliography of pre-2009 items in Icelandic, as well as a full list of Leifs's writings, the reader is advised to consult the Icelandic version of this book, *Jón Leifs—Líf í tónum* (Reykjavík: Mál og menning, 2009).

UNPUBLISHED MATERIAL

National and University Library, Reykjavík, manuscript department (Landsbókasafn Íslands—Háskólabókasafn)

Annie Leifs collection.
Björn Kristjánsson collection.
Halldór Laxness collection.
Jón Leifs collection.
Páll Ísólfsson collection.

Lbs 700 fol.
Þorleifur Jónsson, letters.

Lbs 4067–4072 4to.
Þorleifur Jónsson, letters.

National Archives of Iceland (Þjóðskjalasafn Íslands), Reykjavík

Einkaskjalasafn. Alþingishátíðin 1930. Nr. 7. Minutes of the Preparatory Committee for the 1930 Alþingi Festival.

Einkaskjalasafn. Alþingishátíðin 1930. Nr. 8. Sigfús Einarsson, Notebook and letters relating to the 1930 Alþingi Festival.

Foreign Ministry 1996–B/484. Correspondence with Jón Leifs, January 1944–July 1968.

Foreign Ministry 30L5. Jón Leifs, Report on wartime activities in Germany.

Icelandic Embassy, Paris 1990–B/125. Correspondence with Jón Leifs, April 1946–December 1955.

Ministry of Education 1989–B/1540. Correspondence with Jón Leifs, September 1945–February 1956.

Ministry of Finance 1991–B/713. Correspondence with Jón Leifs, June 1947–July 1954.

Ministry of Finance 1993–71. Werner Gerlach Papers.

Icelandic National Radio Archives (Ríkisútvarpið, safnadeild), Reykjavík

DB-567-1. Composer of the Month, Þorkell Sigurbjörnsson interviews Jón Leifs. First broadcast February 2, 1968.

DB-637. Jón Leifs, introduction to *The Lay of Guðrún*. First broadcast November 19, 1948.

DB-814. Jónas Jónasson interviews Jón Leifs. First broadcast November 14, 1964.

DB-5105. Jón Leifs, "On the Performance of My Works." First broadcast May 7, 1949.

TD-248. Jón Leifs, introduction to the *Saga Symphony*. First broadcast January 23–February 18, 1962.

Icelandic Composers' Society (Tónskáldafélag Íslands), Reykjavík

Minutes of the society, vol. 1 (1945–1951); vol. 2 (1951–1968).

Iceland Symphony Orchestra Archives, Reykjavík

Program note for *Trois peintures abstraites*, performance on December 7, 1961.
Program note for *Galdra-Loftr*, performance on March 21, 1963.

Danish National Archives (Rigsarkivet), Copenhagen

Udenrigsministeriets arkiv, Gruppeordnede sager 1909–1945. 9.U.7. (Jón Leifs, 1934–1945).

Udenrigsministeriets arkiv, Gruppeordnede sager 1909–1945. 41.M.62. (Lübeck: Nordisk musikfest).

Berlin, diplomatisk ræpresentation og militærmission, Gruppeordnede sager 1930–1945. 81.A.10. (Jón Leifs Henvendelse angaaende Islænderes Ophold i Tyskland).
Berlin, diplomatisk ræpresentation og militærmission, Gruppeordnede sager 1930–1945. 81.A.39. (Det islandske Althings 1000-Aars Jubilæum).

Bundesarchiv, Berlin
NS 8/221. Documents regarding Jón Leifs.
NS 15/30. Documents regarding Jón Leifs.

Staatliche Museen zu Berlin, Ethnologisches Museum, Berlin
Berliner Phonogramm-Archiv. 76 wax cylinder recordings made by Jón Leifs in 1926–34.

Stiftung Archiv der Akademie der Künste, Berlin
PrAdK 2.1/059. Minutes of the Prussian Academy of the Arts, 1934–35.
PrAdK 2.1/228. Documents regarding the Prussian Academy of the Arts concert, March 10, 1941.

Archiv Hochschule für Musik und Theater "Felix Mendelssohn Bartholdy," Leipzig
A, I.2, 11925 and 12388. School records for Annie Riethof and Jón Leifs.

State Archives (Staatsarchiv), Hamburg
614-1/26. Documents regarding the Philharmonische Gesellschaft and Verein Hamburger Musikfreunde, 1926.

New York Public Library, New York
Henry Cowell Papers.

UNPUBLISHED THESES

Guðmundsdóttir, Þórunn. "Historical and Stylistic Aspects of the Solo Songs by Páll Ísólfsson and Jón Leifs." PhD diss., University of Illinois, 1999.
Hillenstedt, Michael. "Das 'isländische' als ästhetische Komponente in der Musik von Jón Leifs." Master's thesis, Hamburg University, 1990.
Karlsson, Finnur. "Greining á köflum V og VI í *Eddu II* eftir Jón Leifs." BM thesis, Iceland Academy of the Arts, 2011.
Magnúsdóttir, Ingunn Þóra. "Ágrip af sögu Bandalags íslenskra listamanna frá upphafi og til ársloka 1942." Master's thesis, University of Iceland, 1991.

Ragnarsson, Hjálmar H. "Jón Leifs, Icelandic Composer: Historical Background, Biography, Analysis of Selected Works." MFA thesis, Cornell University, 1980.
Sigmarsdóttir, Sif. "Ómstríð hljómkviða umbótanna." BA thesis, University of Iceland, 2001.
Smith, Frederick Key. "Nordic Myth and Legend in the Music of Jón Leifs." PhD diss., University of Florida, 2003.
Sveinbjörnsson, Bjarki. "Tónlistin á Íslandi á 20. öld, með sérstakri áherslu á upphaf og þróun elektrónískrar tónlistar á árunum 1960–90." PhD diss., Aalborg University, 1997.
Þorvaldsdóttir, Anna. "Three Answers. Submitted for Satisfaction of the Written Portion of the Doctoral Qualifying Exam." PhD diss., University of California, San Diego, 2010.

BOOKS AND ARTICLES

Almgren, Birgitta, Jan Hecker-Stampehl, and Ernst Piper. "Alfred Rosenberg und die Nordische Gesellschaft: Der 'nordische Gedanke' in Theorie und Praxis." *NORDEUROPAforum* 11/2 (2008): 7–51.
Andersson, Theodore M. *The Icelandic Family Saga: An Analytic Reading.* Harvard Studies in Comparative Literature 28, Cambridge, MA: Harvard University Press, 1967.
Andrews, Malcolm. *Landscape and Western Art.* Oxford History of Art. Oxford: Oxford University Press, 1999.
Aster, Misha. *The Reich's Orchestra: The Berlin Philharmonic, 1933–1945.* Oakville, ON: Mosaic, 2012.
Árnason, Jóhann Páll. "Icelandic Anomalies." In *Nordic Paths to Modernity*, edited by Jóhann Páll Árnason and Björn Wittrock, 229–50. New York: Berghahn, 2012.
Benediktsson, Einar. *Harp of the North: Poems by Einar Benediktsson.* Translated by Frederick T. Wood. Charlottesville: University of Virginia Press, 1955.
Bergsson, Snorri G. *Erlendur landshornalýður—Flóttamenn og framandi útlendingar á Íslandi, 1853–1940.* Reykjavík: Almenna bókafélagið, 2017.
Brinkmann, Reinhold. "The Distorted Sublime: Music and National Socialist Ideology—A Sketch." In *Music and Nazism: Art Under Tyranny, 1933–1945*, edited by Michael H. Kater and Albrecht Riethmüller, 43–63. Laaber: Laaber-Verlag, 2003.
Cannady, Kimberly, and Kristín Loftsdóttir. "'A Nation without Music?': Symphonic Music and Nation-Building." In *Sounds Icelandic*, edited by

Þorbjörg Daphne Hall, Nicola Dibben, Árni Heimir Ingólfsson, and Tony Mitchell. Sheffield: Equinox, 2019.

Cohn, Richard. *Audacious Euphony: Chromaticism and the Triad's Second Nature*. New York: Oxford University Press, 2012.

Cowell, Henry. "The Music of Iceland." *The Musical Mercury* 3/3 (September 1936): 50.

Darcy, Warren. *Wagner's Das Rheingold*. Studies in Musical Genesis and Structure. New York: Oxford University Press, 1993.

Dümling, Albrecht, and Peter Girth. *Entartete Musik, Dokumentation und Kommentar zur Düsseldorfer Ausstellung von 1938*. Düsseldorf: dkv—der Kleine Verlag, 1993.

Egilsson, Sveinn Yngvi. *Náttúra ljóðsins. Umhverfi íslenskra skálda*. Reykjavík: Háskólaútáfan, 2014.

Eichner, Barbara. *History in Mighty Sounds: Musical Constructions of German National Identity 1848–1914*. Woodbridge, UK: Boydell, 2012.

Fossler-Lussier, Danielle. *Music in America's Cold War Diplomacy*. Oakland: University of California Press, 2015.

Friedländer, Saul. *The Years of Extermination, Nazi Germany and the Jews 1939–1945*. New York: HarperPerennial, 1998.

Furtwängler, Wilhelm. *Notebooks 1924–1954*. Translated by Shaun Whiteside. London: Quartet, 1989.

Garberding, Petra. "Musik, Moral und Politik: Richard Strauss, Kurt Atterberg und der Ständige Rat für die internationale Zusammenarbeit der Komponisten." In *Richard Strauss im Europäischen Kontext: Richard Strauss-Jahrbuch 2011*, 235–50. Vienna: Richard Strauss-Gesellschaft, 2011.

Gerigk, Herbert. "Triumph nordischer Musik." *Die Musik* 27 (1935): 733–36.

Gervasoni, Pierre. *Henri Dutilleux*. Paris: Actes Sud/Philharmonie de Paris, 2016.

Glahn, Denise Von. *The Sounds of Place: Music and the American Cultural Landscape*. Boston: Northeastern University Press, 2003.

Gleißner, Ruth-Maria. *Der unpolitische Komponist als Politikum*. Frankfurt am Main: Peter Lang, 2002.

Greenfield, Jeanette. *The Return of Cultural Treasures*, 3rd ed. Cambridge, UK: Cambridge University Press, 2007.

Grimley, Daniel M. *Grieg: Music, Landscape, and Norwegian Identity*. Woodbridge, UK: Boydell Press, 2006.

Guðmundsson, Ásgeir. *Berlínar-blús: Íslenskir meðreiðarsveinar og fórnarlömb þýskra nasista*, 2nd ed. Reykjavík: Skrudda, 2009.

Hallberg, Peter. *Halldór Laxness*. Translated by Rory McTurk. New York: Twayne, 1971.

Hálfdanarson, Guðmundur. "Hugmyndir Herders um þjóðina og endalok menningarlegrar þjóðar. http://www.visindavefur.is/article.php?id=38.

———. "Icelandic Modernity and the Role of Nationalism." In *Nordic Paths to Modernity*, edited by Jóhann Páll Árnason and Björn Wittrock, 251–73. New York: Berghahn, 2012.

———. "Þingvellir. An Icelandic 'Lieu de Mémoire.'" *History & Memory* 12 (2000): 4–29.

Hálfdanarson, Guðmundur, and Ólafur Rastrick. "Culture and the Construction of the Icelander in the 20th Century." In *Power and Culture: Hegemony, Interaction and Dissent*, edited by Jonathan Osmond and Ausa Cimdina, 101–17. Pisa: Plus, Pisa University Press, 2006.

Helgason, Jón Karl. *Hetjan og höfundurinn. Brot úr íslenskri menningarsögu.* Reykjavík: Heimskringla, 1998.

Hollander, Lee M. *The Poetic Edda*, 2nd edition. Austin: University of Texas Press, 1962.

Hornbostel, Erich M. von. "Phonographierte isländische Zwiegesänge." In *Deutsche Islandforschung 1930*, vol. 1, edited by Walther Heinrich Vogt, 300–320. Breslau: Ferdinand Hirt, 1930.

Hreinsson, Viðar, ed. *The Complete Sagas of Icelanders*. 5 vols. Reykjavík: Leifur Eiríksson, 1997.

Ingólfsson, Árni Heimir. "Clothing Irons and Whisky Bottles—Creating an Icelandic Musical Avant-Garde." In *A Cultural History of the Avant Garde in the Nordic Countries, 1950–1975*, edited by Tania Ørum and Jesper Olsson, 273–90. Leiden: Brill, 2016.

———. *Jón Leifs—Líf í tónum*. Reykjavík: Mál og menning, 2009.

Jackson, Timothy. "Sibelius the Political." In *Sibelius in the Old and New World: Aspects of His Music, Its Interpretation, and Reception*, edited by Timothy L. Jackson, Veijo Murtomäki, Colin Davis, and Timo Virtanen, Interdisziplinäre Studien zur Musik, edited by Tomi Mäkelä and Tobias R. Klein, vol. 6, 69–123. Frankfurt am Main: Peter Lang, 2010.

Johnson, Julian. *Webern and the Transformation of Nature*. Cambridge, UK: Cambridge University Press, 1999.

Kater, Michael H. *Composers of the Nazi Era: Eight Portraits*. Oxford: Oxford University Press, 2002.

———. *The Twisted Muse: Musicians and Their Music in the Third Reich*. Oxford: Oxford University Press, 1997.

Kater, Michael H., and Albrecht Riethmüller, eds. *Music and Nazism: Art Under Tyranny*. Laaber: Laaber, 2003.

Larrington, Carolyne. *The Poetic Edda*. Oxford: Oxford University Press, 1999.

Leifs, Jón. "Busonis Rasse." *Der Auftakt* 6 (1926): 16–17.

———. "'Deutsche Kammermusik' in Baden-Baden." *Signale für die musikalische Welt* 85 (1927): 1107–08, 1130.
———. "Erinnerungen an Karl Muck." *Zeitschrift für Musik* 107 (1940): 289–91.
———. "Gegen die Romantisierung klassischer Musik." *Zeitschrift für Musik* 92 (1925): 633–39.
———. "Interpretationsstudien." *Neues Beethoven-Jahrbuch* 3 (1927): 62–90.
———. "Island, das Land der Künstler." *Island, Vierteljahrsschrift der Vereinigung der Islandfreunde* 21 (1935): 29–30.
———. "Isländische Volkslieder: Zwei Forschungsberichte." *Zeitschrift für Musikwissenschaft* 11 (1929): 365–73.
———. "Isländische Volkslieder I: Dritter Bericht." *Mitteilungen der Islandfreunde* 19 (1931): 2–12.
———. "Isländische Volkslieder II: Dritter Bericht." *Mitteilungen der Islandfreunde* 19 (1931): 32–41.
———. "Isländische Volksmusik und germanische Empfindungsart." *Die Musik* 16 (1923): 43–52.
———. *Islands künstlerische Anregung. Bekenntnisse eines nordischen Musikers.* Reykjavík: Islandia Edition, 1951 [recte 1950].
———. "Nachdenkliches zum Toscanini-Besuch." *Allgemeine Musikzeitung* 57 (1930): 681–82.
———. "Robert Teichmüller †, Erinnerungen eines Auslands-Schülers." *Zeitschrift für Musik* 106 (1939): 748–49.
———. *Útvarp og tónment: opinber skýrsla.* Reykjavík: Tónlistarvinir í Reykjavík, 1938.
Lutzhöft, Hans-Jürgen. *Der Nordische Gedanke in Deutschland 1920–1940.* Kieler Historische Studien 14. Stuttgart: Ernst Klett, 1971.
Magnason, Andri Snær. *Dreamland: A Self-Help Manual for a Frightened Nation.* Translated by Nicholas Jones. London: Citizen, 2008.
Martin, Benjamin G. *The Nazi-Fascist New Order for European Culture.* Cambridge, MA: Harvard University Press, 2016.
Mitchell, Tony. "Music and Landscape in Iceland." In *The Oxford Handbook of Popular Music in the Nordic Countries,* edited by Fabian Holt and Antti-Ville Kärjä, 145–62. Oxford: Oxford University Press, 2017.
Neijmann, Daisy, ed. *A History of Icelandic Literature.* Histories of Scandinavian Literature, vol. 5. Lincoln: University of Nebraska Press, 2006.
Painter, Karen. "Polyphony and Racial Identity: Schoenberg, Heinrich Berl, and Richard Eichenauer." *Music and Politics* 5, no 2 (2011): 13n49. http://dx.doi.org/10.3998/mp.9460447.0005.203.
Petropoulos, Jonathan. *Artists under Hitler: Collaboration and Survival in Nazi Germany.* New Haven: Yale University Press, 2014.

Pétursson, Sigurður Reynir. *Þú skalt ekki stela. Störf og barátta STEFs í fimm áratugi til verndar og styrktar höfundarétti*. Reykjavík: STEF, 1998.

Pickard, John. "Jón Leifs (1899–1968)." *Tempo*, New Series, No. 208 (April 1999): 9–16.

Potter, Pamela M. *Art of Suppression: Confronting the Nazi Past in Histories of the Visual and Performing Arts*. Oakland: University of California Press, 2016.

———. "The Arts in Nazi Germany: A Silent Debate." *Contemporary European History* 15 (2006): 585–99.

———. *Most German of the Arts: Musicology and Society from the Weimar Republic to the End of Hitler's Reich*. New Haven: Yale University Press, 1998.

———. "What Is 'Nazi Music'?," *The Musical Quarterly* 88 (2005): 428–55.

Prieberg, Fred K. *Handbuch Deutsche Musiker*. Kiel, 2005. CD-ROM.

———. *Musik im NS-Staat*. 2nd ed. Cologne: Dittrich, 2000.

Rastrick, Ólafur. *Háborgin: Menning, fagurfræði og pólitík í upphafi tuttugustu aldar*. Reykjavík: Háskólaútgáfan, 2013.

Rehding, Alexander. "Liszt's Musical Monuments." *19th Century Music* 26 (2002): 52–72.

Rem, Tore. *Knut Hamsun: Reisen til Hitler*. Oslo: Cappelen Damm, 2014.

Rickards, Guy. "Music of Fire and Ice: A Survey of Icelandic Music on Record." *Tempo* 181 (June 1992): 52–56, 58–61, 64.

Riley, Matthew, and Anthony D. Smith. *Nation and Classical Music from Handel to Copland*. Woodbridge, UK: Boydell, 2016.

Ringler, Dick. *Bard of Iceland: Jónas Hallgrímsson, Poet and Scientist*. Madison: University of Wisconsin Press, 2002.

Ross, Alex. *Listen to This*. New York: Farrar, Straus and Giroux, 2011.

———. "Nordic Fire." *The New Yorker*, May 1, 2017, 78–79.

Sachs, Harvey. *Toscanini, Musician of Conscience*. New York: Liveright, 2017.

Sachs, Joel. *Henry Cowell: A Man Made of Music*. New York: Oxford University Press, 2012.

Schaumburg-Lippe, Friedrich Christian Prinz zu. *Zwischen Krone und Kerker*. Wiesbaden: Limes, 1952.

Scherchen, Hermann. *Werke und Briefe*, edited by Joachim Lucchesi. Berlin: P. Lang, 1991.

Schwab, Heinrich. "Jón Leifs und die 'gigantischen Vorgänge eines isländischen Vulkanausbruchs': zum Thema 'Musik und Landschaft' in den skandinavischen Ländern." *Island* 5 (1999): 3–16.

Sadie, Stanley, and John Tyrell, eds. *The New Grove Dictionary of Music and Musicians*. London: Macmillan, 2001.

Sigmundsdóttir, Alda. "Jón Leifs: Iceland's Sanctified Son." *Scandinavian Review* 85 (1997): 64–68.

Simon, Artur, ed. *Das Berliner Phonogramm-Archiv 1900–2000. Sammlungen der Traditionellen Musik der Welt*. Berlin: VWB, Verlag für Wiss. und Bildung, 2000.

Stevens, Patrick J., ed. *Icelandic Writers*. Dictionary of Literary Biography vol. 293. Detroit: Gale, 2004.

Sträßner, Matthias. *Der Dirigent, der nicht mitspielte: Leo Borchard 1899–1945*. Berlin: Lukas, 2017.

Taruskin, Richard. *Music in the Nineteenth Century*. Oxford: Oxford University Press, 2010.

Thimme, Roland. "Jón Leifs, ein isländischer Komponist in Potsdam." *Mitteilungen des Vereins für Kultur und Geschichte Potsdams* 14 (2009): 130–38.

Toliver, Brooks. "Eco-ing in the Canyon: Ferde Grofè's *Grand Canyon Suite* and the Transformation of Wilderness." *Journal of the American Musicological Society* 57 (2004): 325–68.

Torfason, Helgi. *The Great Geysir*. 2nd ed. Reykjavík: Geysir Centre, 2010.

Treutler, Paul. "Islandische Volkslieder." *Zeitschrift für Musik* 100 (1933): 329–33.

Tutenberg, Fritz. "Jón Leifs: Island-Ouvertüre op. 9." *Zeitschrift für Musik* 99 (1932): 1087.

Ziegler, Susanne. *Die Wachszylinder des Berliner Phonogramm-Archivs*. Berlin: Ethnologisches Museum—Staatliche Museen zu Berlin, 2006.

Þorsteinsson, Bjarni. *Íslenzk þjóðlög*. Copenhagen: S.L. Møller, 1906–09.

Åhlén, Carl-Gunnar. *Jón Leifs: Kompositör i motvind*. Stockholm: Atlantis, 2002.

———. *Jón Leifs—Tónskáld í mótbyr*. Reykjavík: Mál og menning, 1999.

INDEX

Abendroth, Walter, 216
Aber, Adolf, 274
Aðils, Jón Jónsson, 80
Albéniz, Isaac, 300
Albertsson, Kristján, 7, 58, 62, 155, 200, 216, 218, 226–27
Allegra, Salvatore, 281
Allt eins og blómstrið eina (chorale), 51, 68–69, 71, 83, 92, 145–47, 153, 336
Altstadt-Schütze, Grete, 177, 219
Alþingi Festival (Alþingishátíð), 117, 134–38, 140–42, 145, 151
Andersson, Theodore, 220–21
Andrews, Malcolm, 313
Armhold, Adalheid, 179
Armstrong, Louis, 323
Atterberg, Kurt, 171, 172, 184, 186, 283n23
Ásgeirsson, Ásgeir, 104
Ásgeirsson, Jón, 330n6, 338
Ásmundsson, Jón, 69

Bach, Johann Sebastian, 24, 29, 30, 41, 44, 62, 64, 123, 145–46, 215
Bahr, Robert von, 337
Barbirolli, John, 186
Barkel, Charles, 259, 260
Bartók, Béla, 5, 49, 74, 86–87, 183
Beckman, Klas, 252

Beethoven, Ludwig van, 12, 21–22, 25, 36, 60, 76, 77, 78, 123, 126, 174, 223, 329; *Appassionata* sonata, 12, 21; *Coriolan* overture, 78, 221; *Egmont* overture, 78, 152; *Hammerklavier* sonata, 38–39; influence on Leifs's works, 109–13; *Moonlight* sonata, 21; Piano Sonata no. 8 in C minor (*Pathétique*), 21, 39; Piano Sonata no. 12 in A-flat major, 21, 39; *Rage over a Lost Penny*, 223; Symphony no. 3 (*Eroica*), 36, 60, 62, 64, 75, 76, 110, 111, 150; Symphony no. 7, 36, 78; Symphony no. 9, 25, 36, 63, 137, 303, 329
Benediktsson, Einar, 46, 71, 114, 116–17; encouragement of Leifs, 46, 59–60, 69, 72; Alþingi cantata competition, 117, 138; Leifs's use of poetry in compositions, 70, 114, 248, 308, 311, 312
Berg, Alban, 87
Berio, Luciano, 322
Berlin, Irving, 198
Berlioz, Hector, 326, 327
Bernburg, Paul, 42
Besch, Otto, 216
Bjarnadóttir, Ragnheiður, 13–14, 15, 16, 31, 84, 159, 297
Bjarnarson, Sigurbjörn, 69

Björk, 340
Blech, Leo, 40
Blöndal, Kristján, 89
Blöndal, Sigfús, 51
Borchard, Leo, 183
Boult, Adrian, 186
Bour, Ernest, 154
Brahms, Johannes, 36, 60, 65, 220, 287
Brecht, Bertolt, 87
Brian, Havergal, 5
Britten, Benjamin, 321
Broman, Sten, 203, 275
Bruckner, Anton, 36, 64, 220, 314
Bull, Ole, 76
Burkhard, Paul, 256
Burnham, Scott, 110
Busch, Adolf, 149, 202, 304
Busoni, Ferruccio, 39, 53n25, 165, 298
Böðvarsson, Gunnar, 226–27
Böttcher, Otto, 58

Cannady, Kimberly, 3
Chamberlain, Houston Stewart, 164
Chopin, Frédéric, 25, 72, 284n58, 298
Christian IX, King of Denmark, 11
Christian X, King of Denmark and Iceland, 42, 75, 141
Cohn, Richard, 124
Corteccia, Francesco, 10
Cowell, Henry, 74, 89, 313, 315
Czerny, Carl, 21

Dante Alighieri, 226
Debussy, Claude, 72, 258
Dennis, David B., 110
Dent, Edward J., 171
Dewing, Richard Henry, 248
Dibben, Nicola, 6
Drewes, Heinz, 204
Drischner, Max, 167
Dubois, Wolfgang, 211, 212, 218
Dutilleux, Henri, 281–82

Edelstein, Heinz, 250
Egge, Klaus, 275–76
Eggen, Erik, 74, 75
Egk, Werner, 281
Ehrling, Sixten, 324
Eichenauer, Richard, 165
Einarsson, Guðmundur, 91
Einarsson, Sigfús, 24, 43, 49, 50–51, 57, 72, 136, 139, 141, 151, 202
Einstein, Alfred, 274
Erlingsson, Þorsteinn, 319
Eulenburg, Ernst, 155, 204

Federation of Icelandic Artists (*Bandalag íslenskra listamanna*), 2, 91, 195, 208, 250
Finnbogadóttir, Vigdís, 257
Finnbogason, Guðmundur, 118
Finsen, Olufa, 11
Frederick VIII, King of Denmark, 18
Freudenthal, Heinz, 296
Furtwängler, Wilhelm, 66, 150, 178, 218

Gade, Jacob, 256
Gade, Niels, 11
Geissmar, Bertha, 218
Gellert, Christian Fürchtegott, 153
Gerigk, Herbert, 166, 177, 179, 211, 218, 237n63
Gerlach, Werner, 202
Gies, Ludwig, 161, 196
Gieseking, Walter, 57
Gleißner, Ruth-Maria, 168
Gobineau, Arthur de, 164
Goebbels, Joseph, 164, 168–69, 170, 177, 200, 201, 203, 208, 219, 231
Goethe, Johann Wolfgang von, 18
Gogh, Vincent van, 272
Graener, Paul, 38, 42, 72, 155, 178, 186, 215, 284n58
Grahl, Hans, 184
Gram, Peder, 208
Grieg, Edvard, 11, 21, 22, 51, 166
Grundherr, Werner von, 226–27

Grøndahl, Launy, 279
Guðjohnsen, Pétur, 10
Guðmundsdóttir, Björk. *See* Björk
Guðmundsson, Valtýr, 15
Guðmundsson, Þórarinn, 42
Guðnason, Svavar, 299
Gunnarsson, Gunnar, 91, 326
Günther, Hans F. K., 165, 166

Haakon VII, King of Norway, 75
Haeser, Kurt, 58
Halldórsson, Jón, 137
Hallgrímsson, Jónas, 50, 114, 231–32, 247, 262, 264, 287, 288–91, 306
Halvorsen, Johan, 177
Hambræus, Bengt, 275
Hamburg Philharmonic Orchestra, 2, 77–78, 80–82, 83, 95, 111, 137, 171, 184, 250
Hammerich, Angul, 46
Hamsun, Knut, 169
Handel, George Frideric, 38, 62, 65, 78, 126
Harris, Roy, 5
Hausegger, Siegmund von, 75, 171
Haydn, Joseph, 76, 204
Heintz, Thea (Althea Maria Duzzina), 251–55, 280
Helgason, Hallgrímur, 39, 294, 330n6
Helgason, Helgi, 109
Helgason, Jónas, 11
Herder, Johann Gottfried, 4
Herzfeld, Friedrich, 183
Heydrich, Reinhard, 228
Hindemith, Paul, 178, 184, 218, 278, 298
Hitler, Adolf, 160, 169, 208, 293
Hofhaimer, Paul, 10
Honegger, Arthur, 128–29
Hornbostel, Erich Moritz von, 82–83, 88, 89, 90, 250
Hovhaness, Alan, 5
Hullebroeck, Emiel, 208
Höller, Karl, 281

Iceland, British occupation of, 212, 226, 310; independence from Denmark, 2, 6, 11–12, 33–34; landscape, 1, 3, 115–16, 117–22, 210; medieval literature, 3, 103–09, 111; musical development of, 9–11, 12; post-World War II era, 250, 296, 310–11
Iceland Symphony Orchestra (*Sinfóníuhljómsveit Íslands*), 43, 274, 280, 282n9, 294, 314, 335, 336, 338
Icelandic Composers' Society (*Tónskáldafélag Íslands*), 2, 255, 278, 287, 322, 324–25, 329
Icelandic Performing Rights Society (STEF), 2, 251, 255–58, 278, 280, 287, 291, 325
Idenstam, Gunnar, 336–37
Indriðason, Kristinn, 88
Ives, Charles, 5
Ísland, farsælda frón (tvísöngur), 48, 50, 51, 57, 58, 73, 79, 80, 115–16, 250, 340
Ísólfsson, Páll, 24, 155, 162, 184, 202, 255, 273, 290, 307, 314, 334n78; Alþingi Festival competition, 136, 137, 138–40, 141, 143; career in Iceland, 58, 249; National Radio and Leifs, 151–52, 174, 181; performer of Leifs's works, 65–66, 145, 153–54, 250; relations with Leifs, 25–26, 152, 278–79, 286n86, 325–26; study years in Leipzig, 29, 30, 31, 36

Jalas, Jussi, 275, 307, 336
James, George Payne Rainsford, 231
Jaritz, Fritz, 62
Jochum, Eugen, 178
Jochumsson, Matthías, 18
Johann II, Prince of Liechtenstein, 75
Johansen, Oscar, 18, 27n17
Johnson, Julian, 121
Jóhannsson, Magnús Blöndal, 298
Jónsson, Hjálmar, 210
Jónsson, Jóhann, 93, 207
Jónsson, Jón, 151
Jónsson, Ragnar, 249

Jónsson, Þorleifur, 13–15, 16, 17, 40, 91–92, 94, 138–39
Jónsson, Þórarinn, 226–27

Kaelin, Bernard, 270
Kagel, Mauricio, 296
Kamban, Guðmundur, 200, 330n12
Karajan, Herbert von, 186
Karlsson, Gunnar, 104
Kempen, Paul van, 186
Keussler, Gerhard von, 215, 216
Killer, Hermann, 166–67, 218, 219
Kilpinen, Yrjö, 171, 186–87
Kistner & Siegel (publishers), 155, 159, 189n33, 196, 199, 204, 220, 233, 236n46
Kjarval, Jóhannes (Sveinsson), 71, 81, 118–19, 155
Kleiber, Erich, 178
Klenau, Paul von, 167
Knudsen, Niels, 247, 248
Krenek, Ernst, 198
Krienitz, Ernst, 209, 225–26
Kroner, Irmgard, 155
Kroner, Klaus, 155

Laborde, Jean-Benjamin de, 54n39, 71
Laxdal, Jón, 23, 109
Laxness, Halldór, 24, 58, 74, 108, 114, 210, 293–94, 314, 326
Leach, Henry Goddard, 274
Lehmann, Else, 198
Leifs, Annie, 34, 35, 41, 59, 70, 74, 75, 78, 84, 85, 92, 93, 159, 172, 176, 184; career as pianist, 37, 43–44, 56, 62–63, 66, 72, 78, 86, 87, 153, 284n58; death of Líf Leifs, 259–62; death of parents, 228–30; Jewish origins of, 161–62, 211–12, 237n63; Leifs household, 61–62, 153; life after World War II, 269–70, 272; marriage to Jón Leifs, 38, 42, 172, 182, 185, 195–96, 242, 252, 259; promotion of Leifs's works, 63, 155, 172, 177; stay in Germany during Nazi era, 162, 182, 196, 231

Leifs, Jón: adoption of surname, 26, 28n38; as author, 43–44, 62, 76; as conductor, 40, 42–43, 52, 60–61, 66, 67, 75–76, 81–82, 83, 152, 216, 294; attempt to secure Icelandic king, 199–201; Berlin Philharmonic, 166, 177–79, 182–83, 201, 211, 215–18, 235n32, 250; Berlin radio collaboration, 226–27, 249, 276; childhood of, 12–14, 16–26, 138; Conseil International des Compositeurs, 281–82; cultural exchange efforts of, 2, 176, 184, 201–02, 212 (*see also* Leifs and Hamburg Philharmonic tour); death of father, 91–92, 95, 138–39, 143; death of parents-in-law, 228–30; financial situation of, 31–32, 63, 85, 86, 228, 242, 257; folk song collecting journeys, 60, 69–71, 82–83, 88–90, 92; Hamburg Philharmonic tour, 76–82, 95, 111, 171, 212, 275; harmonic use, 71, 123–24, 145–48, 211–13, 263–64, 306, 309–10; Icelandic folk music, 4, 45, 46, 49, 51, 56–57, 78–79, 90, 210, 290; Icelandic nationalism, 2–3, 6, 33–34, 36–37, 80, 103–105, 115, 160–61, 201; illness of, 37, 38, 39, 40, 41, 52, 93, 329–30; influence of Beethoven and "heroic" style, 109–13 (*see also* Ludwig van Beethoven); influence of other composers, 36, 64, 126, 128–29, 314; *Islands künstlerische Anregung* (book), 166, 214, 274, 294; journey to Iceland in 1945, 246–48, 249; Jón Leifs Society, 155–56, 184, 199, 212; medieval Icelandic culture, 20, 103–09; marriage to Annie Riethof, 38, 42, 172, 182, 185, 195–96, 242; marriage to Thea Heintz, 251–55, 280; music studies of, 17–18, 21–26, 29–31, 38–42; National Radio work, 150–52, 154, 174–76, 179, 181–82, 184, 195, 250; nature, 4, 20, 22, 117–22, 208–10, 299, 328 (*see also* Þingvellir and individual works); Nazi authorities, 160–61, 190n52,

196–99, 202, 203–04, 208, 213, 226–27, 230, 233, 237n63; Nazi racial theory, influence of, 110, 165–66; Nordic renaissance, 104–05, 110, 160, 233, 252; Permanent Council for International Cooperation among Composers, 170–72, 174, 179, 186, 198, 207–08, 211, 215, 230–31, 255, 281, 316; personality of, 23–24, 272–73, 287; pianist, 17–18, 21, 22, 25, 29–30, 39, 41–42, 44, 56, 71–72, 258; political stance, 159–61, 201, 210, 296–97; reception at Nordic music festivals, 202–03, 275–76, 279–80, 307, 321; reception as composer in Germany, 63, 75, 144, 150, 154, 162–63, 166–67, 169, 177, 178–79, 183, 186–87, 208, 215–20, 225–26, 239n91; reception in Iceland, 5, 57–58, 79–81, 155, 250–51, 274–75, 294, 298, 300, 314–16, 335–41; religious beliefs, 94–95; rumors of Nazi collaboration, 246, 248–49, 254, 276, 294–96; spiritualism, 17, 322; style and compositional method, 122–129; Westdeutsche Orchesterakademie, 83–85; Þingvellir park supervisor application, 291–92, 316

Leifs, Jón, works: A Hymn to the Setting Sun (Sólsetursljóð), 92, 231–32, 290; Baldr, 22, 123, 124, 128, 161, 173, 205, 231, 232, 243–46, 252, 258, 282n12, 297, 301, 335, 337, 338; Baptismal Hymn (Skírnarsálmur), 288; Boy's Song (Strákalag), 298–99; Cadenza for Beethoven's Piano Concerto no. 3, 110; Consolation (Hughreysting), 329; Dance of Sorrow (see Elegies); Dettifoss, 22, 117, 120, 129, 287, 300, 307–11, 312, 319, 339; Edda I—The Creation of the Earth (Sköpun heimsins), 90, 106, 109, 117, 123, 124, 173, 179–81, 184, 195, 204–06, 214, 215, 236n46, 243, 268, 279–80, 292, 320, 326, 336, 338; Edda II—The Lives of the Gods (Líf guðanna), 106, 109, 180, 280, 288, 291, 316–17, 326, 327, 338; Edda III—Twilight of the Gods (Ragnarökr), 106, 109, 122, 123, 124, 180, 288, 291, 326–28, 329, 338; Edda IV—Resurrection (Endurreisn), 180, 329; El Greco (see String Quartet no. 3); Elegies (Erfiljóð), 123, 124, 206, 261, 266, 268–69; Elegies on the Death of Jónas Hallgrímsson, 288; Elegy (Hinsta kveðja), 297; Fine I, 317; Fine II, 317, 324; Four Pieces for Piano (op. 2), 49, 56–57, 63, 72, 73, 74, 79; Galdra-Loftr (incidental music), 67–69, 78, 123, 147, 167, 202–03, 274, 294, 315, 324, 335; Galdra-Loftr (overture), 86, 167, 202–03, 313, 324; Geysir, 4, 22, 117, 120, 129, 287, 300, 301–03, 306, 308, 337, 338, 339; Gróa's Spell (Grógaldr), 106, 321–22, 338; Hafís, 22, 117, 287, 300, 312–13, 338, 339; Hekla, 4, 22, 116, 117, 120, 124, 129, 232, 245, 287, 291, 300, 304–07, 308, 309, 321, 327, 337, 338; Hymns op. 12a (see Three Hymns); Iceland Cantata (Þjóðhvöt), 92, 93, 95, 117, 134, 137–41, 142–44, 167, 178, 182–83, 186, 198, 205, 208, 219, 236n52, 250, 292, 294, 301; Iceland Overture (Minni Íslands), 78–80, 123, 152–53, 163, 166–67, 171–72, 178, 198, 218, 239n91, 250, 274, 294, 296, 301, 315, 324, 335, 336; Icelandic Dances (Íslenzk rímnadanslög), 83, 88, 154, 162, 180, 182, 198, 250, 269; Jónas Hallgrímsson in memoriam, 291; Kyrie for choir and organ prelude op. 5, 63, 64–66, 123, 153, 169; Landfall (Landsýn), 4, 117, 126–27, 128, 247–48, 315; Lay of Guðrún, The (Guðrúnarkviða), 106, 213–14, 273, 278, 320, 339; Lay of Helgi the Hunding-Slayer, The (Helga kviða Hundingsbana), 106, 167, 319, 320–21, 338; Lord's Prayer, The (Faðir vor), 93; Love Verses from the Edda (Ástarvísur úr Eddu), 106; Lullaby (Vögguvísa), 93–94, 124, 142, 199, 214, 262, 263; Mors et vita

Leifs, Jón, works (Cont.)
(see String Quartet no. 1); New Icelandic Dances, 298; Night (Nótt), 123, 291, 317, 319, 321, 335; Nocturne for harp, 173, 199, 315; Old Skaldic Verses from Iceland, 107, 225; Organ Concerto, 51, 66, 83, 86, 93, 123, 134, 144, 145–149, 150, 153, 155, 167, 172, 176–77, 178, 179, 198, 211, 215–20, 225, 236n52, 245, 275, 336–37, 338; Organ Prelude op. 5 (see Kyrie); Poems of Icelanders (Íslendingaljóð), 231, 269, 290; Praeludiae organo (Organ Preludes), 147, 153–54, 180, 336; Prelude and Fughetta, 63, 64, 75, 123, 199, 225–26, 316; Quintet, 297; Réminiscence du Nord, 258, 266, 315; Requiem, 92, 117, 123, 124, 261–65, 267, 268, 269, 288; Reverie/Meditation (Vökudraumur/Hugleiðing), 23, 299; Rise Up, Banner of Young Iceland (Rís þú, unga Íslands merki), 59–60, 70, 79, 80; Saga Symphony (Sinfónía I—Söguhetjur), 6, 109, 123, 128, 129, 161, 180, 205, 214, 220–25, 231, 251, 273, 275–77, 293, 294, 314, 315, 336, 337; Scherzo concreto, 123, 317–18, 319, 327, 328; Song of Dorrud (Darraðarljóð), 109, 124, 125, 319–20, 327, 328, 338; Songs of the People (Alþýðusöngvar), 147; Songs of the Saga Symphony, 107, 224–25; Songs of Þorgerður (Þorgerðarlög), 254–55; Spring Song (Vorvísa), 90, 116, 288, 289–90; Stand, House of Stone (Stattu, steinhús), 288, 290; String Quartet no. 1 (Mors et vita), 90, 125, 161, 206, 210–11, 279; String Quartet no. 2 (Vita et mors), 123, 261, 266–67, 268, 324; String Quartet no. 3 (El Greco), 317, 322, 324; Three Hymns (Kirkjulög) op. 12a, 83, 92, 94, 98n53, 118, 147; Three Icelandic Hymns for Church Use op. 17b, 154; Three Icelandic Organ Preludes (see Praeludiae organo); Three Patriotic Songs, 231; Three Songs from Icelandic Sagas, 107, 224; Three Verses by Jónas Hallgrímsson, 116, 231–32, 250 (see also A Hymn to the Setting Sun); Three Verses from Hávamál, 63, 64, 106, 109, 122, 184, 336; Torrek (op. 1 no. 2), 34–35, 123, 199; Torrek (op. 33a), 35, 109, 124, 261, 265–66; Trilogia piccola, 34–35, 39, 56, 63–64, 75, 86, 182, 202, 336; Trois peintures abstraites, 117, 258, 299–300, 315; 25 Icelandic Folk Songs, 70–72, 74, 79, 139, 146, 148, 199; Two Icelandic Folk Songs, 88, 90; Two Songs op. 14a, 179 (see also Lullaby); Variazioni Pastorali on a Theme by Beethoven, 86, 110, 123, 144, 149, 184, 198, 210, 290, 324; Viking's Answer (Víkingasvar), 38, 291–93; Vita et mors (see String Quartet no. 2); Weather Verses (Veðurvísur), 291

Leifs, Leifur, 288, 289, 298
Leifs, Líf, 93, 185, 209, 242, 259–62, 266–67, 269–70, 280
Leifs, Snót, 61, 66, 84, 85, 92, 185, 209, 242, 259, 260, 261, 270–72, 280, 284n59, 291
Leifs, Þorbjörg (Möller), 273, 289, 290
Lentrodt, Ursula, 172–73
Leschetizky, Theodor, 28n29
Lienhard, Ludwig, 226
Ligeti, György, 154
Linnemann, Carl, 155, 159, 196. See also Kistner & Siegel
Linnemann, Richard, 155, 159. See also Kistner & Siegel
Liszt, Franz, 24, 124, 298, 314; Faust Symphony, 32, 220
Lohse, Otto, 40
lur (instrument), 205, 275, 336
Luther, Martin, 293

Mackenzie, George, 54n39
Magnússon, Jón, 71
Magnússon, Sigurður A., 273
Mahler, Gustav, 36, 66, 148, 314

Mann, Tor, 152
Martinů, Bohuslav, 86
Matthíasdóttir, Herdís, 18, 21, 23
Másson, Áskell, 339
McHugh, Jimmy, 256
Mendelssohn, Felix, 11, 29, 37, 49, 215
Messiaen, Olivier, 275
Methling, Svend, 202
Mixa, Franz, 141, 151
Mohr, Wolfgang, 186
Moorman, Charlotte, 298
Mosolov, Alexander, 129
Moth, Helga, 99n75
Moth, Paul, 99n75
Mozart, Wolfgang Amadeus, 21, 36, 39, 44, 60, 62, 76, 77, 78, 87, 126
Muck, Karl, 40, 63, 77, 82, 180
Munter, Friedrich, 87
Musica Nova, 297–98, 318
Möller, Þorbjörg. *See* Þorbjörg Leifs
Müller, Hans Alexander, 196, 197, 270
Müller, Marie, 34, 161–62, 196, 228, 270

Nagel, Erich, 61
National Radio Broadcasting Service (*Ríkisútvarpið*), 150–52, 174–76, 179, 181, 182, 249, 278, 289–90, 294, 298, 324, 326
Nielsen, Carl, 36, 74, 79, 139, 335
Nietzsche, Friedrich, 63–64, 68, 272
Nikisch, Arthur, 32, 36, 75
Nobile, Umberto, 150
Noetel, Konrad, 184
Nono, Luigi, 322
Nordal, Jón, 280, 298
"Nordic" music and Nazi ideology, 7n2, 62, 110, 160, 163–67, 214, 220, 224
Norðmann, Jón, 39

Oddsson, Búi, 88
Orff, Carl, 274
Ottósson, Róbert Abraham, 250, 335
Ólafsson, Björn, 316

Paik, Nam June, 298
Palestrina, Giovanni Pierluigi da, 126
Pálsdóttir, Þórey, 13
Pálsson, Helgi, 255
Peppermüller, Fritz, 59, 178, 182
Perlman, Gabriele. *See* Gabriele Riethof
Petropoulos, Jonathan, 160
Pétursson, Hallgrímur, 68, 92, 114
Pfitzner, Hans, 40, 167
Pickard, John, 6, 128
Pius XII, Pope, 270
Plenge, Paul, 59
Poll, Willem van de, 89, 90
Potter, Pamela, 199
Puccini, Giacomo, 256
Päsola, Väinö, 275

Rachmaninoff, Sergei, 38
Ragnar, Ragnar H., 248–49
Ragnarsson, Hjálmar H., 249, 336, 337, 339
Rangström, Ture, 36
Rasch, Kurt, 216
Reger, Max, 38, 44, 60, 123, 146
Rehding, Alexander, 5
Reichsmusikkammer, 170, 187, 194n119, 198, 208, 211, 212, 234n20
Reichwein, Leopold, 86
Reinecke, Carl, 11
Reinhardt, Max, 87
Reykjavík Music Society (*Tónlistarfélagið í Reykjavík*), 184, 202, 249, 294
Reykjavík Orchestra, The (*Hljómsveit Reykjavíkur*), 43, 76, 141, 151
Reykjavík Town Band (*Lúðrasveit Reykjavíkur*), 58, 66–67
Reznicek, Emil Nikolaus von, 171, 186, 201, 215
Ribbentrop, Joachim von, 200
Richter, Hans, 40
Rickards, Guy, 263
Rieckmann, Johannes, 100n78
Riemann, Hugo, 124
Riethof, Annie. *See* Annie Leifs

Riethof, Edwin, 34, 38, 66, 67, 87, 228
Riethof, Gabriele, 34, 38, 228–30, 231
Riethof, Marie. *See* Marie Müller
Riethof, Sofie, 229
Riisager, Knudåge, 176–77
Rimsky-Korsakov, Nikolai, 124
Rindskopf, Josef, 34
rímur, 46–48, 59, 64, 69, 71, 79, 83, 86, 88, 111, 120, 147, 149, 154, 221, 223, 292, 298
Rode, Viktor, 229
Rolland, Romain, 168
Rosenberg, Alfred, 160, 166, 169, 177, 197, 211, 218, 224
Ross, Alex, 340
Ruggles, Carl, 5
Runólfsson, Karl Ottó, 202, 255

Salonen, Esa-Pekka, 337
Salter, Norbert, 66
Samúelsson, Guðjón, 119–20
Schacht, Ernst, 59
Schaeffer, Pierre, 317
Schattuck, Arthur, 28n29
Schaumburg-Lippe, Prince Friederich Christian, 200–01
Scherchen, Hermann, 40, 56, 60–61, 76, 171
Schmidt-Isserstedt, Hans, 184
Schoenberg, Arnold, 73, 170, 215
Schreker, Franz, 40
Schubert, Franz, 38, 62, 77, 171
Schuller, Gunther, 318
Schultz-Dornburg, Rudolf, 204
Schumann, Georg, 194n119, 215, 216
Schumann, Robert, 29, 38, 49
Schuricht, Carl, 172
Schweyda, Willibald, 225
Segerstam, Leif, 337
Senfl, Ludwig, 10
Serkin, Rudolf, 202
Shakespeare, William, 226
Sibelius, Jean, 5, 36, 52n19, 160, 166, 168, 171, 176, 184, 275, 335
Sigur Rós, 340

Sigurðsson, Haraldur, 23, 28n29, 139, 141
Sigurðsson, Jón, 11
Sigurgeirsson, Oddur, 90
Sigurjónsson, Jóhann, 67–68, 87
Sigurjónsson, Rögnvaldur, 298
Sinding, Christian, 187
Sittard, Alfred, 150
Skagfield, Sigurður, 230
Skallagrímsson, Egill, 114, 265
Skúlason, Þorvaldur, 299
Smetana, Bedřich, 300: *The Moldau (Vltava)*, 129
Spengler, Oswald, 164–65
Stalin, Josef, 293
Stange, Hermann, 178, 179
STEF. *See* Icelandic Performing Rights Society
Stefánsson, Davíð, 95, 138, 142, 143
Stefánsson, Eggert, 198, 250
Stege, Fritz, 166, 178, 219, 239n91, 275
Stephensen, Magnús, 10
Stephensen, Martha María, 18
Stockhausen, Karlheinz, 296, 322
Straube, Karl, 30
Strauss, Johann (Jr.), 78
Strauss, Richard, 170, 171, 179, 231, 314; *Eine Alpensinfonie*, 36, 129; *Die Frau ohne Schatten*, 40; *Guntram*, 230; *Josephslegende*, 243
Stravinsky, Igor, 170, 205
Strickland, William, 315
Strindberg, August, 272
Stumpf, Carl, 82
Sturluson, Snorri, 105
Sveinbjörnsson, Sveinbjörn, 11, 50, 55n52, 63, 73, 130n20
Szendrei, Aladár, 38

Tchaikovsky, Pyotr Ilyich, 152
Teichmüller, Robert, 30, 34, 40, 42, 56, 58, 155
Telmányi, Emil, 74
Theotokópoulos, Doménikos, 322
Thierfelder, Helmuth, 176

Thoroddsen, Emil, 73–74, 80, 111, 155
Thoroddsen, Theodóra, 264
Thorsteinson, Árni, 11, 72, 80, 109
Toini, Antonietta, *179*
Toscanini, Arturo, 149–50, 165
Tómasson, Haukur, 339
Tómasson, Helgi, 272
Treutler, Paul, 163
Trotha, Thilo von, 160
Turski, Zbigniew, 246
Tutenberg, Fritz, 163, 274
Tveitt, Geirr, 203
tvísöngur, 46, 48–49, 50, 54n49, 56–57, 70, 73, 79, 83, 88, 89, 115, 120, 124, 147, 204, 292, 319, 339, 340

Urbancic, Victor, 250
Utz, Kurt, 145, 176, 215, 216

Varèse, Edgard, 129, 275
Verdi, Giuseppe, 165, 326
Viðar, Jórunn, 338
Vollerthun, Georg, 167
Vänskä, Osmo, 337, 338

Wagner, Oskar, 281
Wagner, Richard, 36, 40, 77, 124, 165, 182–83, 222, 226; *Das Rheingold*, 204, 303; *Siegfried*, 40, 180; *Siegfried Idyll*, 78; *The Ring Cycle*, 167, 180, 193n91, 213, 243, 324
Wallner, Bo, 276
Walter, Bruno, 40, 86
Walters, Thorstina Jackson, 74
Warrack, Guy, 281
Weber, Carl Maria von, 78

Webern, Anton, 122, 170, 318
Weill, Kurt, 87, 198
Weiss, Edward, 28n29
Weisshaus, Imre, 74
Whitehead, Þór, 169
Wiechert, Ernst, 259
Wilhelm II, Emperor of Prussia, 166
Winter, Paul, 167
Wolfurt, Kurt von, 219

Zapp, Frieda, 61
Zingel, Rudolf Ewald, 144
Zukofsky, Paul, 246, 337
Züchner, Ernst, 168–69, 177, 197–98, 203, 211, 233

Þingvellir, 115, 117, 122, 134–136, 138, 140, 142, 181, 184, 195, 251, 291–92, 301, 304
Þorbergsson, Jónas, 151, 175–76, 181
Þorláksson, Böðvar, 89
Þorláksson, Jóhannes, 71
Þorleifsdóttir (Nagel), Salóme, 15, *16*, 61
Þorleifsdóttir, Þórey, 15, 16, 17, 155, 297
Þorleifsson, Bjarni, 14, 16
Þorleifsson, Páll, 16
Þorsteinsson, Bjarni, 11, 23, 45–46, 48, 49, 50, 51, 56, 57, 71, 79, 88–89, 154
Þorvaldsdóttir, Anna, 339
Þórarinsson, Jón, 278, 298, 300, 315, 325–26
Þórarinsson, Leifur, 298, 307, 318, 336
Þórðarson, Bjarni, 13
Þórðarson, Sigurður, 29, 42, 202, 255, 330n6

Åhlén, Carl-Gunnar, 39, 252, 336–37, 338

ÁRNI HEIMIR INGÓLFSSON is Artistic Advisor of the Iceland Symphony Orchestra, Visiting Professor at the Iceland University of the Arts, and past British Academy Visiting Fellow at Oxford University. He is author of *Jón Leifs—Líf í tónum*, which was nominated for the Icelandic Book Award.

www.ingramcontent.com/pod-product-compliance
Lightning Source LLC
Chambersburg PA
CBHW030430300426
44112CB00009B/940